Identity Politics Inside Out

Identity Politics Inside Out

National Identity Contestation and Foreign Policy in Turkey

LISEL HINTZ

OXFORD
UNIVERSITY PRESS

OXFORD
UNIVERSITY PRESS

Oxford University Press is a department of the University of Oxford. It furthers
the University's objective of excellence in research, scholarship, and education
by publishing worldwide. Oxford is a registered trade mark of Oxford University
Press in the UK and certain other countries.

Published in the United States of America by Oxford University Press
198 Madison Avenue, New York, NY 10016, United States of America.

© Oxford University Press 2018

CIP data is on file at the Library of Congress
ISBN 978–0–19–065597–6

1 3 5 7 9 8 6 4 2
Printed by Sheridan Books, Inc., United States of America

CONTENTS

ACKNOWLEDGMENTS

This book is the cumulative product not only of years of research and writing on domestic politics and foreign policy, but also of decades of curiosity about the role of identities: how groups of "us" and "them" take shape, how we choose to present ourselves in different environments, what elements remain nonnegotiable no matter the situation, and how others' perceptions of us shape the way we are treated. I am greatly indebted to countless people who have shaped—consciously or not—the construction of my identity, helping me to reach this point in my personal life and professional career.

For giving me a boundless love of all things readable, I am eternally grateful to my mother Tori and my late grandmother Vicki. Thank you for the endless story times, the thrill of wandering library stacks, the fun of making lists and memorizing facts, the belief that there will always be more fascinating things I need to learn (probably in another language). I am also extremely grateful for the opportunity to travel internationally with my mother from a young age, accompanying her while she managed International Workshops conferences to absorb so much of the many cultures I encountered. Back home my father's drive and determination were formidable, and I hope at least some rubbed off on me.

I will always be grateful to Jarrod Wiener, who supported me on the academic side by suggesting I return to graduate school, helping to put me on the doctoral path, and being a steady source of encouragement over the span of a decade. I thank everyone at the Brussels School of International Studies, where I taught my first course on nationalism and identity, for their support, particularly Harm Schepel, Yutaka Arai, Tom Casier, Milo Jones, Amanda Klekowski von Koppenfels, and Anja Sablon.

Marc Lynch was the best adviser I could ask for, providing invaluable support coupled with the still-daunting reminder: "Do or do not. There is no try." His guidance as I negotiated every aspect of the transition from student to professor cannot be overstated. Martha Finnemore's big-picture thinking helped my initially narrowly focused work grow by leaps and bounds; Henry Hale's fine-grained analysis and enthusiasm for my project made sure I was on track in many ways. I greatly benefited from Nathan Brown and Sultan Tepe's comments as excellent external committee members. Among GW's outstanding faculty, I especially thank Bruce Dickson, Kimberly Morgan, Harris Mylonas, and Evgeny Finkel for their support of my progress through the program. The encouragement and solidarity of friends like Julia, Katie, Kelly, Fouad, Kerry, Rachel, and Tristan will always be greatly appreciated.

For assisting me in preparing for fieldwork, I thank Zeynep Gür and Sylvia Önder for their superb efforts in teaching a difficult language. During my fieldwork in Turkey I benefited immensely from the generosity of the people I met. I am grateful to Metin Heper and Alev Çınar for granting me multiple stays as a visiting research fellow at Bilkent University, and to the US State Department Critical Language Scholarship Program for two summers of intensive language immersion in Bursa and Ankara. Özge Tekin was my fearless first Turkish friend and guide, Güneş Ertan my Ankara and Karadeniz partner in crime and fascinating discussions. Berk Esen's sharp wit and limitless knowledge gave me unparalleled insight into Turkey's tumult. I am deeply indebted to Hakan Övünç Ongur for his dear friendship, unwavering support, and detailed feedback on my writing. I thank Sinan Ciddi for all his caring efforts on innumerable fronts throughout the last three years of my doctoral work and subsequent positions; *sensiz yapamazdım.* For assistance with contacts for interviews and numerous discussions ranging from Gezi to Gaza, I am grateful to Arife, Aylan, Berkay, Burak, Gamze, Murat, Nigar, Önder, Şebnem, Tuba, and Zeki.

The dissertation writing grant I received from the Institute of Turkish Studies provided crucial support in completing my doctoral program, and my postdoctoral fellowship at Cornell, under the superb guidance of Peter Katzenstein, gave me the space for writing this book. I am grateful for the opportunity to have been a member of Barnard College's Political Science Department and to teach outstanding undergrads, and now to find my home for research, writing, and teaching in Johns Hopkins University's School of Advanced International Studies. Working with Alice, Cristina, and Erik in European and Eurasian studies is an honor.

Finally, I thank everyone dedicated enough to read the endnotes in this book. *Herkese çok teşekkürler!*

Identity Politics Inside Out

1

Introduction

Turning Identity Politics Inside Out

In the early 2000s Turkey's foreign policy orientation swung enthusiastically toward the European Union (EU), just at the moment when a party with roots in an explicitly anti-Western tradition of political Islam assumed power. The Justice and Development Party (Adalet ve Kalkınma Partisi, AKP) proclaimed EU membership to be one of its primary foreign policy goals, undertook massive political and economic reforms in line with EU accession, and employed optimistic and cordial rhetoric in dozens of meetings with its presumably future partners. As quickly as Ankara's decision makers had turned toward the EU, however, they then veered sharply away in favor of deeper ties with former Ottoman territories and other Muslim states. Reforms mandated by the EU slowed to a snail's pace, and relations with Brussels soured, resembling "a marriage gone wrong."[1] In addition to the increasing acrimony in EU-level relations, bilateral tensions reached crisis mode when Turkish president and AKP cofounder Recep Tayyip Erdoğan claimed the Dutch and German governments were run by "Nazis" and "fascists"[2] when AKP politicians were denied entry into those countries to campaign in the run-up to the April 2017 constitutional referendum. In conjunction with these diplomatic unravelings, the AKP was quick to proclaim Turkey's new role as savior of Palestinians in the occupied territories, defender of the Muslim Brotherhood in Egypt, and generous host to Syrian refugees fleeing civil war and Islamic State violence.[3] In brief, the AKP and its supporters presented themselves as resuscitators of long-lost historical and cultural bonds they believed to have been unwisely, and unjustly, severed by the secular, Western-oriented republican regime of founding father Mustafa Kemal Atatürk.

From a broader historical perspective, Turkey's policy and discursive shifts to the East are as surprising as they are rapid. As a staunch North Atlantic Treaty Organization (NATO) ally and longtime partner in US efforts in the Middle East, Turkey seemed firmly embedded in the Western security community.

Given this institutionalized Western orientation, Turkey's defiance of US and European practices through initiatives such as its cooperation with traditional archenemy Iran in an attempted nuclear deal, its prolonged support of the Syrian regime despite President Bashar al-Assad's brutal crackdown during the Arab uprisings, and its deluge of virulently hostile rhetoric directed toward former close ally Israel—all three of which have spectacularly imploded[4]—are thus genuinely puzzling.

The animosity shown to Israel, and later Iran and Syria as well, challenges otherwise compelling arguments claiming that Turkey is pursuing a role as a regional powerbroker,[5] while its lifting of visa requirements and friendly overtures to neighboring Muslim states complicate regional hegemony explanations.[6] Also confounding security perspectives, Turkey has demonstrated a flagrant disregard for its NATO alliance commitments by pursuing missile defense negotiations with China[7] and Russia,[8] as well as a willingness to instigate conflicts on its own borders, as seen in its false-flag activities vis-à-vis Syria.[9] The Turkish military's campaign against Syrian Kurdish militia forces the US was arming against the Islamic State—support that was viewed by Turkey as meddling worthy of the infamous "Ottoman slap"[10]—when combined with other disputes arguably brought US-Turkish relations to an all-time low in early 2018.[11]

Returning specifically to Turkey-EU relations, institutional approaches combining Turkey's foreign policy with its domestic politics account for the initiation of EU-based domestic reforms in Turkey but prove lacking when considering that the implementation of reforms markedly slowed at nearly the same time that the EU opened official accession negotiations with Turkey in 2005; frustrated with Turkey's lack of progress, the EU called a halt to negotiations one year later.[12] The timing of this slowdown also challenges economic approaches that cite the 2008 EU financial crisis as motivating Turkey's shift eastward.[13] Finding security, institutional, and economic explanations for Turkey's foreign policy shifts unsatisfactory, recent commentary assumes these reorientations are manifestations of Turkey's increasingly Islamist political identity.[14] Pointing to the Islamist background of AKP members, leader-centric identity arguments cite the religious background of top party figures such as President Erdoğan,[15] former prime minister Ahmet Davutoğlu,[16] and former president Abdullah Gül[17] as driving Turkey's apparent reorientation toward its Muslim neighbors. But how could domestic Islamism explain both the Western and the Eastern trajectories under the same party's rule, and with the same party leaders?

Other explanations claim to identify broader societal trends of "Middle Easternization"[18] or "neo-Ottomanism"[19] in shaping both Turkey's domestic and foreign policies. While many of these arguments are less rigorous than rhetorical,[20] such explanations gain plausibility with the surge of Islam- and Ottoman-based public discourse at both elite and society levels within Turkey.

This spread is evident in the number of references to Ottoman history in billboard advertisements for products ranging from chewing gum to luxury housing; in dozens of recent novels and films celebrating the heroic wresting of Constantinople (Istanbul) from the infidels; in architecture, in political speeches, and in the educational system—in short, in every facet of the public sphere.

As clear as the rise in fascination with Ottoman culture and history has become in large swathes of Turkey's society, as has the presence of some sort of Ottoman-based understanding of Turkey's identity in shaping its recent foreign policy reorientation, neither of these shifts coincided with the AKP coming to power in 2002 with a strong capacity to legislate as it pleased. Receiving 34.3% of the vote, the AKP not only won an extraordinarily large share for a party established just a year before the election, but also gained an unprecedented parliamentary majority that greatly strengthened its ruling capacity. This surprising electoral outcome stemmed from the country's system of proportional representation, with an extremely high (10%) threshold that kept smaller parties out of parliament, and voters' frustration with multiple coalition governments' instability and inability to handle the 2001 economic crisis that erupted under their leadership. As the AKP was thus equipped from a legislative perspective to quickly realize the interests generated by what I term its "Ottoman Islamist" identity in practice, domestic politics explanations cannot account for the rise of Ottoman Islamism in domestic and foreign policy only during the AKP's second, and especially third and fourth, terms.

Finally, the Welfare Party (Refah Partisi, RP), a predecessor of the AKP that shared its Ottoman Islamist understanding of Turkish identity, had been devastatingly thwarted just a decade earlier in its attempts to enact policies including forming a Muslim-states version of NATO and instituting an Islamic currency union. As suggested previously, the Ottoman and Islamist identity elements apparently reorienting Turkey's policies today are fundamentally at odds with the state's own previously dominant, Western-modeled understanding of Turkishness, which I refer to in this book as "Republican Nationalism."[21] The now frequent references to Turkey's glorious Ottoman past and conservative values of Islam as the basis of societal interaction are antithetical to the Republican Nationalist concept of the "model citizen": Western, modern, and secular.[22] As evidence of the previous power wielded by supporters of this Republican Nationalist understanding of identity, the Ottoman Islamist RP was forced out of power by Turkey's military and shut down by its judicial institutions the following year; RP leader Necmettin Erbakan was banned from politics. These measures and others comprised part of a far-reaching process of secularization efforts to suppress political Islam, known to every citizen of Turkey as simply 28 Şubat (February 28), marking the day the National Security

Council issued an ultimatum to the RP.[23] As one columnist phrased it, "Turkey's generals declared war on the country's Islamic movement."[24] How, then, does an Ottoman Islamist understanding begin to spread throughout Turkey's public sphere and institutions of governance as it has under AKP just ten years later?

As this book emphasizes, getting a firm analytical grip on the intricate complexity that constitutes various contemporary understandings of Turkishness— or of any national identity—sheds immense empirical light on what initially appears to be an impenetrable web of puzzling and shifting policies. Identity is indeed deeply important for understanding foreign policy, but existing accounts citing identity-based factors fail effectively to link Turkey's domestic discursive struggles with its multiple, varied international outcomes. Understanding the why, the when, and the how of these dynamics over time requires moving beyond the scholarly advances in studies of identity made in the often discretely bounded realms of comparative politics and international relations (IR). Specifically, this book demonstrates that the answers to these questions lie in the complex role that foreign policy plays in domestic struggles over identity politics. I argue that foreign policy serves as an alternative arena to domestic politics in which these contests over identity take place.

In the course of outlining this conceptualization of a subject traditionally treated as a strategy for competing against international counterparts, I illustrate how foreign policy preferences are organically, intrinsically linked with conceptions of national identity. I specify the particular red lines of contestation among the various proposals for identity on domestic and foreign policy issues, illuminating how actors and institutions imbued with one proposal can serve as obstacles to the spread of competing proposals. I examine contestation as a mechanism for change, accounting for the rise and fall of support for particular "proposals,"[25] defined as suggested understandings of identity that prescribe and proscribe specific standards of behavior and compete to establish a particular national identity. I demonstrate that contestation among identity proposals, rather than being a phenomenon bounded within the domestic arena, both shapes and is shaped by foreign policy gambits whose domestic identity components might not be immediately observable. Further, although I employ the concept of red lines, I emphasize that it is a fundamental error to assume that internal identity divisions are the result of natural cultural "fault lines," doomed forever to produce instability and destruction among bounded "civilizations."[26] In contrast, red lines can harden and soften, emerge and disappear through processes of contestation.

To get at the dynamics of this relationship, in this book I develop a theory of inside-out identity contestation that specifies the conditions under which, and the avenues through which, interaction among groups with competing proposals for identity spill over into foreign policy. I argue that supporters seek the benefits believed to come with achieving a goal that I term "identity hegemony"—ranging from the ontological security generated by seeing their own understanding of identity accepted as the "right" understanding by others to the policy advantages obtained through dominance in institutions used to spread beliefs about identity, including the media and the educational system—by competing to spread their own proposal for national identity across a population. Precisely because of the appeal of these benefits, however, supporters may be blocked in their pursuit of hegemony by those who fundamentally object to their proposal for who "we" should be. These objections may come from individuals, who can use their votes as electoral obstacles to an identity proposal's promulgation, or from institutions, which can act as veto powers through legal and bureaucratic channels. Inside-out identity contestation theory contends that elites who face obstacles or threats to their attempts to spread their own proposal in the domestic political arena choose to take their struggle outside to the foreign policy arena. The theory also suggests that actors who have achieved their goal of neutralizing the power of opponents back home may lose enthusiasm for or even abandon the foreign policy initiative motivated by domestic political ambitions. As a result of this process of externalizing contestation, interactions at the international level have distinctive, often counterintuitive effects on the contours of domestic identity discourses. In sum, inside-out identity contestation theory seeks to explain the timing of and motivations behind the spillovers of identity politics into foreign policy.

To facilitate the type of intensive study necessary to understand these struggles and their effects, this book employs a clear, explicit, and replicable framework of identity content that systematically breaks down proposals into their constitutive elements. In order to gain access to the various proposals competing to define national identity in Turkey, I have developed an original methodology that applies intertextual analysis to oral, written, and symbolic texts gathered from sources chosen to reflect various, often conflicting understandings of identity. I derive these texts from traditional sources such as governmental archives and news media, but also from novels, films, and television series that allow the researcher access to debates about religion, ethnicity, class, gender, and other identity-based relations in Turkey that one might not otherwise be able to witness. I supplement these with an in-depth study of the user-generated platform of social media, whose ardent debates facilitate immensely valuable insight into identity discourses present in Turkey. I also employ interviews with politicians, grassroots activists, civil servants, retired military officers, academics, journalists, and members of the business community; extended questionnaires covering issues of foreign policy and identity debates; and a survey of 175 university students asking what television characters serve as the best and worst role models for citizens of Turkey, and why. Finally, I incorporate participant observation of events such as political rallies, protests, holiday observances, and everyday practices to gain insight into the various proposals for national identity present in Turkey.

The analysis of identity contestation and foreign policy presented in this book derives from an in-depth case study of Turkey, whose national identity has long been hotly contested in scholarship as well as in practice.[27] While empirically rich, such discussions generally lack clear, systematic delineation of what Turkish identity actually consists of (i.e., how we know it when we see it), and what specific issues are at stake in identity debates, such as why issues of foreign policy seem so vital to questions of who "we," not "they," are. Breaking down proposals for national identity into their constitutive elements and specifying their identity red lines—the elements deemed fundamentally inappropriate to the point of being intolerable for supporters of competing proposals—facilitate the study of these questions. The theory of inside-out contestation, the identity content framework, and the conceptualization of foreign policy as an alternative arena for identity politics developed in this book help to make sense of otherwise inchoate sets of behaviors in a state's international relations. From this perspective, the AKP's initial pursuit of EU accession becomes comprehensible as a foreign policy variant of strategies used to pursue hegemony for a particular identity proposal. By examining the institutional legacies of a domestic strategy used to pursue hegemony, carried out through a massive nationalization campaign by Republican Nationalists when they founded the Turkish Republic, the book's argument makes clear why the most viable strategy available to the AKP was taking its identity fight "outside" to the foreign policy arena. The inside-out theory of identity contestation that the book develops also accounts for the timing of the AKP's turn away from the EU, that is, once it had sufficiently reduced the role of veto players in the domestic arena that could block the dissemination of its identity proposal.

As a NATO ally, EU-candidate country, Organisation of Islamic Cooperation (OIC) leader, and aspiring regional powerbroker, Turkey offers an excellent empirical window on how identity debates spill over into foreign policy, but these implications extend far beyond Turkey itself. Indeed, some version of these dynamics pervades the foreign policy of all states; Benjamin Netanyahu's March 2015 address to US lawmakers, which emphasized Iran's "oldest hatred" of "the one and only Jewish state,"[28] serves as a topical example of the foreign policy arena's appeal to elites for advocating their version of identity, given not only its timing shortly before Israel's national elections but also Netanyahu's deeply ingrained perception of Iran as an existential threat he fears not enough Israelis recognize. The initial foreign policy steps taken by India under Narendra Modi and his Hindu nationalist Bharatiya Janata Party (BJP) include a more "muscular" foreign policy toward Muslim-majority neighbor Pakistan and elimination of the mention of Palestine—"one of the touchstones of Indian foreign policy vis-à-vis the Middle East-Asia"[29]—from a recent resolution. These shifts, particularly for a state whose foreign policy is "characterized more by continuity than by change,"[30] suggest that the BJP may be taking the opportunity while in power to realize some of its Hindutva ideology-based interests outside the reach (at least until the next election) of India's Muslim population. As explored throughout the chapters in this book, elites facing obstacles to spreading their proposal for identity back home can circumvent these obstacles through foreign policy in several ways; viewing foreign policy as an arena for identity contestation—rather than solely as a source or product of identity—facilitates understanding how.

In addition to its empirical insights into identity and foreign policy shifts in Turkey, the book therefore strives to make several theoretical contributions of value to broader studies of one or both of these subjects. First, the concept of identity red lines that I introduce here[31] enables us analytically to parse those elements of identity that generate conflict between individuals holding specific understandings of identity and those who do not. As a brief example on which the following chapters elaborate, for some people in Turkey the political recognition of ethnic identities other than their own is a violation of a red line, for others a red line is crossed when politicizing any ethnicity, and still others see no problem in politically recognizing multiple ethnicities but have red lines among themselves on other identity-related issues. As the breakdown of identity content in chapter 3 makes clear, Pan-Turkic Nationalists celebrate the ethnic and cultural components of Turkishness and their ties to Turkic populations but find even informal acknowledgement of Kurdish identity intolerable; Republican Nationalists find the politicization of all ethnic identities dangerous and intolerable. Western Liberalists and Ottoman Islamists are tolerant of political recognition of ethnic identities but have identity red lines between them on issues such as gender relations and sexual identities.

In the foreign policy realm, some citizens of Turkey find close ties with the Turkic states of the former Soviet Union to be necessary, some would find a deepening of relations acceptable, and others would deem such a foreign policy initiative unpalatable. The same is true for beliefs about relations with the EU, but the groups delineated by their views toward relations with Central Asia do not match up with the groups advocating, tolerating, and denouncing EU membership. Briefly, Pan-Turkic Nationalists believe close relations with Turkic states are necessary, Ottoman Islamists and Western Liberalists find them acceptable but not a priority (Ottoman Islamists would include other Muslim-majority states and Ottoman territories as well), and Republican Nationalists view a deepening of ties with what they view as "backward" states as foolish and potentially dangerous in provoking Russia's ire on its borders, if not necessarily intolerable. In the EU case, Western Liberalists find EU membership an institutional anchor necessary for advancing the freedoms and rights they see as lacking, Republican Nationalists generally favor EU membership but are wary of all international entanglements, and Ottoman Islamists and Pan-Turkic Nationalists tend to reject Turkey's place in the West (even though both groups have benefited from the economic integration facilitated by joining the Customs Union in 1995). Breaking down the nebulous concept of identity into its constituent parts and identifying red lines among various proposals enables us to make sense of this dizzyingly complex map of domestic and foreign policy preferences.

Second, my approach specifies how institutions of governance and nation-building such as the military, the judiciary, and the educational system in which identity proposals can become embedded—as was Republican Nationalism up until the AKP period—are able to block contestation efforts by supporters of competing proposals. For inside-out theory, institutional rules and the individuals tasked to uphold these rules function as the guardians of a particular proposal, vigilantly on the lookout for violations of identity red lines such as infractions regarding religious principles or, conversely, the public practice of those principles. When such institutions become weakened in capacity and no longer hold any authority, as was the case for the Ottoman caliphate and sultanate, they can be circumvented or even dismantled by supporters of competing proposals. Finally, conceptualizing foreign policy as an arena of identity contestation moves beyond monodirectional explanations that assume one factor produces or is produced by the other, instead providing a way of understanding the mutually constitutive relationship between the two. A constitutive approach can help to provide insight into the hegemonic motivations behind otherwise puzzling foreign policy initiatives, as well as facilitate an understanding of how an identity proposal long dormant or suppressed within a state rapidly gains public support and spreads to state institutions. As chapter 7 suggests in its discussion of other cases, for example, the institutionalized racism and the identity-based obstacles put in place by the National Party in South Africa motivated the African National Congress to take its fight outside and engage international civil society; international normative pressure, in turn, helped shape the conditions that made the transition to native rule possible, as suggested by scholars such as Audie Klotz.[32] Viewing foreign policy as an arena allows us to better understand the dynamics of the whole South African picture and recognize similar dynamics in other cases. Finally, the theory of identity contestation presented here and its use of identity-based obstacles provide an institutional account of why some attempts by supporters to spread their identity proposal to the public sphere are blocked and others are not.

In presenting its theoretical and empirical contributions to the case of Turkey and beyond, the rest of this book is structured in the following manner. Chapter 2 outlines the inside-out theory of contestation developed through this study in detail. It specifies the goal of actors' contestation as identity hegemony, defining this goal's parameters as the power wielded and legitimacy enjoyed by an identity proposal that is widespread (a) in terms of support across a population and presence in domestic institutions and (b) to the point of being "relatively stable and unquestioned."[33] The chapter also details individuals' motivations for pursuing hegemony and explains my choice to conceptualize foreign policy as an arena, alternative to domestic politics, for the contestation through which they can do so. As the chapter demonstrates, externalizing contestation in the foreign policy arena can serve as a highly successful strategy for advancing identity proposals when there are entrenched, identity-based obstacles to these proposals back home, because the rules and contenders in the foreign policy contest differ. First, engaging in foreign policy provides a means of circumventing opponents who vehemently defend their own understandings of identity and thus attempt to block the pursuit of interests defined by another proposal. Second, those who support that proposal but live abroad, such as diaspora and migrant worker communities, can serve as sources of financial support or external legitimacy for contestation back home.[34] Third, and relatedly, targeting transnational civil society as a foreign policy strategy can generate naming and shaming mechanisms[35] that persuade domestic actors to modify or remove the identity-based obstacles they have put in place, such as bans on ethnic or religious groups, in line with prevailing international norms.[36] Fourth, international organizations can provide the resources and justification for adjusting the roles, power, and policies of domestic institutions in line with accession criteria.[37] Elites can strategically use these constraints to their own advantage, having conditionality at their disposal to weaken institutional obstacles to their proposal. Finally, foreign policy is treated here not solely as the realm of governmental elites, but as a forum in which leaders of an identity-based movement (e.g., minority or civil rights) may attempt to spread international awareness of their proposal when their contestation attempts are—given their relative disadvantage vis-à-vis institutional access—often blocked at home.

The second chapter also presents a clear and cohesive framework for parsing out the content of various identity proposals whose supporters compete among each other for hegemony. This framework breaks down identity into four elements of content: constitutive norms, social purpose, relational meaning, and cognitive worldview. Specifying the "stuff" that members of a certain in-group share with each other about who they are and how they behave facilitates the comparison of content elements across proposals and the identification of red lines of contestation among them. This specificity the framework allows also provides a tool for systematic cross-case analysis.

Finally, the chapter details the methods used to identify proposals for national identity present in Turkey's society and thus to trace the rise and fall of support for these proposals over time. The chapter outlines (1) the multiple, varied sources used to collect evidence of beliefs about identity that might otherwise be inaccessible to the researcher; (2) the intertextual analysis approach used to extract proposals for national identity from these sources; and (3) the process tracing method employed to assess the change in levels of support for particular identities, evaluated in terms of their presence in public discourse and domestic institutions.

Chapter 3 presents the four proposals for Turkey's national identity analyzed in this book in rich empirical detail. I extract these proposals from data gathered during fieldwork in Turkey over a period of eighteen months from 2012 to 2015, research that I supplemented with follow-up visits and online data collection. While bearing in mind that this categorization is not exhaustive, and that there may be overlap of content elements across categories—the relational meaning of belonging within the Western world and the social purpose of modernization, for example, may be shared among texts that differ greatly in constitutive norms of human rights and various freedoms of expression[38]—the evidence collected from texts coalesces around four general sets of elements that can be considered coherent identity proposals: Ottoman Islamism, Republican Nationalism, Western Liberalism, and Pan-Turkic Nationalism. The chapter presents the identity content for each of the four proposals held by members of Turkey's contemporary society in each of the four content categories noted above. This enables the parsing out of the domestic and foreign policy interests generated by each proposal and the identification of the red lines among them.

Chapter 4 details the processes of identity formation prior to, during, and immediately following the founding of the Turkish Republic in 1923. I trace the emergence and development of Republican Nationalism, focusing on the constitutive effects of the collapse of the Ottoman Empire and the War of Liberation against the Allied powers on the content of the proposal. I highlight how these experiences shaped the proposal's constitutive norms of nonethnic membership and a secular lifestyle; its social purpose of protecting the principles of the republic's founder and first president, Atatürk; its relational meaning of rightful inclusion in, but suspicion of, the West; and its cognitive worldview of Turkey as the secular guard of the modern world order in a tumultuous region. The chapter then analyzes the strategies by which supporters of Republican Nationalism in its earliest iteration pursued hegemony for their proposal over the contemporary versions of Ottoman Islamism and Pan-Turkic Nationalism, as well as the non-Turkish proposal of Kurdish nationalism. Finally, the chapter examines challenges that arose to counter this pursuit of hegemony in the period following Turkey's most drastic, far-reaching military coup, in 1980. I analyze internal and external events—including the reverberations of the harsh crackdown itself, the development of the Turkish-Islamist synthesis, and the collapse of the Soviet Union and the Cold War order—that paved the way for supporters of Ottoman Islamism, Pan-Turkic Nationalism, and the newly emerging Western Liberalism to contest against Republican Nationalism. The chapter concludes by suggesting that despite sweeping reforms that abolished the already decrepit Ottoman Islamist institutions of the caliphate and the sultanate, which were specifically tailored to create a modern, secular, civic identity for the citizens of the new republic, the content of Republican Nationalism and the militant way in which this content was spread planted the seeds of future resistance against it.

As noted previously, unlike the AKP's successful efforts to spread Ottoman Islamism in the public sphere and institutions of governance, the RP's Ottoman Islamist attempts just a decade previously were short-lived and powerfully suppressed. To provide understanding of these dramatically different outcomes, chapter 5 investigates the institutionalized legacies of Republican Nationalism. The chapter first outlines the utility of conceptualizing institutions such as the military, judicial, and educational systems not only as conduits through which to disseminate a particular understanding of national identity, as traditional nation-alization arguments contend,[39] but also as defensive, identity-based obstacles to the spread of proposals with identity content deemed intolerable. The chapter examines the internalization of Republican Nationalism, arguably the only identity proposal to come close to becoming hegemonic in Turkey's history, in bodies erected to protect its specific, identity-generated principles, including the Turkish Armed Forces (Türk Silahlı Kuvvetleri, TSK), the Constitutional Court (Anayasa Mahkemesi), and the position of university rector. While Republican Nationalism faced many challenges to its position, as highlighted in the previous chapter, this chapter demonstrates how its institutionalized presence constituted an identity-based obstacle to Ottoman Islamism in the 1990s.

Chapter 6 traces how the AKP was able to circumvent these Republican Nationalist domestic institutions, taking its identity contest to the foreign policy arena to engage with an international institution that plays by different rules. I show how, by initially embracing the EU accession process and selec-tively applying its democratization criteria during its first term, the AKP was able to reconfigure the domestic playing field, weakening or reconfiguring the Republican Nationalist obstacles that had served to obstruct previous Ottoman Islamist gambits. This chapter focuses on how the AKP's identity contestation in the foreign policy arena made it safer to spread its own identity proposal back home in its second and third terms. Illuminating the counterintuitive finding that Turkey's EU-oriented foreign policy made the subsequent rise of Ottoman Islamism possible, the chapter then illustrates the AKP's efforts to realize in practice its domestic and foreign policy interests—including constitutive norms of piety and social conservatism, a social purpose of increasing the presence of Sunni Islam in the public sphere, a relational meaning of deeper integration with Muslim and former Ottoman lands, and a cognitive worldview of Turkey as the legitimate inheritor of the Ottoman legacy and head of the Muslim world—once it had successfully taken its identity contestation "outside" to the foreign policy arena. In terms of foreign policy shifts that have resulted from the AKP's ability to enact initiatives in line with the behavior prescribed by its identity, the chapter focuses particularly on the drastic shifts in policy toward Israel and Syria. In the case of Israel, seen as the oppressor of Ottoman Islamists' Muslim brothers, the AKP's rhetoric became increasingly hostile following the attacks on Gaza in 2008 and culminated in an effective severing of diplomatic relations with a country that Turkey had been the first in the Muslim world to recognize. The Syrian case is more complex, including a rapid warming of relations under former foreign minister and later prime minister Davutoğlu's Ottoman Islamist strategic depth doctrine, followed by a re-escalation when Ankara quickly changed its position in August 2011 and called for Assad's ouster when he refused to adhere to Erdoğan's demands. As the chapter discusses, this dramatic change of approach makes sense when applying an Ottoman Islamist identity framework, which prescribes that Turkey's role in the region be that of legitimate leader and rule-setter, as in an idealized version of Ottoman times.

Chapter 7 explores how the inside-out theory of contestation developed in the book extends to cases outside of Turkey, helping us better understand how identity struggles spill over into foreign policy in other environments and then shape the playing field back home. Demonstrating that inside-out contestation occurs irrespective of regime type and region, I focus on examining the externalization of identity struggles in two authoritarian regimes, Iran and apartheid South Africa, and two democratic regimes, Israel and India. Extending the framework outside of the EU context in which Turkey's dynamics are intertwined challenges suppositions that the EU is sui generis not only in its institutional make-up but also in its ability to mold domestic structures and identities.[40] Further, the framework's focus on identity proposals rather than states allows us to analyze cases of identity politics "inside out," involving actors that do not enjoy the power of the state. Exploring this perspective, the chapter demonstrates how non-state groups can also use foreign policy as an arena via various mechanisms—institutional support (if not conditionality), diaspora groups, transnational advocacy networks (TANs)—to circumvent identity-based obstacles back home. The authoritarian cases of Iran and apartheid South Africa explored here illustrate the foreign policy strategies of non-state actors, but I deliberately do not draw links between regime type and actor type, as far-right parties in European democracies, for example, reach out to like-minded groups abroad in their efforts to advance their own proposals back home.[41] To round out this claim, the chapter concludes by turning back to the case of Turkey to explore the efforts of Turkey's Kurdish and Gülen movements in contestation against Republican Nationalism through outreach abroad.

Chapter 8 reviews the book's findings, emphasizing the analytical utility to be gained by examining Turkey's domestic and foreign policy shifts from an inside-out identity hegemony perspective. The chapter evaluates the potential for a hybrid identity to form out of the proposals that united in their contestation against the AKP government and its attempts to infuse Sunni Islam into Turkey's domestic public sphere and foreign policy. Of the many dynamics that emerged in contestation against Ottoman Islamism, the chapter focuses on the two conceptual strands exemplified by the hybridization of the 2013 Gezi Park protests and the polarization of the 2013 Gülen movement's split from the AKP. The months-long and nationwide demonstrations catalyzed by police violence against peaceful environmental demonstrators, and the media silence that followed the crackdown, represent an unprecedented uniting of, in very large part, politically apathetic individuals supporting Republican Nationalist, Western Liberalist, and Pan-Turkic Nationalist identity proposals. This joining of rivals and the new forms of interaction in which they engage created the (as yet unrealized) possibility for a hybrid proposal to develop out of their mutual contestation against Ottoman Islamism. In contrast, the sudden and quite vehement revocation of support for the AKP's Ottoman Islamist pursuits by followers of Islamic cleric Fethullah Gülen is presented as a conduit for a new, Turkish Calvinist identity proposal to emerge. Focusing on the analytical tool of identity red lines I develop, this chapter highlights the hybridization and polarization of Turkey's existing identity proposals through these episodes of contestation taking place just in the last few years.

Linking Identity Politics and Foreign Policy

An Inside-Out Theory of Identity Contestation

Introduction

When considering the relationship between identity and international relations, are foreign policy initiatives best conceived as outcomes of domestic identity politics or as factors contributing to them? Why do elites choose to politicize national identity debates at the foreign policy level, and with what consequences? At a more basic level, why is foreign policy such a hotly contested component of what are essentially national questions of who "we"—not "they"—are? Despite numerous studies by comparativist and IR scholars on identity politics and foreign policy, the relative disconnect between the two literatures creates a gap in understanding the relationship between them. In teasing out this complex link throughout the course of this book, I conceptualize foreign policy as an alternative arena in which the supporters of a particular proposal for national identity compete in struggles to advance the spread of their proposal across a state's population.

To analyze these struggles and their inextricable relationship with foreign policy, in this chapter I develop an inside-out theory of identity contestation. The theory posits that supporters engage in a process of contestation among competing proposals, identifying a mechanism that accounts both for changes within a particular group's understanding of the proposal and in the relative distribution of support for identity proposals across a population over time. Engaging social psychological studies of identity grounded in experimental research, the chapter outlines the reasons that supporters of a particular proposal pursue what I term *identity hegemony*. I then draw from both comparativist and IR literatures to specify the strategies of contestation used in this pursuit. Stipulating the conditions under which domestic and international arenas are chosen for contesting against competing proposals, inside-out theory argues that political elites choose to take this identity contestation "outside" to the foreign policy arena when identity gambits at the domestic level are blocked.

To build the foundation for the theoretical argument I advance in this book, the following section briefly reviews the available literature on identity and foreign policy. I then outline inside-out theory, providing definitions of the key terms it engages, such as *identity proposal, contestation,* and *hegemony.* The theory section also outlines the framework I use to break down the content of various identity proposals and identify points of intolerability—or what I term *red lines*—among them. This framework facilitates identifying which content elements may be most intensely contested and thus pose threats to supporters' advancement of their proposal at the domestic level by those who find its content fundamentally unacceptable. The chapter concludes by outlining the dual methodology used to examine processes of identity contestation in Turkey. I outline the use of intertextual analysis to extract identity proposals present in Turkish society and explain why resources as various as archives, surveys, social media, and television shows were chosen as sources of the texts analyzed. I then describe the method of process tracing I use to track changes in levels of support among competing proposals as well as changes within proposals in terms of identity content, and to identify the emergence of new, hybrid proposals formed through mutual contestation against an intolerable proposal.

Identity and Foreign Policy

While the "constructivist turn" in IR scholarship[1] sought to unpack the concept of identity, attempts to problematize this previously bracketed element have been, in a word, problematic. The use of identity as a variable in IR is fraught with analytical obstacles, normative objections, and—in the words of scholars attempting to address such challenges—"definitional anarchy."[2] The task of formulating, much less agreeing on, a workable definition for such a nebulous concept has proved so formidable that some have called for abandoning the terminology of identity altogether.[3] Others have argued that existing identity-based explanations reify precisely that which scholars attempting to offer such explanations argue is intersubjective.[4] Objections also arise in critiques of the generalization and determinism of arguments explaining behavior in terms of identity.[5]

Even if all these obstacles to the study of identity can be overcome, one also must question whether identity is actually doing any constitutive or causal work in the cases we seek to understand. As Henry Hale's discussion of "ethnicity-as-epiphenomenal" theories explains,[6] epiphenomenal arguments pointing to causal mechanisms ranging from elite manipulation[7] to political action coordination[8] assert that identities such as ethnicity and other commonly shared understandings of group membership have no intrinsic value, but rather serve as tools in the pursuit of (largely) material interests such as power, resources, and security. All of these arguments could ostensibly apply to Turkey, as a state that has at different times contested Shi'i-majority Iran and Eastern Orthodox–majority Russia for dominance in the Middle East, made Pan-Turkic overtures to the newly independent Central Asian republics in hope of obtaining further pipeline access and establishing new markets for its goods, and lobbied to secure its legitimate place in the transatlantic security community through NATO membership. Indeed, these whiplash-inducing switches among Sunni Muslim, Pan-Turkic, and Western identity appeals seem to lend credence to arguments that states can select from a "menu of choices" for national identity[9] or perhaps a state-based version of the "identity repertoire" that Daniel Posner outlines, which provides an "inventory of ethnic group memberships that individuals possess."[10]

As an analytical heuristic, Posner's conceptually spare treatment of identity is tidy,[11] but such rationalist approaches omit elements essential for understanding behavior such as the ontological and emotional importance of identities and the actor-specific interests they generate. Constructivist arguments, in brief, account for factors that fundamentally shape ideas about what is possible, desirable, and necessary, prescribing and proscribing behaviors based on understandings of identities and interests that purely rationalist arguments do not problematize. That a gun in the hand of a friend differs from a gun in the hand of an enemy is commonsensical. The explanation for this lies not in distributions of material capabilities, but in the intersubjective understandings that give meaning to relationships between actors.[12] Those rationalist arguments explicitly incorporating information variables and signaling mechanisms[13] offer much more nuanced explanations of interactions in international politics than previous theories in the realist family but cannot account for the constitutive and constraining effects of identities in the international system. Liberalist approaches and schools of international political economy (IPE), in turn, acknowledge that domestic institutions and actors' interests shape states' options at the international level,[14] but their focus on material factors occludes the powerful identity-based constraints on what domestic actors are willing to tolerate, what they desire, and what they see as necessary in terms of foreign policy.

Several recent works of constructivism addressing the challenges enumerated above directly engage the role of norms and identity in foreign policy and thus provide guidance for developing an overarching analysis of the relationship between domestic identity politics and foreign policy. Michael Barnett's temporal analysis, for example, examines how normative structures of Arab politics shaped the social interactions between Arab states in different periods, demonstrating how dialogues between these states created moments of transformation in which the rules of the game of Arab politics were open to change.[15] Marc Lynch also examines how norms and identities can change, arguing that shifts in international and domestic public spheres altered the contours of internal debates over Jordan's identity.[16] Barnett and Shibley Telhami's edited volume explores the function of an identity "menu of choices" at the disposal of elites noted above, while Rawi Abdelal adds a nationalist perspective to the study of IPE by demonstrating that national identities constrain interest perception by ruling out particular foreign policy possibilities, such as developing economic interdependence with a state perceived as an "Other."[17] David Campbell explores foreign policy's role in constructing threats that legitimate the existence of the state,[18] while Ted Hopf's study of Soviet and Russian foreign policy fleshes out the mechanisms by which identities can influence foreign policy, including conditioning the policies that leaders can entertain as possible and legitimate choices, raising the costs of policies pursued for reasons other than identity, and delineating potential allies and enemies.

This book incorporates and builds on insights from this foundational scholarship, developing a well-grounded study newly examining the foreign policy arena as a locus of national identity contestation. In doing so, I develop a theory that identifies the underlying sources of what may otherwise appear to be inchoate sets of pick-a-mix foreign policy strategies. This theory moves beyond prominent approaches noted above that assume elites choose foreign policy strategies either constrained or facilitated by an identity "menu of choices." I not only demonstrate how menus become constituted in the first place, but also identify the specific mechanisms of contestation at the domestic and international levels by which the contours of such menus can change. Finally, I provide systematic analysis of the actual "stuff" of identities by breaking down this concept into content elements within a cohesive and replicable framework for comparing and contrasting proposals competing to define the appropriate national identity for the citizens of their state. Employing this framework not only facilitates fleshing out the identity content constitutive of current understandings of Turkishness, but also specifies their points of fundamental disagreement, or "red lines" of prescribed behavior, whose violation supporters of competing identity proposals deem intolerable.

Inside-Out Theory of Identity Contestation

With the goal of providing a more comprehensive analysis of the relationship between domestic identity politics and foreign policy, this book conceptualizes foreign policy as a locus of identity contestation, defined as ongoing processes of debate and pushback among groups holding differing understandings of what constitutes the appropriate national identity for their state. This approach offers a broader lens for the analysis of the relationship between national identity debates and foreign policy than those viewing the latter solely as an outcome of struggles among competing identity groups or as the source of those struggles.[19] Academic work examining these issues generally employs what IR scholars have termed either "second image" or "second image reversed" approaches.[20] The argument advanced here not only synthesizes these two approaches—examining the reasons national identity contestation takes place in the foreign policy arena and in turn how foreign policy practices shape the contours of identity debates back home—but also develops a theory of identity contestation that accounts for otherwise inexplicable shifts at both levels of analysis.

Rather than being a theory of domestic politics explaining struggles over economic resources or other forms of material power, inside-out identity contestation theory analyzes struggles to define the appropriate identity for a particular social group. These struggles carry immense ontological significance, as groups compete against each other to delineate, among other standards, the boundaries of inclusion and exclusion, desired goals of the group, and friends and enemies—essentially who "we" are and how we should behave. The ability to be in a position to define these standards for the whole carries with it benefits intimately connected to individuals' own sense of self, as well as those individuals' prospects of improving their well-being and success—or "life chances" in the Weberian sense.[21] Practical examples related to both personal identity and structural life chances—such as the language of education,[22] the existence of an official religion,[23] the level of women's access to politics,[24] and level of rights provision for LGBTQ individuals and couples[25]—all represent intersections of the two and thus can form the basis of intense political contestation among those who differ about appropriate standards of behavior vis-à-vis these issues. The achievement of identity hegemony by a group sharing a collective understanding of an extended self—a "we-ness"—not only ensures that the group could put its own standards of appropriate behavior into practice through institutions of governance, but also limits the possibility that dissenters would challenge the appropriateness of the group's actions and push to institute policies based on an alternative version of "we-ness." *Hegemony* as I use it here thus constitutes not just the governing power to delimit and enforce norms of prescribed and proscribed behavior; it also entails an ontological fulfilling of groups' sense of existence by being able to realize their (identity-based) interests in practice.

Drawing on insights from experimental research in social psychology regarding the ontological function of social identities, inside-out theory assumes that supporters of a particular identity proposal—defined here as a suggested understanding of the appropriate content of a national identity for citizens of a state—seek to increase support for their proposal by spreading its acceptance to more individuals. Social identity, defined by Henri Tajfel as "that part of an individual's self-concept which derives from his knowledge of his membership in a social group . . . together with the value and emotional significance attached to that membership,"[26] provides individuals with a mechanism for generating self-esteem by fulfilling a need not only for distinctiveness but for positive distinctiveness.[27] These ontological needs for group membership and positive distinctiveness serve as the "motivational underpinnings" of social identities.[28] Individuals seek to fulfill these needs through intergroup evaluation of and competition among various social identities, treated here as processes of contestation. National identity proposals, as social identities especially "thick"[29] with historical and political meaning, particularly function to provide legitimacy and esteem to in-group members (supporters of the same proposal) and thus are expected to be highly contested among supporters of different proposals. Inside-out theory also assumes that in-group members share a desire to realize in practice the goals envisioned by their identity. In constructivist IR terms, this is equivalent to an actor fulfilling the interests generated by his or her identity.[30] The theory posits that individuals believe the more widely supported their identity proposal is, the more likely they will be able to access the requisite institutions to facilitate achieving the goals their identity prescribes. Individuals—and particularly elites, who may be better equipped with financial tools and skill sets—thus strive for hegemony of their proposals to satisfy personal needs and realize group interests.

While acknowledging that hegemony is a loaded term, I select it to connote the power wielded and legitimacy enjoyed by an identity proposal that has achieved a certain status. A hegemonic proposal is an understanding of a national identity that is widespread, in terms of distribution across a population, to the point of being "relatively stable and unquestioned."[31] Supporters of a hegemonic proposal therefore wield the capacity to dictate political and societal rules within the state as well as the behavior of the state—from the lifestyles of its citizens to foreign policy preferences—in line with ideas about appropriate behavior stemming from its identity.[32] This capacity to shape a population's understanding of its identity is undergirded by a complex confluence of both ideational and material factors, such as those captured in Max Weber's ideas on various forms of legitimacy and Antonio Gramsci's critique of wealth's positional advantages in generating consent.[33]

Indeed, this formulation of identity-power relations shares some assumptions with Gramsci's conception of cultural hegemony, in that identity hegemony also involves support among in-group members for an overarching social structure of norms and rules that shape everyday life. However, it departs from Gramsci's assumption that hegemony comes about by a passive revolution.[34] In contrast, inside-out theory assumes that the struggle to achieve hegemony is often met with active and sustained resistance to an identity proposal ascending by acquiring widespread support, and that acquiescence—required to constitute a hegemonic structure of relations among actors[35]—is nearly impossible to attain due to the ontological importance of identities to individuals, noted above. Hegemony is thus a goal for which supporters of competing identity proposals strive but rarely if ever achieve. As this book's case study of Turkey makes clear, hegemony can prove elusive despite the most ardent efforts to spread and institutionalize a particular understanding of identity; on the contrary, the more ardent the pursuit in eliminating rival proposals to achieve hegemony for one's own, the more elusive the goal.

To provide deeper insight into why this is the case, the inside-out theory of identity contestation developed here identifies strategies that various proposals' supporters use in their pursuit of hegemony. Such strategies take various forms, ranging from the exclusion or annihilation of "Outgroup(s)"[36] to nationalizing practices aimed at assimilation,[37] defamation campaigns seeking to delegitimize identity components associated with those in the out-group, persuasion campaigns inundating popular media with propaganda positively depicting elements of a proposal to reinforce loyalty of existing supporters as well as gain new supporters, and institutional reform that seeks to alter the distribution of competing identity proposals by advancing the relative position and appeal of one's own.

As another theoretical contribution, I also identify the conditions under which this identity contestation takes place outside, rather than inside, the state. By conceptualizing foreign policy as a locus of national identity contestation, the theory I develop identifies an additional, and counterintuitive, site in which supporters of identity proposals attempt to advance these proposals toward hegemony other than within the domestic sphere. In contrast to rationalist IR theories' views of foreign policy as a tool of institutionalized bureaucracies serving the (fixed) interests of a (black-boxed and unitary) state,[38] inside-out theory's challenge to these assumptions reveals the mechanism by which national identity debates spill over into foreign policy. Specifically, given the ontological importance of identity and thus the potential gains to be had by increasing one's own proposal's share in the distribution of identities across a population, the theory assumes that when supporters of identity proposals find their struggle to achieve hegemony obstructed at the domestic level, they take their contestation battle to the foreign policy arena. Further, foreign policy is treated here not solely as the realm of governmental elites, but also as a site in which identity proposal supporters who are not in power may also attempt to spread awareness of the legitimacy of their understanding of national identity when their contestation attempts are (more frequently, given their relative disadvantage vis-à-vis institutional access) blocked at home.

Externalizing contestation in the foreign policy arena can serve as a highly successful strategy for advancing identity proposals when there are major domestic obstacles to these proposals, because the contenders and rules in the foreign policy contest differ. Crucially, there is no pushback from opponents who vehemently defend competing proposals for the same identity, whose content may fundamentally conflict with that of the proposal being advanced and therefore be viewed as intolerable. The ontological commitments to particular components of a national identity are much weaker, if present at all, for interlocutors in foreign policy than they are in the domestic arena, because they have much less stake in the identity content of the in-group. Supporters of an identity proposal may therefore use the foreign policy arena to pursue hegemony if doing so at home risks posing an organizational (or even existential) threat to the in-group. Political or religious groups that have been forced to disband, for example, but whose members have reconstituted a moderated version of the group, may be more likely to fight in the foreign policy arena due to past experiences and fear of future repression from those who find the content of their identity proposal intolerable.

In addition, in drawing on both comparativist and IR literatures, we can identify several mechanisms by which supporters not only circumvent obstacles but also benefit from opportunities available in the foreign policy arena. Engaging diaspora communities, ethnic kin groups, and even their host countries' governments can provide material sources of support for,[39] as well as draw valuable attention to, the plight of groups whose identity contestation efforts are blocked or suppressed. Individual nongovernmental organizations (NGOs) and transnational advocacy networks (TANs) more broadly may also serve as efficient fora in which to raise awareness and generate "boomerang" pressure for change back home.[40] Finally, the constraints generated by international organizations' accession criteria can serve as a tool to alter the relative power of domestic actors in the name of gains to be made through membership.[41] In necessitating institutional and legislative change—for example, reducing the influence of particular institutions such as the military or religious authorities over politics, broadening constitutional definitions of citizenship, and raising electoral quotas or lowering thresholds—a proposal's supporters can strategically employ conditionality to alter the contours of identity contestation at the domestic level to their own advantage.

With the mechanism of contestation used to advance the spread of identity proposals across a population having been outlined, the last part of this section presents a framework for analyzing the identity content specific to each proposal. Identity content represents the "stuff" of identity: the elements supporters of an identity proposal share that form an in-group among them and differentiate them from other out-groups. This shared content—such as beliefs about membership in and desired goals of the in-group, as well as how the in-group should relate to others—is difficult to determine empirically and even more difficult to capture analytically. Inside-out contestation theory therefore utilizes a replicable framework, first proposed in an interdisciplinary and mixed-methods volume by Abdelal, Yoshiko Herrera, Alastair Iain Johnston, and Rose McDermott,[42] that breaks down identity content into four components, thus making the nebulous concept of identity easier to grasp. First, constitutive norms provide guidelines for membership within and appropriate behavior for the in-group, defining who "we" are and how we should behave. Second, the social purpose component defines group interests, the goals that the in-group believes it should achieve. The third component of relational meanings defines the in-group's relation to various out-groups; some of these relations may be friendly while others may be hostile, fearful, and so forth. Finally, the cognitive worldview component provides an overarching sense of the group's role in the international sphere.

Importantly, this framework does not posit that any of these elements are fixed; rather, through processes of contestation both within an in-group and among an in-group and its various out-groups, these components can change. This framework therefore facilitates the analysis of such topics as a change in the norms of behavior for a specific identity proposal over time (e.g., what it means to be Western or liberal), changes in how an in-group views its relations with a particular out-group (e.g., a shift from viewing "Europe" as an enemy to viewing it as a partner), and changes in relative distribution of proposals across a population (e.g., a shift from a high amount of support for a "Western" proposal to high support for an "Eastern" proposal).

This framework also facilitates identifying clear red lines of seeming intolerability among proposals. I theorize that supporters of competing proposals run up against issues that appear to be unsolvable and thus object to norms of prescribed behavior that are not only inappropriate but unacceptable to supporters of a rival proposal:[43] for example, is Europe our friend or enemy, are we pacific or bellicose? The qualifier "seeming" is used here to emphasize the constructed and malleable nature of identities and their constitutive components, no matter how intractable contestation over particular components may appear at a given time. Some components of identity content may be shared across proposals (e.g., two proposals with a common cognitive worldview of being a global human rights norm entrepreneur) and others may differ but not *necessarily* conflict (e.g., Proposal A's constitutive norm of religious freedom and Proposal B's constitutive norm of piety), allowing for collaboration, or at least peaceful coexistence, among groups. Proposals with components that are intolerable vis-à-vis each other (e.g., social purposes of spreading capitalism versus communism), however, pose ontological threats to supporters' sense of who they are as individuals and as a group, leading supporters to use all available strategies of contestation to prevent such proposals from becoming more widespread and, when possible, to increase the spread of their own proposal.

Identifying intolerable components among proposals thus provides insight into why supporters of a proposal may encounter challenges that block their pursuit of hegemony in the domestic arena. To understand how blockage functions, I conceptualize those challenges powerful enough to thwart such pursuits as identity-based obstacles. Outlined in detail in chapter 5's discussion of Republican Nationalist obstacles, these consist of institutions established, at least in part, to ensure that red lines of intolerability are not crossed. The form, authority, and enforcement capacity of these obstacles may vary across cases, but they can consist of institutions as varied as militaries, police forces and other forms of civilian patrol (one can think here of Iran's so-called morality police), judicial bodies, educational systems, language institutes, constitutions, and the media. I demonstrate that pursuits of hegemony that are ultimately thwarted by the presence of identity-based obstacles lead supporters to take their identity contestation outside through foreign policy.

In sum, the framework developed here specifies content components of identity proposals and highlights points of intolerability among proposals. The framework is used in conjunction with the specified mechanism of contestation, which allows for both the content of particular proposals to change and levels of support to shift from one proposal to another over time. As such, the framework provides a basis for replicability within cases and cross-case comparison of identity proposals in future scholarship.

Methodology

Vital to constructing and applying any theory of identity contestation is developing a method for identifying and distinguishing among competing identity proposals. In basic terms, how do we know an identity proposal when we see it? Using the explicit framework of identity content outlined above enables a delineation of the particular components that make up each identity proposal—that is, specifying the "stuff" that members of a certain in-group share with each other about who they are and how they behave. This step allows for the analytical assembly of the bits of identity stuff into coherent and cohesive concepts once located, but the task of determining how to collect and interpret these bits remains. Searching for evidence of certain identities could easily prejudice the findings in numerous ways, such as by creating predetermined notions of what particular statements or actions mean that lead to misinterpretations or by creating blinders that inhibit the capture of identities that are present in society but not familiar to the researcher.

Rather than engage, therefore, in basic ascriptive classification, I employ an intertextual analysis approach that seeks to extract existing proposals for national identity content from discourse. This approach deliberately avoids application of identities specified a priori by initiating investigation agnostic about the understandings of identity content expected to be found. Intertextual analysis involves inductively recovering existing but potentially obscured identities from oral, written, and symbolic texts,[44] organically constructing collective identities that cohere around shared understandings. The sources used to extract various identity proposals in this study include texts found in print and online news media; social media sites; and government archives, including minutes from parliamentary debates, party platforms, and legislation published in the *Official Gazette* (*Resmi Gazete*).

In line with Hopf's assumption that novels depict background daily practices and everyday dimensions of interpersonal relations in which "incidental asides to identity" are likely to be found,[45] I also drew on texts of popular novels. Novels can serve as an extraordinarily useful vehicle for gaining insight into the contours of identity debates, providing a forum in which overt discussions of normally taboo issues regarding identity can take place. Through analyzing such texts, the researcher—particularly one not native to the country of study—becomes privy to scenes one might not otherwise be able to observe. Further, sifting through various public reactions to controversial novels also provides insight into the reasons particular subjects are taboo. Author Elif Şafak, for example, garnered popular and critical acclaim within Turkey as well from international audiences for her novel *The Bastard of Istanbul* (*Baba ve Piç*),[46] which directly takes up the highly contested issue of the atrocities/ genocide committed against Armenians through its interwoven stories of families affected by the events of 1915 in Turkey, both at home and in the diaspora. For her portrayal of events, Şafak was charged with violating article 301 of the Turkish Penal Code (*Türk Ceza Kanunu*) by expressing an "insult to Turkishness" (*"Türklüğe hakaret"*).[47] Analyzing responses to the novel and the indictment of Şafak, who was born in France and lived many years outside of Turkey, published in newspaper columns and blogs sheds further light on various understandings of identity in Turkey, ranging from overtly pro- to vehemently anti-Western. A post on the media site Bianet.org (Bağımsız İletişim Ağı, Independent Communication Network), which I classify as containing Western Liberalist texts, praises Şafak's selection as cultural ambassador by the European Culture Foundation.[48] In stark contrast from an identity perspective, the late leader of the ultranationalist Great Union Party (Büyük Birlik Partisi,

BBP) Muhsin Yazıcıoğlu, whom I classify as Pan-Turkic Nationalist, posted a piece in which he directly references the title of the novel when criticizing both Şafak and the European community for defending her. He states: "Europe needs bastards; if there is a bastard, [Europeans] will embrace it. If [the bastard] betrays the Turkish state and is opposed to its territorial unity (*bütünlüğü*), if this individual tries to separate the nation, all of them will protect it, embrace it. It's completely natural for them to endorse this."[49] Yazıcıoğlu's comments in reaction to the controversy generated by a subject long considered "off limits" in the public sphere provide insight into the content of the identity proposal he supports. While territorial unity for and defense of the Turkish nation will be seen to be a primary constitutive norm of both Republican Nationalism and Pan-Turkic Nationalism in the following chapter, the aggressively anti-European stance he displays and his many references to being Turkish as *Türklük*, which carries an ethnic or racial connotation in defining Turkishness, are elements Republican Nationalists reject.

Further, novels can contain scenes in which contrasting attitudes toward highly contested issues face off against each other in a microcosm of wider debates. Characters may serve as mouthpieces for arguments authors wish to see expressed to and understood by wider audiences. The Kurdish nationalist romance novel *Bir Dava, İki Sevda* (*One Cause, Two Loves*) provides an excellent example of such a debate, as Kurdish high-school friends Bedri and Ruken try to convince Turkish classmate Özgür that the struggle of the Kurds for independence is a valid cause given the tyranny they have faced at the hands of the Turkish state and its military. Excerpts from the dialogue that ensues when Özgür suggests that the grievances propelling some of Turkey's Kurds to "go to the mountain" (*dağa çıkmak*, a euphemism for joining the Partiya Karkaren Kurdistani [PKK]'s mountain-based camps) are not ethnic, but are rather "the result of ignorance (*cahillik*) and feudalism (*feodalite*)," make clear the point the author wishes to convey:

> **Bedri:** Özgür, the subject isn't that simple. . . . Even children from well-off families are on the mountain. What's happening is the result of an unsolved problem that has been around since the founding of the republic.
>
> **Özgür:** There's no need to go to the mountain. If Kurdish and Turkish workers struggle together the problem will be solved. Those who are defending their [Turkish] homeland can shoot together at those wandering around up there with guns.
>
> **Bedri:** Özgür my friend, no one goes to the mountain or risks death for fun. Since the beginning the state has denied the existence of the Kurds, trying to get rid of the problem by assimilating them like the

other minority Muslim groups. . . . Kurds want the problem solved in a democratic and peaceful way more than anyone. . . . Ruken and I just want to enjoy the same rights as you do. If you [Turks] would show a little empathy . . .

Özgür: When we can live together under a Turkish identity (*Türk kimliği altında birlikte yaşamak varken*), it's hard to understand why Kurds separate themselves. . . . You can be a prime minister or president, what else do you want?[50]

During the discussion, Alevi Kurd Ruken remains mostly silent. The reader learns this is likely because she is struggling with her own sense of identity, having been raised speaking Turkish at home but discovering her Kurdishness through interactions with her friends. The Kurdish characters face numerous hardships throughout the novel, including abduction and torture in addition to their personal identity crises, creating the "empathy" in the reader that Bedri requests. The arguments put forward by Özgür (whose name, meaning "free/at liberty" in Turkish, may have been chosen to imply he is the character who is most "free" as opposed to the Kurdish characters), in turn, are emblematic of narratives expressed by Republican Nationalists in their desire to modernize all citizens of Turkey, but their fear of ethnicity as a destructive, separatist (*bölücü*) force destroying the process. The presence of such debates in novels, clearly attempting to persuade the reader, also allows contrasting viewpoints to unfold and thus become accessible to the researcher.

Finally, novels can set the stage for discussions drawing together multiple strands of identity that the researcher might not otherwise be able to untangle. Ömer Zülfü Livaneli's widely popular works, for example, regularly insert questions of identity into conversations among characters seemingly juxtaposed precisely to illustrate such complexity. For example, in Livaneli's novel *Mutluluk* (*Bliss*), an American journalist seeking to understand the left-right struggles of the 1970s, the secularism debate, and the Kurdish question attempts to interview a disparate group of passengers in the train car in which he is seated. Introducing a question to one of the passengers through an interpreter, the journalist states that he has found there are three poles (*kutuplar*) in Turkey: Turkish nationalism, Kurdish nationalism, and political Islam. He asks whether the man agrees, to which he receives the outraged and emphatic reply that the Turkish Republic is not at all separated (*bölünmüş*) along such poles; there are only Turks, and the Kurds and Islamists who try to destroy them. The journalist is bewildered and turns to ask a female passenger who had earlier stated she is from southeastern Turkey—an area densely populated by Kurds that has been plagued for decades by armed conflict—whether she is Turkish or Kurdish. Terrified at being caught in the middle of this identity debate, the woman falls back on a phrase she has heard repeated since she was born: "*Elhamdülillah Müslüman'ım*! (Praise be to God, I'm a Muslim!)"[51] The scene serves as an encapsulation of the complexity of (some of the many) various lines of identification in Turkey—a veritable word of warning to the researcher against adopting pregiven understandings of the contours and ramifications of these debates.

In selecting the novels to be used in this study, I consulted best-seller lists, books listed by the university student participants in my popular culture survey (discussed below), books displayed prominently on stands at bus stations and airports, and recommendations solicited or offered in the course of informal conversations. I also drew on monographs, a popular and relatively accessible form of conveying one's ideas through local publishers such as Hemen Kitap, GOA Yayınarı, İleri Yayınları, and Şule Yayınları.[52] Of course novels are not the only cultural medium in which debates of such utility to the researcher seeking to extract identity proposals take place. Working under the assumption that all forms of popular fiction constitute a particularly important source of identity and its discursive practices, I expanded the breadth and variety of texts used in Hopf's approach to analyze the content of television series and films. Including these serves to extract texts from media consumed by a much broader swath of the population than just readers; a large majority of university students, for example, indicated on a survey I conducted that they do not read novels. Guided by this important if somewhat depressing insight, I built on work demonstrating how broad social issues such as modernity, religion, and gender roles are engaged, contested, and shaped via diverse forms of pop culture media.[53] As media anthropologist Hikmet Kocamaner notes, the Turkish state has used mass media as a form of governance and nation-building since the formation in 1964 of the state-owned Turkish Radio and Television Corporation. Until the privatization of television broadcasting in the 1990s under President Turgut Özal, whose leadership as prime minister in the 1980s oversaw a massive neo-liberal economic opening, the state wielded television programming as a platform for spreading a Republican Nationalist identity proposal. In Kocamaner's words, "only those who fit the state's definition of an *ideal Turkish citizen* were represented on state TV, and those outside of it were virtually invisible. Thus, TV audiences could only watch educated, urbane, secular Turks, while ethnic and religious minorities, and non-secular Muslims were nearly absent from TV screens."[54] Just as visual entertainment media serve as an effective tool of the government, here state-approved programming provides insight for the researcher into ideas about who constitutes the "ideal Turkish citizen" mentioned in the quote.

In terms of entertainment media consulted, the samples I chose (a) had high viewer ratings and box-office sales numbers and (b) were cited frequently in a survey of university students, who might be more likely to access such media through YouTube or other online sources. Due to factors related to Turkey's system of sorting university applicants, the students I surveyed at Bilkent and TOBB universities in Ankara and Gebze Technical University in Kocaeli (a province neighboring Istanbul) represented a wide variety of socioeconomic backgrounds.[55] I asked the survey's 175 university-level participants to list the novel, television, and film characters they believed represented the ideal example of who a Turkish citizen should be, and well as which characters they thought represented the worst possible example, and why. In addition to collecting a set of mostly television series and films (if not many novels) for analysis, the survey thus also proved extremely useful in generating highly contrasting beliefs about what constitutes the ideal citizen of Turkey without directly asking the question—which, especially in a university setting, might have generated rote answers directly tied to the national(ist) education they received.

I further broadened the collection of texts by conducting more than fifty semi-structured interviews with political party members and government officials, NGO workers, cultural association members, civil servants, retired military personnel, business community members, street activists, academics, journalists, and other citizens of Turkey. Nearly all interviews were conducted in Turkish, and they lasted from thirty minutes to two hours. Several interviews, including those conducted at the Ankara headquarters of the Alevi Pir Sultan Abdal Cultural Association and the Giresun branch of the Idealist Hearths (Ülkü Ocakları), were group interviews that enabled me to record responses to statements made by other participants in the conversation, as well as to gain insight into debates internal to the group. I also analyzed the texts of more than sixty responses to an extended written questionnaire, in which I included questions such as whether Turkey has any natural allies, what the most salient line of identity debate is in Turkey, and what the most important components of Turkishness are, and why. Finally, as a supplement to my other methods, I have drawn on the ethnographic observation I engaged in over the course of twenty months in 2012–2016. I primarily conducted this observation while based as a visiting researcher at Bilkent University in Ankara, but also broadened the scope of my observations by conducting research in Antalya, Eskişehir, Giresun, Istanbul, Konya, Marmaris, and Trabzon.[56] This, and the timing of my fieldwork in Turkey, allowed me to record diverse observances filled with texts related to identity debates, such as a march on Republic Day (Cumhuriyet Bayramı) in Ankara, numerous demonstrations in the Gezi Park protests in Ankara and Istanbul, local election campaigning by the Nationalist Action Party (Milliyetçi Hareket Partisi) and the Felicity Party (Saadet Partisi) in Trabzon and Giresun, attitudes toward European and Russian tourists in Marmaris, and the observance of Ramadan in highly conservative Konya.

From this cumulative body of material, the identity content framework outlined above provides a guide for making analytical sense of the discursive practices extracted from these texts, creating composite understandings of identity that cohere around shared constitutive norms, relational meanings, social purposes, and cognitive worldviews. This framework thus functions here in reverse of the order that I originally intended: that is, to parse out the content among competing identity proposals that have already been determined. In contrast, these four content elements serve as a useful framework on which to drape the discursive practices observed to discern whether they do in fact flesh out into coherent identity proposals as expected. Bearing in mind the complexity of identity in practice, this extraction of identity proposals does not claim to be able to capture perfectly neat boxes into which all content elements discretely and uniformly fall, even in the necessarily finite number of texts analyzed here. There is, for example, some overlap among elements of the four identity proposals that emerged from this process. The relational meaning of belonging within the Western world and the social purpose of modernization, for example, may be shared among texts that differ greatly in constitutive norms of human rights and various freedoms of expression.[57] Nonetheless, the four proposals extracted and examined in detail throughout this study represent distinct constellations of the four categories of identity content I employ.

Indeed, despite the overlap I encountered, general patterns of correspondence among content elements clearly emerged. As an example, texts containing both the constitutive norms of piety and belief in an overtly strong ruler also tended to exhibit a social purpose of increasing space for Islam in the public sphere, a relational meaning of brotherhood and solidarity with other Muslim countries, and a cognitive worldview of Turkey as a revered cultural and military power in line with its imperial legacy. Further, after I established how the identity content present in the texts I was analyzing tended to coalesce into four distinct patterns—each containing clear norms of membership and appropriate behavior, desired goals for the group, beliefs about relations with others, and overall views of the group's place in the world—examinations of new texts produced similar alignments of content into the patterns I refer to here as identity proposals. In this study I name the four proposals that collectively capture the most widespread understandings of Turkey's national identity today— Pan-Turkic Nationalism, Western Liberalism, Republican Nationalism, and Ottoman Islamism—based on their key constitutive identity components. By distinguishing specific and easily identifiable criteria that make up each composite proposal, this process of identity extraction once completed greatly eases the task of answering the question "How do we know it when we see it," justifiably posed by those asked to consider complicating their already overflowing analytical toolboxes with a new concept (especially one as intangible as identity) for this study and beyond.

Once having achieved a highly detailed, systematically organized catalog of the content of each of these proposals, I use process tracing to identify the causal mechanisms of contestation at work in shaping the contours of the competition among supporters of each, as well as to evaluate the effects of this contestation. As David Collier notes, descriptive inference is a fundamental, if sometimes underappreciated, tool of social science research that facilitates understanding change in our subjects of interest over time through the comparison of carefully assembled snapshots.[58] That is, in order to characterize a process and flesh out the mechanisms driving it, the researcher must develop a way of capturing the key steps in the process.

Whereas intertextual analysis facilitates the extraction of identity proposals from discourses present in Turkey's society, I employ process tracing to highlight diagnostic evidence bolstering my argument that supporters use both the domestic *and* the foreign policy arenas to pursue hegemony for their proposals. Tracing the pursuit by Republican Nationalist supporters in the domestic arena, for example, as well as the limited levels of foreign engagement prescribed by the content of the identity, reveals the extraordinary measures used in an attempt to eradicate the Ottoman Islamist, Pan-Turkic Nationalist, and Kurdish identity ties left over from the Ottoman Empire and seen to be not only undesirable but fundamentally intolerable by the founders of the republic. Despite the Republican Nationalists' massive campaign to institutionalize a new identity, process tracing that draws from a wide variety of sources demonstrates that their pursuit of hegemony ultimately falls short, revealing evidence of numerous lingering challenges from supporters of competing proposals. As historians have noted, "lived memories of the once glorious empire did not simply evaporate . . . the imperial legacy could not be erased."[59] Digging deep into the contestation over the different understandings of identity using novels and newspapers, for example, provides empirical insight into lingering narratives of Ottoman Islamism onto which future adherents could graft and build by taking their fight outside.[60] Process tracing also proves useful in uncovering this strategy of contestation that I argue enabled the AKP to circumvent and then weaken Republican Nationalist obstacles to its own pursuit of hegemony. I trace how the AKP, whose key founding members initially opposed membership in the European Union, utilized the EU accession process and specific elements of its democratization criteria to contest identity-based obstacles such as the military and the Constitutional Court in a much safer environment—that of the foreign policy arena—than its predecessors had occupied.

Conclusion

The relative dearth of inter-subfield communication within political science leaves the relationship between identity politics and foreign policy—often considered to be under the sole jurisdiction of comparativist and IR scholars, respectively—undertheorized and thus underexplored. In seeking to fill this gap, this chapter also highlights the inability of rationalist explanations—both comparative theories of identity politics and IR theories of foreign policy—to account for the ontological importance of identities for individuals and groups and the function of identities in shaping the realms of the desirable, the possible, and the necessary in terms of policy choices.

In an effort to capture the significance of all of these elements, I combine insights from comparativist, IR, and social psychology literatures in an inter-disciplinary approach to the study of the interactive relationship between iden-tity and foreign policy. Aiming to fill the existing analytical gap by closing the identity–foreign policy circle, this chapter offers an inside-out theory of identity contestation that analytically links the means by which national identity debates spill over into foreign policy with the means by which foreign policy serves as a strategy for advancing a particular group's position in these debates. Arguing that individuals fulfill their innate social psychological need for group belonging and self-esteem through intergroup comparative evaluation, the theory of iden-tity contestation developed here posits that individuals seek to advance the spread of their own proposal for national identity across as wide a distribution of the population as is possible. According to this theory, the larger the distribu-tion of this proposal relative to other competing proposals for national identity, the more able supporters are to realize the interests prescribed by that proposal. While rarely if ever achieving their goal due to the ontological importance of individuals' deeply held beliefs about who they are and how they should behave, supporters of particular identity proposals engage in various strategies of contes-tation in pursuit of hegemony for their particular proposals.

Seeking to flesh out the relationship between domestic identity debates and foreign policy, this chapter conceptualizes the latter as both a particularly hotly debated component of national identity and an alternative arena in which iden-tity proposals are contested. Inside-out theory stipulates the conditions under which supporters of identity proposals employ strategies of contestation at the domestic versus the international level, positing that political elites choose to take this identity contestation "outside" to the foreign policy arena when identity gambits at the domestic level are blocked by the presence and actions of identity-based obstacles. A process tracing–based focus on contestation as a mechanism for change enables analysis of both changes within these identity proposals over time, as well as changes in the relative level of support for identities across the population.

The following chapter presents the content of the four identity proposals extracted by using intertextual analysis to examine texts collected from a variety of archival, media, and participant-based sources such as surveys, interviews, and ethnographic observation. Breaking down each of the composite proposals of Pan-Turkic Nationalism, Western Liberalism, Republican Nationalism, and Ottoman Islamism into their constituent components as outlined above facilitates the specification of identity red lines used to locate particular points of contestation among the proposals. This specification assists in conceptualizing the identity-based obstacles formed during the pursuit of identity hegemony by supporters of Republican Nationalism outlined in chapters 4 and 5, as well as how these obstacles will be circumvented by supporters of Ottoman Islamism, analyzed in chapter 6.

3

National Identities in Turkey

Four Competing Proposals

Introduction

This chapter presents the main body of empirical evidence gathered for this study, providing a detailed examination of the four identity proposals I extracted from these data. By analyzing written, oral, and symbolic discourses collected from interviews, surveys, and participant observation, as well as popular culture, news, and social media, I located four internally coherent, repeatedly manifested patterns of beliefs about the proper identity for Turkey's citizens. I then operationalized these patterns as proposals in line with Abdelal et al.'s contribution toward conceptual congruity and replicability in studies of identity.[1] I conducted the majority of the research for this project as a visiting researcher at Bilkent University in Ankara, Turkey's capital city and political center, but I also include data from research conducted in Antalya, Bursa, Eskişehir, Giresun, Istanbul, Marmaris, and Trabzon. This facilitated my accumulation of a wide variety of perspectives in a country in which understandings of identity, despite wide internal migration, still tend to be regionally concentrated.

The proposals I identify here are not intended to be exhaustive, nor could they be in a country of nearly eighty million people. Rather, they analytically capture the four understandings of identity most widely held in Turkey's contemporary society, based on eighteen months of fieldwork. Although initially intended as a point-in-time snapshot to ascertain the content of these proposals, a main contribution of this book is to identify the processes by which support for competing proposals can change over time. As the following chapters illustrate, those who support varying proposals engage in identity contestation at every level. From coffeehouse griping about politicians to the gambits of the politicians themselves, ordinary citizens and elites delegitimize and discredit what they consider to be flawed and even offensive ideas about Turkishness, consciously or unconsciously striving for the hegemony of their own idea of what Turkey's national identity should be.

This is far from the first study to give names to various understandings of identity in Turkey, nor is it likely to be the last. Turkey serves as a fascinating and exceedingly useful empirical window into processes of identity contestation precisely because of its highly contentious relations along multiple, often complexly overlapping lines of identification—Turks and Kurds, Alevis and Sunnis, Muslims and non-Muslims, pious and secularists, urbanites and new migrants from rural villages—and academics willing to wade into these ontologically and methodologically murky waters offer many descriptors for classifying these group dynamics. Soner Çağaptay's study—appropriately subtitled "Who Is a Turk?"—investigates how proponents of what he calls Turkish nationalism grappled with Islam, secularism, and ethnic identity to forge a cohesive nation.[2] Jenny White's richly detailed study of Muslim nationalism provides excellent insight into the seemingly strange bedfellows of political liberalism and cultural conservatism comprising the mindset of what she calls "the new Turks."[3] Among those who cite multiple, competing versions of Turkish nationalism, Tanıl Bora names four: official/Atatürk, Kemalist, liberal, and Turkist radical nationalisms;[4] Şener Aktürk points to the same number of "intellectual movements": Pan-Islamism, Pan-Turkism, Westernism, and Eurasianism.[5] Given this proliferation of classifications of identity and identities in Turkey, why bother offering up another?

While similarities do exist among my identity proposals and those listed above—what I term Pan-Turkic Nationalism in the discussion below, for example, is close to both Bora's Turkist radical nationalism and Aktürk's Pan-Turkism—substantial and important differences exist in my formulation and treatment of not just contrasting but *competing* proposals for Turkey's identity that uniquely facilitate this project's study of when and how national identity contestation takes place in the foreign policy arena. First, the method and data I use to extract the four identity proposals that serve as the analytical focal point of this study provide the distinct advantage of accessing and recording beliefs about identity from the average citizen to the most powerful elite. Second, I specifically included questions related to foreign policy in all interviews and surveys and focused my analysis of written sources on discussions of Turkey's friends, foes, and ideal future in the international community. Third, I organically assembled these proposals, aware that numerous descriptive classifications existed but deliberately avoiding them, remaining as agnostic as possible about what I would find. In doing so, I have generated a widely comprehensive, richly detailed, and societally reflective picture that can serve as the basis for analysis of change within and among proposals, rather than a description of their differences. Finally, and crucially from a theory-building perspective, this book's engagement with the framework introduced in the previous chapter newly enables the speci-fication of points of intolerability among them. The systematic, element-by-element breakdown of proposals in this chapter reveals those intolerable, unacceptable behaviors that I classify as red lines of identity content, as well as elements of content that overlap across proposals. Red lines indi-cate points of intense contestation, which serve as the ideational founda-tion of identity-based obstacles erected to prevent the spread of competing proposals. In contrast, overlapping elements may provide the groundwork for hybrid identity proposals to develop in the future among previous rival supporters.

As mentioned previously, the four proposals I extracted from my research as coherent sets of identity content elements represent the four most widely held understandings of Turkey's national identity: Pan-Turkic Nationalism, Western Liberalism, Republican Nationalism, and Ottoman Islamism. I selected the name of each proposal to capture as accurately as possible the content constitutive of its supporters' beliefs about themselves, members of their in-group, and various out-groups. The first half of each proposal's name represents the historical, cultural, and/or geographical space that orients its supporters in the wider world. This orientation provides onto-logical security through a sense of rootedness and legitimacy in a commu-nity. For Ottoman Islamists, for example, "Ottoman" signifies a historical rootedness of centuries of existence, a cultural magnificence from military might to law and order, and a legitimacy of domination over a wide swath of the Balkans, Caucasus, and Middle East. This signifier also differentiates the Ottoman proposal I discuss from traditions of Islamism anchored in other historical or geographical orientations; the particularly Turkish form of Islamism espoused by members of the Gülen movement, discussed in the concluding chapter as a proposal I term "Turkish Calvinism," is one ex-ample of this. The "Republican" in Republican Nationalism signifies some-thing quite different: a newly forged, territorially based civic community whose legitimacy comes from struggle and revolution, one that is made up of citizens sharing civic principles rather than imperial subjects organized by *millet* (confessional group). The second half of each proposal signifies the value system that provides guidance for supporters in terms of appropriate norms of behavior. Pan-Turkic Nationalists thus expect fellow members to defend the honor and existence of the Turkic nation above all others, broadly conceived as discussed below, while Western Liberalists consider protecting liberal values and freedoms the standard to uphold. To assist readers in navigating the complexity of the content that follows and to allow for a side-by-side comparison of each identity proposal, a summary of the content of the four proposals is presented in table 3.1.

Table 3.1. **Table of Identity Proposals**

	Pan-Turkic Nationalism	Western Liberalism	Republican Nationalism	Ottoman Islamism
CN	Ethnic/cultural Turkish membership; Sunni Muslim faith, deeper roots in Central Asia	Nonethnic, nonlinguistic, nonreligious membership; embrace diversity, liberties	Nonethnic, linguistic and territorial membership; must call oneself Turk; embrace principles of Ataturk	Sunni Muslim; piety; deference of women; absolute authority; Ottoman rule as greatest era
SP	Enrich and protect Turkish culture; eradicate Kurdish, Armenian claims that threaten this culture; realize some form of union with Turkic populations	Protect rights, liberties, equality (esp. minorities, women, LGBTQs); promote freedom of expression in all forms	Uphold Ataturk's principles; protect secularism and territory at all costs; retain Western orientation	Spread Islam in public sphere; provide aid to and deepen ties with Muslim, Ottoman peoples; regain Ottoman glory
RM	Natural brotherhood with Turkic peoples; hostile relationship with the West; suspicion of Arab peoples	Natural kinship with West, Europe as civilizational home; no inherent hostility toward any peoples or regimes	Natural Western orientation but suspicious view of Western regimes as imperialist (Sèvres); cautious relations due to fear of entanglement, border compromise; Muslim peoples seen as backward/ignorant	Natural kinship with Muslim peoples, possibility of good relations with other former Ottoman territories; hostility toward West; enmity toward Israel as Palestine oppressor
CW	Natural big brotherhood to and savior of Turkic peoples (Central Asia, Uyghurs, Tatars)	Natural place in modern, liberal, Western world; Turkey should be example of peace, freedom, liberty and rights recognition	Secular guard of modern lifestyle in region of Islamic fundamentalism; Turkey as a nonaggressor state	Turkey as legitimate inheritor of Ottoman legacies, power; leader of Islamic world, Palestinian protector

CN = constitutive norms of membership (in-group boundary criteria), prescribed and proscribed behaviors

SP = social purpose (interests of group)

RM = relational meaning (view of relations vis-à-vis various out-groups)

CW = cognitive worldview (general role, beliefs about position in space and time)

Pan-Turkic Nationalism

Of those proposals that I extracted from discourse and analyzed in this study, Pan-Turkic Nationalism was the least prevalent of the four. This relatively low level of support is likely due to the fact that it represents a highly exclusive understanding of national identity. Further, while some supporters of this proposal could be classified as ardent enthusiasts of cultural Turkism, others, who are clearly situated in the realm of neo-fascism and openly support violence[6] as detailed below, lead many to judge Pan-Turkic Nationalists as a whole to be overtly extremist. In terms of the framework employed in this study, this means that the constitutive norms of the Pan-Turkic Nationalist proposal for Turkish identity are narrow in scope. Supporters believe that all Turks' roots lie in Central Asia, thus delimiting at least in some sense who can be a Turk according to Pan-Turkic Nationalists' understanding of *Türklük*, or Turkishness.[7] In addition to Turkic peoples of the five former Soviet republics considered to have large Turkic populations (Azerbaijan, Kazakhstan, Kyrgyzstan, Turkmenistan, and Uzbekistan), a strong connection also exists for Pan-Turkic Nationalists with Turkic populations such as the Uyghurs in China (as well as those diasporic Uyghurs in states such as Tajikistan, whose population is not generally considered by scholars of Pan-Turkic movements because of Tajikistan's primarily Persian cultural heritage),[8] Crimean Tatars, and Turkmens concentrated in cities such as Mosul, Iraq.[9]

Shared cultural symbols displayed on social media sites created by Pan-Turkic Nationalists provide effective visual representation of the constitutive norms of membership for this identity proposal. One prominent symbol is the *bozkurt*, or grey wolf, which according to a founding myth guided Turkic peoples into safety in Anatolia; the Grey Wolves (Bozkurtlar) is used as the name of the ultra-right-wing militant arm of the Nationalist Action Party (Milliyetçi Hareket Partisi, MHP). Facebook pages mourning the killing of Pan-Turkic Nationalist Fırat Yılmaz Çakıroğlu, believed to have been stabbed to death by student sympathizers of the PKK (Turkey's Kurdish nationalist militant wing, classified as a terrorist group by Turkey, the United States, and the EU), display images of the grey wolf, as well as photos of supporters making the well-recognized Grey Wolves hand gesture.[10] The flag of what Pan-Turkic Nationalists refer to as East Turkestan, the Xinjiang region of China, which is highly populated by Turkic-Muslim Uyghurs, is identical to the Turkish flag except that it is pale blue instead of red. This symbol is also displayed on social media and at rallies to indicate a constitutive norm of shared Turkic membership. One interviewee's Facebook page includes a photo, shared in solidarity with Uyghurs, in which the red Turkish flag melds with the blue flag of East Turkestan. The photo contains the caption: "We are one nation, two states. My brother, resist the slaughter committed by China in East Turkestan. . . . East Turkestan, the bleeding wound of the Turk."[11]

Some older generations of Pan-Turkic Nationalism supporters define membership within the Turkish nation as blood or race based;[12] a group of interviewees in Turkey's Black Sea region repeatedly emphasized that "Turks come from a definitive progeny" and "the Turks are our race."[13] Overall, however, explicitly race-based (and racist) understandings of a common Pan-Turkic identity, informed in large part by the writings of author and activist Nihal Atsız, are relatively rare.[14] Many younger supporters deliberately specify that the ties they share with their Turkic brothers are cultural rather than strictly ethnic or racial in terms of blood lineage. One member of the ultra-right-wing Ülkü Ocakları in his mid-twenties commented that upholding such a criterion of membership would be ridiculous given the migration and intermarriages that constitute Turkey's demographic history.[15] For him and many others in the newer generation of Pan-Turkic Nationalism, a belief in shared culture is a much more important— and practical—constitutive norm. When pressed to define the specific "stuff" of this shared culture, interviewees and survey participants cited elements such as Turkish-based language, Islam, history dating to pre-Ottoman times, nomadic origins in Central Asia, and conservative lifestyle.[16]

Particular to the membership norm of this identity proposal according to all supporters is the belief that Kurds also belong, even if they themselves do not believe they do. More precisely, for Pan-Turkic Nationalists, Kurds are not Kurds, but are rather Turks who have been conned into believing they constitute a separate ethnicity. As MHP leader Devlet Bahçeli has stated numerous times, particularly when issues of granting cultural rights to the Kurds are raised: "There is no Kurdish problem."[17] An important point for the membership element of this identity proposal is that Bahçeli does not believe that the Kurds do not have problems; he, along with other Pan-Turkic Nationalists, believes they should accept that they are Turks and live as such rather than trying to differentiate themselves as Kurds. Examples of Pan-Turkic Nationalist literature making claims such as "In Kurdish there is no such word as 'Kurd',"[18] "There are no architectural remains belonging to Kurds,"[19] and "There is no such thing as Kurdish literature"[20] vehemently articulate the Pan-Turkic Nationalist belief that a separate Kurdish identity is fictitious (*yapay*, or "invented/fake"), but Turkic identity is "real" (*gerçek*).

The norms of appropriate behavior for Pan-Turkic Nationalism require protecting by whatever means necessary the Turkish nation's people and borders from any threat.[21] These threats can be material or ideational and have historically included the West's "blood-thirsty imperialism,"[22] communism, and the promotion of human rights that may lead Kurds to agitate for secession—all of which would rupture the Turkish nation in the Pan-Turkic Nationalist line of thinking. Organizations in addition to the Ülkü Ocakları, mentioned above, such as the Association of Idealist Workers (Ülkücü İşçiler Derneği) and the Association of Turkists and Turanists (Türkçü Turancılar Derneği), have thus been set up to "protect" Turks against intellectual and moral corruption and to produce "quality Muslim Turks" who appreciate their shared heritage with their Turkic brethren.[23] Attaining the honor of being an intellectual about the history of Turkic peoples and contributing to the dissemination of inherited "truths"[24]—which for more militant Pan-Turkic Nationalists may involve violently obstructing the proliferation of "untruths" by Kurds and Americans[25]— constitutes a highly important norm of behavior for supporters of this identity proposal.[26]

There is a strongly militant constitutive norm of protecting the Turkish nation from external threats, perhaps most prominent in the *Valley of the Wolves* (*Kurtlar Vadisi*) television and film series. This series, in which Turkish hero Polat Alemdar battles primarily against American and Israeli villains,[27] was cited frequently in surveys conducted with university students as both the best example of an ideal Turk—"because he is a person who is tied to his values about his religion and homeland";[28] "because he is a patriot and exhibits many of our meaningful values"[29]—and as the worst example "because he uses violence in any situation he wants to and tries to solve problems with weapons."[30] The first two fit within the Pan-Turkic Nationalist proposal for identity content, while the third is consistent with the Western Liberalist proposal's support of peaceful conflict resolution.

The social purpose of Pan-Turkic Nationalism is similar to the constitutive norm of protecting the Turkish nation but extends to the wider promotion of the welfare of all Turkic peoples in Europe and Central Asia and to striving for unity among these members.[31] While a single political institution governing all Turkic peoples may never materialize out of the Pan-Turkic Nationalist "romantic desire for Turkish unity,"[32] subscribers to this identity understanding share a belief in the desirability and even the naturalness of a union of Turkic peoples. The freeing of Turkic populations from what was viewed as Soviet victimization provided supporters of this proposal with optimism for a regeneration of the Turkic nation. Rory Finnin's study of novels written during the Soviet era and targeted at readers whom I categorize as supporting a Pan-Turkic Nationalist identity proposal, for example, highlights the plight of Crimean Tatars and urges readers to agitate for their freedom.[33] The need to assist Turkic populations was evidenced in the "strong support felt for Uyghurs" in China and in the "euphoria" felt by Pan-Turkic Nationalists following the independence of former Soviet Central Asian republics.[34] This responsibility to aid Turkic brethren continues to manifest itself today in the Pan-Turkic Nationalist understanding of Turkey's social purpose as inextricably linked with assisting Turkey's Eastern neighbors, most recently in the cases of Turkic Crimean Tatars following Russia's annexation of Crimea and of the Turkmen population of Mosul, in the wake of the Islamic State's invasion.

The relational meaning of this proposal includes suspicion of and enmity against the United States in particular but also the EU,[35] as well as any groups these actors may support at the perceived expense of the Turks, such as Armenians or Kurds. While Pan-Turkic Nationalists view Kurds as brainwashed Turks, as discussed above, they view Armenians as a traitorous enemy, blaming them for the betrayal of the Turkish nation by forming paramilitary groups in conjunction with Russian moves to further weaken the crumbling Ottoman Empire. The efforts by US and European lawmakers to recognize the subsequent massacres and forced displacement carried out against hundreds of thousands of Armenians in 1915 as a genocide stoke Pan-Turkic Nationalists' resentment against these foreign actors as meddlers in issues that are none of their business. Along the same lines, Armenia is also to blame for its territorial conflict with Azerbaijan, Turkey's closest cultural brother for Pan-Turkic Nationalists, over the Nagorno-Karabakh region. The 1992 massacre in Khojali (Hocalı), in which hundreds of Azerbaijani civilians were killed in a particularly bloody episode in the conflict, is commemorated annually through social media and billboards that denounce the slaughter of "our blood brothers" (soydaşlarımız) and rally demonstrators to call for the recognition of the massacre as a genocide.[36] Hinted at above in the militancy justified to protect the Turkish nation, this sentiment comes through in the novel Metal Storm (Metal Fırtına), in which Turks scramble to defend themselves from an American ambush in northern Iraq and recover from an attack that destroys Anıtkabir, Atatürk's mausoleum and the most important monument in Turkey for nationalists (both Pan-Turkic and Republican).[37] Conveying smug US delight in the destruction, after former US defense secretary Donald Rumsfeld learns that the surprise attack has been carried out from his adviser, Jack Argosian (a surname recognizable to Turks as Armenian), "a calm smile appears" on his face.[38]

In terms of both social purpose and relational meaning, it is important to note that some Pan-Turkic Nationalists are quick to emphasize that they do not harbor enmity for or seek to act against all Armenians (or Kurds) in general; one interviewee emphasized that an Armenian from Istanbul was running as a candidate in local elections for the party he supported, the MHP. Tellingly, however, he emphasized that the candidate was openly proud of also being Turkish, which seemed to make the otherwise unpalatable candidate acceptable.[39] Indeed, there is, however, widespread and very publicly displayed evidence of hate speech and violence against Armenians who are deemed to be overly emphasizing their Armenian background, especially those calling for genocide recognition, on Pan-Turkic Nationalist social media sites. Following director Fatih Akın's efforts to cast someone to play the role of Armenian journalist Hrant Dink,[40] who was murdered outside his *Agos* newspaper office in 2007, affiliates of the Türkçü Turancılar Derneği tweeted what amounted to death threats aimed at *Agos* and Akın. Referencing multiple elements of Pan-Turkic Nationalist identity content, the tweet stated "we are following you with our flag of Azerbaijan and our white berets" (*beyaz berelimiz*, a nod to the headwear sported by Dink's assassin Ogün Samast); the post also implied Akın was Kurdish.[41] A Facebook group with the name "Grey Wolf Castle" (Bozkurt Kalesi, another use of the grey wolf symbol) posted a retrospective congratulatory message to Samast: "On the seventh anniversary of Hrant Dink's death, we congratulate Oğuz Samast with respect, love, and adoration."[42]

The cognitive worldview of a Pan-Turkic Nationalist identity understanding conceives of Turkey's role in the region as that of "big brother" (*ağabey*) to its long-lost Turkic siblings of the former Soviet Union. References to the "rebirth" of the five "brotherly republics" and a "genuine spirit of pride"[43] were aimed at stirring up fraternal connections to legitimate Turkey's guiding role in Central Asia. The concept of rebirth that emerged out of the collapse of the Soviet Union stems from the widespread narrative among Pan-Turkic Nationalists that views Turks' history and the history of the Turkish state as uninterrupted (*kesintisiz*),[44] rather than broken up into periods such as Central Asian, Ottoman, and Republican periods. This continuous narrative of Turkic peoples, according to Pan-Turkic Nationalists, gives gravitas to their history and legitimates the reuniting of Turkey with its former brothers.[45] Turkey's efforts to guide the Turkic republics in their initial years as independent states—including providing economic aid, founding an international Turkish broadcasting channel, and establishing schools and universities to "teach" the Turkic republics how they should behave as newly restored members of a Turkic in-group—reflected initiatives trying to nurture this connection. However, as this book demonstrates, these outreaches were relatively limited and met with significant backlash from supporters of competing identity proposals, preventing Turkey's relationships with the Turkic republics from deepening to the degree desired by Pan-Turkic Nationalists.

Western Liberalism

In stark contrast to Pan-Turkic Nationalism, Western Liberalism is the least exclusive of Turkey's national identity proposals. The constitutive norms of membership, for example, are quite broad and have no ethnic, religious, or even linguistic criteria, as do all three other proposals outlined here. One survey respondent whose responses formed a composite Western Liberalist identity explicitly stated that, to avoid any intimation of exclusionary criteria, she tries to say "people in Turkey" (*"Türkiye'deki insanlar"*) rather than "Turks"

("*Türkler*") in referring to her co-nationals.[46] The contrast between this understanding of identity and others in Turkey is illustrated clearly in the novel
Serenad's (*Serenade*) dialogue between university administrator Maya and her
military officer brother, who is ashamed by the news that their grandmother
was Armenian and who defends the killings of Armenians in the name of the
Turkish nation. Horrified, Maya shouts: "When you look at people you see
uniforms, flags, and religion." When her brother asks, "Well, what do you see?,"
Maya replies "a person, just a person."[47] No matter their ethnic background or
religious persuasion, citizens of Turkey who define themselves as modern, supportive of individual rights and freedoms, and embodying Western values fall
into this in-group.[48] In terms of membership, for reasons related to the identity
content of the other three proposals I present in this study, many individuals
who are Laz, Kurdish, LGBTQ, and/or Alevi (non-Sunni Muslims), as well
as many non-Muslims such as Jews, Christians, and atheists, support the
Western Liberalist proposal partly because of what they are not, such as ethnically Turkish, socially conservative, and/or Sunni Muslim. Interviewees of
Turkey's non-Turkish and non-Sunni Muslim populations defined themselves
using the discourse of this identity proposal, finding both traditionally hegemonic Republican Nationalist references to all citizens as Turks offensive and
newly rising Ottoman Islamism's heavy use of religious language exclusionary.
One Laz interviewee, for example, stated that he was "insulted" by the word
"Turk" and refused to be defined as such by any government.[49] While some
non-Muslims and Alevis support Republican Nationalism precisely because
of its social purpose of removing religion of any kind from the public sphere
and thus are happy to call themselves "*Türk*" ("Turkish") in the civic sense,
Western Liberalists believe in distancing themselves further from the ethnic
connotations of the term and prefer the newly emerging term "*Türkiyeli*" ("one
who is of Turkey").[50]

The name of the newly formed and aspiring catch-all Peoples' Democratic
Party (Halkların Demokratik Partisi, HDP), despite its Kurdish roots,
underscores the principle of diversity generally absent from other parties
with the pluralistic use of "peoples." The name stands in stark contrast to
that of the main opposition Republican People's Party; in this case, a seemingly innocuous apostrophe's placement represents an entirely different
conceptualization of identity. The more broadly inclusive HDP represents
the most recent iteration of the Kurdish political movement in the wake of
the previous parties, such as the People's Labor Party (Halkın Emek Partisi), the
Democracy Party (Demokrasi Partisi), the People's Democracy Party (Halkın
Demokrasi Partisi, HADEP), and the Democratic Society Party (Demokratik
Toplum Partisi), all of which were banned by Turkey's Constitutional Court
for their supposed links to the PKK, as well as the Peace and Democracy Party

(Barış ve Demokrasi Partisi), which merged in 2014 with the explicitly non-Kurdish HDP at the national level but continued to operate at the local level in the Kurdish-dominated southeastern region of Turkey. While being a natural political home for Kurds supporting a Western Liberalist identity proposal for Turkey—as opposed to Kurdish nationalists, who support a proposal of identity for a separate Kurdistan, a subject outside the scope of this study[51]—the HDP also serves as the first electorally viable party with a platform explicitly advocating the expansion of individual and group rights, liberties, and diversity that has been embraced by non-Kurds as well. Former HDP cochairman Selahattin Demirtaş received nearly 10% of the vote in the 2014 presidential election, indicating that the party may have a chance to cross the uniquely high 10% threshold to be able to enter into parliament as a party.[52] Another explicitly Western Liberalist party, the Liberal Democratic Party, has never received more than .5% of the vote. As many Western Liberalists find the Republican Nationalist legacy of the Republican People's Party (Cumhuriyet Halk Partisi, CHP) too restrictive identity-wise, discussed below, Western Liberalists hope that the HDP has truly detached itself from its Kurdish nationalist roots and can advocate rights and liberties for all groups and individuals.[53] The facts that another former HDP cochairman is a non-Kurdish woman raised in a Sunni family,[54] that the party's bylaws specifically mention supporting disabled and LGBTQ rights,[55] and that half of the candidates on the HDP's party list for the 2015 elections were women[56] while one was an LGBTQ individual,[57] seem to support this hope.

The protection of group rights such as minority and women's rights along with individual freedoms such as those of religion and expression constitutes Western Liberalism's social purpose. There is a strong focus on the importance of women's equality and the advancement of rights of the LGBTQ community, as these communities are suffering particular hardships in Turkey. At a recent seminar in Istanbul, Aylin Nazlıaka—a Western Liberalist CHP representative working to shed some of the party's more exclusionary Republican Nationalist baggage[58]—expressed the grievances of her female constituents: "They tell me: 'I want to work, but my family doesn't let me,' because parents say they are less valuable as a marriage candidate."[59] Women's labor force participation is the lowest in European countries by far—the EU's aim for its 2020 strategy is 75% while Turkey's is 35%[60]—and gender equality and violence against women still remain woefully in need of major attention and reform.[61] Women protesting the rape and murder of university student Özgecan Aslan on a minibus, as well as the attitude manifested in ensuing comments implying that she "had it coming" (*oh olsun*) because she (a) was a young female traveling alone at night and (b) resisted the rape, were targeted with profanity and threats by police while being taken into custody.[62] The identity factors involved in beliefs about relations between sexes, gender equality, and sexual orientation that underlie the contestation of these issues in Turkey are discussed further in the presentation of Ottoman Islamism, below.

Improving opportunities for and treatment of Turkey's LGBTQ community is an even tougher social purpose to achieve than improving the condition of women. Many texts I collected containing elements of Western Liberalism indicated a desire for, but relative lack of optimism about, change in this area. Identifying as LGBTQ has long been a very widespread taboo in Turkey, something intolerable for supporters of identity proposals other than Western Liberalism.[63] A 2011 World Values Survey report found that 84% of Turkey's citizens did not want to live next to a gay neighbor; to provide a sense of the extent of this prejudice, other groups subject to discrimination in Turkey, such as atheists, Jews, and Christians, garnered far lower percentages of respondents who would not be willing to have them as neighbors (64%, 54%, and 48%, respectively).[64] Prospects for progress toward expanding LGBTQ rights and freedoms appeared to be diminishing as the AKP strove to spread its Ottoman Islamist proposal throughout Turkey's society and its institutions of governance (discussed in detail in chapter 5); former prime minister, current president, and AKP cofounder Erdoğan is well-known for asserting that homosexuality is contrary to Islamic morals. For example, when commenting on a Turkish boy who had been placed in the adoptive care of a lesbian couple in the Netherlands, he stated: "If [a child] is Muslim it should be given to a Muslim family. . . . I'm saying this for the culture of a people whose majority is Muslim: to hand over a child to a homosexual family is contrary to the moral rules and beliefs about values in that society."[65] Supporters of a Western Liberalist identity proposal, however, expressed great hope at the newly created space for expressing LGBTQ grievances and being able to openly include LGBTQ voices as a legitimate part of a wider opposition movement during the 2013 Gezi Park protests. One activist quoted in a newspaper interview stated that "Gezi did in three weeks what otherwise would have taken us three years."[66] Two Gezi participants I interviewed emphasized the novelty of the communal and supportive atmosphere among those demonstrating against the government, noting that Gezi provided a newly safe space within the public sphere for people to whom "solidarity means a lot."[67]

The relational meaning component, as indicated by the discussion above, consists of geographical and cultural inclusion in, or at least close relations with, the West and/or Europe. This component supports continued engagement with Western institutions such as NATO and the EU, even if EU membership is never fully realized.[68] This Western orientation is often articulated as fervently European; former opposition MP and staunch human rights advocate Şafak Pavey stated that her "*kible* is the European Union."[69] As the *kible* (or *qibla*, in Arabic) is the arrow that orients Muslims toward Mecca, in explaining that the

EU is her point of reference Pavey was demonstrating the fundamental importance of international orientation and foreign policy in her identity.

From a broader perspective, a cognitive worldview separate from Turkey's
place in Western civilization and modernity seems to be unclear at present.
Roles have included Turkey's position as a buffer zone or defender of the West
against any forms of authoritarianism or fundamentalism, most recently in the
form of radical Islam. Currently the clearest points are that Turkey should constitute a full and legitimate member of the Western liberal order and strive to be
a model of democracy for the region.

Republican Nationalism

Republican Nationalism is also a relatively new proposal compared to Pan-
Turkic Nationalism and Ottoman Islamism. Members who support the identity
proposal outlined below are often referred to as "Kemalists" but are referred to
here as Republican Nationalists for two reasons. First, "Kemalist" has become
a moniker used pejoratively to denote individuals who are dogmatic in their
beliefs and fawning in their admiration for the republic's founder and first president, Mustafa Kemal, who later took the surname Atatürk, or "Father of the
Turks." Second, several of the components of identity content shared by the
original, more hardcore Atatürkçüler ("followers of Atatürk") who might reasonably have been deemed Kemalist have transformed over the years. Republican
Nationalists still view themselves as guardians of Atatürk's legacy, to the point
where a "scandal" erupted when an answer given on a television game show
called into question the leader's original last name. On an episode of the popular
Turkish version of *Who Wants to Be a Millionaire* (*Kim Milyoner Olmak İster*),
the correct response to the question "What was Mustafa Kemal's last name before the surname law came into effect?" was given as "Öz," meaning "genuine"
or "original." The supposed mix-up occurred due to an incorrect reading of a
document stating "The Republican leader originally named Kemal" but that was
interpreted as "The Republican leader Kemal, with the last name of Original."[70]

Despite this fastidiousness when it comes to the legacy of the country's
founder, the beliefs of the majority of Republican Nationalists have become
moderated over time, as discussed in the following chapter, such that it is justi-
fiable to eschew using the term Kemalist.[71] Republican Nationalism is used here
to describe those who, broadly, are highly patriotic and still concerned about
protecting Turkey's borders and values as prescribed by Atatürk—outlined at
immense length in an epic, six-day speech (*Nutuk*) in 1927[72] that became known
as the "sacred text" of Turkey[73]—but are relatively more flexible and open to discussion about how to go about ensuring that protection.

The norm of membership for Republican Nationalism is broad but contains the caveat that its members must consider themselves Turkish, must honor Atatürk and the Turkish flag, and must speak Turkish. In a survey conducted to extract identity understandings as part of the intertextual analysis method I use in this study, "Being Atatürk's children" was one respondent's first answer to the question "What are the three most important elements of Turkish national identity?"[74] Another survey respondent stated that "the most important, of course, is loving Atatürk," explicitly emphasizing this hierarchy of identity elements.[75] Atatürk's phrase *"Ne Mutlu Türk'üm Diyene"* (How happy is he/she that says 'I am a Turk'") fills texts collected from social media feeds around holidays associated with the republic. A declaration of the vital importance of saving the Turkish language from the yoke of foreign languages in protecting the country's independence is engraved in Atatürk's handwriting on the side of the Turkish Language Institute (Türk Dil Kurumu).[76] As an acquirable component that can thus be taught, language was viewed as a better criterion for identity membership than ethnic descent or even religion[77] during the nationalization campaign carried out to spread Republican Nationalism to the republic's new citizens, a strategy for pursuing identity hegemony noted in the previous chapter.

Important for the discussion of identity red lines, not only is Republican Nationalism a civic understanding of Turkishness, rather than an ethnic understanding such as that of many Pan-Turkic Nationalists, but I argue that its supporters believe it is explicitly "anti-ethnic."[78] Although Western Liberalists such as the Laz interviewee mentioned above would vehemently disagree, saying that Turkish ethnicity lies at the core of Republican Nationalism's ideal and quite rightly pointing to instances of discrimination against non-Turks in practice, supporters of the latter argue that when language and territorial belonging are accepted as supplanting ethnic origin, the source of such discrimination disappears. In turn, Republican Nationalism's anti-ethnic membership criterion entails that ethnicity should not be officially recognized and in practice often means that references to and displays of ethnicity are prohibited or censured. Supporters of the proposal's earlier hegemonic iteration undertook nationalizing projects[79] that sought to erase ethnic divides and other potential avenues of mobilization along identity lines believed to be lethal to the Turkish Republic, most prominently among its Kurdish population. Republican Nationalists view ethnic identification itself as a destructive force fueled by Greek, Bulgarian, Serbian, and other nationalisms that led to massive losses of precious territory and lives. This causal belief between competing identity proposals and dissolution of territory—pervasive in many Turks' descriptions of the Balkan Wars and other conflicts that led to a massive territorial "dismember[ment]" in the Ottoman Empire's final years[80]—has manifested itself in a desire among Republican Nationalists to create an overarching, civic identity that can prevent the emergence of divisions believed to be inherently dangerous. The experiences of the Ottoman Empire's resounding defeat in World War I were also highly formative, instilling in Republican Nationalists the need for a complete lack of dependence on external powers, including the United States and the EU.[81] This narrative of dismemberment emerged many times in interviews and surveys from those I categorized as Republican Nationalist as a vital—even existential—lesson learned both from the territorial pieces perceived as having been ripped away from the body of the Ottoman state through various nationalist wars as well as the territories that were intended to be carved up by the Allied powers through the Treaty of Sèvres in 1920.[82]

A main social purpose of Republican Nationalists is to protect the guiding principles Atatürk established to shape and cultivate his vision of the ideal Turkish nation and modern, developed state. While some of these concepts (such as populism and statism) have become relaxed in the transformation from Kemalism to Republican Nationalism, others, particularly secularism, have remained firmly in place. Two slogans chanted repeatedly at the celebration of Republic Day on October 29, 2012, when a large crowd gathered at the site of the Republic of Turkey's first parliament in the Ulus neighborhood of Ankara for the annual march to Atatürk's Anıtkabir memorial, illustrate well this social purpose: "*Mustafa Kemal'in askerleriyiz!*" ("We are Mustafa Kemal's soldiers!") and "*Türkiye laiktir laik kalacak!*" ("Turkey is secular and will remain secular!").[83] For Republican Nationalists, the protection of secularism against the threat of Islam increasing its presence in the public sphere and especially in institutions of governance—a lesson, like the dangers of ethnic nationalism and international entanglements, learned from Ottoman collapse—is essential for creating a "utopia of modernization" in the positive sense of the expression.[84] Directly engaging the language of preserving secularism in Atatürk's name, one social media site dedicated to his memory uses clever Turkish wordplay in its group name: "*Laiksiz Türkiye, Atatürk'e layık değildir*" ("A non-secular Turkey isn't worthy of Atatürk").[85] Similar to the Turkish Language Institute, which was established according to Atatürk's personal instructions in 1932 to institutionalize and protect a modern form of Turkish "cleansed of words with foreign roots"[86] such as Arabic and Farsi (i.e., languages associated with the Islamic world), other protective institutions such as the TSK, the judiciary (particularly the Constitutional Court), and a constitution explicitly referencing the republic's foundational principles, are explained in detail in the following chapter. As chapter 6 demonstrates, the strength of many of these institutions has since been eroded due to the AKP's efforts to weaken their power as identity-based obstacles.

Another fundamental social purpose of all supporters of a Republican Nationalist proposal is the absolute maintenance of Turkey's territory and borders. As both a domestic politics and a foreign policy issue, territorial border maintenance is deeply ingrained in Republican Nationalists' identities as indicated above. A natural goal with the TSK as a main institutional defender of Republican Nationalism—guaranteeing the preservation of precious territory and the integrity of Turkey's borders—is a deep-seated interest among all supporters of this identity proposal. In addition to these supporters' consternation over Kurds who agitate for official recognition of their ethnic identity, which is perceived as threatening the integrity of the civic understanding of Turkishness advocated by Atatürk, Republican Nationalists share intense hostility for those separatist Kurds (*bölücüler*) who are pushing for outright secession from Turkey and thus pose a direct threat to Turkey's borders. This focus on maintenance of borders generates relatively isolationist foreign policy implications, with a few notable exceptions that inside-out theory accounts for, as discussed in the following chapter. Border integrity as a social purpose also led Republican Nationalists to be extremely wary of the AKP's deliberate shift toward a more aggressive, potentially irredentist policy of foreign engagement, seeing the active courting of Syria and this initiative's subsequent and dangerous demise in particular as a clear threat to Turkey's land and borders. The text of a *Cumhuriyet* (*Republic*) article entitled "Fake Victory," for example, vilified the operation to move the remains of the grandfather of the Ottoman Empire's founder inside Turkey to protect them as an act that compromised the "only single piece of Turkish territory" outside its borders.[87]

Moving to relational meaning, Republican Nationalists adhere to Atatürk's vision for the Republic in viewing Turkey as oriented firmly toward the West and away from its Ottoman legacies.[88] This relational meaning derives from Atatürk's vision of Turkey's natural place in the West, manifested in numerous reforms enacted following the declaration of the republic in 1923, including abolishing the caliphate, mandating a switch from the Ottoman to the Latin script, banning the fez, changing the day of rest from work from Friday to Sunday, and instituting national beauty pageants for women to provide an idealized standard of Western dress as well as to present to Europeans an image of a Turkish woman who looked just like them.[89]

While struggling to remain neutral during World War II, Turkey later demonstrated its Western commitment by sending troops to the Korean War in the hopes of being admitted to NATO as a much-needed guarantee against Soviet encroachment along its borders, as well as to secure its place as a legitimate member of the Western security alliance structure. Republican Nationalists today remain supportive of Turkey's general Western orientation but are hesitant over Turkish EU membership, for fear of the consequences of dependence as discussed below. The most common overarching them found in the Republican Nationalist texts gathered is the imperative not to shift Turkey's focus southeastward, or "backward," to the lands of the Ottoman Empire.[90]

Finally, the cognitive worldview component is tricky, given the traditional, primarily inward focus of Republican Nationalism's roots in the Kemalist practices intended to shield Turkey from the outside and develop it into a modern, prosperous state on the inside. Turkey as an independent nonaggressor would have been a fair characterization of the early republican view. This is demonstrated by the willingness to accept, and then defend as sacred, the borders established by the 1923 Treaty of Lausanne (with the exception of Hatay, a southeastern province self-annexed to Turkey in 1939 via referendum but whose belonging to Turkey was long disputed by Syria), absent any irredentism or overt attempts to influence its neighbors that could provoke a conflict and endanger its borders. Today's Republican Nationalists are still wary of being entangled with or "operated by" foreign powers[91] and thus strongly believe in the need to remain an example of independence, while sometimes willing to accede to international treaties and organizations that are not seen to threaten this independence.[92] For this reason, Republican Nationalists are divided on the issue of EU accession, with the more hardcore, Atatürkçü-leaning supporters (*ulusalcılar*)[93] highly wary of the effects of voluntarily relinquishing aspects of Turkey's sovereignty on Atatürk's legacy, and particularly his emphasis on republicanism and nationalism, embodied in the name given to this identity proposal. One top EU ministry official, whom I characterize as Republican Nationalist based on his responses to questions in multiple interviews, stressed that Turkey is at its core "not an aggressive state" and could best advance its interests in modernization and Westernization through participation in international institutions without compromising its identity or endangering its borders.[94] Citing the example that World War II could have served as the pretext to go to Mosul to gain sovereignty over Turkmen populations—as a Pan-Turkic Nationalist clearly would have advocated—the official emphasized that (the social purpose of) protecting Turkey's borders was much more important than waging risky wars. The official provided a succinct definition of the cognitive worldview of Turkey shared by supporters of a Republican Nationalist identity proposal by stating that Turkey serves as the "guard of the Western world,"[95] particularly in Turkey's volatile and often stridently anti-Western neighborhood.

Ottoman Islamism

Finally, Ottoman Islamism as a proposed understanding of Turkish national identity contains clearly understood but not clearly expressed constitutive norms of membership. These norms, as in the Republican Nationalist identity proposal, are intertwined with behavior but stand in direct contrast to that proposal's norms rooted in secularism, modernity, and civic belonging as a loyal

citizen of the Turkish Republic. Here, the membership criteria for identity primarily include being a pious Muslim and revering the glory of the Ottoman
Empire, as opposed to the achievements of the republic. In addition to being de-
vout in belief and practice, including daily prayer (*namaz*) and abstinence from
alcohol consumption,[96] the constitutive norm of piety prescribes clear standards
of moral (*ahlaki*) behavior. These in turn enable the clear identification of those
committing immoral behavior such as adultery or, for women, acting in a "loose"
(*serbest*) or "vulgar" (*edepsiz*) manner.[97] Survey respondents naming Bilal, of
the morality-laden *Huzur Sokağı* (*Tranquility Street*), as the television character
representing an ideal model for citizens of Turkey stated they chose him because he was righteous (*dürüst*)[98] and had morals.[99] Based on a novel written
by a pious, headscarved woman so close to Erdoğan that she introduced him
to his wife,[100] *Huzur Sokağı*'s heroes and heroines embody norms of piety that
Ottoman Islamist viewers and readers can emulate while also learning from the
characters' mistakes. Bilal, for example, is initially attracted to headstrong, feminist, mini-skirt-wearing Feyza, but eventually realizes his true love is modest,
family-prioritizing, headscarf-wearing Şükran. Survey respondents selecting
Bilal also often cited Bihter, from the series *Aşk-ı Memnu* (*Forbidden Love*), as
the worst role model, for being an unfaithful wife (*sadık bir eş olmaması*)[101]
and corrupting the gender-specific familial values of modesty (*ar*) and honor
(*namus*).[102]

The primacy of the norm of piety is found throughout Erdoğan's speeches,
many of which explicitly reference his desire to raise a pious generation.
Expressed in many forms, but perhaps most directly with the assertion that
"there is the cultivation of a pious youth. . . . I am behind this,"[103] Erdoğan in-
variably receives widespread applause from supporters who appreciate his emphasis on this constitutive norm of piety and his desire to spread it to a larger
percentage of the population—a desire in line with this study's focus on groups'
pursuit of identity hegemony. In one direct example of identity contestation,
Erdoğan rhetorically asks CHP leader Kemal Kılıçdaroğlu, "Are you waiting for
the *Ak Parti*, which holds a conservative democratic identity, to raise atheists?
Fine, that might be your work; that might be your goal. But we have no such goal
like that."[104] Answering himself, he notes that he wishes to raise a generation of
citizens who have internalized "conservative and democratic values and principles derived from our nation's and our homeland's history."[105]

In another speech Erdoğan addresses critiques of his vision for a pious
generation as being out of line with the lifestyle choices of many citizens of
Turkey by wondering, "Can't a pious generation be modern?" and receiving
enthusiastic applause from his audience.[106] Precisely this question, however, calls into question points of seeming intractability among supporters
of Ottoman Islamism and competing proposals regarding constitutive

norms of appropriate behavior—and particularly what is appropriate for the "modern" citizens the AKP wishes to cultivate. Alcohol consumption, for example, is a red line for Ottoman Islamists; when justifying new restrictions on alcohol sales, Erdoğan referred to all those who imbibe "alcoholics" as "immoral."[107] Pious novel character Atila highlights the ruination alcohol can bring, accusing the state of being a historical proprietor of liquor shops that ignores the consequences and demanding: "Haven't families fallen apart and people died, all because of alcohol?"[108] Questioning the judgment of those in positions of authority—"*Haddini bil!*" is a typically wielded phrase, meaning "Know your place!"[109]—constitutes another red line for Ottoman Islamists, as does disrespecting the principles of Sunni Islam. On a test in a religion class in Van in 2015, four pictures were presented underneath the question: "In which of the images below are the actions of prayer (*namazdaki hareketler*) wrongly represented?" Three of the images depict a drawing of a boy performing the *namaz* according to standard practice, while one of the images is a photograph of Ali İsmail Korkmaz, an Alevi (non-Sunni) participant in the Gezi Park protests who was beaten to death by police in Eskişehir. Korkmaz is represented as disrespecting the principles of Sunni Islam for being an Alevi, as well as for challenging the authority of the AKP government by protesting.[110]

Other behaviors found to be inappropriate and thus punishable according to the Ottoman Islamist identity proposal include showing too much cleavage,[111] wearing red lipstick,[112] and insulting Islam on television.[113] Indeed, television content is highly regulated through the AKP's pressure on Turkey's Radio and Television Supreme Council (Radyo ve Televizyon Üst Kurulu, RTÜK), revealing an attempt to spread the behavioral norms of Ottoman Islamism to its public via a vernacular venue and limits on content considered to violate the proposal's red lines. State-run television shows, one of the popular culture sources of data chosen for this project precisely because they provide a forum in which beliefs about identity are not only reflected but shaped and disseminated, regularly depict and thus repeatedly reinforce norms of piety, charity, reverence for a strong leader, and a family-centered focus.[114] In the television drama *Kızımı Yaşatmak için Öldüremem* (*I Can't Kill to Keep My Daughter Alive*), for example, pious community members show a father who strayed from Islam to join a drug-running gang but is now forced to either kill a man or witness his daughter's execution; even in seemingly hopeless circumstances, turning back to the guidance of the Koran can provide a solution. Cooking shows, highly popular on daytime programming, also provide a forum through which Ottoman Islamist norms are transmitted. The emphasis on the role of women as those responsible for prioritizing cooking, hosting, childrearing, and maintaining a conservative family lifestyle that takes priority over work or education outside the home is evidenced in programs such as *Bence Benim Annem* (*I Think It's My Mom*), *Misafir Ol Bana* (*Be My Guest*), *Yemekteyiz* (*We're at Dinner*), and *Sofradayiz* (*We're at the Table*). Alcohol is never discussed or present at any of the dinner tables, and women preparing the dishes are frequently asked how many children they have. During the Muslim holy month of Ramadan, food is not tasted as it is at other times of the year, in accordance with fasting practices, and many references are made to the importance to Muslims of the fast-breaking *iftar* meal. In the many *iftar* programs aired live during the run-up to these meals, such as an immensely popular program hosted by Nihat Hatipoğlu,[115] audience members ask Islamic scholars questions such as whether they have sinned and how to prevent their children from sinning in a forum specifically designed to articulate Ottoman Islamism's standards of appropriate behavior.

Multiple issues of contestation against Ottoman Islamism revolve around relations between the sexes and women's appropriate role in society. Comments from Ottoman Islamist supporters regarding appropriate constitutive norms of behavior for women may sometimes be headline grabbing in their blatant patriarchy and paternalism. Examples include the imam who, during an *iftar* program on a state-sponsored channel, suggested that pregnant women created an "unaesthetic" image and therefore should not walk around in public,[116] and the AKP deputy chairman who stated that women should not laugh out loud but should rather be much more modest (*iffetli*) in their behavior when in public.[117] The concept of *iffet*, meaning chastity as well as modesty, cited in a pro-AKP newspaper column as one of Islam's fundamental moral values,[118] is used frequently in pro-government media to praise acts of women deemed to be adhering to this principle and chastise those who are not. Such interpretations of women's actions are prescribed by socially conservative norms that run much deeper and are more pervasive than these seemingly extreme cases might suggest. These constitutive norms of behavior *for* women, and of what is acceptable behavior *toward* women, have generated far-reaching societal consequences, ranging from very low participation of women in the labor force[119] to high levels of violence against women, including "honor killings,"[120] the forced marriage of child brides,[121] and increasing rates of murder of women.[122]

Although the emphasis on the constitutive norms of conservatism and piety—and particularly the standards of behavior that are appropriate for women—constitutes a clear point of intolerability among Republican Nationalists and Western Liberalists, supporters of Ottoman Islamism as promulgated by the AKP embrace the fact that someone is finally speaking to "us."[123] As the discourse used by Erdoğan frequently employs "Us" and "Them" categories, it is important to examine not only who is a member of the in-group according to the norms of membership, but also who does not belong. An implicit but evident constitutive norm of the Ottoman-Islamist proposal is its Sunni component of membership. That is, individuals supporting this identity understand Turkishness to include being a Sunni Muslim and thus believe non-Sunni Muslims, such as Alevis, are part of "Them" (or at the very least misguided, heretical parts of "Us" in need of persuasion). While even among Alevis themselves there are disputes about whether Alevism is a syncretic and Shiʿa-based form of Islamic faith, a religion outside of Islam, or not a religion at all but a lifestyle, Alevis are often proudly Turkish and thus frustrated with the AKP government's nonrecognition of them in their own state. One prominent activist noted that, in the AKP's view, "Turks are Muslims. There are no Alevis."[124] Indicative of the Alevis' exclusion and "Other-ization" under the AKP government, Erdoğan made disparaging innuendoes toward CHP leader Kemal Kılıçdaroglu's Alevism at campaign events during the general election in 2011, announcing: "We know Mr. Kılıçdaroğlu is . . . an Alevi" (*Biliyoruz ki Sayın Kılıçdaroğlu bir . . . Alevidir*" and then waiting for the crowd's jeering response.[125] Alevis are also institutionally discriminated against, as their places of congress and worship (*cemevleri*) do not receive funding through the Directorate of Religious Affairs (Diyanet İşleri Bakanlığı) as mosques do.

The Alevi case is one of many narratives—including those of atheists, non-Muslims, LBGTQ individuals, and those who are outspoken against the government (particularly women, as this represents a defiance of the prescribed role of women, discussed above[126])—that is not located within the government's definition of who demonstrates appropriate behavior as a citizen of Turkey. However, especially noteworthy in its relation to recent policymaking efforts vis-à-vis Turkey's Kurdish population is the absence of either an ethnic or an "anti-ethnic" constitutive norm of membership in Ottoman Islamism. That is, Kurds are not excluded from Ottoman Islamism based on their ethnicity—although an Alevi Kurd would be excluded based on being non-Sunni, and a liberal Kurd would not adhere to the proposal's conservative norms of behavior. Ottoman Islamism's lack of prohibition of ethnic identity is in distinct contrast to the identity content of Pan-Turkic Nationalism, at least implicitly, while such a prohibition is a strong, explicit component of Republican Nationalism, as discussed above. Although Erdoğan stated early in his role as prime minister that ethnic nationalism, in terms of the politicization of ethnicity for secessionist goals, is "one of the red lines of politics" for his party,[127] there is no red line, in the language used in this study, of self-identification on an ethnic basis for Ottoman Islamism. Rather, in striking continuity with the *millet* system of classification used during the Ottoman Empire,[128] which sorted individuals based on religion and allowed non-Muslims to conduct some of their affairs relatively autonomously from the sultanate, ethnicity—whether Kurdish, Laz, Circassian, Arab, or other—can be one form of identification under an overarching umbrella of religious identification. As *millet* carries the meaning of "nation," the population under the rule of the Ottoman Empire was essentially categorized into nations consisting of confessional communities.

Although improving the socioeconomic conditions and freedoms of cultural expression of Turkey's Kurdish population is not a social purpose of Ottoman Islamism as it is for Western Liberalists—the AKP government refused domestic and international demands, for example, to provide assistance to support Syrian Kurds under attack in Kobani[129]—the fact that the identity proposal contains no ethnic Turkish or anti-ethnic red lines entails that the AKP can make outreach efforts to the Kurds when it is politically expedient to do so. To make the theoretical assumptions undergirding this study's argument explicit here, in the case of the Kurds, ethnic identity poses no ideational constraint on Ottoman Islamists as it does for Pan-Turkic and Republican Nationalists. This permits Ottoman Islamists to curry the favor of ethnic groups such as Kurds when doing so serves electoral or other interests. Just over a month before the June 2015 general elections, for example, the AKP released a campaign song in Kurdish titled *"Carek Dî"* ("One More") that contained the lyrics "our path is brotherhood, we are one big nation," in the hopes of garnering votes from those who might otherwise vote for the HDP. As an anecdotal illustration of the contestation such Kurdish-themed appeals can generate, a government-led "Kurdish Opening" (*Kürt Açılımı*) announced by President Abdullah Gül in 2009 immediately followed the AKP's defeat in local elections held in such largely Kurdish-populated provinces as Batman, Diyarbakır, Siirt, and Şanlıurfa. This outreach was rejected by the CHP and the MHP, understandably from an identity hegemony perspective, and was later framed as a nationwide democratic opening (*Demokratik Açılım*),[130] but ultimately came to a halt when widespread television images of Kurdish crowds jubilantly welcoming released PKK fighters as heroes arguably led to the AKP's abandonment of its initiative.[131] A mostly secretly conducted "solution process" (*çözüm süreci*), developed in early 2013 and including direct negotiations with imprisoned PKK leader Abdullah Öcalan, demonstrated relatively more success in persuading PKK fighters to leave Turkey. Fascinatingly, and in line with the assumptions of this book's theory of identity contestation, Öcalan's 2013 Kurdish New Year (*Newroz*) speech[132] contained for the first time explicit references to Islam as a centuries-old, overarching identity for Kurds as well as Turks, as well as references to both Ottoman decrees and Muslim prophets in a positive light.[133] Assumed to be a condition of the now defunct negotiations with the AKP government, these references—along with research indicating that Kurdish nationalists were viewing Islam with an increasingly favorable attitude that constitutes a puzzling shift for a movement with secular Marxist roots[134]—can be interpreted as the effects of the AKP's efforts to pursue identity hegemony, discussed in detail in chapter 6.

To move to the social purposes that *are* constitutive of Ottoman Islamist identity, the two main interests include increasing the space allowed for Islam in the domestic public sphere and acting in solidarity with Turkey's Muslim brothers internationally. In the run-up to the release of a 2013 democratization package—in which the ban on headscarves in parliament and other public buildings would be lifted (Law 8/5105 on Public Institutions), thus testing Turkey's tolerance for what is still perceived by some hardcore Republican Nationalists in the CHP (*ulusalcılar*) as an unacceptable incursion on the principle of secularism—state-run stations frequently showed discussions of the issue between covered and noncovered women, as well as between covered women and men. The texts of the dialogue included direct discussions of potential problems that could arise and suggested solutions to overcome these problems—by framing the debate as one of women's equality or gender justice[135] rather than of religious expression, for example. In frequent speeches, Erdoğan laments that his two daughters, along with thousands of other Turkish girls, "were forced to attend foreign universities"[136] so as not to compromise their religious beliefs by uncovering, as was demanded by many traditionally Republican Nationalist university rectors until Ottoman Islamism's presence in the public sphere increased during the AKP's third term. Internationally, the social purpose extends the piety norm of charity to other Muslim countries in the form of humanitarian, development, and disaster aid through multiple private and governmental channels.[137] A survey respondent emphasized the importance of this aid, stating that the teachers in the (Gülen-sponsored) film *Selam* (*Greetings of Peace*) "best represent the Turkish character" as they provide education to needy Muslim populations in Bosnia-Herzegovina, Afghanistan, and Senegal.[138] In addition to these forms of assistance, major nongovernmental aid organization IHH Humanitarian Relief Foundation (İnsan Hak ve Hürriyetleri ve İnsani Yardım Vakfı) strives to fulfill both social purposes by providing funding for the protection of Islamic culture and Muslims globally. Most famous for being the owner and operator of the Mavi Marmara flotilla's ships sent to break the Gaza blockade in 2010, the foundation also funds Islamic cultural centers in areas such as Bosnia that were in its words "orphaned by the fall of the Ottoman Empire"[139] and raises awareness and funds for securing the religious and cultural rights of minority-Muslim populations in places as diverse as Brazil[140] and Vietnam.[141]

The relational meaning of the Ottoman Islamist identity proposal orients Turkey away from close ties with Europe. Its supporters believe strongly in the need for Turkey to define itself and its relations independent of European standards of culture and civilization. Former foreign minister and later prime minister Ahmet Davutoğlu and his team at the International Strategic Research Organization build explicitly on the geohistorical and geocultural legacies Turkey inherited from the Ottoman Empire. Davutoğlu argued extensively in the journals of MÜSİAD (Association of Independent Industrialists and Businessmen)—the business group interest organization formed by pious members of the business community in opposition to TÜSİAD (Turkish Industrialists and Businessmen's Association), the traditional institution of secularists—that "the Ottoman Empire constituted the political structure of the only civilization that succeeded in establishing its rule directly against Europe,"[142] and that Turkey's flirtation with Europe and the West was an "aberration from a historically predetermined developmental trajectory."[143] Contrary to arguments that Turkey's turn away from the EU resulted primarily from a sense of frustration with the process or from the financial crisis of 2008, which hit Europe particularly hard, examining previous texts that outline Ottoman Islamists' beliefs about the relational meaning between Turkey and Europe demonstrates that the roots of Turkey's shift to reorient foreign policy toward the what the AKP considers to be its cultural and historical brothers lie mainly in these views.

The cognitive worldview of this proposal considers Turkey's role as legitimate inheritor of Ottoman legacies and, in turn, the former home of the caliphate; this positions Turkey as a regional power to be feared and admired.[144] These themes are rife in hundreds of novels and films with titles such as *1453 Fetih* (*Conquest*) that laud the heroic conquering of Constantinople by Fatih Sultan Mehmet and his immediate transformation of the great Hagia Sophia church into a mosque. Television comedies such as *Harem* bring palace intrigues and military might to life through slapstick humor, and the immensely popular *Muhteşem Yüzyıl* (*The Magnificent Century*) is a dramatic series based on the life of Süleyman the Magnificent. Tellingly, though dealing with subject material in line with the ruling party's identity proposal, the series was criticized by Erdoğan for presenting an "inaccurate" depiction of history and loose moral behavior because of its frequent depictions of harem infighting, lustful encounters, and alcohol consumption. The charges of insulting the sultan's legacy brought against the cast and crew of the series are a powerful indication of the control the AKP wishes to retain over the content of the identity proposal it supports.[145] Many survey respondents also listed *Muhteşem Yüzyıl*'s Sultan Süleyman as the television character who set the worst example for Turkey's citizens in terms of identity and values, listing the character's "personal and cultural traits"[146] as not only negative but also a "completely untrue"[147] portrayal of the sultan. One stated that the show was "ruining our history."[148] In contrast, the high-budgeted and state-funded *Filinta*, proclaimed by its producers and sponsors to be television's first Ottoman-themed police detective drama,[149] received praise from government-friendly media for relegating its portrayal of crime and intrigue to scenes involving mafia-type figures.[150] The trajectory of the show's aspiring grand vizier, Esad Paşa, who escapes from an impoverished childhood to become an ambitious (if merciless) rising figure in the Ottoman government, closely mirrors that of Erdoğan, who transcended his humble beginnings in the gritty Kasımpaşa district of Istanbul to become the soaring political star of the Islamist Refah Partisi (RP) and, later, the leading cofounder of the AKP.

In sum, the identity proposal of Ottoman Islamism contains constitutive norms of pious Sunni Muslim membership and reverence for the Ottoman Empire's glory and wide-reaching authority, the social purposes of spreading Sunni Islam in the domestic sphere and strengthening ties with Muslim and former Ottoman populations, a relational meaning of Europe (and "the West") in general as the salient out-group, and a cognitive worldview of Turkey as the legitimate inheritor of Ottoman legacies and leader of the Islamic world.

Conclusion

To facilitate analysis of how this mechanism of contestation shapes the contours of domestic identity debates, this chapter has outlined in detail four competing proposals for Turkish national identity that were assembled based on analysis of texts extracted from interviews, surveys, archives, news and social media, popular culture sources, and ethnographic observation. While sometimes sharing overlapping elements, Pan-Turkic Nationalism, Western Liberalism, Republican Nationalism, and Ottoman Islamism as composites represent mutually exclusive understandings of the appropriate content of Turkey's national identity. The specification of red lines among them provides a useful focus for understanding the processes of contestation that take place in the course of Turkey's history, with various groups vying to achieve identity hegemony by circumventing identity-based obstacles established by supporters of competing proposals.

The following chapter opens this book's chronological analysis of the contours of national identity debates in Turkey and their link with Turkish foreign policy. The chapter focuses on contestation of what the appropriate definition of Turkish national identity should be surrounding the founding of the republic in 1923. It analyzes how the foreign policies of the Ottoman Empire and their outcomes fundamentally shaped a new proposal for Turkish identity that eschewed as anathema the identity red lines of ethnicity, Islam, and foreign entanglement.

4

Forging a Nation from Within

Republican Nationalism's Fight for Hegemony at Home

Introduction

This chapter serves as the analytical entry point to the book's examination of the deeply rooted, hotly contested, and ever-evolving struggle to define, establish, and disseminate a particular understanding of Turkish national identity. As outlined in the discussion in chapter 2 of the theoretical precepts undergirding this study and the framework employed in chapter 3 to make sense of the competitors in this intricate contest, whose contours are continually shifting, this and the case study chapters that follow begin with several key assumptions that are worth reiterating and summarizing here. My analysis posits that (a) multiple proposals for national identity exist among the citizenry of a state;[1] (b) individuals hold deep-seated ontological commitments to the particular identity proposal they support; (c) these proposals often contain elements of identity content that are considered intolerable (or exceedingly inappropriate, to employ the traditional constructivist terminology engaging logics of appropriateness) to supporters of other proposals; and (d) rival supporters therefore compete in a contest for identity hegemony so as to prevent intolerable violations of the standards of belonging and behavior that are constitutive of their own identity proposal. In sum, supporters fight to spread acceptance of their proposal to as much of the population as possible, thus gaining popular support for and institutional access to the means for realizing the interests generated by their identity.

As the analysis I undertake in this study is structured chronologically—allowing me to delineate periods of intense contestation among rival proposals against relative hegemony, as well as historical openings through which supporters of previously marginalized proposals found new ways to strengthen their position in the contest—this case study chapter commences its exploration with the struggle to establish a founding identity for the newly established Republic of Turkey. After a devastating and fundamentally transformative loss in

World War I, followed by a surprising victory against the Allied powers in what is generally known as the War of Liberation (Kurtuluş Savaşı) in Turkish, war hero and first president Mustafa Kemal (Atatürk) proclaimed Turkey to be an independent state on October 29, 1923. Neither Turkey's domestic contest to define its new national identity nor the nature of its relations with foreign powers would start from zero on what would come to be called Republic Day, however. As commonsensical as it may sound, it is worth emphasizing—particularly given prominent constructivist Alexander Wendt's assertion, presumably hypothetical but nevertheless discussed at length—that "states do not have conceptions of self and other before their first encounter with each other."[2] Wendt's nuanced discussion of the corporate agency of the state and his breakdown of states' identities into those more related to conceptions of Self (personal/corporate, type) and those defined more in terms of Others (role, collective)[3] acknowledge the importance of unit-specific cultural and historical factors shaping states' self-perceptions. However, his attempt to correct for a perceived surfeit of domestic politics accounts of state formation can arguably lead to an overbalance in favor of structure, glossing over the ways in which perceptions of a state's interests can be shaped prior to its emergence as a sovereign state.[4] As the subject of this study's subnational, constructivist analysis of national identity contestation and foreign policy, Turkey sheds immensely useful light on how various understandings of identity and the relations among them come to take shape. The roots of the proposals competing to establish Turkey's internal (defining the Self) and external (defining relations with Others) identities were planted long before Turkey officially became one of the "people" of international society, entered a "state of nature," or confronted something in between, depending on one's ontological approach to the study of IR.

This chapter therefore specifically takes up an investigation of the dynamics of contestation to establish those who would come to constitute the citizenry of the Republic of Turkey, as well as the events and interactions that shaped these understandings. Although an assumption that there is any clear beginning at which to start or any definitive end at which to stop would do serious harm to the study of identity formation and transformation, this chapter explores the relationship among three identity proposals that were contenders for hegemony during the republic's foundational years: Pan-Turkic Nationalism, Ottoman Islamism, and Republican Nationalism. While the first two are historically rooted, or perhaps precisely because of the challenges these roots are seen to generate, Republican Nationalism rises above them in its pursuit of hegemony.

This chapter analyzes the strategies used by supporters of Republican Nationalism to compete for and attain hegemony for their identity proposal. I demonstrate that by intensively employing a combination of delegitimization of alternative proposals, propaganda campaigns designed to laud the merits of being a "model citizen"[5] (i.e., modern, Western, educated, and secular in terms of lifestyle), and methods of forced assimilation, supporters of Republican Nationalism aimed to achieve identity hegemony. Defining a hegemonic proposal as an understanding of a national identity that is widely distributed across a population, to the point of being "relatively stable and unquestioned,"[6] I argue that this is a status no other proposal has come as close to attaining in the history of the republic. My analysis of these strategies and use of a framework that allows for specification of the red lines among competing proposals help to make sense—if by no means to morally justify—the extraordinarily far-reaching and heavy-handed measures that were used to disseminate the identity content of Republican Nationalism and quash resistance to it. As the chapter highlights, guidelines for appropriate behavior based on religion—as was the case for Ottoman Islamism—and definitions of identity content based on ethnicity—as was the case for Kurdish nationalism, which does not constitute a proposal for Turkish identity but was the target of aggressive assimilation measures—were anathema to the largely militarily oriented elite. These elites had witnessed the dismemberment and ultimate collapse of a previously formidable imperial power, due in part to misplaced reliance on the guiding will of Allah, the defection of Muslim Arab populations from the Ottomans to assist the Allied powers in their fight, and ethnic nationalism.

Starting from the September 12, 1980 coup and the social and political chaos that followed the handover of governmental control to civilians in 1983, the chapter then analyzes the contestation advanced by those critical of Republican Nationalism's pursuit of hegemony. The extended ideational and material control the Republican Nationalists had seemed to exercise in their governance of Turkey became the target of multiple challenges in the public sphere, but came much more slowly from an institutional perspective (as explored in the next chapter). To account for the multifront assault on the dominance of Republican Nationalism, I identify the domestic and international factors that created new openings for the limited numbers of supporters of the previously suppressed Ottoman Islamism and Pan-Turkic Nationalism. These factors—including reactionary sentiment directed against the leaders of the 1980 military coup, the development of the Turkish-Islamist synthesis, and the collapse of the Soviet Union—created challenges to the hegemonic aspirations of Republican Nationalists, leading some, the so-called Second Republicans (İkinci Cumhuriyetçiler), to contest Republican Nationalism from the inside. A focus on these developments also provides an account of how Western Liberalism, not present in any significant or identifiable way in previous periods in Turkey, emerged as a distinct proposal for national identity. Finally, this analysis sheds light on the doors that opened to allow levels of support for Ottoman Islamism to rise, as well as the stunted nature of Pan-Turkic Nationalists' attempts to convince others that the former Soviet Turkic Republics are Turkey's natural allies. To understand how these periods of stability and shift became possible, however, it is imperative to begin by providing an understanding of how the contours of identity debates in the new Republic of Turkey took shape.

No newly formed state in the international system—whether that state is produced as a result of independence struggles, (re)unification, the collapse of imperial or colonial structures, or some other process producing a shift in borders—emerges absent any understanding of what or who it is or of how its relations with other states may develop. While the constitutive act of becoming a sovereign member of the international community certainly shapes a new state's understanding of itself and the community's understanding of it, as well as endowing it with new capacities by virtue of being such a member, the individuals contained within its newly established borders bring with them preformed understandings of who they are, what they want, and how they view their neighbors. Indeed, there are quite likely numerous proposals for what the identity of the state and its citizens should be. Whether or not those proposals ever become widely spread across the state's population or manifested in state institutions and policies depends on a multitude of factors, not least of which is the map of existing identity proposals at the moment the state is formed.

Turkey provides an outstanding empirical window for understanding the dynamics of this process, as a state with a definitive sovereign starting point at which a clear proposal for identity was promulgated to suppress competing identities; an imperial past in which religious identity was primarily salient both within the empire and in its external relations; and a process of gaining sovereignty through war that profoundly shaped the military elites' perceptions of ethnic/tribal, religious/imperial, and civic/Western identities. The Republic of Turkey, emerging out of dual processes of defeat and victory, would be governed with an extremely firm hand by elites supporting an identity proposal constituted in great part by these experiences. Recalling the identity content framework outlined in the previous chapter, as an embodiment of the military elites' beliefs about the appropriate membership and behavior norms, goals, relations, and role of Turkey and its citizens, Republican Nationalism provided a clear blueprint for national identity to be disseminated throughout the new state's population. In doing so, Republican Nationalists engaged directly in an identity contestation battle against the competing proposals for Turkey's national identity, Ottoman Islamism and Pan-Turkic Nationalism. Ahmet Davutoğlu's account of the geopolitical landscape surrounding Turkey's entrance into the world of sovereign states sums up well the reasons neither Pan-Turkic Nationalism nor Ottoman Islamism held up as legitimate proposals to guide the domestic and foreign policies of the new republic, providing a good starting point for this chapter's analysis of Republican Nationalism's rise:

> During those years [of Ottoman collapse], the most crisis-filled period in the history of the Islamic world took place, and every area experienced a process of dramatic shrinking in size. As for the Turkic world, it had fallen completely under the grip of slavery after the Bolshevik Revolution. In this way, Islamism and Turkism, considered to be the two important bases for the claim of the Anatolian-Balkan- and Istanbul-based basins of political strength on which the Ottoman state rested to create an international "*hinterland*," were seen as having lost their importance in any real sense.[7]

Pursuing Hegemony for Republican Nationalism

The steps undertaken by the newly established state's elites to spread their Republican Nationalist proposal for Turkish identity, well documented by both academics[8] and activist Republican Nationalists in associations such as ATAMER (Atatürk İlkeleri ve İnkılâp Tarihi Araştırma Merkezi, Center for Research on the History of Atatürk's Principles and Revolution),[9] closely adhere to the behaviors of what Rogers Brubaker terms a nationalizing state.[10] While those devising the nationalizing measures used to advance this proposal were governing a newly independent state, as Brubaker suggests, their implementation was portrayed by elites as "reforms" (*ıslahatlar*), rather than as new regulations for behavior. Understanding these practices as a pursuit of hegemony for the Republican Nationalist identity proposal goes beyond what can be gleaned from an analysis of nationalizing practices, helping to provide increased insight into the ontological motivations behind the pursuit, the material and ideational gains to be had if hegemony were achieved, and the red lines of intolerability that form particular points of contestation among supporters of competing proposals.

All steps taken to bring about a change in the way the citizens of the new republic should be and behave were conceived of as a rollback of intolerable, wrongly guided formal legislation and informal customary rules; the impetus behind these steps was based on the Republican Nationalist belief that endowing religious and ethnic identities with political importance could be perilous.[11] One seeming exception to these beliefs is the so-called Sun Language Theory (*Güneş Dil Teorisi*), a pseudoscientific approach to the world's great linguistic variety that claimed all languages were rooted in a form of proto-Turkic language developed among peoples of Central Asia who wanted to give voice to their recognition of the sun as the source of human creation. The theory's precepts first appeared in an unsigned column sponsored by the Turkish Language Society in Ankara's *Ulus* newspaper on November 2, 1935. The thesis, supported by Atatürk, conveniently explained away concerns emerging during debates over the institutionalization of the Turkish language about which words could be considered "pure Turkish" by asserting "the words of all languages are Turkish anyway." While there is a decidedly descendence-based component to this approach to language more reminiscent of Pan-Turkic Nationalism, the emphasis here is on the ultimate universality of language rather than on ethnicity as a divider and thus fits well within Republican Nationalism's constitutive norms of membership, even if the thesis seems at odds with the proposal's emphasis on positivism and modernity. The promulgation of the theory represents one of the many strategic inventions and uses of cultural symbolism to advance the proposal's pursuit of identity hegemony analyzed in this chapter.

In advocating for the spread of this understanding of identity, Republican Nationalist elites argued that existing practices were in dire need of fundamental transformation. These purported relics of governance and societal ordering were portrayed as stemming from an archaic set of factors presided over by egotistical sultanic rule; a website dedicated to the study and preservation of Atatürk's legacy, for example, cites intolerance, envy, enmity, and personal interests as the causes of many of the problems experienced during the reign of Mahmut II.[12] Key among these factors was a government bound by religion and its ties to the Islamic world. A summary of the law abolishing the caliphate on the website of Sakarya University's ATAMER provides insight into this, noting that Atatürk realized that the old regime "had begun to take on the airs of being the leader of the Islamic world," and that such a position "could be dangerous" for the newly established republic's government.[13] Republican Nationalists also blamed pernicious ethnic ties for weak governance structures. As discussed above, the Balkan Wars in particular, as well as what was viewed as treason by the Ottoman Empire's Arab population, led to a belief that ethnic identification was a red line whose crossing must not be allowed.[14] Finally, the newly ruling elites disparaged rural feudalities as guilty of depriving society of legal structures needed to modernize. In a critique of the "Ottoman feudal order's" ignorance, Republican Nationalist lawyer Vural Savaş emphasizes that "Ataturkist ideology, which was responsible for implementing a land-register survey and distributing land to landless peasants . . . embodied the principle of personal property" necessary for economic development.[15]

Indeed, the reforms that Atatürk viewed as necessary for shaping a modern, Western, literate population, which included both a fundamental interest in producing the ideal citizen and a derivative interest in generating the workforce necessary to rapidly achieve desperately needed economic development, were depicted as constituting Atatürk's "revolutions" (*Atatürk'ün İnkılâpları*) for society. These revolutions can best be understood as Republican Nationalist attempts to decimate existing religious/imperial and ethnic/tribal identifications in order to pursue hegemony for what was seen by the proposal's supporters as the appropriate, legitimate understanding of Turkish national identity. The following two subsections discuss these efforts directed toward competing identity proposals, focusing on Ottoman Islamism as the main competitor to define Turkish national identity and Kurdish nationalism as the chief proposal for a separate, non-Turkish identity. This analysis facilitates an overall understanding of the societal, institutional, and foreign policy changes made following the establishment of the republic that surpasses existing accounts focused primarily on secularism, economic modernization, and Westernization, with each factor often used as an explanatory variable of the other.[16]

Contesting Alternative Proposals for Turkish National Identity

The revolution was explicitly intended to constitute a clear and clean break between the institutions of the old Ottoman Empire and the new republic, sweeping out the old, inappropriate standards of governance and lifestyle to usher in the new. In the form of a literal separation, Atatürk's Republican Nationalist elite cadre presided over the deliberate and strategic move of the capital of the new republic away from Istanbul. The former Byzantine hub and then capital of the Sunni Islamic world represented Fatih Sultan Mehmet's defeat of the infidel and conquering of the world's most wondrous city in 1453. Istanbul served as the base from which the Ottoman Empire expanded its territory and inhabitants while experiencing a "golden age" of civilizational development, as well as the rightful resting place of precious holy relics housed in mosques and former Ottoman palaces.[17] Resulullah.org, an Ottoman Islamist website on Islamic relics whose name means "The Prophet," conveys the emotional connection to religion that the city evokes: "Even though most of us are aware of places to experience this feeling [of awe], just in Istanbul alone there are dozens of mosques, mausoleums, and museums protecting holy relics." These items include coverings of the Kabe (or Ka'aba), the cube-shaped structure at the center of al-Masjid al-Haram mosque in Mecca displayed in Ayasofya (the monumetal Hagia Sophia that Fatih Sultan Mehmet converted from a church into a mosque, now a museum); footprints of the Prophet embedded on stone, available for viewing in the Ottoman palace Topkapı Sarayı; and hair and beard fragments of the Prophet on display in the Vakıf Hat Sanatları Müzesi (Calligraphy Museum).

Istanbul was thus imbued with a holy symbolism of its own because of the culture, history, and religion that combined to define its unique past. The powerful appeal of this symbolism is effectively reflected in the interest in

Ottoman-themed pop culture forms celebrating Istanbul that has blossomed under the Ottoman Islamist AKP's rule. In one of the many popular novels bringing to life the "impossible conquest" of the city that many powers had tried in vain to capture, *1453 Fetih* (*1453 Conquest*) depicts the sultan proclaiming before the battle: "This city is the love of my dreams, my unconquered ground."[18] Among detective novelist Ahmet Ümit's best-selling works are *İstanbul Hatırası* (Memory of Istanbul, 2010) and *Sultanı Öldürmek* (*To Kill a Sultan*, 2012).[19] Interest has arisen also in late Ottoman-era writings such as *Memleket Hikayeleri* (*Hometown Stories*, 1919) and *İstanbul'un Bir Yüzü* (*A Face of Istanbul*, 1920), whose author, Refik Halit Karay, opposed the Committee of Union and Progress and was exiled to Anatolia in 1913.[20] The immense popularity of the *Muhteşem Yüzyıl* television series, based on the life of Sultan Süleyman the Magnificent and discussed in the previous chapter, perhaps best captures precisely the nostalgic sentiments Republican Nationalists sought to eradicate.

Cultural symbolism, as powerful as it can be, was not the only driving force behind the selection of Ankara as Turkey's capital rather than Istanbul. Also thinking in geostrategic terms, and motivated by the sacredness of borders outlined in the previous chapter, top military commander-turned-politician and chief negotiator of the Lausanne Treaty İsmet Paşa (who was given the surname İnönü by Atatürk for his military victory in the city of the same name) recognized that Istanbul was extremely difficult to defend given its easy access via multiple water routes. Indeed, the city had been invaded by the Allied powers, who made Istanbul their temporary home while they decided how to carve up and distribute the empire's territory. Ankara, in contrast, represented a relatively blank canvas from a symbolic standpoint and was situated in the steppes of central Anatolia, providing a much more easily defensible location as well as one that held very little of the geostrategic importance, transportation potential, or purely aesthetic appeal that Istanbul had for centuries in the eyes of its would-be conquerors. As İnönü argued in the newly established (first) Turkish parliament:[21]

> I am meeting with the Western world's executives, specialists, and diplomats in Lausanne. They desire that the new state be established according to the people who know the Istanbul government and Istanbul's surroundings. I understand this from every angle. From our perspective there are more substantial and varied fronts to the issue. Once the Bosporus Straits are completely clear of military patrol, they are completely insecure. We are facing this legacy. The outcomes and the historical conditions we achieved through the Lausanne Treaty give us cause for worry. We want to be located in the middle of Anatolia and run our new state as an Anatolian government.[22]

Moving the capital to Ankara constituted a way to distance the government from the caliphate, stripping it of its political power before eventually abolishing the institution completely. Although İnönü argued that there was no direct relationship between the two, he also stated that "we do not consider the Caliphate to be a permanent institution. Ankara will be the center of government and the Caliphate will be centered in Istanbul; this will also be a basic means for getting rid of it."[23] Creating physical distance between the seat of government and the caliphate could also create symbolic distance for the new republic's citizens when they considered the authorities by which they should be governed.

Along these lines of thinking, Republican Nationalists had already abolished the institution of the sultanate and sent Sultan Mehmet VI, the thirty-sixth and last *padişah* (ruler) of the empire, into exile in Malta in 1922. This move, which marked the end of an empire that was established in 1299 and was once one of the most formidable and accomplished world powers, was carried out based on Atatürk's request to the Turkish parliament in November 1922. Viewing Mehmet VI as a weak capitulator willing to hand over great swathes of territory in accordance with the Treaty of Sèvres, Atatürk finally decided to put an end to the de facto dual system of government to make clear that Ankara was the sole and legitimate seat of power in the republic. As Mehmet VI fled Istanbul in fear of reprisal for his concessions to the Allies, boarding a British destroyer on November 16, the image of the "sultan taking refuge with the enemies of the nation"[24] worked in the Republican Nationalists' favor by swiftly delegitimizing the sultan and his legacy in the eyes of many Turks.[25]

In the opening paragraph of his *Nutuk* speech, Atatürk lambasts the sultan's behavior in his final days as a "degenerate" who was "searching for some sneaky measure by which to save himself and his lonely throne, the only things he worried about."[26] From an identity contestation perspective that specifies a goal of hegemony, any form of delegitimization of the content of a proposal or of leading figures associated with it constitutes a positive development for competing proposals. Individuals who previously defined themselves by that content or identified with those leading figures may gradually find themselves shifting their support to another proposal by coming to accept that its norms of membership and prescribed standards of behavior are appropriate. In this case, some of those who had supported Ottoman Islamism because they revered the empire's glory and believed the sultanate to be a divinely legitimized form of rule may have changed their beliefs upon seeing the empire crumble in defeat and the sultan take refuge with his purported enemies.

Similar to the fate of the sultanate, the caliphate was also abolished, but only after incrementally separating it from the body of the sultan himself and then from the seat of government following its transfer to Ankara, as discussed above. Upon the removal of the sultan from power and his hasty exit from Istanbul, his first cousin, Abdülmecid Efendi, was selected as caliph by the Turkish parliament, "becoming the only hope" for those close to the old regime who hoped that the shift to republicanism was temporary and sought to retain Islamic rule.[27] Abdülmecid's brief rule as supreme clerical authority in the Sunni Islamic world experienced swift changes, with reforms taken to constrict its power. Having gradually detached the caliphate from its previous institutionalized authority and changed its administration, the Turkish parliament then abolished it in March 1924. The removal of this institution served both Republican Nationalist social purposes of dislodging Islam's grasp on governance and of officially distancing the republic from the rest of the Islamic world.

In *Nutuk*, Atatürk makes this purpose clear: "It is never an acceptable mindset or logic for any Muslim state to give the authority of administering and governing the affairs of the entire Islamic world to one person."[28] He also explicitly warns of the danger of ignorance, which had allowed Muslims to get caught up in the caliph's intrigues: "Gentlemen, I must say this quite clearly and with certainty: the Muslim people find themselves tangled in the efforts of the specter of a caliph to plague and deceive them. . . . [T]hese are the enemies of Turkey especially."[29] Finally, he underlines the necessity of removing the caliphate to achieve the goals of Republican Nationalism: "It doesn't require great wisdom to understand that a form of government that demands unconditional adherence to the Caliphate cannot be a republic."[30]

Having completed these major institutional shifts to distance the new republic from its Ottoman and Islamist past, Atatürk's revolution then rolled swiftly on to affect many aspects of the new citizens' daily lives and spread the Republican Nationalist identity proposal throughout the public sphere. To encourage Turkey's population to internalize an identity proposal whose relational meaning situated Turkey firmly in the West, basic but far-reaching reforms such as institutionalizing a dress code were of great importance to Republican Nationalists. In the words of a scholar from Turkey writing in English, and thus presumably for a Western audience, at the time of its founding, "Turkey was considered morally and religiously backward, and its traditional ways and costumes, particularly the *fez*, became objects of derision" in the eyes of the "West, confident in its material and spiritual superiority."[31] Consequently, the so-called Hat and Dress Revolutions (Şapka ve Kıyafet İnkılâpları or Devrimleri; the former is an Ottoman Turkish word, the latter modern Turkish) of 1925 included the banning of the backwardness-connoting fez. The law on headgear (*Şapka İktisası Hakkında Kanun*) mandated that individuals working in the parliament and the civil service were required to cover their heads, and that the common headgear of the Turkish people would be the hat.[32] Parliament also sought ways in which to encourage both men and women to dress in a modern (*çağdaş*) style, with the unveiling of women in line with modern European norms of dress a preeminent goal. Although a law to this effect was prepared, parliament was unable to come to a decision on its content; numerous local governments, however, passed laws criminalizing the wearing of religious body-covering robes (*çarşaflar*, commonly referred to in today's debates on religious garments as the *burka/burqa*) and veils (*peçeler*). A proposal prepared by the government emphasizes the Republican Nationalists' belief in the importance of the relationship between clothes and identity:

> The separation of the state and religion and keeping religious values out of the state's functioning must not remain only a quality of one's con-science. . . . That is, the government of the Republic, whose revolution is based on secularism and which recognizes secularism as a primary principle, saw the addressing the subject of the clothing that spiritual individuals wear during religious rituals as well as what every individual can wear outside of rituals as a natural outcome and need of the steps taken on this path.[33]

In addition to changes in permissible clothing, Republican Nationalist reforms included changing the day of rest from Friday to Sunday, the replacement of Islamic canon law with a system based on the Swiss code, mandating that all citizens of Turkey take up a surname, a ban on the public practices of religious scholars (*ulema*), changing the call to prayer (*ezan*) from Arabic to Turkish,[34] and instituting legal equality of the sexes. Arguably the reform that would have the greatest effect in creating distance between Ottoman- and Muslim-based identification and in shaping the content of the new identity in line with a Western model, however, was the shifting of the alphabet from Arabic to Latin script in August 1928. Ottoman Turkish (*Osmanlıca*), written with Arabic letters but adhering to the grammatical structure found in the language used by Turkic tribes before they were conquered and converted to Islam (*eski Türkçe*), was purged of its thousands of Arabic and Persian words to create the modern Turkish language. As İnönü stated in his memoirs: "One of the most fundamental goals of the revolution was to close to the doors of the past to new generations, sever ties with the Arab-Islam world, and weaken the influence of religion on society."[35] This "most important" process of "cleans[ing] the Turkish mind from its Arabic roots"[36] was overseen by the Turkish Language Institute (Türk Dil Kurumu, TDK), put in place by Atatürk to formulate, disseminate, and vigilantly maintain a language unique to Turks, seen as a vital component of defining and protecting the nation, as indicated by survey responses cited in the previous chapter's outline of the identity proposal's content. The home page of the TDK's website, for example, displays one of the many famous statements by Atatürk related to language and the nation, written in his own penmanship: "The

Turkish nation, having known how to protect its country and its supreme freedom, must also save itself from the yoke of foreign languages."[37] Symbolically representing this need to preserve the Turkish nation from foreign influence, a cartoon subtitled "The Triumph of 31 August 1928" depicts a giant figure of Atatürk standing imposingly on top of a mound of crushed Arabic letters, with the phrase "New Turkish Letters" (*"Yeni Türk Harfleri"*) inscribed over a brightly rising sun.[38]

Given this imperative, it may seem surprising that so many French words remained in the language institutionalized by the TDK and were given Turkish spelling. Atatürk's affinity for the language and the intellectual and philosophical movements associated with it suggest that he found French, as a language indicative of a sophisticated, modern, European identity, to be a more appropriate linguistic source than the languages of Turkey's Muslim, Middle Eastern neighbors. As his biographer notes, Atatürk would frequently slip French words into conversation and was particularly enamored of the word *"déjà."*[39] However, many Turks may be unaware of the "foreign," Western-derived imports present in Turkish, such as *mayo* (swimsuit, from *maillot*), *egzersiz* (exercise, from *exercice*), and *burjuvazi* (from *bourgeoisie*, a transliteration guaranteed to trip up any French speaker when learning Turkish). This highlights somewhat of a double standard in the objections by some virulently anti-imperialist Republican Nationalists to the encroachment of English on modern Turkish in today's increasingly globalized media environment.[40] The website *Türkçesi Varken* (Since It Exists in Turkish), for example, encourages visitors to commit to using Turkish words rather than foreign imports, particularly from English. Such supporters view English words and expressions—even as innocuous as "bye-bye," articulated by millions of Turks when ending a telephone call as *"hadi bye-bye"* ("come on then, goodbye")—as threats to the Turkish nation, thus provoking the ire expressed by those resentful of foreigners "ruining [their] language."[41]

The best-selling book *Bye-Bye Türkçe*,[42] first published in 2000 but reissued in multiple editions, articulates this resentment particularly well. Framed as the imperialism of English and American culture, the book opens with an imaginary "New York Dream" (*"Nev-York Rüyası"*) sequence, which portrays how strange and unnatural it would seem to wander around a major American city plastered with ads written in Turkish, satirizing the English-language product, store, and café names in cultural capitals such as Istanbul. The imaginary protagonist speaks with an American who bemoans the profusion of education in "foreign" languages, noting with embarrassment "as the sick obsession with foreign education rapidly increased, the level of America's science, technology, and literature really dropped." This implies a criticism of the transition of many of the most prominent private universities in Turkey's major cities—such as Sabancı and Koç (both in Istanbul) and Bilkent and Middle East Technical University (both in Ankara)—to all-English language education. The quote on the front cover of the book sums up the Republican Nationalist view of the link between language and nation: "If Turkish goes, Turkey will go!"

While English is increasingly present in various sectors of Turkey's population but particularly among youth, and is thus represented in entertainment media forms aiming to appeal to this population, thousands of Arabic and Farsi words were eliminated from the average speaker's usage along with the switch to the Latin script, so that understanding Ottoman Turkish would require learning a new vocabulary as well as a new alphabet. Indeed, Turkish-language scholars and commentators note that Turks today could not read Atatürk's *Nutuk* speech as it was originally written in the Arabic- and Farsi-infused Turkish of the time. There is an irony here, in that not being able to read *Nutuk* as an indirect result of Atatürk's language reforms and the population's increasing contact with Western media[43] means "not listening to how the Republic was founded from Mustafa Kemal."

As Ottoman Islamists would later lament in the course of their efforts to spread their own proposal for Turkish national identity, the Republican Nationalist strategy to switch scripts and purge the language of foreign—that is, Arabic and Farsi—words produced the intended situation in which younger generations of Turkey's population were unable to connect with their past via Ottoman literature without the help of translation, appreciate the Ottoman art of calligraphy (*hat sanatı*),[44] or even read the inscriptions on their ancestors' gravestones.[45] Demonstrating the affective nature of these debates, one language professor vociferously derides the "ignorant" mentality of "20th century dinosaurs" who oppose the mandatory teaching of Ottoman language as an ideological step backward.[46] Another academic similarly points out that Republican Nationalists are the ones who are truly backward, calling Ottoman classes a "long overdue introduction" to Turkey's education system.[47] In direct contestation of this perspective, however, former director of the Turkish History Institute (Türk Tarihi Kurumu) Yusuf Halaçoğlu vocalizes support of the logic behind Atatürk's language reform. In his criticism of the newly passed legislation mandating Ottoman Turkish courses for all high school students, Halaçoğlu wonders: "Poor kids—by teaching them Ottoman Turkish are they going to travel to outer space? Are they going to save Turkey?"[48] Halaçoğlu admits he himself struggles in reading Ottoman Turkish and sees the mandatory implementation of high school courses in the language foolish. The discourse used in these different reactions to the introduction of Ottoman Turkish into the curriculum highlights the strength of individuals' convictions regarding aspects of identity content, including constitutive norms of behavior and cognitive worldview. Atatürk and his elite team of reformers were just as convinced that a modern and Westernized Turkish language, along with great improvements in levels of literacy across the country, were inexorable in creating generations of citizens capable of leading Turkey to its rightful place in the world as an economically developed and legitimately Western state.

Contesting a Proposal for Non-Turkish Identity

Apart from efforts to destroy the religious and imperial ties the republic's new citizens had with their past, the state's elites were also greatly focused on eradicating the ethnic identities they saw as destructive to the health of the Turkish nation. Thus, while language reforms were used to cleave Turkey away from its Ottoman and Islamist past, the Law on the Adoption and Implementation of Turkish Letters (*Türk Harflerinin Kabul ve Tatbiki Hakkında Kanun*) of 1928 also forbade the use of Kurdish letters, officially excluding the letters q, w, and x from acceptable uses of the alphabet.[49] As the Republican Nationalist constitutive norm of membership can be considered "nonethnic" and even "anti-ethnic" in prohibiting the expression of ethnic identity, as discussed in the previous chapter, the exclusion of Kurdish letters and prohibition of the use of the Kurdish language in public was one of many reforms enacted to prevent the expression of Kurdish identity,[50] seen as embodying an inherently separatist (*bölücü*) ethnic identity. In combination with laws against the use of the Kurdish language, thousands of Kurdish place names were changed. A parliamentary request submitted by an MP of the Kurdish Peace and Democracy Party (Barış ve Demokrasi Partisi, BDP) asking for the name of Bingöl province to be changed to the Kurdish name Çewlig claims that more than thirty thousand places with Kurdish, Armenian, Greek, Laz, Circassian, Arabic, and other names had been renamed beginning in 1921;[51] more than twelve thousand of these changes were to the names of Kurdish villages, a figure that a recent independent report confirms.[52] The report notes that these changes were formalized with Memorandum 8589 from the Ministry of the Interior in 1940, which stated "the names of both places of relocation and natural places that come from foreign languages and roots, and whose usage opens the path to great unrest, are replaced with Turkish names."[53]

Parents were also forbidden to give their children Kurdish names in efforts to remove potential challenges to a Republican Nationalist identity, a ban that continues in practice despite the official lifting of the prohibition of Kurdish letters as outlined in the AKP's democratization package of 2013. A registrar in Bismil recently told a Kurdish family attempting to give their newborn the name Cigerxwîn: "Give your child a different name."[54] The title of an article in which this anecdote is cited, "This Is Turkey, Kurdish Is Forbidden," captures the Kurdish movement's frustration with the continual challenges they face in obtaining minority rights and freedom of expression.

Such cases of what international human rights law deems minority rights abuses abound, with many receiving international criticism due to recent actions by the Kurdish diaspora to engage transnational civil society's attention in their bid to increase freedom of cultural expression, a strategy of taking an identity contest "outside" (discussed in chapter 7). As a few examples, (1) a worker in the densely Kurdish-populated province of Batman tried to give his daughter the name "Asiwa" (using the forbidden letter "w"), but the registrar refused to record the name; (2) a Turkish-origin Swedish citizen tried to give his daughter the same name, deciding to give her Swedish citizenship when Turkish citizenship was refused on the basis of the use of the letter "w" rather than to choose a different name; and (3) when a Malatya resident tried to register his daughter as "Clara Xazal," the municipal registrar noted that "one of the names was German, the other an unknown language."[55]

In one of the most drastic measures used to spread Republican Nationalism and replace existing identifications, the forced resettlement of many Kurds from their traditional homelands in southeastern Turkey was intended to disrupt cultural and clan ties that could act as a barrier to accepting an overarching Turkish identity. As a part of this campaign, millions of Kurds were displaced during the early years of the republic in efforts to break up Kurdish solidarity and extinguish the potentially border-threatening ethnic separatism that Republican Nationalists associated with Kurdish identity. Yet other Kurds migrated in later years not because of specific government decrees or campaigns, but to escape dangerous environments, including widely imposed states of emergency (*Olağanüstü Hal*, OHAL) that were used to justify harsh repressive measures against Kurds as well as violent acts carried out by Kurds themselves. Many Kurdish-populated towns and villages were continually tense with the fear of reprisals by the Turkish military and its various militant groups for acts perceived as separatist. The novel *One Cause, Two Loves* (*Bir Dava İki Sevda*) illustrates the outcomes of fleeing one's homeland in extensive and affective detail.[56] One of the two protagonists, an Alevi Kurdish girl named Ruken, leaves Tunceli[57] with her family to escape violent activism, relocating in the Mediterranean region of Çukurova as a child. In a conversation with Zeriye, an imam's daughter who was raised as a pious Sunni Kurd in Hakkari (near the Syrian borer), Ruken reflects despairingly on the loss of her own Kurdish identity, illustrating in part the intended outcome of Republican Nationalists' contestation of this non-Turkish proposal:

> I like my name. In any case my only tie to Kurdishness is my name. My name is Kurdish but I don't know the Kurdish language or Kurdish history. Actually, we don't know ourselves as people. We have become strangers to ourselves (*kendimize yabancılaştık*).[58]

Hegemony in Question: Challenges
to Republican Nationalism

As the preceding quote implies, the pursuit of identity hegemony for Republican Nationalism entailed efforts to erode ethnic and religious ties within Turkey's population, in the belief that they posed threats to the social purpose of protecting the principles of Atatürk. Islam was systematically removed from the public sphere and then put under the government's control—later to be wielded as a tool in the fight against leftism—and Pan-Turkic and Kurdish identifications were dismissed as backward-looking, romantic foolishness or were openly suppressed. Realizing Republican Nationalist interests at the foreign policy level took the initial form of "active neutrality" during World War II,[59] with President İsmet İnönü maneuvering to obtain aid from both sides of the conflict while avoiding entanglements that could threaten Turkey's borders or damage the socioeconomic modernization program Atatürk envisioned. The Turkish military's firm hold over politics and governments that were in large part Republican Nationalist, at the very least in terms of foreign policy but arguably in most aspects of domestic politics as well,[60] ensured that Turkey's orientation became firmly Western while remaining as independent as possible. Turkey's NATO membership, though potentially threatening for Republican Nationalists by creating the possibility of being pulled into conflicts, was ultimately judged necessary to protect against the looming Soviet threat on Turkey's eastern border.[61] Republican Nationalism had become widely spread throughout the public sphere as a result of the implementation and upholding of Atatürk's reforms and was embedded in guardianship institutions whose role is analyzed in the following chapter.

However, internal and external events following the military's sweeping coup in September 1980, which uncharacteristically put in place a military government power for three years and left Chief of the General Staff Kenan Evren as president until 1989, began to pose significant threats to Republican Nationalism's pursuit of hegemony. The "outside-in" challenge created by the neoliberal economic opening begun under Prime Minister Turgut Özal in the 1980s and carried on under the AKP,[62] and the "inside-out" challenge posed to Republican Nationalism by the increase in international attention focused on the Kurdish issue as a result of Kurds' engagement with transnational civil society,[63] inserted new dynamics into the contest to define Turkey's national identity by importing new discourses regarding human rights into the country while exporting its goods and expanding its dialogue with European institutions.[64] The following subsections focus on three challenges undoubtedly connected to these wider events, but worthy of analysis from an identity contestation perspective for understanding how Republican Nationalism evolved, Western Liberalism emerged, Pan-Turkic Nationalism remained stagnant, and Ottoman Islamism gained the support that would propel its own pursuit of identity hegemony, as discussed in chapter 6.

Contestation from Within: Second Republicans (İkinci Cumhuriyetçiler)

[handwritten annotation: offshoot of R.N.]
[handwritten annotation: 1]

In the aftermath of the 1980 coup and the institutionalization of the extraordinarily strict constitution of 1982,[65] one of the most intriguing challenges to Republican Nationalism was that posed by Republican Nationalists themselves. The theory of inside-out identity contestation I develop in this book, particularly its focus on contestation as a mechanism for change in both the content of proposals as well the levels of support each proposal enjoys, facilitates an understanding of this challenge and the changes it would produce. Infighting occurred among supporters of Republican Nationalism, generated by those who believed the oppressive measures taken to ensure that such a drastic intervention on the part of the military would not be necessary again would eventually produce a moderation of Republican Nationalists' stance toward protecting the red lines of secularism and civic identity. This moderation also included an increased willingness to acknowledge and address the brutal measures used in the past to dismantle religious and ethnic forms of identification, seen as threats to Republican Nationalism's hegemony pursuit, and a greater openness toward international engagement, previously seen as highly risky due to the potential for increased interdependence in the international arena that would lead to entanglements that could threaten Turkey's borders. These moderations in the Republican Nationalist identity proposal are admittedly analytically inseparable from other challenges created by internal and external events mentioned in the introduction to this section. Here, I focus on the Second Republicans (İkinci Cumhuriyetçiler) to demonstrate that it was not external pressure alone that generated the observed modifications in the proposal supported by the great majority of Republican Nationalists, but rather a process marked by extensive contestation from within. Finally, this contestation can also be seen as contributing to the emergence of Turkey's Western Liberalists, formed by İkinci Cumhuriyetçiler and others unsatisfied with many of Republican Nationalists' abilities or willingness to admit responsibility for atrocities committed against groups such as Kurds and Armenians during Republican Nationalism's pursuit of hegemony.

As explored in further detail in the following chapter's analysis of various Republican Nationalist institutions as identity-based obstacles to the spread of alternative identity proposals, the Turkish military served, in Atatürk's own words, as "the leader of movements to achieve lofty ideals . . . as the guardian of [the Turkish nation's] ideals."[66] As such, questioning the military's actions or even being critical of the institution in general could mark individuals as traitors to their nation (*vatan hainleri*). Beginning on the day of the 1980 coup, hundreds of thousands of those who had expressed criticism and/or engaged in what was believed to be seditious politics were rounded up by the military to be imprisoned, tortured, and/or killed. The destruction of the individual and the rending apart of families in Turkey during the period after the coup come to life in the widely popular film *Babam ve Oğlum* (*My Father and My Son*), in which protagonist Sadık's wife dies while giving birth to her son because no medical personnel can be found on the morning of the September 12, 1980 coup. Following years of imprisonment and torture for his leftist political views, which leave him terminally ill, Sadık takes his son Deniz to live with his father, Hüseyin, who had disowned Sadık for his leftist agitation.[67]

The harsh portrayal of the coup's devastating aftermath in the film, released in 2005, reveals over two decades of critical reflection upon and debate about the role of the military in politics in the public sphere. Criticism also began to arise regarding the dogmatic nature of Republican Nationalists' commitments to the principles of Atatürk, and in particular how this dogmatism shaped perceptions of what constituted threats to the republican regime. As former CHP general secretary Ertuğrul Günay argued, "forty years of a continuously reinvented politics of antagonism and debates about threats to the regime will not lead anywhere."[68] Günay's expulsion from the party shortly after he made these comments suggests there was still resistance to internal criticism in 2004, but many Republican Nationalists seemed to agree that a rethinking of what the party of Atatürk stood for was in order. The İkinci Cumhuriyetçiler movement, spearheaded by self-described Marxist-liberal Mehmet Altan and his brother Ahmet,[69] encouraged critical reflection to correct what its members perceived as doctrinaire thinking that produced reflexive defense of antiquated "taboos and red lines."[70] As Mehmet Altan argues, the single-minded focus on carrying out Atatürk's prescribed principles for the nation produced a denial of forms of identification that had been seen as anathema to Republican Nationalists: "There is a Kurdish problem, but official ideology assumes that such a problem does not exist. There is also a problem relating to Islam; that is to say, as a culture, Islam has been rejected."[71] The title of the column in which Altan expresses these views is telling: "Turkey's Entire Problem Is That It Has Not Been Able to Shift from Being a Political State to a Liberal State." The most poignant criticism voiced by İkinci Cumhuriyetçiler emphasized that the hardcore interpretation of Atatürk's views for the nation, and the measures used to combat perceived threats to this vision, prevented the emergence of a liberal democracy that acknowledged and respected diversity.

The İkinci Cumhuriyetçiler also made a point of discussing previously taboo subjects in Turkey, encouraging the open debate the movement believed was necessary to bring about this type of new regime. Ahmet Altan, novelist and founder of the liberal and openly pro-Kurdish newspaper *Taraf Gazetesi*, was fired from his position at *Milliyet Gazetesi* for publishing a column titled "*Ataküt*," a play on Atatürk's name inserting "Kurd" for "Turk."[72] Altan imagined an alternative course of Turkey's history in which Atatürk was an Ottoman general from Mosul who advocated a twist on his original phrase: "How Happy Is He/She That Says 'I Am a Kurd.'" In line with this study's analysis of Republican Nationalism, the column was a highly controversial breach of a Republican Nationalist red line and thus was precisely what Altan had envisioned in terms of broaching traditionally untouchable subjects. He continued to push the boundaries of acceptable discourse, receiving both praise and censure. Altan was charged in 2008 under article 301 of Turkey's Penal Code for an article titled "Oh, My Brother,"[73] which was "dedicated to the victims of the 'Armenian genocide'" but was deemed an "insult to Turkishness" (*Türklüğe hakaret*), and he was named Turkey's "Man of the Year" by the Gülen-owned English-language newspaper *Today's Zaman* in 2010 specifically for his struggles to "break taboos."[74] The Altan brothers provide an apt example of the risks of challenging orthodox Republican Nationalist principles as well as the fickle nature of political favor; in February 2018 both were sentenced to life imprisonment on charges on conspiring with Gülen to overthrow the AKP, but received little sympathy from Republican Nationalists who largely blamed the two journalists for enabling the AKP's rise in the first place.[75]

The effects of the intellectual movement led by the İkinci Cumhuriyetçiler on the contours of Turkey's identity debates, although inextricably linked to the developments outlined in the discussion of contestation from alternative proposals below, cannot be overestimated. Many individuals who identify strongly with Atatürk have moderated their views of what constitutes a threat to his legacy. As a columnist for the Republican Nationalist *Cumhuriyet* (*Republic*) recalls from his early days at the newspaper: "Most of the columnists were staunch Kemalists but some were beginning to defend rights for Kurds [and thought] that the headscarf [issue] should be solved in a democratic way."[76] Deniz Baykal, another former CHP general secretary, noted how in the pursuit of Atatürk's principles, the social leftism and populism that were originally inherent in them had been trodden on by dogmatic suppression of beliefs. He stated that at "the root of social democracy lies freedom of thought, belief, and worship,"[77] demonstrating a much more broad-minded perspective than in previous years.[78] Former members of the military have also noted changes in the level of flexibility that many individuals who still see themselves as loyal to Atatürk now apply to issues of diversity in identity, as well as to the desirability of Turkey's deepening of ties with the EU. In a discussion of why he supported EU membership for Turkey, while doubting its eventual realization under the current AKP government, a retired officer asserted in an interview that "being a modern Turk is being a good European."[79] As a product of being pushed to reflect upon the identity content of Republican Nationalism by İkinci Cumhuriyetçiler, most supporters demonstrate a less rigid (even if only slightly), more tolerant view of the expression of ethnic identity and religion as well as more willingness to relax the inward-focused relational meaning and cognitive worldview of the proposal, to see increased international engagement as less threatening.

In contrast, those Republican Nationalists whose views on ethnic identity, religious expression, and international interdependence did not evolve as a result of this contestation from within have come to be known as *ulusalcılar*—a specific form of hardcore nationalist discussed in the previous chapter—and recently took institutional form under *ulusalcı* politician Emine Ülker Tarhan as the Anadolu Partisi, which split from the CHP.[80] On the other side of the spectrum, the İkinci Cumhuriyetçiler—along with the Yetmez Ama Evetçi'ler (Those Who Say It's Not Enough but Yes) movement, discussed in chapter 6, and other individuals who had struggled to express their diverse identities, such as Kurds and LGBTQ individuals—are supporters of what now merits discrete identification as a Western Liberalist proposal for Turkey's national identity. While devising a categorical separation between moderated Republican Nationalists and Western Liberalists can be quite problematic in practice, the main difference would be between those who have developed a less stringent attitude toward the securitization of Atatürk's principles and those, like many among the İkinci Cumhuriyetçiler, who believe "the republican modernity project was a mistake from the start."[81]

Contestation from Alternative Proposals: Ottoman Islamism

Despite all of the Republican Nationalists' efforts to change the makeup of citizens of Turkey—spreading an understanding of identity proposing that reliance on Islam as a guiding principle was backward—their strategy to combat another threat to the Turkish nation would inadvertently spur a return of religion to the public sphere. Whereas Republican Nationalists' actions following the 1980 coup created criticism from within as discussed in the previous section, by instituting what was known as the Turkish Islamic Synthesis (*Türk İslam Sentezi*) in order to staunch the spread of destabilizing leftist radicalism,[82] Republican Nationalists created a conduit for contestation from without, unwittingly providing an intellectual basis for the relegitimation of Islamic identity. Viewing the social upheaval witnessed during the left-right ideological clashes of the 1970s that prompted the coup as reactionary civil disobedience by individuals who had been brainwashed by aculturalist Marxism, elites including Chief of the General Staff and President Evren, Prime Minister Özal, and the ministers of culture and education decided at a meeting in 1986 that Turks needed culture to restore their morality.[83] In consultation with the sociopolitical group known as the Intellectuals' Hearths (Aydınlar Ocakları),[84] these elites located in Turkishness and Sunni Islam the sources of the culture they believed was needed as a "binding agent" (yapıştırıcı) for a moral society.[85]

This new legitimizing ideology for the republic and its identity-based foundations in content traditionally found in the identity proposals of Ottoman Islamism and Pan-Turkic Nationalism represent a tactical move by the government and its military president to curb leftist threats but is also indicative of the state of flux in which Republican Nationalism found itself. Its supporters had exercised control over Islam in multiple ways before, making clear that Turkey's somewhat puzzling laicist version of secularism (laiklik) entails state control over religion rather than a mere separation of the two,[86] creating the Directorate of Religious Affairs (Diyanet İşleri Bakanlığı) as an institution for overseeing the practice of Islam, and officially banning religious brotherhoods (tarikatlar) such as the Bektaşi and the Nakşibendi. In this instance, however, the process of disseminating the Turkish Islamic Synthesis, as seen in a revised national education curriculum that aimed to "invoke the positivism in Islamic sciences all the while disassociating scientific reasoning from secularism and the West,"[87] constituted a break from the policies prescribed by Republican Nationalist identity content. Despite the military's claim that the synthesis was ideologically rooted in their overarching goal of protecting the Turkish nation,[88] the mandatory religious classes that were instituted at all levels of education to promote Sunni Islam as a source of guidance and morality, the encouragement of religious groups' organization, and Kenan Evren's recitation of verses from Muslim holy scripture during speeches[89] all constituted red lines for Republican Nationalists.

The crossing of these lines, in addition to the brutal nature of the 1980 coup, contributed to opening the door to contestation among supporters of Republican Nationalism about what exactly their shared identity content consisted of: what norms of behavior are appropriate for them, what their goals should be, and so forth. The return to a focus on Islam in the public sphere also served as a constitutive act that provided supporters of Ottoman Islamism as well as pious Pan-Turkic Nationalists Islamists with an intellectual doctrine to legitimize their beliefs. While Ottoman Islamists often refer to the aftermath of the 1980 coup as a period of mağduriyet (victimization or unjust treatment),[90] the Turkish Islamic Synthesis implemented at that time to generate an Islamic sense of community to prevent a recurrence of the ideological clashes and political violence that marred the 1970s would actually empower Ottoman Islamists,[91] such that the AKP would become "one of the biggest long-term beneficiaries" of the military intervention.[92]

The AKP, formed in 2002, would not only have to wait decades after the events of September 12 to advance its spread of Ottoman Islamism as a proposal for Turkish national identity, but would also have to employ a strategy this study conceptualizes as taking its identity contest outside to the foreign policy arena. In the meantime, successive Islamist parties, led by Necmettin Erbakan and representing a political incarnation of the National Outlook Movement (Milli Görüş Hareketi), faced severe sanctioning, and each party was subsequently banned. The account of the institutionalization of identity-based obstacles offered in the following chapter accounts for why Ottoman Islamist gambits in the domestic arena were thwarted prior to the AKP, but understanding the constitutive effects of the Turkish Islamic Synthesis provides insight into what would eventually become the most powerful challenge to Republican Nationalism's pursuit of hegemony. The Motherland Party (Anavatan Partisi, ANAP) of Özal, which was the most successful of the three allowed to run in the post-coup 1983 elections, was a catch-all party that combined economic ne-oliberalism with Islamic conservatism. Özal himself had run on the ticket of the National Salvation Party (Milli Selamet Partisi, one of the parties formed out of the Milli Görüş Hareketi) in Izmir in 1977 but failed to garner enough votes.[93] The newly established RP was banned from running in the hope of producing a stable government and received only 7% of the vote in 1987, not enough to cross the extremely high 10% threshold and enter parliament.[94] By allying with the right-wing Nationalist Work Party (Milliyetçi Çalışma Partisi, an iteration of the Milliyetçi Hareket Partisi) and Reformist Democracy Party (Islahatçı Demokrasi Partisi) in 1991, however, the RP both gained parliamentary seats for an overtly Ottoman Islamist party and made connections with political players who shared an "ideological affinity [centered] around the role of Islam."[95] The RP continued to benefit electorally from the increased presence of Islam in the public sphere, with its candidate, Erdoğan, becoming the first Islamist mayor of Istanbul in the 1994 local elections and the party garnering the largest amount of votes in the 1995 general elections. This unprecedented political success of an Islamist party, while clearly influenced by capital contributed by conservative Anatolian businessmen, the distribution of patronage in the form of coal and food packages during the holy month of Ramadan, and the organizational efforts of groups using Islam as a tool of mobilization,[96] owes much to the Turkish Islamic Synthesis, which lent legitimacy to such activities.

The challenge that the 1994 and 1995 electoral gains represented generated a strong backlash against the apparently increasing support for Ottoman Islamism, with schoolbooks being re-rewritten with more emphasis on

Republican Nationalist principles to correct for the insertion of Islam into the national curriculum during the heyday of the synthesis. The "counter-reaction" publicly manifested by concerned citizens ranged from the increased display of Atatürk portraits in windows to schoolchildren being told not to talk with RP supporters, as Jenny White's ethnographic study relates.[97] This display of Republican Nationalist symbolism in the public sphere, and the reactive steps taken through institutional channels discussed in the following chapter, provide strong evidence that supporters of Republican Nationalism recognized the challenges facing their attempts to achieve hegemony.

Contestation from Alternative Proposals: Pan-Turkic Nationalism

Intertwined with the contestation of Republican Nationalism advanced by Ottoman Islamists was that carried out by supporters of Pan-Turkic Nationalism, another proposal whose content was legitimized by the Turkish Islamic Synthesis. Already bolstered by the doctrine's new focus on pre-Islamic Turkic culture and history along with the new emphasis on Islam, which fit well with many of its supporters' pious sensibilities, this challenge to Western-oriented Republican Nationalism experienced an unexpected and intense revitalization with the sudden liberation of the Turkic Socialist Republics from Soviet rule. With the dissolution of the USSR in late 1991, Pan-Turkic Nationalists viewed the new independence of the states of Azerbaijan, Kazakhstan, Kyrgyzstan, Turkmenistan, and Uzbekistan as an ideal window in which to realize their social purpose of establishing close ties with Turkic states and their cognitive worldview of serving as a mentoring older brother (*ağabey*). While other parts of what supporters conceive of as the Turkic world (*Türk dünyası*) remained inaccessible, such as the Uyghur-populated Xinjiang region of China, known to Pan-Turkic Nationalists as East Turkistan (Doğu Turkestan), and Crimea, home of the Turkic Tatars but part of the Slavic Ukrainian state (later annexed by Russia), international dynamics had changed such that the five Turkic states could now develop their own independent foreign policies.

As discussed in the previous chapter's outline of identity proposals, the concept of rebirth as related by Pan-Turkic Nationalists stems from the widespread narrative that views Turks' history and the history of the Turkic/Turkish state as an uninterrupted (*kesintisiz*) and glorious path from their pre-Islamic origins in Central Asia to the present. The cultural and religious ties that bind Turkic peoples, according to this narrative, were the victims of a history rife with "unjust practices" (*mağduriyet*) that erected "ridiculous" (*saçma*) walls between brothers.[98] Interviewees emphasized that while some Turks seem to need to choose between glorifying Atatürk (as Republican Nationalists might do) or the Ottoman Empire (as Ottoman Islamists might do), there is no need for such divisive dispute because they are both part of Turks' continuously illustrious history.[99] This continuous narrative of Turkic peoples, according to Pan-Turkic Nationalists, gives gravitas to their history and legitimates the reuniting of Turkey with its former brothers.[100]

Pan-Turkic Nationalists interviewed lament that they were unable to more successfully contest Turkey's Republican Nationalist, Western-oriented foreign policy at the time. In what would turn out to be the largely unwarranted hope that the Turkic republics wanted an *ağabey* as much as Pan-Turkic Nationalists wanted to be one and thus would adjust their foreign policies accordingly, supporters intended to channel the euphoria experienced following the collapse of the USSR into some form of institutionalized relationship with the Turkic states. Multiple interviewees noted that this relationship need not have been a political union, but could have been—and still should be—economic or cultural. The loose consortia established thus far however, such as the Turkic States' and Communities' Friendship, Fraternity, and Cooperation Foundation (Türk Devlet ve Toplulukları Dostluk, Kardeşlik ve İşbirliği Kurultayı), remain unsatisfactory to those interviewed. Indicative of Pan-Turkic Nationalism's anti-Westward orientation, several interviewees expressed frustration with Turkey fruitless and "misguided" pursuit of EU membership and disregard for some form of union of Turkic states, which they believed would be more appropriate.[101]

When asked to speculate on why Turkey's government failed to engage more deeply with the Turkic republics following their independence, a consistent narrative running through the statements of Pan-Turkic Nationalist interviewees was: "We weren't ready" (*"Hazır değildik"*), with some implying that their supporters had been unable to spread their vision for Turkey to the point where it would be taken seriously by the government. Indeed, by the time of the Soviet Union's collapse, there were few supporters of Pan-Turkic Nationalism, due in part to the ideological cleansing of rightist and (mostly) leftist elements that took place following the 1980 coup,[102] and the foreign policy orientation they supported was viewed by Republican Nationalists as fanciful at best and possibly even perilous.

The ethnic constitutive norm of Pan-Turkic Nationalism and the foreign entanglement that might stem from acting upon it represent potential dangers to the borders of Turkey in the same manner as Kurdish nationalism (if by irredentism rather than separatism), a red line for Republican Nationalists. The concern that an activist foreign policy in Central Asia and the Caucasus "would not only be a futile attempt, but also one to further polarize the region on ethnic and religious lines and thus sever the painstakingly established *organic* ties with Europe"[103] highlights the Republican Nationalist belief in both a natural relationship between Turkey and Europe and the lack of a need to maintain close ties with the Turkic republics. The social purpose component of Republican Nationalism clearly defined a primary goal of the Turkish state as full membership in the European Union (European Community at the time) to fit with its particular worldview, as prescribed by its constitutive norm of European membership, outlined above. The cognitive worldview component can be expressed by Atatürk's aphorism *Yurtta sulh, cihanda sulh* (Peace at home, peace in the world), prescribing a noninterventionist policy for Turkey and thus proscribing deep relations with states in Russia's sphere of influence. The proposal's stridently anti-Western relational meaning also marks a distinct contrast from the Republican Nationalist conceptualization of the need to embrace "an 'authentic' modern identity" by securing its rightful place in Europe.[104]

The sentiments of unpreparedness expressed by Pan-Turkic Nationalists stem from a failure to spread their proposal's identity content to more of Turkey's population, an indication that the challenge posed to Republican Nationalism by its supporters is relatively minimal. As noted in the previous chapter, organizations such as the Türk Ocakları and Ülkü Ocakları were founded to educate Turks about their history and how proper Turks should behave. Along with the Turkish Islamic Synthesis's effects of making Turkish culture and Islam more salient for citizens of Turkey, these organizations also strive to teach Turks about their nomadic origins in Central Asia, their uninterrupted history as a glorious state, and their natural bonds with other Turkic populations. When the window of opportunity for a long-awaited union with these fraternal populations opened in late 1991, not enough Turks believed that such brotherhoods had any meaningful importance.[105]

In comparison with this relative paucity of support, Republican Nationalism's presence in institutions such as the military and its own popular support proved resilient against any substantial contestation by Pan-Turkic Nationalist supporters in what could have been the ideal opportunity to advance their proposal. Instead, the limited partnership established by the ruling coalition of the True Path Party (Doğru Yol Partisi, DYP) and ANAP with the Turkic republics—notably referred to in a negative light by critics of the policy as "impoverished Kyrgyzstan" and "under-populated Turkmenistan"[106]—encountered significant backlash and even ridicule. Republican Nationalist supporters favoring a more modern, Western-oriented foreign policy thus deplored the DYP/ANAP's decision to invest in such "economic backwaters."[107] Despite these efforts to reach out to the Turkic republics of the former Soviet Union, the initial period of " "romanticism" was followed by a "face the facts" period instigated by supporters of more widely spread Republican Nationalism,[108] whose understanding of Turkishness fundamentally conflicted with Pan-Turkic aspirations. Following the collapse of the DYP/ANAP coalition and its flirtation with the Turkic republics, future governments refrained from developing more sustained and meaningful alliances with the Turkic world.

Conclusion

This chapter's exploration of the motivating sources of and competitors with Republican Nationalism laid the groundwork for understanding its pursuit of hegemony, a goal that is ultimately unrealized. By focusing on contestation as a mechanism of change for the content of existing proposals, for the relative levels of support across proposals, and for the emergence of hybrid or entirely new proposals, the chapter provides significant insight into the dynamics of interplay among supporters of competing proposals during the formative years of the Republic of Turkey. Applying a framework of identity contestation that specifies the red lines of identity content that constitute major points of contestation among competing proposals facilitates understanding why particular precepts of Pan-Turkic Nationalism and Ottoman Islamism were anathema to Republican Nationalists and thus why identity-based obstacles were put in place to protect against any spread of two proposals. A contestation-based perspective also helps to illuminate the challenges posed to Republican Nationalists' pursuit of hegemony, including contestation from within its own ranks as well as by supporters of competing proposals.

In the following chapter I examine the main institutions of governance in which Republican Nationalism was embedded, demonstrating both the initial victory of this identity proposal's supporters over its rivals and the means by which Republican Nationalists sought to secure the interests generated by the proposal against future incursions. The chapter provides an in-depth investigation of the Turkish military, the judicial system (particularly the Constitutional Court), and university rectors, conceptualizing these institutions as identity-based obstacles to gambits by supporters of competing proposals. I illustrate how these institutions, as agents themselves, view their organizational identity to be tasked with upholding the founding principles of the republic as delineated by the individual who would become known as Father of the Turks. Building on the current chapter's examination of Republican Nationalism's pursuit of hegemony, I argue in the following chapter that this institutionalization of Republican Nationalism guaranteed the resilience of the proposal's defense of its prescribed standards of behavior against the challenges of Ottoman Islamist supporters. As chapter 6 illustrates, however, Republican Nationalist–infused institutions of guardianship could only prove resilient until the AKP chose to circumvent these obstacles, taking its contestation to the foreign policy arena.

5

Stuck Inside

Obstacles to Ottoman Islamism at Home

Introduction

The theory of identity contestation developed in this book posits that for both sociopsychological reasons related to belonging and self-esteem and institutional reasons related to gaining access to realize the interests generated by a particular proposal, supporters of identity proposals aim to spread their understanding of identity as far as possible across a population, ultimately in pursuit of hegemony. The theory also stipulates that when efforts to disseminate an identity proposal face obstacles at the domestic level, supporters utilize an "inside-out" strategy of contestation, taking their identity struggle to the foreign policy arena instead. This chapter explores the role of identity-based obstacles, which represent the institutionalization of an identity proposal in a guardianship role intended to prevent the dissemination of alternative, competing proposals.

The power of such institutions is by no means permanent or uncontested, as the following chapter examines in detail by tracing the strategic contest to spread Ottoman Islamism. To lay the groundwork for its analysis of the AKP's seemingly counterintuitive strategy of pursuing hegemony for Ottoman Islamism through an EU-oriented foreign policy, this chapter identifies the formidable obstacles to supporters of Ottoman Islamism in the domestic arena. While the previous chapter outlined internal and external factors posing challenges to Republican Nationalism's grip on hegemony—including the intensification of the Kurdish problem (*Kürt sorunu*), the neoliberal economic opening pushed forward by former Prime Minister and President Turgut Özal, and the collapse of the Cold War order and Soviet regime—the identity-based obstacles instituted as guardians of the identity proposal remained largely in place. As this chapter highlights, the defensive power of these obstacles in protecting Republican Nationalism was particularly evident during the so-called February 28 Process, during which the efforts of Islamist politician Necmettin Erbakan and his RP to realize Ottoman Islamist interests at the domestic and foreign policy levels were deemed to be threats and thus were quickly thwarted.

Identifying Identity Obstacles

The use of the concept of identity red lines as developed in chapter 2 and fleshed out empirically in the Turkish case in chapter 3 facilitates the specification of particular elements of identity content—beliefs about norms of membership and behavior, interests and goals, the definition of allies and enemies, and a country's overarching role in the international system—that can be considered intolerable by supporters of an opposing proposal. In this study I conceptualize identity-based obstacles as institutions established, at least in part, to ensure that red lines are not crossed. The form, authority, and enforcement capacity of these obstacles may vary across cases, but identity-based guardians can consist of institutions as varied as militaries, judicial courts, educational systems, language institutes, constitutions, and the media.

Much work has been done examining such sites for defining and spreading a particular understanding of national identity throughout a population. Sam Kaplan's analysis of national education curricula;[1] Ronald Krebs's study of the military and conscription;[2] John Gillis's edited volume on official commemorations;[3] and Benedict Anderson's discussion of censuses, maps, and museums[4] focus on specific institutions or sets of practices designed to articulate and instill a clear vision of the model citizen, as well as defining who belongs inside and outside of that group. Considered as a whole, these sites and the others noted above can also usefully be conceptualized as guardians of that vision against the incursion of competing proposals for national identity, with all of the standards of appropriate and inappropriate behavior those proposals define. While some entities may be more explicitly defensive in their stance toward the spread of identity proposals whose content they deem intolerable— national militaries tasked to define and defend against internal as well as external threats, for example—courts' decisions on the permissibility of ethnic parties, constitutions' delineation of the criteria of citizenship, and universities' prohibitions on the wearing of religious garments on campus all exemplify the acts of institutions seeking to protect a particular understanding of identity by preserving its hegemony.

Placing a focus on institutions as identity-based obstacles helps to facilitate analytical capture of the distribution of support for identity proposals across a population, which is combined in this study with an investigation of support displayed for various proposals in the public sphere. This focus also aids in tracing shifts generated by processes of a form of "institutional capture,"[5] by which supporters of a competing identity proposal appropriate an institution such as the judicial or educational systems or the national media. In taking away control, the process of capture enables those striving to dislodge the material and ideational capacity for authority wielded by supporters of a rival proposal to use the institution as a forum for the pursuit of hegemony for their own proposal. From the opposite perspective, an institutional lens also assists in making sense of the longevity of widespread support for some proposals over others before they are captured by supporters who, blocked in their identity gambits at the domestic level, take their contestation outside to the foreign policy arena. Finally, examining the institutionalization of an identity proposal helps in understanding the particular elements of identity content that are deemed to be in need of defense and thus become points of intense contestation—such as secularism, respect for Atatürk, or Western orientation—as opposed to elements that constitute red lines for supporters of other proposals, such as a social purpose of promoting LGBTQ rights or ethnicity as the constitutive norm of membership.

Western Liberalists, for example, could be expected to object to the advancement of any identity proposal that contains membership norms based on religion and submission to an authoritarian leader, which are directly opposed to their own constitutive norms of diverse inclusivity and protection of liberties. Pan-Turkic Nationalists, while sharing some elements of identity content with Ottoman Islamists, such as constitutive norms rooted in reverence for Turkey's ancestors and an anti-Western relational meaning, strongly oppose Ottoman Islamists' social purpose of promoting the welfare of all Muslims without prioritizing Turkic Muslims and their tolerance of the expression of ethnic identities other than that of "Türk." Finally, the Republican Nationalist social purpose of protecting the founding principles of Atatürk—and particularly the principle of secularism—fundamentally conflicts with the Ottoman Islamist social purpose of increasing space for Islam in the public sphere. Identity proposals with content elements that are seemingly incompatible with one another—for example, beliefs about appropriate behavior for group members (constitutive norms) or what the group's goals (social purpose) should be appear to be irreconcilable—can be expected to have supporters who clash with each other as well. While all three of these identity proposals contain points of incompatibility with Ottoman Islamism, given its much more widespread and institutionalized support base, Republican Nationalism posed the largest obstacle to any attempt by the AKP to pursue identity hegemony during its first term.

By turning the focus to an examination of identity-based obstacles, it becomes clear that Republican Nationalism was the far stronger contender in the fight. Since the founding of the Turkish Republic, Republican Nationalism had been embodied in institutions such as the TSK, the Constitutional Court and other high courts, and the university rectorship (*rektörlük*). Individuals within the first two institutions viewed themselves as morally tasked to uphold the republic's founding Atatürkist principles, as discussed in the previous chapter.[6] Many university rectors also shared this sense of duty; further, following the 1980 coup state university rectors were selected and supervised in conjunction with the state's Higher Education Council (Yükseköğretim Kurulu, YÖK). Unlike the relatively less widespread Pan-Turkic Nationalism and Western Liberalism, however, Republican Nationalism's supporters had institutional tools with which to combat attempts to advance the spread of Ottoman Islamism throughout the population and achieve the interests it prescribes. The following sections examine these institutionalized, identity-based obstacles in detail, focusing on their defensive role in the February 28 Process. This examination serves to undergird the argument elaborated upon in the following chapter that, even though the AKP received enough votes to form a single-party government just months after being established, the party was far from free to realize the interests generated by its Ottoman Islamist identity proposal upon coming to power in 2002.

The analysis that follows in this chapter is intended to be illustrative rather than exhaustive of the Republican Nationalist institutions that posed obstacles to the spread of Ottoman Islamism. The majority of major media outlets prior to the 2000s, for example, were highly Republican Nationalist in ownership, and thus their content often focused on the legacies of Atatürk, perceived threats to secularism, and the dangers of an anti-Western foreign policy. A few select media sources as of writing are still overtly Republican Nationalist, such as *Cumhuriyet Gazetesi, Aydınlık Gazetesi*, and *Ulusal Kanal*, but most of the mainstream newspaper and television outlets have been consolidated by massive media groups under the influence of AKP supporters. This consolidation of media ownership and messaging turned into a full-blown purge following the split between the AKP and followers of exiled Islamic cleric Fethullah Gülen's Hizmet (Service) movement in 2013, with Gülenist-owned outlets such as *Zaman* and its English affiliate *Today's Zaman* being taken over by the government. The closure of Kurdish television networks and other media broadcasters following the 2015 breakdown of peace talks between the AKP government and the PKK, when combined with dozens of closures carried out in the wake of the July 15, 2016 coup attempt,[7] served to narrow significantly the amount of non-state-sponsored content and thus to limit the extent to which those opposed to the AKP's promulgation of its Ottoman Islamist proposal can reach the general public.

When asked why opposition parties in general, and the main opposition CHP in particular, did so poorly in elections, Eskişehir CHP MP and Republican Nationalist Kazım Kurt stated: "We don't stand a chance; we don't have any media left to broadcast our message."[8] Commenting on a government decree stripping the Supreme Election Board of the right to issue penalties for one-sided and/or biased propaganda in the run-up to the April 16, 2017 constitutional referendum, CHP leader Kemal Kılıçdaroğlu similarly argued in a tweet that "only [AKP] voices will be heard until the referendum; only one side will be able to make free broadcasts."[9] News media can clearly serve as a powerful institution, either blocking or facilitating the spread of an identity proposal. This power will vary across cases, however, based on the extent to which supporters of a particular proposal have consolidated ownership of and influence over media outlets. For example, the liberalization of broadcasting in Turkey in 1990 opened up space for the dissemination of Ottoman Islamist–themed content, and the following discussion illustrates the power of the Turkish military— which issued an ultimatum to twenty television stations as part of a Republican Nationalist–led purge beginning in 1997[10]—to combat perceived threats to secularism in privately owned fora such as news and entertainment media. The three institutions I explore in this chapter represent those in the Turkish case through which Republican Nationalists were most effective in infusing and consolidating their proposal in identity-based institutional obstacles of governance and societal control.

Turkish Armed Forces (TSK)

With 600,000 personnel prior to the post-putsch purges, the TSK ranked as the eleventh largest army in the world, second only to Russia's armed forces in Europe.[11] For reasons understandable from an identity contestation perspective, the TSK has long striven to be as influential as an identity-based obstacle to competing proposals in domestic politics as it is in guarding Turkey's borders from external threats. Since the founding of the Turkish Republic in 1923, following the collapse of the Ottoman Empire and an astonishingly successful national independence campaign against Allied powers who sought further further divide the territory of what is modern-day Turkey among themselves, the TSK served as a highly powerful institution. This power manifested itself not only in terms of numbers and responsibilities delegated by the state.[12] The TSK has historically been the institution most fervently dedicated to—and effective in—upholding and protecting the principles of Atatürk, in particular his vision for the national identity of the new republic's citizens. This inextricable, affective link among the military, Atatürk, and identity makes sense when examining the founding narrative of Republican Nationalists,[13] in which all three are deeply imbricated.

Atatürk is lauded not only as the founder (*Kurucu*), but also as the warrior (*Gazi*), savior (*Kurtarıcı*), and superhuman (*Fevkalbeşer*) of the republic.[14] Given the singular name of Mustafa, in the fashion typical of foundational narratives, he is rumored to have been given the second name of Kemal (meaning "perfection" in Ottoman Turkish) by a mathematics professor who was also called Mustafa but was so impressed by his student that he bestowed upon him this praiseworthy distinguisher.[15] The man who would later become Atatürk distinguished himself in numerous military campaigns, winning national acclaim at Çanakkale (Gallipoli) during World War I and later leading his troops to victory against the Allies in what is often referred to in Turkish as the *Kurtuluş Savaşı* (War of Liberation). While the 1919–1922 war is generally referred to in English as Turkey's War of Independence or War of Resistance, both of which labels connote large-scale, bottom-up movements, the Turkish usage notably depicts Atatürk as the liberator or emancipator of the masses, saving them from occupying forces intent upon rending apart what increasingly became seen as the Turkish nation. This connotation positions him singularly to become the Father (*Ata*) of the Turkish people (*Türk halkı*), hence the surname of Atatürk, which he acquired upon making surnames mandatory for all citizens of Turkey.[16] His military heroism in the face of seemingly insurmountable obstacles has become the stuff of legend. The story of how the pocket watch Atatürk was wearing saved his life by protecting his heart from shrapnel is one of the highlights of tours of the battlefields at Çanakkale. The search for the "watch that changed the fate of a country," which was lost during World War II after being gifted to Atatürk's field marshall Otto Liman von Sanders, makes national headlines.[17] Atatürk is repeatedly compared to legends both for his bravery and for his anguish in times of struggle; his adopted daughter famously compared his eyes to the "eyes of those burning in Dante's hell" to describe his suffering on behalf of the nation.[18] His military experiences formatively impacted his understanding of his own personal identity and thus his role as a political leader; he used the title of *Gazi*—a signifier that traditionally carried the meaning of "holy warrior" but became "republicanized"[19] during the processes analyzed in the previous chapter—for the rest of his life.[20]

Respect for Atatürk's achievements as a war hero and father of a nation, defending it against seemingly overwhelming odds, has traditionally imbued the country's armed forces with a strong sense of legitimacy—understood here as a normative belief that an institution should be obeyed[21]—for much of Turkey's population. A study published in 2004 notes that public opinion polls show Turkey's citizens at that time had more confidence in the military than in any other political institution.[22] These beliefs about legitimacy and confidence in the TSK, which played a significant constitutive part in its ability to act as an authoritative guardian of Republican Nationalism, derive in great part from a national educational system that had been designed to produce both patriotic citizens and soldiers. As Michael Wuttrich's study of the Turkish military rightly emphasizes, Turkey's educational system has traditionally reinforced the "organic" link between Turkish society and its armed forces.[23] A common Turkish phrase expresses this well: *"Her Türk asker doğar"* ("Every Turk is born a sol-dier"). Military service (*askerlik*) for young males, mandatory until the AKP introduced a concession that allowed individuals to pay a fee to be exempt, is seen as a rite of passage in Turkish culture, as traditional as the male circumcision ceremony (*sünnet*). Young men leaving to perform their *askerlik* are sent off with rowdy processions, and (primarily Republican Nationalist and Pan-Turkic Nationalist) families express pride in their young sons' future duties as much as they express worry about the dangers they may face.[24] As Sam Kaplan found in his fascinating ethnographic study and work as a teacher in Turkey, third graders, for example, read that "We Turks give importance to military service. We are even known by the world nations as a nation of soldiers (*asker bir millet*)," bound by duty and honor to follow in Atatürk's footsteps.[25] In reflecting upon an older student's essay on "The Turkish Person," in which the student wrote that Atatürk "was a very brave, knowledgeable, and very good commander" who "would think more about his country than himself," Kaplan highlights the student's belief that Atatürk's military career was "central to the creation of a uniform national identity in the educational system."[26]

The TSK and the segment of the population that the pre-AKP national educational system was able to mold successfully thus see the armed forces as the outgrowth of Atatürk himself, a "defender of Kemalism"[27] institutionally tasked to protect the legacy and vision of Turkey's liberator and founder.[28] As discussed in chapter 3, the main principles that supporters of Republican Nationalism in general—and the TSK as a guardian institution in particular—believe are in need of protection are republicanism (against the threat of imperialism from within and externally), secularism (against the threat of Islamism), and nationalism (against the threat of Kurdish ethnonationalism). By looking at the breakdown of identity content for Ottoman Islamism—indeed, by looking at its name alone—we see that this proposal and its supporters clearly constitute threats to the first two of these three principles.[29] By looking at the strength of the military in Turkey we see that the TSK becomes and remains well positioned to combat these threats—until the AKP's EU-derived reforms, examined in chapter 6.

As discussed in the previous chapter, the TSK carved out a sphere of autonomy, intervening in politics in the form of formal military coups (1960 and 1980) and less formal interventions (1971) for a number of reasons, ranging from massive corruption and loss of democratic legitimacy to a complete breakdown of civil order. The "postmodern coup" of 1997,[30] however, was overwhelmingly motivated by the perception that the principle of secularism was under threat. Crucially, this determination of threat and the authority to devise a response to this threat lay in the hands of the TSK rather than civilian authorities, per article 35 of the military's Internal Service Law (*İç Hizmet Kanunu*), which was enacted following the 1960 coup.[31] While the era of Prime

Minister Turgut Özal (1983–1989) saw efforts to reassert measures of civilian control over the military, most likely in an attempt to increase global perceptions of Turkey as a stable investment opportunity and reliable trade partner during his neoliberal economic opening, successive prime ministers Süleyman Demirel and Tansu Çiller formed alliances with the TSK that effectively "strengthen[ed] the military's domestic hand."[32]

The electoral gains of Islamists in the local elections of 1994 and the general elections of 1995 also contributed to the military's perception that its influence was needed to protect the Turkish Republic from the domestic threat of incursions against secularism. The RP won municipal elections in six major cities in 1994, including the important bellwethers of Ankara and Istanbul, and received the most votes for any religious party in Turkey's history (21.8%) in 1995.[33] As a result, the TSK once again reconsolidated its political power (after having handed the government back to civilians in 1983) and was again prepared to intervene. The TSK kept a close watch on what it perceived as a rising Islamist threat, which can be seen as pre-AKP Ottoman Islamists' attempts at political contestation in the mid-1990s, culminating in Turkey's first Islamist-led coalition government under Erbakan's RP in 1996. This attempt, however, would soon be thwarted, leaving transformational lessons for the AKP on the dangers of contesting Ottoman Islamism in the domestic arena.

These efforts to derail Erbakan and his party's perceived incursion on the red lines of Republican Nationalism became known collectively as the February 28 Process, referring to the many steps taken to securitize Islam and roll back all advancements made by political Islamists in the mid-1990s, discussed in the previous chapter.[34] The process may have been sparked by an Iranian ambassador's speech demanding that Turks obey the "precepts of Islam" at a rally just outside of Ankara,[35] at which Hamas and Hezbollah banners were waved, but it had deeper historical roots. As the founder and leading figure of the Islamist National Outlook Movement (Milli Görüş Hareketi, MGH), Erbakan had seen his National Order Party (Milli Nizam Partisi, MNP) and National Salvation Party (Milli Selâmet Partisi, MSP) shut down following the previous coups and had been banned from politics himself. Reorganizing and mobilizing the extensive and extremely efficient networks of the MGH around the newly founded RP,[36] Erbakan achieved what was unthinkable for Republican Nationalists, becoming Turkey's first Islamist prime minister in 1996. A sample of newspaper headlines from the (very brief) Erbakan period is telling in this respect: "Our 70-year Image Was All for Naught," "Secularism Warning," "The Army Is Uncomfortable," "The Last Warning to Refah."[37]

Seeing some of their worst fears progressively realized—the increased presence of Islam in the educational system, civil society, and the business community; personal appeals by Erbakan for jihad and for the instatement of sharia law;[38] a state visit to Libya; Arab sheiks visiting the Prime Ministry; and the explicit rejection of a Western orientation for Turkey in favor of membership in an international Islamic Union—on February 28, 1997, members of the highly powerful National Security Council (Milli Güvenlik Kurulu, MGK) delivered a set of eighteen directives to Erbakan's cabinet. Each was designed to roll back what the TSK perceived as encroachments on Turkey's inviolably secular nature.[39] After multiple TSK-led press briefings stressing the perils of Islamic reactionism (*irtica*)—at one of which the military for the first time declared this threat to be a greater danger to Turkey than any external threat or even separatist terrorism[40]—and pressure on actors such as Gülen and RP coalition partner the True Path Party (Doğru Yol Partisi) to revoke their support of the RP,[41] Erbakan finally resigned and the RP-led coalition collapsed on June 18, 1997.

Having succeeded in removing Turkey's first Islamist head of government, the military continued in its efforts to eradicate perceived threats to secularism through the forum of Turkey's military-run State Security Courts, trying even Gülen on charges of trying to alter the secular nature of the republic.[42] Fittingly, in a speech delivered on August 30 at a Victory Day celebration (*Zafer Bayramı*, commemorating the victory of Atatürk's forces in the decisive Battle of Dumlupınar, near the end of the *Kurtuluş Savaşı*), the chief of general staff announced that there were "thousands of reactionary civil servants" just like Gülen who were plotting to establish a theocratic state, and that the TSK had already identified and thrown numerous "*Fethullahçılar*" out of its own ranks.[43] The theme of *Fethullahçılar* infiltrating Turkey's secularist institutions to eventually take power and Islamicize the country is a popular one in pop culture, catering to the widespread penchant for conspiracy theory but also striking a chord with those fearful of being caught unaware by creeping Islamicization. The novel *Devşirme* (*Recruitment*), named for the boys who were taken from Christian homes and forced to convert to Islam to be part of the Ottoman Janissary corps, illustrates this fear and suspicion well. In a plot oozing conspiracy theory, young Atilla is taken from his home by seeming benefactor Lütfü Bey, a prominent brotherhood (*cemaat*) member who raises Atilla to be a pious Muslim along with hundreds of other young boys similarly recruited. Atilla later learns that his future as orchestrated by Lütfü Bey is to infiltrate the CHP by first becoming head of its branch Kadıköy—likely chosen by the author as a particular bastion of leftism and secularism in Istanbul—and eventually by becoming a pious prime minister unwittingly elected by secularist voters fooled by the scheming of treacherous Islamists.

In addition to routing out perceived real-life schemers in the form of Gülen supporters and shutting down their foundations (*vakıflar*), the military also ordered the closing of hundreds of media outlets and schools thought to constitute an Islamist threat. The TSK, most prominently through its highly powerful organ the MGK, had essentially declared Islamists the greatest enemy of the state and demonstrated its power to crush those who posed a threat to the principle of secularism that it was tasked to protect.

Constitutional Court

Though not as explicitly or to the same degree as the Turkish armed forces, Turkey's judicial system in general, and the Constitutional Court in particular, has also served as a traditional repository of Republican Nationalism. Generally adopting a highly conservative approach of protecting rather than interpreting Turkey's highest laws, for over three decades the Constitutional Court has used as its baseline the constitution drafted by the military during its rule in 1982. A good portion of this conservatism was deliberately built into the constitution by its military drafters; Article 4 states that articles 1 through 3, which deal with characteristics of the republic such as its language and its citizens' loyalty to Atatürk, "cannot be amended and no amendments can be proposed."[44] While amendments have been made to the 1982 constitution, and the most substantial constitutional reform process in the republic's history has been under way for the last several years,[45] the military constitution has remained in place.

Even had the Constitutional Court not historically represented a manifestation of Republican Nationalism—both in terms of its institutional identity and the identity proposal supported by its individual members[46]—the discussion above indicates that the document that serves as its highest legal point of reference was written by members of a staunchly Republican Nationalist institution. Furthermore, the 1982 constitution stipulated that the right to appoint all members of the Constitutional Court and other important judicial bodies lay with the president,[47] an office traditionally held by Republican Nationalist supporters. The last president before AKP founding member Abdullah Gül became Turkey's first Islamist president was Ahmet Necdet Sezer, a staunch secularist who declared that "a task that has fallen on all of us today is to carry Ataturkism into the future."[48] In an interesting twist, before serving as president, Sezer was the chief justice of the Constitutional Court, underlining again the Republican Nationalist hold on institutions before the AKP period. Finally, the constitution's preamble declares the document itself to be in the service of the "understanding of nationalism specified by Atatürk, the eternal leader and unparalleled hero, the founder of the Republic of Turkey."[49]

This study's breakdown of the form of nationalism referred to in the constitution makes clear the points of seeming incompatibility—the red lines— between its supporters and those of Ottoman Islamism. Understanding the identity proposal institutionalized in the constitution and the court that was established to protect its principles provides insight into many of the Constitutional Court's decisions that seem to be incongruent with other states' high appellate courts. Despite high courts' progressive rulings on civil liberties cases in countries stretching from southern Africa and Eastern Europe to Asia and the Middle East in the 1990s, Turkey's Constitutional Court seemed to be "swimming against the international tide" by closing down fifteen political parties with explicit ethnic or religious affiliations.[50] Examining Republican Nationalism's constitutive norm of membership based solely on linguistic-civic-territorial identity and its social purpose of protecting the public sphere from any encroachments on the principle of secularism helps to make sense of this anomaly. For the Constitutional Court, official recognition of an ethnic or religious political party constitutes a red line whose crossing would represent not only a violation of the constitution but, more important, an existential failure of the institution and its members.

The Constitutional Court, in both its commitment to pursuing Republican Nationalist interests and its institutional power, was thus perfectly poised to act as an obstacle to supporters of Ottoman Islamism. Indeed, as briefly referenced above, the court shut down a number of political parties on the grounds that they violated the fourth clause of article 68 of the constitution, which states that political parties and their platforms "may not be contrary to the democratic and secular principles of the Republic."[51] Article 69 states that parties violating this clause will be subject to a closure decision. The MNP—the first of the parties generated by Erbakan's Milli Görüş movement—was closed in 1971 for "behaviors contrary to the principle of secularism specified by the constitution of the Republic of Turkey," for making references to Islam and Ottoman sultans and welcoming the crowd with the Islamic greeting "Esselamünaleyküm" "Peace be with you" in speeches at various meetings.[52]

The MSP was established a year later by many of the same members, including Erbakan, who served as its party chairman, but it engaged in more overt subversion of the secularist system than its predecessor, even attacking Atatürk directly.[53] The MSP was thus in line for closure by the Constitutional Court, but it was closed along with all political parties according to Law 2533 by a military court in 1981.[54] Not discouraged, but also failing to internalize an important lesson that the AKP would learn, Erbakan and other supporters of Ottoman Islamism founded the RP in 1983 and, thanks to a massive mobilization effort geared toward the pious and economically disadvantaged under the slogan "Just Order" (Adil Düzen), became the victor in the 1995 general elections.[55] Shortly after the resignation of Erbakan as prime minister and the dissolution of the RP-led coalition government under military pressure discussed above, the Constitutional Court closed down the RP in January 1998 during the course of purges known collectively as the February 28 Process, on the charge that "its activities in contradiction of the principle of secularism had become a focus" of the party.[56]

Established a month before its predecessor was officially shut down and, on the recommendation of Erbakan, daring enough to run a headscarved candidate in the 1999 general elections,[57] the Virtue Party (Fazilet Partisi, FP) survived several closure indictments before finally being closed down in 2001 for the same violations of secularism as the other parties in its Ottoman Islamist lineage.[58] Like the military, the Constitutional Court proved itself to be a formidable obstacle to the pursuit of hegemony for Ottoman Islamism in the domestic arena. The AKP, founded directly after the shutting down of the FP by several of its leading figures—but not, crucially, by Erbakan, who founded the Felicity Party (Saadet Partisi) along with other Islamist hardliners[59]—recognized the pattern of threats directed toward parties advancing Ottoman Islamist agendas and would change tactics upon coming to power in the following year. As the next chapter demonstrates in line with this book's argument, however, the Constitutional Court remained a sticky institutional obstacle against domestic moves to open the public sphere to ideas that challenge secularism. In early 2005, for example, the court ruled 23–4 to uphold the conviction of a *Milli Gazete* columnist accused of inciting conflict based on religious ideas.[60] Only after the AKP's use of an EU-oriented foreign policy and its entailed reforms began to erode the hegemonic grip Republican Nationalism had on Turkey's institutions of governance and the prevailing discourse in the public sphere did the Constitutional Court recede from its position as guardian against Ottoman Islamist incursions.

University Rectors

While not a typical institution of study—and in many senses not a singular institution at all—the position of university rector in Turkey both represents and constitutes political power. Despite this relative dearth of study of rectors, the position has been a target of identity contestation in popular culture materials, one of the primary sources used in extracting identity proposals for the purposes of this study. In a March 2008 episode of the police action series *Kollama* (*Cover/ Protection*) later made into a film, a wine-drinking, Western-music-loving university rector is gunned down by a clandestine organization seeking to blame the assassinations of prominent secularists on pious actors.[61] Events unfolding in the series resemble the claims made against defendants accused of being members of an organization seeking to destabilize Turkish politics and thus topple the AKP in the *Ergenekon* and *Balyoz* trials. Certainly, much controversy exists about the connection between fiction and reality in the cases themselves, not to mention the *Kollama* series; the show aired on the Samanyolu channel owned by Gülen, whose supporters in the police and judiciary were involved in collecting evidence and prosecuting the case against suspected Ergenekon members. Nevertheless the political power of a seemingly Western- and secular-friendly rector that makes him a symbolic target for those seeking to agitate Turkey's secular-pious divide is clear.

Rectors' power and that of other education administrators came under close state control following the 1980 coup as part of the military-led government's efforts to curtail the violent leftist revolutionary–rightist fascist clashes that left thousands dead. Here too, Kaplan's *The Pedagogical State* provides unparalleled insight into the contests over national identity that took place during this period among the secular military (Republican Nationalists), neoliberal secularists (most of whose identity content would coalesce into a commonly shared Western Liberalism through processes of Turkey's globalization), and religious nationalists (comprised of Ottoman Islamists and Pan-Turkic Nationalists).[62] Among other outcomes relevant to our study, he demonstrates how a mutual fear of radical leftism, the military's ardent desire to maintain control of what form of religion was being taught in schools so as to prevent deviations, and a bureaucratic politics of compromise produced the Turkish Islamic Synthesis, which entailed mandatory religious education in all schools and the establishment of hundreds of religious vocational (*imam hatip*) schools. As noted above, this compromise inadvertently initiated a legitimization of the role of Islam in the public sphere, a slow-building trend that would empower members of movements such as the MGH by giving them give them state-sanctioned materials and institutions with which to justify their existence.[63]

Turning back to the post-1980 coup era, while the military-led restructuring reached all levels of education, there was a strong focus on universities as hotbeds of political agitation. To ensure that the position of the rector was filled with individuals committed to Atatürkist principles, beginning in 1992 rectors of public universities were appointed by the president of the Turkish Republic based on a list of four nominations from YÖK.[64] Rectors were appointed for a five-year term and enjoyed wide-ranging powers as heads of both administration and academic instruction. With the final say on rectors under the purview of the traditionally Republican Nationalist institution of the presidency—and solely so now, following Erdoğan's post-July 15, 2016 restructuring of the appointment process[65]—it is unsurprising that in that period Republican Nationalists were installed as heads of Turkey's state-run universities. This presence was further reinforced following the onset of the February 28 Process, in which the military and Constitutional Court purged those Islamists who had been able to achieve positions of power.[66] While the most notable example of this was the 1997 "postmodern" coup by memorandum, the military's and Constitutional Court's steps to oust from power and then close the Islamist RP, as discussed above, Republican Nationalists also took this opportunity to remove university rectors deemed to have demonstrated Islamist sympathies during their period of service. Beşir Atalay, for example, was the rector of Kırıkkale University until he was dismissed by YÖK for alleged Islamic activism in 1997 (tellingly, he was later appointed minister of the interior under the AKP government).[67] Harran University rector Servet Armağan was also removed from his position by YÖK in September 1997, for "turning a blind eye" to the wearing of the Islamic headscarf and the formation of religious cadres on campus;[68] President Demirel removed Mahmut Sert from the same position and on the same grounds in 1998.[69]

Ultra-secularist President Sezer, known for refusing to invite headscarved wives of AKP ministers to the presidential residence for important events,[70] wielded his power of rectorship appointment to protect Republican Nationalist principles from potential threats by overturning many of the university-level elections while he was in office (2000–2007). Although he won the overwhelming majority of the votes as a candidate for the rectorship of Kastamonu University, for example, Mustafa Safran was overlooked by Sezer in favor of Bahri Gökçebay (who received two votes, including Sezer's). Safran later protested the decision, claiming he was not chosen because he went to Friday prayers, even though he declared himself a "secular individual"; Safran claimed that Sezer "paid no attention to any criterion other than secularism" in making his decision.[71] Sezer also appointed as rector a former military official (Osman Metin Öztürk, who had eight votes) in place of an acting rector (Mehmet Tüfekçi, who had twenty-five votes) at Giresun University,[72] further institutionalizing Republican Nationalist preferences for staunch secularists in that position.

Those supportive of creating a large space for the expression of Islam in the public sphere criticized the position of university rectors, particularly what they saw as their rectors' focus on secularism. One journalist stated that "if we can find any rector who—without using words like Atatürk's principles, *irtica, sharia,* secularism, headscarf, national interests, enemy, republic, or sublime army— can succeed in putting together a logical sentence, let's entrust him to a university."[73] On an education-themed social media site, a user who is also critical of university rectors' defensive role questions those who state "we are protecting Atatürk's principles; we are the guardians of secularism (*laikliğin bekçisiyiz*)," arguing that rectors should "concern themselves with knowledge and shouldn't practice politics."[74] However, knowledge and politics are intricately interwoven, with each greatly influencing the other in theory and practice. As university rectors have traditionally acted not as bureaucratic administrators of the objective transmission of knowledge, but rather of knowledge shaped by standards of appropriateness prescribed by Republican Nationalism, I include them in my analysis.

In addition to making administrative hiring choices and shaping university curricula, the most visible way in which university rectors have served as the gatekeepers of Republican Nationalist principles is, quite literally, as gatekeepers. Taking a cue from the Dress and Appearance Regulation's ban on the wearing of the headscarf by civil servants in public institutions,[75] which was put in place by the military government in 1982 along with many other reforms aimed at protecting the principle of secularism, and following several incidents of students being denied access to university libraries or graduation ceremonies in the mid-1980s,[76] rectors began to install checkpoints at the entrance gates of their universities. Beginning with sporadic implementation in the period following the 1980 coup and then nearly universally in the late 1990s, security teams were tasked by rectors with preventing female students wearing the Islamic headscarf (*türban* or *başörtüsü*)[77] and male students who had the rounded beards symbolic of pious Muslims[78] from entering their campuses.

While there was never a law explicitly prohibiting the wearing of the headscarf—despite many references in Western and Turkish media alike to a "headscarf ban" in Turkey's universities—headscarved women were denied entrance to public buildings such as universities through the internal policing of their institutions. By the mid-1990s these checkpoints had become the overwhelming norm, so that one could speak of a de facto headscarf ban; the decision to enforce this ban, however, lay with the rectors. Required to remove their headscarves before entering campus, many students donned wigs or stocking caps to cover their hair; those whose families could afford it went abroad for university education.[79] In countless speeches, Erdoğan laments that his own two daughters, along with thousands of other Turkish girls, "were forced to attend foreign universities" so as not to compromise their religious beliefs by uncovering.[80] From the personal level to the identity proposal level, therefore, university rectors proved to be a powerful identity-based obstacle to the spread of Ottoman Islamism and the realization of its interests. As the following chapter shows, the AKP has worked ardently to shift the identity proposal embedded in the *rektörlük*, both by supporting the establishment of dozens of new universities with rectors who are supportive of Ottoman Islamism and by using the power imbued in the position of Turkey's president to select sympathetic rectors for existing universities.

Conclusion

This chapter is intended to lay the analytical and empirical foundations for understanding the contours of identity debates in the pre-AKP era. Delineating the concept of identity-based obstacles as institutions established not only to spread but also to defend a particular understanding of identity against competing proposals sharpens the focus on processes of contestation over identity. Specifying the red lines of identity content for particular proposals in terms of constitutive norms, social purpose, relational meaning, and cognitive worldviews that are deemed intolerable by supporters of a rival proposal also helps to hone in on the particular domestic- and foreign policy-related identity issues—ethnic and religious expression, Western and non-Western allies and enemies—that become the most hotly debated points of contestation.

Examining the degree to which the Republican Nationalist identity proposal was embedded in the institutions of the military (particularly the MGK), the judicial system (particularly the Constitutional Court), and the national educational system (particularly the position of university rector) makes clear the obstacles faced by supporters of Ottoman Islamism. Despite the various internal and external challenges to Republican Nationalism's pursuit of hegemony detailed in the previous chapter, its institutional legacies embodied in these identity-based obstacles enabled its supporters to thwart through the February 28 Process the perceived Islamist threat posed by Erbakan and his string of MGH–based parties. Just ten years later, however, the AKP—also a branch of the Milli Görüş tradition—would signal a major, previously unthinkable shift by successfully nominating an Islamist candidate to another previously Republican Nationalist institution: the presidency. The AKP's ability to accomplish this form of institutional capture despite the strong objections of the military indicated that the contours of the domestic identity contestation field had been altered. To understand how this rapid and dramatic transformation became possible, the following chapter analyzes the AKP's decision to circumvent Republican Nationalist obstacles by taking its fight for Ottoman Islamism outside to the foreign policy arena.

Ottoman Islamism Inside Out

Identity Contestation through EU-Based Foreign Policy

Introduction

The meteoric rise and spread of the Ottoman Islamist proposal for Turkey's national identity throughout the public sphere beginning around 2010 became a subject of great interest for scholars and residents of Turkey alike. The character Sultan Süleyman "The Magnificent" waged tremendous military campaigns on television screens, restaurants opened that attempted to recreate dishes served in Ottoman palaces, and candidates for local elections posed for press photos in colorful (pseudo)Ottoman garb. A show dubbed the Turkish "Game of Thrones" inspiring fans to reenact battle scenes in their homes celebrated the victories of the father of Osman I, the founder of the empire.[1] Sometimes characterized as "Ottomania,"[2] this phenomenon represents much more than a passing fad of fascination with Turkey's imperial forefathers. While references to all things Ottoman now permeate everything from pop culture to political campaigns, I observed a more profound transformation in the prevailing understanding of Turkishness, in policy and practice, that inspired the basis for this book. How could a largely Western-clad, devoutly secular population that appeared to vehemently reject any association with Ottomanism as backward delusions of Islamist grandeur so quickly embrace the country's imperial past as a model for its glorious future? How could a state deeply embedded in the transatlantic alliance structure and EU accession process so dramatically uproot its foreign policy tradition and replant it in the Middle East? How was such a drastic reorientation of Turkey—inside and out—possible under the AKP? Finally, if the AKP wanted to spread Ottoman Islamism at home and behave according to its precepts abroad, why did it not do so immediately upon coming to power with an unprecedented parliamentary majority?

This chapter seeks to provide answers to these questions by analytically unpacking the processes of identity contestation in which the AKP engaged.

Before tackling these puzzles, however, a brief note on the relationship between identity proposals as I employ the term and party identity is important here. As chapters 2 and 3 of this book make clear, identity proposals do not always map neatly onto political party membership; therefore, party membership cannot generally be considered a reliable indicator of identity proposal. Within the main opposition CHP, founded by Mustafa Kemal (later named Atatürk) and a traditional repository of Atatürkist thought, I identified both Western Liberalists and Republican Nationalists, including the few hardcore Atatürkist nationalists (*ulusalcılar*) unaffected by the intraproposal transformation discussed in chapter 4. I also identified highly pious individuals within all four identity proposal collectivities, dispelling the idea that all pious Muslims are AKP supporters. Employing the identity content framework developed in this study facilitates a much more nuanced and useful understanding of competing identities, and thus of the intricate dynamics of identity debates, than studies based on party or religious affiliation can provide.

However, in the case of the AKP, the party and the identity proposal are often one and the same; as of this writing, to support the AKP is to at least publically support Ottoman Islamism, and vice versa. As a new party founded in 2001 and initially supported by many individuals who I classify as Western Liberalists[3] as well as Ottoman Islamists, this congruence of party and identity proposal solidified as the AKP became an increasingly hierarchical, patriarchal, and personalistic organization that refuses to tolerate public questioning of any of its actions, including its efforts to spread a particular understanding of identity throughout Turkey's population. As is the case in any attempt to group individuals within a collectivity, there will always be outliers. There are certainly individuals who joined the AKP in the hopes of obtaining personal economic or political gain, rather than for any strong convictions about the identity proposal the party sought to develop and disseminate. Former EU minister Egemen Bağış, for example, was caught on tape allegedly mocking the Koran in a conversation with a journalist[4] and ran up an exceedingly large minibar tab during a hotel stay in London.[5] As making fun of holy verses and alcohol consumption are both clear red lines for supporters of Ottoman Islamism, this suggests that Bağış did not internalize Ottoman Islamist constitutive norms of behavior. However, the AKP has been quick to tamp down or correct any public behavior perceived to be contradictory to any of the identity components of Ottoman Islamism. Shortly after the recording claiming to show Bağış ridiculing the Koran was released, he was very publicly shown off as Erdoğan's guest at Friday prayers. This public practice, and Erdoğan's claim that the recording was a fake—"*montaj, dublaj*" (montage, voice-over taping)—as he claimed all the other incriminating recordings also were, suggests that Erdoğan maintains a vested interest in the consistent and public representation of the Ottoman Islamism he wishes to promulgate from the top down.[6]

As this study is concerned primarily with contestation of identity in the public sphere, rather than with differentiating what individuals "really" believe in terms of what they have internalized versus the identity proposal they outwardly support—a highly worthwhile task for future research—Bağış's many public demonstrations of behavior in line with Ottoman Islamist norms are crucial to note. What is important here is that members of the AKP, whether or not they have internalized the components of Ottoman Islamism, are expected by those who have internalized them and intend to disseminate them to act in line with the proposal's prescribed behavior. Furthermore, it is difficult to conceive of an individual who would support Ottoman Islamism but not support its greatest champion. In brief, today's Ottoman Islamism can be thought of as the identity project of the AKP.

This chapter demonstrates that the AKP—the most recent iteration of a string of parties generated by the wider Milli Görüş religious movement and subsequently shut down, as this chapter discusses in detail—as an institution took on the cause of promoting the Ottoman Islamist proposal for Turkish identity supported by these earlier parties as its primary motivating task. When examining this claim of party-identity proposal overlap along with the AKP's assumption of power in 2002 in particular, the puzzle of the timing in policy shifts suggested above arises. Using the identity content framework of chapter 2 facilitates a clear breakdown of what these policies would be, but there was no move toward realizing any of the interests generated by an Ottoman Islamist identity until well into the AKP's second term. Applying an inside-out identity contestation perspective, this chapter demonstrates that the AKP could take none of the steps prescribed by Ottoman Islamism because it faced an organizational threat within the domestic arena upon coming to power in 2002.

The following section briefly reviews the obstacles posed to Ottoman Islamism by supporters of Republican Nationalism and the organizational bodies in which this latter proposal had become institutionalized. The section highlights the historical challenges to pre-AKP iterations of Ottoman Islamism, highlighting how the fate of these parties and individuals served as a deterrent, obstructing the immediate pursuit of hegemony by the AKP. The main claim of inside-out identity contestation theory is that actors, when faced with obstacles to their identity gambits at the domestic level, will take their fight to advance a particular identity proposal outside to the foreign policy arena. By doing so, actors may be able to garner outside support for use in their domestic identity struggles—from actors in the diaspora[7] or sympathetic international actors and transnational coalitions,[8] for example—or may be able to use international institutions as an anchor for their own domestic identity projects. The third section therefore analyzes the AKP's pursuit of EU membership as identity contestation of Ottoman Islamism in an alternative arena. It examines the elements of EU-oriented foreign policy that reduced traditional obstacles to Ottoman Islamism, such as the military and the Constitutional Court, by mandating the democratization of civil-military relations and the reconfiguration of the judicial system in line with the EU's Copenhagen accession criteria. The assumptions of inside-out theory help in understanding both the timing of the AKP's foreign policy swing toward the EU immediately upon coming to power and its swing away, beginning in the late 2000s. This assumption of the need to initially circumvent and, if possible, marginalize the influence of supporters of competing identity proposals also explains the delay in the AKP's implementation of Ottoman Islamist policies at home. The fourth section investigates the period in which the AKP has finally become positioned to initiate this pursuit. Having reduced the power of traditionally Republican Nationalist institutions, the AKP has unfurled domestic and foreign policy agendas that are in line with the behaviors prescribed by Ottoman Islamism. Accompanied by spikes in pop culture consumption of everything Ottoman, what some have somewhat anachronistically described as "neo-Ottomanism,"[9] actually represents an unprecedented but deep-rooted—if by no means permanent—shift in support for a very different understanding of national identity for Turkey, in many ways incompatible with the previously dominant Republican Nationalist understanding. This chapter demonstrates clearly how national identity contestation spills over into foreign policy agendas and how initiatives in foreign policy, in turn, shape the dynamics of identity debates back home.

Contesting Republican Nationalism on the Outside

As the successor to a string of parties that had all been shut down only to re-open under a new name each time, the AKP acted pragmatically and cautiously upon coming to power in 2002. Its leadership worked under the knowledge that policies seen to threaten secularism domestically or to alter Turkey's historically Western foreign policy orientation, as Erbakan was determined to do, could be seen as provocation by the military and thus cause for intervention and possible overthrow of the government. Party leaders emphasized that the term "conservative democrat" best encapsulated the identity that shaped their political platform, shying away from the term "moderate Islamist."

The February 28 Process, discussed in the previous chapter, exemplifies the immediate factors underlying much of this cautiousness. As noted in detail, the RP was pressured out of power by the military in 1997 and closed down by the Constitutional Court in 1998. The constitutive effect the process had on former RP members held particular resonance for Erdoğan, who as an RP member and mayor of Istanbul was arrested for reciting a poem that was claimed to incite religious hatred.[10] He spent four months in prison and was temporarily barred from politics, delaying his assumption of Turkey's premiership until 2003, despite his party coming to power in 2002.

Due to this organizational threat presented by institutions of aspiring hegemon Republican Nationalism, in its first years in power the AKP was unable to employ domestic-level identity hegemony practices, including nationalizing projects (e.g., the early republican period's policies of "Turkification" along linguistic and civic lines) and delegitimization campaigns, against supporters of alternative proposals. A prime example of such efforts is a YouTube video campaign sponsored by the Republican Nationalist newspaper *Cumhuriyet*. One of the videos, meant to appear ominous, shows a woman with her hair uncovered in one frame and covered by a *niqab* (face veil) in the next, while a voice intones "Are You Aware of the Danger?" (*"Tehlikenin Farkında Mısınız?"*), illustrating the imminent nature of a perceived Islamist threat.[11] There was also an inherently foreign, and thus (for Republican Nationalists) un-Turkish dynamic to this threat, as in general even Turkey's pious women would cover their hair only with a headscarf, not a *niqab*. An alternative to such practices of nationalizing through media-based delegitimization is institutional change, a tool probably only available to an in-group that is rising toward or has achieved hegemony. The AKP embraced this tool with gusto, but given the domestic obstacles to Ottoman Islamism posed by the Republican Nationalist institutions discussed above, took its efforts to enact institutional change to the foreign policy arena.

In a 180-degree departure from the "Islamic Union" foreign policy orientation pursued by Erbakan, and seemingly in direct contradiction to the behaviors prescribed by Ottoman Islamism, the AKP immediately declared Turkey's membership in the EU to be a primary pillar of foreign policy. The AKP also started working diligently to implement political and economic reforms that were in line with the accession criteria of the EU's Copenhagen Agreement, as if trying to prove to skeptics citing the Milli Görüş heritage of the party's founding members that the AKP was completely different and that its intentions were genuine. Republican Nationalists and some Western Liberalists doubted the AKP's commitment to EU accession just as they doubted its professed commitment to democratization, pointing to numerous public speeches made by Erdoğan during his time as RP mayor of Istanbul just five years earlier. His statement that "for us, democracy can never be a goal" but merely a vehicle is exemplary of the sources of these doubts.[12] Other Western Liberalists were willing to give the AKP the benefit of the doubt, accepting its repeated declarations that it was a conservative democratic party rather than a party with any ties to Islam, and that it was fully dedicated to achieving EU membership. The well-known journalists and public intellectuals among these were later dubbed "*Yetmez Ama Evet*"*çiler*—those who say "It's not enough but yes"—to indicate they were happy with the path the AKP was on but expected more.[13] The term came into use after the 2010 referendum on a package of constitutional amendments proposed by the AKP but has come to refer to anyone who stood up against criticism of the party during its first two terms.

Despite this support, there are many legitimate reasons to doubt the AKP's commitment to both democratization and EU membership that have come to light in its third and fourth terms (2011–present). Nearly all of the "*Yetmez Ama Evet*"*çiler* came to criticize the AKP, if not to directly admit that they were wrong in trusting the party in the first place—a particularly bitter sticking point for Republican Nationalists who believed they knew best all along. An EU ministerial official interviewed made the lack of connection between the reforms the AKP had been pushing through and the EU accession process quite clear, stating that a constitutional amendments package had nothing to do with the EU; it was already on the ministry's desk and needed to be justified as part of the EU process.[14] In the same way, the AKP was able to target obstacles to its pursuit of Ottoman Islamist hegemony by shifting the arena of contestation to the EU process. By engaging ardently in EU negotiations and citing the need to demonstrate Turkey's commitment to the accession process, the AKP was able to justify the need for civil-military and judicial reforms, thus taking on the most powerful obstacles to Ottoman Islamism in an arena in which the military and the courts couldn't compete. Through its reforms, the AKP worked to significantly reduce the role of the military in politics; change the powers and makeup of the judicial system; and, relatedly, reduce the influence of traditionally Republican Nationalist rectors, thus weakening their power as identity-based obstacles.

Although the EU officially opened accession negotiations in October 2005, Turkey had already undertaken significant reforms to get to that point. Indeed, and important for the timing element of this book's argument, reforms in line with EU membership criteria undertaken by the AKP slowed dramatically, and the EU froze talks in December 2006. By adhering to the civil-military reforms necessitated by the EU's Copenhagen Agreement during its first few years in power, however, the AKP was able to institutionalize civil authority over the military and remove its "special status," legislating a total of nine harmonization packages between 2002 and 2004.[15] In its 2004 Regular Report, the European Commission noted that "over the past year the Turkish government has shown great determination in accelerating the pace of reforms," showing enthusiastic approval of reforms targeted toward "civilian control of the military."[16]

Arguably the most effective step toward reducing threats from an autonomous, staunchly Republican Nationalist institution was taking control of the MGK, the body that forced the RP to step down in 1997 and the "main tool for shaping politics" in the pre-AKP era.[17] The influence of this pre-viously powerful body was greatly constricted through these reforms, to making recommendations to the Council of Ministers in a "purely consulta-tive function."[18] Before these reforms, article 118 of the 1982 constitution had stipulated that the government would give priority (öncelik) to decisions made by the MGK.[19] Further, the MGK was removed as a member of YÖK and the Higher Council of Radio and Television (Radyo ve Televizyon Üst Kurulu, RTÜK),[20] shrinking the power it wielded over university life and curricula and the content broadcast by the media, respectively. In critically evaluating the impact these EU-mandated changes would have on the military's influence over the people of Turkey, a Republican Nationalist blogger warned that the army was being "liquidated" along the path to EU democracy.[21]

The reforms also included making a civilian the head of the MGK for the first time and increasing the number of civilians within the institution, changing its makeup as well as its influence. The 2007 EU Progress Report—published at the beginning of the AKP's second term in power—praised the MGK's "new role," the drastic reduction in its overall size, and the halving of the number of military personnel on the MGK.[22] Tellingly, those areas in which successive reports have criticized a lack of progress, including civilian control over the gendarmerie and civilian oversight over defense expenditures, involved issues that did not consti-tute direct threats to AKP rule. The report also criticized the Turkish military's statement against AKP Islamist presidential candidate Abdullah Gül in 2007,[23] a move that could have posed a threat to the AKP in the past, when the military had stronger influence over politics. Gül's conservative upbringing, career in the Milli Görüş tradition of political Islam, and, particularly, his wife's wearing of the headscarf represented red lines for Republican Nationalists' social purpose of protecting Atatürk's principle of secularism. That nothing came of the military's famous "e-memorandum" warning of a possible intervention if the candidacy of Gül was not rescinded, that soldiers stayed in their barracks instead, testifies to the AKP's success in reducing the role of a Republican Nationalist institution through foreign policy channels.

Emboldened by these institutional reforms mandated by the AKP's EU-oriented foreign policy, which made possible the election of Gül despite the open objection of the military, supporters of an Ottoman Islamist proposal went fur-ther in applying EU democratization criteria to the military obstacle. One of the most sweeping instances of this is the investigations and prosecutions over the course of 2008–2012 that comprised the Ergenekon and Balyoz trials, labeled by media outlet Al Jazeera as "Islamists' revenge against the army."[24] The hundreds of individuals charged in these cases—including then-serving and former mili-tary personnel, journalists, and politicians—were accused of forming a clandes-tine secularist organization that sought the overthrow of the AKP government by inciting terror throughout society. Including indictment titles such as "Plan to Intervene in Democracy" (*Demokrasiye Müdahale Planı*), the two cases centered around the claims that those accused were part of a "deep state" organization plotting to create chaos through bombings and assassinations. These attacks, the indictments argued, would show the public that the AKP was unable or unwilling to provide for the security of its opposition and thus would justify a military coup against the democratically elected government. Prosecutors attempted to draw links among attacks such as the 2006 assassination of a Council of State judge and the bombing of *Cumhuriyet* (Republic) newspaper, and evidence of planned assassinations of navy admirals, the Greek patriarch, and non-Muslim minorities.

Initially heralded as a step forward in the democratization of civil-military relations by applying the rule of law even to former chief of general staff and president of Turkey Kenan Evren, the trials came to be seen as a way of obviating the threat of powerful individuals, as well as tarnishing the institutional credibility of the armed forces, secular newspapers, and other disparate institutions and individuals united only in their opposition to the AKP. Signs that evidence used in the trials was illegally gathered and even manufactured—supposedly damning CDs containing plans written during the Balyoz coup plot in 2003 were written in Calibri, a font Microsoft only released as part of Windows 2007[25]— also pointed to the cases serving more as a platform for political targeting than for the objective application of due process. The strong presence of members of the Gülen movement (a brotherhood or *cemaat*) in the police and the judicial institutions responsible for gathering evidence and prosecuting the cases also raised suspicions about the motivations behind the trials.

The Gülen network's spiritual head is Islamic cleric Fethullah Gülen, who emigrated to the United States in 1999, citing the need for medical treatment but also likely fleeing an impending trial as part of the February 28 Process— thus quite literally taking his fight outside, as the next chapter examines in detail. Although hailing from a different (*Nurcu*) Islamist tradition than the AKP's predominantly Milli Görüş followers, the Gülenists' Turkish Calvinist identity proposal (also discussed in the following chapter) has much of the same content as Ottoman Islamism—particularly the constitutive norm of Sunni Islam as a membership criterion and the social purpose of spreading Sunni Islam at home and cultivating ties with Muslim populations abroad. This confluence of content made possible a temporary alliance among Gülenists and the AKP that manifested itself most clearly in the prosecution and imprisonment of Republican Nationalists. As further indication that Gülenists were key to the trials' targeting of opponents of the AKP, a few months after the AKP-Gülen alliance dissolved into intense acrimony and the AKP began purging Gülenists from their positions of authority, courts began releasing those convicted of involvement in the alleged coup plots. This thumb in the eye to Gülenists was hailed as a "Freedom Holiday" (*Özgürlük Bayramı*) by Republican Nationalists skeptical of the timing of the decision but nevertheless grateful for their release.[26]

Whether the trials were motivated more by a desire for revenge against the institution that instigated the February 28 Process and its ensuing purge of Islamists or deliberately to remove the military as a player from the political chessboard, the resulting weakening of the military's reputation and influence, even prior to the purges following the July 15, 2016 coup attempt, is clear. According to a multiple-year survey conducted by Kadir Has University in Istanbul, the percentage of respondents stating that they didn't trust or definitely didn't trust the military rose from 19.6% in 2011 to 31.9% in 2013.[27] What makes these numbers intriguing is that we can assume many Ottoman Islamists already deeply mistrusted the military; the *Ergenekon* and *Balyoz* trials succeeded in eroding the confidence of those who might otherwise have defended the military's intervention in politics. As a collection of letters published with the subtitle "Letters of Support Sent to Turkish Officers Wronged by *Balyoz*" shows, however, some Republican Nationalist loyalists remained unswayed by the accusations. Letters including phrases such as "as a child of Atatürk"; "the struggle will continue; this homeland is ours, this glorious army is ours too"; and "as long as I can remember, as long as I've been able to understand Atatürk, my heritage, my country, my nation, as a Turkish girl I've known that I am always indebted to you" evince strong Republican Nationalist identity content.[28]

In the survey cited above, moving from trust to beliefs about capacity, the percentage of respondents who stated in 2013 that the influence of the military in politics had decreased or definitely decreased in the recent period was 54.9%.[29] Apart from societal reactions, the weakened influence of the military in Turkey was also demonstrated by a general continuation of politics as usual following the resignation of the chief of general staff as well as the leaders of the army, navy, and air force in protest against the trials in 2011. Erdoğan's immediate acceptance of the resignations and appointment of his own choice for chief of general staff, Necdet Özel, served to make the domestic arena safer for the contestation of national identity by the AKP in its third term. The establishment of the National Defense University in 2016 represents the consolidation of military institutions of instruction under one government-supervised umbrella. Replacing all of Turkey's military academies, which were closed in the wake of the coup attempt, facilitates the AKP's design, implementation, and monitoring of a singular curriculum for all students headed for service in the TSK. After weakening the institutional obstacle's influence over politics in line with EU civil-military relations criteria, the AKP took advantage of a domestic crisis to reconstitute and control the military according to its own preferences.

Also as part of its EU foreign policy, the AKP pushed through judicial reform that ended the jurisdiction of military courts over civilians and abolished the State Security Court used to try crimes against the state, including violations of the principle of secularism. It was the State Security Court that had sentenced Erdoğan to prison for reading an allegedly Islamist reactionary (*irticai*) poem and had him temporarily banned from politics.[30] The Constitutional Court, another looming obstacle to the AKP's pursuit of hegemony for Ottoman Islamism, also became a target of the judicial reforms carried out in line with EU accession criteria. The AKP began to move forward in these reforms after its amendment meant to override the decisions of university rectors[31]—the third obstacle addressed in this chapter—and guarantee the right of university students to wear the headscarf was overturned by the court in 2008. Further, the party barely survived a closure case in the same year thanks to the last-minute vote of the court's new president and then AKP sympathizer Haşim Kılıç.[32] While the AKP gained an automatic advantage when Gül became president, as the president selects all the members of the Constitutional Court, the AKP strove to quickly change the makeup of the court by proposing seventeen regular justices rather than the existing eleven regular and four substitute justices. While the reform was in "harmony" with the EU standard of delimiting justices' term limits to twelve years,[33] it simultaneously set up the AKP to rotate out justices nominated by previous Republican Nationalist president Sezer and replace them with AKP-friendly justices. Further, all justices will continue to be selected by the president or by the parliament over which Erdoğan is projected to retain influence at least in the near future. These institutional reforms, ostensibly taken in pursuit of EU membership, also greatly advanced the AKP's prospects for contesting national identity back home.

The AKP's battle with the third obstacle of university rectors is indirectly related to its EU foreign policy strategy. While the exponential growth in the number of new universities established over the last ten years—many of them by AKP supporters—certainly helps to ease Turkey's problems with access to higher education and thus is in line with the EU's emphasis on the right to education, it would be stretching the argument too far to say that the subsequent decrease in the proportion of university rectors who are Republican Nationalists is a result of foreign policy. Rather, the AKP became much better equipped to tackle the obstacle of university rectors because it first tackled the obstacle of the military. By swiftly reducing the role of the military in politics through EU-mandated reforms, the AKP facilitated the confirmation of Gül as president, despite the now-weakened military's objections. The formerly Republican Nationalist institution of the presidency holds the authority to appoint the head of YÖK, the council responsible for both state and private universities, as well as to appoint heads of the former. By clearing the way for an Ottoman Islamist president through EU reforms, the AKP thus ensured that at least for the time being, a supporter of its identity proposal would wield a significant amount of power over Turkey's university rectors.

Upon becoming the first popularly elected president in 2014, Erdoğan actively used his authority in choosing rectors to weaken the Republican Nationalist domination of the influential institution of the university rector. As one columnist put it, university rectors became the "next domino in Erdoğan's path" toward eliminating dissension and filling these powerful positions with supporters willing to implement his wishes.[34] Although this institutional restacking of the deck has been particularly prominent since the July 2016 coup attempt, multiple instances of Erdoğan hand-selecting university rectors occurred prior to the state of emergency that followed it. Overriding the 1,202 votes cast in April 2015 by "social democrats" (*sosyal demokratlar*, a political affiliation that would generally be found among Republican Nationalists and Western Liberalists) in support of Raşit Tükel for the position of rector at Istanbul University, Erdoğan instead appointed Mahmut Ak,[35] who received 908 votes and was supported by the "conservative" (*muhafazakar*) segment of the university's voters.[36] Similarly, Erdoğan appointed conservative candidate Yusuf Ulcay, who received 265 votes for the rectorship of Uludağ University in Bursa, over sitting rector Kamil Dilek, who received 576 votes.[37] Ramazan Taşaltın, a rumored member of the Hayrat Vakfı,[38] an Islamic foundation dedicated to promoting study of the Koran and the learning of Ottoman Turkish,[39] received the fifth-lowest number of votes (58) for the position of rector at Harran University in Şanlıurfa, yet he was appointed rector over candidates who received 96, 67, 67, and 62 votes, respectively.[40] The AKP further facilitated the spread of Ottoman Islamism in universities by restricting the autonomy of "board selection in private universities, tenure and promotion reviews, and granting of equivalency to degrees obtained abroad."[41] Having essentially neutralized the main institutional threats to Ottoman Islamism, the AKP continued comfortably to consolidate its hold over higher education.

With Executive Order 676, issued October 29, 2016, as one of many preventative/punitive measures taken following the coup attempt, Erdoğan institutionalized complete control over the administration of higher education in Turkey in the executive by granting the president the power to appoint private as well as state university rectors.[42] Further, the intra-university vote has been eliminated in public universities; the president now chooses whomever he wishes without input from the faculty. Erdoğan's first such appointment is an indication that he will act solely according to his own will. Rather than select then Boğaziçi University rector Gülay Barbarosoğlu, who received a record-breaking 86% of the faculty vote held several days before the coup attempt, Erdoğan appointed Mehmed Özkan, a biomedical engineering professor who was not a candidate in the election by faculty and whose sister is an AKP parlia-mentarian.[43] The overlooking of Barbarosoğlu, a prominent female figure and strong women's rights advocate, is objectionable to Republican Nationalists and Western Liberalists not only because Erdoğan passes women over but appoints men such as Mustafa Talha Gönüllü, a rector at Adıyaman University, who stated that shaking hands with a woman who is not a relative is "more horrific than holding fire."[44]

In an ironic illustration of the "plus ça change" adage,[45] the system under Erdoğan's presidential rule now resembles (or as some argue even surpasses)[46] in form, if decidedly not in content, the centralization put in place by President/General Evren's military government to consolidate Republican Nationalism, discussed in the previous chapter. Indicative of what this book describes as the moderation of Republican Nationalism, CHP chairman Kemal Kılıçdaroğlu, a non-*ulusalcı* supporter of this identity proposal, is one of the strongest in vocalizing this comparison between military junta- and AKP-led takeovers of higher education.[47]

Realizing Ottoman Islamist Interests Abroad

Having reduced the main threats to its advance of Ottoman Islamism, the AKP became able to act on both foreign policy and domestic goals that are incom-patible with the Republican Nationalist proposal for Turkish identity. The EU accession process ground to a halt in practice, particularly following the AKP's victory in a 2010 referendum enabling it to make amendments to the constitu-tion and its 2011 election victory, in which it garnered a higher percentage of the votes than in 2002 and 2007. As a 2013 EU Progress Report notes: "Turkey froze its relations with the Presidency of the Council of the EU during the second half of 2012 and did not align itself with EU positions or statements in international fora."[48]

The foreign policy goals prescribed by Ottoman Islamism involved increasing engagement with other Muslim states, such as Iran, and territories of the former Ottoman Empire in the Middle East and the Balkans with a view to achieving "zero problems with neighbors" (*"komşularla sıfır sorun"*). In his *Strategic Depth (Stratejik Derinlik)* manifesto, notably subtitled "Turkey's International Position," foreign policy architect and former foreign and prime minister Ahmet Davutoğlu claimed that the pursuit of strategic depth—that is, taking advan-tage of the geocultural legacies a state has inherited—could only be undertaken once security threats in the region had been removed.[49] Erdoğan's speeches often specifically engage Turkey's Ottoman legacies, reaching out to former im-perial territories that he believes are eagerly watching Turkey. As Ayşe Zarakol notes, Erdoğan's 2011 general election victory speeches included blatant out-reach to former Ottoman territories: "Sarajevo has won as much as Istanbul; Beirut as much as Izmir; West Bank and Gaza as much as Diyarbakır."[50] In actual policy terms, acts such as lifting visa requirements for countries such as Iran and Yemen; opening multiple Turkish Airlines routes between Turkey and Iran, Iraq, and North Africa;[51] taking on leadership of the OIC; and particularly providing development, humanitarian, and "cultural protection" aid to Muslim countries[52] are all elements in line with the Ottoman Islamist social purpose of extending piety to fellow Muslim populations, a relational meaning of orientation toward former Ottoman territories, and a cognitive worldview of Turkey as the rightful leader of the Islamic world.

Perhaps one of the clearest foreign policy shifts generated by pursuit of Ottoman Islamist interests by the newly emboldened AKP can be seen in the rapid deterioration of relations with Israel, Turkey's former close ally. Turkey was the first Muslim-majority state to recognize Israel as a state in 1949 under the Republican Nationalist CHP and maintained close economic, diplomatic, and security ties for over fifty years despite hiccups, including Israel's worries over Turkey's fidelity upon its signing of the Baghdad Pact (1955) and the tempo-rary downgrading of relations in the wake of the Suez crisis (1956).[53] Following the Six-Day War in 1967, Turkey refused to condemn Israel as an "aggressor state," although other states in the Muslim world did so, and opposed severing diplomatic ties with Israel at a meeting of the (then-titled) Organization of the Islamic Conference, demonstrating no solidarity with fellow Muslim states. As Ottoman Islamism prescribes a view of Israelis as oppressors of fellow Muslim Palestinians, however, Israel became an explicit target of animosity during the AKP's second and third terms, culminating in an effective severing of diplomatic relations. Erdoğan's berating of Israeli president Shimon Peres for Israel's attacks against Palestinians during the 2008–2009 Gaza War—shouting "you know well how to kill"—before storming off the stage at the 2009 World Economic Forum was met with jubilation by supporters, who proclaimed him the "Fatih of Davos" for his willingness to stand up to Israel and his support for the Palestinian cause. The choice of fatih (conqueror) here is telling in its invocation of Ottoman im-agery, particularly of Fatih Sultan Mehmet's conquering of Istanbul to wrest the city from the (Christian) infidel, in support of Erdoğan's actions.[54] As one ministerial official put it, Palestinians love Erdoğan because of his "anti-Israeli stance . . . his image of being a strong Muslim leader, not a Turkish leader."[55]

Erdoğan has wielded his rhetorical criticism of Israel on visits throughout the Muslim world—particularly following the 2010 raid on the Gaza-bound Turkish flotilla Mavi Marmara, in which nine Turkish activists were killed—which in turn increases his legitimacy as defender of Turkey's Muslim brothers back home.[56] As one journalist noted in an interview, Erdoğan's (waxing and waning) popularity in the Arab street is a result of his anti-Israeli stance, "not any Ottoman history," hinting at the limits of Ottoman Islamism's popularity in terms of other foreign policy issues in the region.[57] The legitimacy element is key here to a constructivist analysis of Ottoman Islamism or of any identity proposal. As identity constrains what is possible as much as it prescribes what is desirable, Ottoman Islamist supporters can legitimately claim to empathize with their Muslim brothers in the Palestine-Israel conflict, but cannot do the same for Jews. Red lines in place within Ottoman Islamism's identity content constrain their supporters from being able to express solidarity and brotherhood with Jews, nor would an international audience be likely to buy into such expressions. This does not mean that identities cannot be wielded in strategic ways, of course, as long as they resonate with those to whom claims about one's own identity are being made. Arguably hoping to benefit again from Turkey's self-declared role as the protector of Muslims and enemy of those who would persecute them, Erdoğan exponentially strengthened his criticism of Israel in response to the attacks launched on Gaza in July 2014 and during the run-up to his bid to become Turkey's first popularly elected president the following month. In a sense, Erdoğan had already set the parameters for acceptable delegitimization of Israelis and Jews several months earlier when he assaulted a protester demanding justice for the victims of the May 2014 mining disaster in Soma by slapping him and then appearing to use a strongly anti-Semitic epithet.[58]

Anti-Semitism is by no means new to Turkey;[59] however, the expression of animosity toward Jews appears to have become newly acceptable and more frequently cited in the public sphere by some supporters of Ottoman Islamism under AKP rule. In 2012 the Turkish Jewish community made repeated requests to remove a Biomen Shampoo advertisement depicting Hitler shouting at men not to use women's shampoo.[60] Racist rhetoric manifesting a virulently acrimonious relational meaning with Jews and the state of Israel increased following the onset of the 2014 Israel-Gaza War. A Facebook group page with the name "We are Ottoman Grandchildren for Stubbornness's Sake" includes a photo of a dog urinating on an Israeli flag, posted on July 11, 2014.[61] The page also displays a photo of a *Daily Telegraph* headline stating "The Turkish Empire Is Coming," with a comment posted underneath that reads "God willing, with God's permission we will be liberated from rule by the Jews and we will advance on the path of my ancestor!"[62] Moving to the more formal realm of publications, the pro-AKP newspaper *Yeni Akit's* July 19, 2014, crossword puzzle included a photograph of Hitler with the written clue "We are searching for you."[63] Further, after singer Yıldız Tilbe tweeted multiple anti-Semitic statements, including "May God be pleased with Hitler, he even did little to [Jews]" and "Muslims will bring about these Jews' end,"[64] AKP mayor of Ankara Melih Gökçek retweeted several of Tilbe's tweets. One of Gökçek's retweets included the comment "a query full of intelligence from Tilbe," leaving no question as to his approval of the singer's support for Hitler.[65] His support, in turn, was reported positively by pro-AKP newspaper *Yeni Şafak*, which cited the number of Palestinian deaths framed around the question of why the world was keeping silent with no criticism of the reference to Hitler.[66] Gökçek was not the only AKP official to openly make racist remarks against Jews, who after many waves of emigration, including one inspired by rising anti-Semitism in conjunction with Turkey's increasingly hostile relationship with Israel under the AKP, now comprise only 20,000–25,000 Turkish citizens. Nesim Güveniş, deputy chairman of the Association of Turkish Jews in Israel, echoed other non-Sunni Muslim populations' concerns in Turkey: "We are uncomfortable with being 'othered.' "[67]

Given the hardening of this hostile relational meaning, it is unsurprising that Turkey's rapprochement (*uzlaşma*) with Israel in June 2016 carried no friendly overtures. Prompted by Turkey's need for energy and its desire to be a natural gas hub in the region, as well as Israel's need for routes to export its gas, the normalization of ties evidences pure realpolitik at work. Prior to the rapprochement, posters commissioned by Gökçek and displayed across Ankara depicted a large, stoic image of Erdoğan towering over a small, grimacing Netanyahu and touted Israel's formal apology in 2013 for the flotilla incident. The text reads: "Dear Prime Minister, we are grateful for the pride you have made us experience."[68] In reporting on the normalization, pro-government media outlets emphasized the concessions Israel would be forced to make, including making financial reparations and allowing Turkey access to provide humanitarian aid to Gaza. A *Yeni Şafak* headline expresses this view well: "Israel's Press: We Surrendered, Hamas and Turkey Won."[69] Two other journalists posed the question of whether Turkey's negotiated achievement should be deemed a "victory" (*zafer*) or a "thrashing" (*hezimet*).[70] Following the rapprochement, Turkish Jews continued to emigrate, citing a discriminating environment in general and threats via social media specifically.[71] Far from an amicable reconciliation, the new state of relations between Turkey and Israel was portrayed as Turkey's moral and political triumph over a contrite enemy.

In addition to the sharp decline in relations with Israel, foreign policy swings toward and then away from Syria under the AKP also become comprehensible through inside-out contestation theory. Turkey has only been able to pursue Ottoman Islamist interests abroad after weakening or reconfiguring Republican Nationalist obstacles. The rapid and intense warming of ties between the AKP and Bashar al-Assad's Alawite (non-Sunni Muslim) regime stands in stark contrast to previous relations between the two countries, historically plagued by Syrian Arab resentment of Ottoman domination, differing Cold War alignments, water politics, border disputes, and Syria's support for the PKK in its own northern Kurdish region of Rojava and the Syrian-controlled Bekaa Valley in

Lebanon. In terms of the more current, pressing issues, the water politics issue favors Turkey's economic development, and the border dispute over the south-eastern province of Hatay, which separated itself from Syria's French mandate in 1938 under circumstances Syrians find dubious, was effectively settled in Turkey's favor when residents in the province voted to join Turkey via refer-endum in 1939, leading to a formal annexation (a decision that was recognized by the Syrian government, if not its people, in 2004). Given the dimensions of these conflicts, the dispute posing the greatest threat to Turkey in the eyes of for-merly dominant Republican Nationalists was Syria's intermittent playing of the Kurdish card, including supporting training camps for PKK fighters within its own borders and hosting PKK leader and, for Republican Nationalists, terrorist fugitive Abdullah Öcalan. Recalling the Republican Nationalist identity pro-posal outlined in chapter 3, threats to Turkey's territory and borders, as well as recognition of and support for Kurdish ethnic identity, were red lines that could not be tolerated.

While Turkey was thus on the brink of war with Syria in 1998—until cred-ible threats made primarily by TSK chief of staff Hüseyin Kıvrıkoğlu persuaded then Syrian president Hafez al-Assad to sign the Adana Agreement and, cru-cially, expel Öcalan from Syrian territory—relations transformed from civil to warm under the AKP's regional "zero problems with neighbors" policy. Eager to expand Turkey's influence into Muslim and former Ottoman territories, the AKP-led government lifted visa restrictions on Syria, as it did with other Muslim neighbors,[72] as part of an overall plan quickly to improve and deepen relations be-tween "peoples who had lived as friends and brothers for centuries."[73] Following the significant presidential visits between the countries in 2009, the Turkey-Syria High Level Strategic Cooperation Council was established. The close, personal relationship that developed between Erdoğan and Bashar al-Assad was demonstrated by the former's repeated reference to the latter as his brother and the vacation their families took together in Bodrum[74]—a dramatic shift in rela-tions over a decade that was to be followed by another, even more dramatic shift as Erdoğan realized Assad was unwilling to recognize Turkey as the legitimate leader of and rule giver for the region, as Ottoman Islamism prescribes.

The seemingly overnight shift from being close friends experiencing a "golden age"[75] to bitter enemies poised for war, which took place in August 2011, is a puzzle to both makers and observers of Turkish foreign policy.[76] Suggested explanations offered during interviews and conferences attended in-clude the accruing international institutional condemnations against Syria; a buildup of frustration over political capital apparently wasted in trying to per-suade Assad to accept reforms (including an alleged seven-hour meeting be-tween Davutoğlu and Assad);[77] and the beginning of the Muslim holy month of Ramadan on August 1, 2011, which may have increased Turks' sensitivity to the slaughter of Muslims by a government led by a non-Sunni president. While it is likely that all of these factors played a role in the rapid shift to calls for Assad to step down, analyzing the decision-making from an identity proposal perspective helps to make more comprehensive sense of Turkey's swing toward and then away from Syria under the same AKP rule. Near the end of its first term and well into its second, the AKP, after weakening Republican Nationalist institutions to the point where it was politically safe to pursue policies prescribed by Ottoman Islamism both at home and abroad, began to act in line with Davutoğlu's strategic depth doctrine, whose geocultural foundations had been prepared in Islamist MÜSİAD journals and the monograph of the same name years before the AKP came to power. In order to re-establish Turkey's roles as inheritor of the Ottoman legacy of regional rule and the legitimate center of the Muslim world, as it had been while hosting the caliphate, the AKP sought to spread its influence and leadership authority across former Ottoman lands. In keeping with Ottoman tradition, this would include influence over territories not controlled by Sunni Muslims, such as Alawite-ruled Syria. Having established close ties, interviewees emphasized that Erdoğan and Davutoğlu believed they had established the authority necessary to convince Assad to concede to enacting reforms. Upon realizing that exercising Turkey's influence over Syria was no longer possible, Erdoğan quickly reversed his position and condemned Assad as a brutal dictator, using every international means possible to try to push him out of power. This included making Turkey's participation in international efforts against ISIL contingent upon Assad's removal. In order to realize Ottoman Islamist interests in the region, AKP leaders had finally decided Assad was an irredeemable obstacle that needed to go.

Turkey has gone to great lengths to bring about this desired change of power. Quite literally taking outside its fight to realize Ottoman Islamist interests abroad, the Turkish government enlisted the services of its now relatively pacified military and other institutions to wage war against the Assad regime inside Syria. Turkish journalists arrested on spying charges revealed photographic evidence that Turkey's National Intelligence Organization (MİT) was using the convoys of the country's largest humanitarian aid organization (İHH) to secretly ship weapons to Jabhat al Nusra.[78] The group was al-Qaeda's Syrian-based affiliate until its members split from their parent organization and rebranded themselves as Jabhat Fateh al-Sham in July 2016; they later merged once again with al-Qaeda and other Salafist jihadists to form Hay'at Tahrir al-Sham.[79] While then prime minister Davutoğlu at first declared the weapons were being sent to the Free Syrian Army, later changing his statement to claim that they were headed to Syrian Turkmens, the location where the trucks were discovered and the vehemence of the AKP's reaction suggest that Turkey was arming jihadist rebels. Further, the AKP had ignored warnings from the United States to patrol its five-hundred-mile border with Syria more effectively for years, leaving a porous space through which ISIL fighters, arms, and oil could easily flow.[80]

Thus, while Turkey has been rightly lauded for hosting the over three million Syrian refugees who had sought asylum within its borders by the end of 2017, it is also at least somewhat complicit in causing the conditions that forced the Syrians to flee. Syrians caught in the crossfire of ISIL and other jihadist groups, Russian-backed Syrian government forces, and US-backed rebel groups such as the Free Syrian Army and the Kurdish People's Protection Units (YPG) have paid a staggering human cost. According to the London-based Syrian Observatory for Human Rights, as of March 2017 approximately 465,000 Syrians had been killed;[81] the Pew Research Center estimated in January 2018 that nearly 13 million are either internally displaced or have fled the country.[82]

As a final and most prominent example of the AKP realizing its Ottoman Islamist interests abroad, in October 2016 Erdoğan took advantage of the US-led coalition's fight to take back Mosul from ISIL to question the current state of Turkey's borders. Erdoğan explicitly expressed his concern for "our Sunni Arab brothers, our Turkmen brothers" in announcing that Turkey would join in anti-ISIL airstrikes in Mosul.[83] Having earlier criticized the Treaty of Lausanne's prime negotiator İsmet İnönü and Atatürk as "two drunkards" (*iki ayyaş*) whose ineptness allowed Turkey's borders to be drawn too narrowly,[84] Erdoğan shifted from rhetoric that demonstrated solidarity with these former Ottoman Muslim populations to articulating seemingly irredentist aspirations. As historian and map aficionado Nicholas Danforth notes, Turkey's borders may not be changing in the near future, but the newly drawn maps displayed in pro-AKP media show what for Ottoman Islamists would be a "new and improved Turkey."[85] These maps include not only Mosul, which has a large ethnic Turkmen population, but also the Kurdish cities of Erbil and Kirkuk, territories outlined in the National Pact (*Misak-ı Milli*) announced by the Ottoman parliament in February 1920. A series of events that followed, including the Allied occupation of Istanbul, the signing of the Treaty of Sèvres by Ottoman Sultan Mehmet VI, and the War of Liberation led by Atatürk in nationalist reaction against the territorial concessions the Treaty would have entailed, led to the Treaty of Lausanne in July 1923. With the exception of the province of Hatay, which was annexed by Turkey via referendum in 1939, the latter treaty defined Turkey's current borders— borders that Turkey's Republican Nationalist founders believed were realistically defensible and should comprise the national homeland (*vatan*). Erdoğan's speech on Mosul directly undermined the borders settled on at Lausanne: "The goal of those [leaders] who wanted to imprison Turkey in a vicious circle was to make us forget our Selçuk and Ottoman past. We cannot act in 2016 with the psychology of 1923; to insist on [1923 borders] would be the greatest injustice to our country and our nation (*millet*)."[86] Recalling the importance of maintaining and protecting these borders as one of the core social purposes of Republican Nationalism, such Ottoman Islamist–oriented, irredentist rhetoric constitutes a red line for supporters of the former identity proposal.

Realizing Ottoman Islamist Interests at Home

In addition to pursuing foreign policy interests generated by its Ottoman Islamist understanding of identity, the AKP also was able to move forward on the so-cial purpose of increasing space for Islam in the public sphere domestically—another red line incompatible with previously more widespread Republican Nationalism. Advancing this social purpose entails enacting legislation to change behavior in varied aspects of citizens' lives, as did the reforms pushed forward by Atatürk discussed in chapter 4. One Republican Nationalist critic of Ottoman Islamism stated in an interview that the AKP's "religious mindset . . . shapes eve-rything: the education of children, [positions toward] alcohol and abortion, women's issues";[87] in a sense, the many sweeping reforms aimed at spreading Ottoman Islamism and particularly increasing Islam's presence represent an effort to roll back the at least equally sweeping reforms during the early years of the republic.

Under the AKP the educational system was reconfigured to effectively in-crease the number of children attending clerical (*imam hatip*) schools, an outcome the military explicitly tried to prevent in pressuring the RP out of gov-ernment in 1997. The so-called 4 + 4 + 4 system—mandating four years each of primary-, middle-, and high-school education—introduces elective courses, including religious courses, at the middle-school level. The system ostensibly aimed to provide early vocational training, but its detractors claim it is a method of increasing the exposure of children to religious instruction at a younger age and thus increasing the number of those who will attend an *imam hatip* high school. Originally established to train (male) students to become imams, male and female graduates of *imam hatip* schools—including Erdoğan—now work in many sectors, a source of consternation for adamant defenders of secularism, such as the Republican Nationalists discussed in this book. The recent statement by AKP MP Ali Boğa following the new education law's passage that "we have in our hands the chance to make all schools *imam hatip*" schools—echoing comments repeatedly made by Erdoğan when he was mayor of Istanbul—thus understandably provoked outrage among supporters of the Republican Nationalist identity proposal.[88]

Also in line with spreading the constitutive norms and social purpose of Ottoman Islamism in the realm of education, the number of Ottoman Turkish classes offered is multiplying in private institutions, and Ottoman Turkish courses are now taught in public as well as private high schools. The AKP's legis-lation to make Ottoman Turkish a required course for all high-school students—denounced as "backward" by Republican Nationalists[89]—is intended to spread knowledge of and access to Ottoman Islamism's historical sources among young generations even further. The law was approved by a majority at the nineteenth meeting of the National Education Council (Milli Eğitim Şurası) in December 2014, its advocates stressing that "the Turkish people are the only nation that cannot read the gravestones of their grandfathers, and a demand for Ottoman Turkish exists in Turkey's society."[90] As mentioned in the discussion of Atatürk's language reforms in chapter 4, supporters of Ottoman Islamism have publicly lamented the distance they perceived as imposed upon them by the manda-tory switch to the Latin script and the purging of Arabic and Farsi words from Turkish carried out by the Turkish Language Institute. A distant grandson of the last Ottoman emperor, Abdülhamid Kayıhan Osmanoğlu, praised the National Education Council's decision, and Erdoğan personally, for spearheading the move to make Ottoman Turkish a requirement, stating that "the Ottoman was just sleeping, and opened his eyes after a nice little nap."[91]

Many of the dozens of new universities being opened by AKP supporters have names referencing figures from the Ottoman period, such as Orhangazi, Fatih Sultan Mehmet, Süleyman Şah, and Yıldırım Beyazıt,[92] and honoring key advocates of Ottoman Islamism, such as Konya Necmettin Erbakan Üniversitesi. Rectors of these universities, and new rectors who have moved into the tradi-tionally Republican Nationalist institution of the rectorship at well-established state universities, have used their substantial influence to shape the political cul-ture of their student bodies in line with Ottoman Islamist constitutive norms. Following Erdoğan's call for a mosque to be built on every university campus, Istanbul Technical University rector Mehmet Karaca announced that his uni-versity would be the first to construct a mosque, citing overwhelming demand from the student body. The title of a piece critiquing the plans for the mosque is telling: "The Sultan Commanded, the Rector Announced: A Mosque Is Coming to ITU."[93] Rectors have also worked to ban alcohol sales in on-campus social facilities[94] and to segregate male and female workspaces.[95] The ban on sales of alcohol on university campuses was made a national regulation by YÖK after Erdoğan declared that the consumption of alcohol on university campuses was wrong, rhetorically asking: "Will students absorb alcohol and clown around or will they absorb knowledge [*ilim*] and find themselves?"[96] Erdoğan's use of the word *ilim*—preferred by pious individuals and distinct from *bilim*, in some contexts connoting scientific knowledge and preferred by secularists—is note-worthy here in terms of his view of what university students should be learning.[97]

Suggested in the discussion of university housing above, relations between the sexes have become a primary target of efforts by Ottoman Islamists to spread their own proposal for identity throughout the public sphere. One way of framing these relations, suggested by Ottoman Islamists such as E. Sare Aydın Yılmaz, is to shift current debates away from gender equality and toward gender justice.[98] Yılmaz served as president of the Women and Democracy Association (Kadın ve Demokrasi Derneği, KADEM), an organization known for its promotion of conservative values, which has been repeatedly praised by Erdoğan. At a recent KADEM-organized event, Erdoğan controversially declared, "You cannot bring women and men to an equal position because that is contrary to their natural make-up [fıtrat]."[99] The word fıtrat, another word like ilim that carries an Islamic connotation, along with its meaning of "nature" or "given destiny," has become something of a code word for Ottoman Islamists, used to explain away tragedies because they were destined to happen given an individual or group's nature (fıtratında var).[100] The word is also used to justify forms of behavior toward women, because it is in their nature to be treated as such. The appeal for Ottoman Islamists of the idea that particular standards of behavior toward women are appropriate or natural, as suggested by the concept of fıtrat, manifests itself in recent statements by Uğur Işılak, an AKP candidate in the June 2015 elections, a popular folk singer, and the writer of Erdoğan's presidential campaign theme song "Dombra"—the Kazakh word for a stringed musical instrument resembling a lute, and likely as a song title chosen to appeal to Pan-Turkic Nationalist voters. Işılak suggested during a television appearance that "being a slave to men was in women's nature" ("Kadının fıtratında erkeğe köle olmak var"). Understandably upsetting Western Liberals and Republican Nationalists, but using a discourse to which Ottoman Islamists and many Pan-Turkic Nationalists are sympathetic, Işılak's statement, worth quoting at length, follows:

> In every feminist's heart there is a sentiment of being captivated by a husband, of being his slave, to be his individual, to belong to him—if there is not then let them come out against me. This is inherent in every woman's nature. To act like this isn't the case and this isn't contrary to their nature means that they are definitely not happy. I don't think those feminists are happy. Women's nature is to be connected to something, to belong to something. A man's nature isn't like that. Men don't belong to women, they own them. Some women mix this up; I will own you, you will belong.[101]

Moving from gender relations to the architectural arena, another acknowledged domestic space for spreading a specific understanding of identity, dozens of public buildings and private housing complexes began being remade in the Ottoman style, and the new mosques constructed under the greatly increased budget of the Directorate of Religious Affairs (Diyanet İşleri Bakanlığı) are all reminiscent of the Ottoman era.[102] In terms of spreading the Ottoman Islamist identity proposal, the number of the mosques constructed in Alevi neighborhoods under the AKP has been criticized as "a concerted interruption in the governance of an Alevi space."[103] Further, in a highly controversial move, the AKP decided to name the new "third bridge" that carries traffic across the Bosporus the Yavuz Sultan Selim Köprüsü, one more move that provoked outrage within the Alevi community. Sultan Selim the Ferocious (Yavuz) got his name in part from the massive slaughter of Alevis, whom he believed to be infidels, during his "Sunni-fication" of the empire in the late fifteenth and early sixteenth centuries. Many Alevis (and others) believe that the selection of the bridge's name was a symbolic gesture foreshadowing even more attempts at Sunni-fication.[104] Although the AKP pledged to recognize *cemevleri*, when a long-awaited democratization package introduced by the AKP on September 30, 2013, did not contain this recognition, the Alevi community interpreted this as further evidence of the AKP's vision of spreading Ottoman Islamism across Turkey at the expense of those who are excluded from this proposal. The deputy chairman of one of Turkey's largest Alevi associations stated: "we couldn't see anything in that package for Alevis. . . . It's as though [the AKP] didn't take the tiniest step."[105]

Non-Muslims, especially Turkey's Christian minorities, were frustrated and surprised by the democratization package's lack of attention to their demands. Indeed, many of Turkey's Christians have until recently been relatively supportive of the AKP. Former Representative of Minority Religions, General Directorate for Foundations Laki Vingas, for example, once argued that a "demarginalization of non-Muslim minorities in Turkey" over the last decade allowed groups such as Greeks, Armenians, and Jews to prosper economically and enjoy religious freedoms they were denied before the AKP came to power.[106] This position seems to make little sense given the party's promotion of Sunni Islam. The specification of Turkey's cognitive worldview as the inheritor of Ottoman legacies presented in this study provides insight into this favorable view, as the Ottoman Empire's *millet* system entailed a substantial level of self-government for non-Muslim religious minorities, who could be considered religious out-groups within an Ottoman in-group. However, setbacks including the removal of non-Muslim names from the national record of those who died while fighting Allied forces at Gallipoli in 1915[107] and the blatant anti-Semitism displayed by AKP supporters during the 2014 Gaza War, both of which seem to indicate an intensification of the focus on Islam as the most salient point of identification. The unexpected holes in the democratization package thus contributed to a wave of disenchantment growing among non-Muslims. Having promised to reopen the Halki seminary (Ruhban Okulu in Turkish, located on the island of Heybeliada)—the main theological school of Eastern Orthodox Christianity, which was closed in 1971 in the wake of disputes with Greece over the status of Cyprus's Turkish population and whose opening was a major demand of Turkey's Greek Orthodox (Rum) population—the AKP failed to fulfill its commitment; in a fiery speech justifying the decision, Erdoğan cited the need for reciprocation from Greece on issues such as granting the Muslim population of Western Thrace the right to select its own mufti (Islamic scholar) and permitting Turkey to reopen two mosques that had been closed in Athens, before the school could be opened, despite the government's previous promise.[108] The democratization package that promised to correct many of these injustices was thus disappointing to the Western Liberalists among Turkey's Alevis, Kurds, Christians, and individuals of other ethnic and religious identifications, as well as to Turkey's interlocutors in the EU. The 2013 Progress Report included quite measured language in reference to the package and hinted at the need to focus on implementation of those reforms that were proposed, stating that the package's measures "hold out the prospect to address concerns covered in more detail below";[109] a top EU Ministry official directly involved in the negotiations stated in an interview that the Turkish delegation had to work hard to soften the language of the report in the wake of the European Commission's criticisms.[110]

As much criticism as the democratization package received from both internal and external sources, its reforms represented a victory of great magnitude for Ottoman Islamists. The package included a provision removing phrases such as "the head will always be uncovered in the place of work" from a law regulating dress code for civil servants including teachers, ministry employees, and parliamentarians.[111] Women who no longer had to remove their headscarves before entering the buildings in which they worked welcomed the decision with such expressions as "I feel very free"[112] and, typifying the personalization of the AKP in its leader, "when I learned that a change was going to be made in this area thanks to our [then] Prime Minister, I felt as the though the weight of the world fell off me."[113]

This extension of the spaces in which the Islamic headscarf could be worn was particularly celebrated by the AKP on October 31, 2013, when four headscarved AKP MPs entered parliament. The relative lack of hostility with which their entrance was met contrasted sharply with the experience of Merve Kavakçı's, a headscarved FP MP who had been booed so vociferously for being an "agent" of Islamism upon entering in May 1999 that she was unable to take her oath or return to parliament.[114] While the headscarved deputies took their oaths unobstructed in 2013, the act was perceived by some as a breach of secularism (Republican Nationalists) and by others as the increasing spread of subjugating forces disguised as women's empowerment (Western Liberalists). CHP deputy chairman and human rights activist Şafak Pavey, for example, addressing parliament after the headscarved deputies entered, noted critical areas in which women's rights that intersect with Islam have not been advanced, such as some girls being forced to cover at the age of five and marry at age fifteen. Pavey, like Kavakçı before her, was labeled an agent provocateur and subjected to antifeminist character defamation by pro-government media sources. Casting doubts on whether Pavey actually lost her left arm and leg by trying to assist a wheelchair-bound friend onto a train or in fact purposefully hurled herself under the train in order to leave her husband,[115] AKP-endorsed *Sabah* journalist Sevilay Yükselir viciously called into question a female deputy's credibility by reducing her identity to that of a disobedient wife. The application of a trope familiar to those supporting the Ottoman Islamist identity's constitutive norms regarding the proper role and treatment of women suggests an increasingly intolerable divide on gender equality norms among Ottoman Islamism on one side and Republican Nationalism and Western Liberalism on the other.

Some Ottoman Islamists, however, believe that the legislation did not go far enough in guaranteeing the right of all females to cover. Critically citing the inability of most middle-school and high-school female students to attend classes wearing the headscarf—as the law is vague on this, the decision is left up to school administrators, much the same as the decision to allow headscarved students to enter university campuses was left up to rectors—the director of the Association for Free Thinking and Education Rights (Özgür Düşünce ve Eğitim Hakları Derneği) argued that "our religious beliefs, our identity are not open to negotiation."[116] This statement perfectly encapsulates the ontological significance of identities and the behaviors they prescribe as argued in this study, as well as how red lines of contestation can form when competing proposals prescribe incompatible behaviors.

The government has continued to stoke the public's fascination with Turkey's imperial history through its use of words and symbols. The period-costumed guards flanking Erdoğan when he welcomed Palestinian Authority president Mahmoud Abbas to his newly constructed complex referred to as "Ak Saray." Literally "White Palace," a term playing off the AKP's usage of a word that connotes "pure" (its preferred moniker is Ak Parti), the massive residence received public acclaim by AKP supporters as a display reminiscent of Ottoman power, even if this interpretation was historically inaccurate, as dissenters eagerly noted.[117] One YouTube user, with the username Reis İzindeyiz (We Are on the Leader's Track), shared a video of the event titled *"Osmanlı'nın Ayak Sesleri"* ("The Ottomans' Footsteps").[118] Continuing with the theme of historical cosplay, Turkish police celebrated the 170th anniversary of the founding of the internal security force following the abolition of the Janissaries in 1826 by welcoming Davutoğlu and Deputy Prime Minister Yalçın Akdoğan to the Ak Saray in full Ottoman regalia and false beards. Akdoğan tweeted a photograph of the costumed policemen with the all-capitals caption "Our history is our pride."[119] The previous day he had tweeted: "Many years to our security forces, which come from a glorious tradition—may my Lord protect them."[120]

A wave of revived historical-cultural interest, discouraged for decades under Republican Nationalist pressure, is evident in the number of references to Ottoman history in advertisements from chewing gum to cell phone carriers to luxury housing complexes, which are designed to reflect consumer preferences.[121] The state sponsorship of television series such as the Ottoman-themed detective drama *Filinta*, discussed in chapter 3, and the AKP's public criticism of Ottoman era–based forms of entertainment media whose scenes seem to contradict the Ottoman Islamist norms of modesty for women and piety, such as *Muhteşem Yüzyıl*, demonstrate the AKP's recognition that popular culture is a powerful conduit for spreading an identity proposal, as well as its desire firmly to control the content of the proposal being spread. In turn, and as a fundamental principle of the methodology undertaken in this study, popular culture media forms such as television, film, and novels serve as a reflection of identity proposals that have been internalized, thus creating a demand for materials to whose themes individuals can relate and with whose characters they can identify.

In addition to these forms of pop culture, the platform of social media also provides useful empirical insight into how the AKP's efforts to spread Ottoman Islamism work in practice. Millions of images glorifying Ottoman imperial times and celebrating norms of Islamic piety have been posted, tweeted, and tagged. Perhaps even more directly than traditional consumer-targeted media, the user-generated content of social media reflects the rise in the magnitude of support for Ottoman Islamism as the appropriate definition of Turkish identity during the AKP's later years. The launch of a "halal" (*helal*, permissible according to the principles of Islam) version of Facebook in Istanbul during the month of Ramadan in 2012 was intended to meet a growing demand to be able to share and view social media content generated by Muslims for Muslims, while avoiding content deemed "inappropriate" for Muslim society.[122]

This proliferation of public expressions of Islam indicates at least some success in the AKP's efforts to encourage individuals' identification with and incorporation of norms constitutive of Ottoman Islamism in their daily lives. The policing of the behaviors the proposal prescribes, as seen in Erdoğan's criticism of *Muhteşem Yüzyıl*, indicates the ontological importance of protecting the content from anything that could degrade its perceived authenticity or legitimacy. Such policing can also be seen with regard to novel forms of celebration related to Islam that have emerged in the past few years. One of pro-AKP columnist Fatma Barbarosoğlu's readers[123] wrote to inform her of a new "head covering ceremony" (*baş örtme töreni*), which she claimed is becoming a rite of passage for pious adolescent girls. In the opulent ceremonies the reader described in her letter, after verses are read from the Koran the girl stands while being covered with a headscarf for the first time in front of her party guests, who then present her with gifts reminiscent of a wedding. Barbarosoğlu used her piece, "A New Custom Every Day: Head Covering Ceremonies," to disparage such ceremonies as Western imitations and express concern about the piety of future generations, stating that "these are the baby-shower-throwing daughters and granddaughters of radical Islamists who said the holiday celebrating the birth of the Prophet (*Mevlit Kandili*) was a sinful innovation (*bidat*)."[124] Emphasizing her conservative approach to the practice of Islam, she also laments the fate of Turkey's males growing up with Westernized celebrations: "They've married fundamentally secular (*kökten seküler*) girls and started to pray where they won't be seen."[125]

Novel celebrations of the Blessed Birth Week (Kutlu Doğum Haftası), a holiday similar to Mevlit Kandili that was established in 1994 to observe the Prophet's birth according to the Gregorian calendar as well, have also generated a backlash from Ottoman Islamists aiming to police inappropriate behavior. In April 2015 an official inquiry was launched to investigate why a birthday-style cake in the shape of the Koran, decorated with verses piped in icing, was served during a course dedicated to the study of the holy text in Turkey's Black Sea province of Tokat in April 2013.[126] The Diyanet criticized the edible Koran via tweet, stating that this form of celebration "is never appropriate for the spirit (*ruh*) and the holiness (*mehabet*) of the Blessed Birth and the Koran."[127] In the same week, the religious authority also condemned the construction of a portable replica of the Ka'aba (Kabe)—the cube-shaped structure in Mecca around which Muslim pilgrims walk seven times as part of completing the religious duty of the hajj—by officials in Üsküdar and Tuzla, two municipalities of Istanbul.[128] The Diyanet declared through its Hello Fatwah Line (*Alo Fetva Hattı*)[129] that the replicas, likely installed to win support from pious voters in the upcoming June 2015 general elections, were a "great sin" ("*büyük vebal*").[130] While the emergence of novel celebrations provides evidence of the spread of Ottoman Islamism to the public sphere, the censure against those that are deemed to be imitating Western consumerism or disrespectful to Islam provides useful empirical insight into the ontological significance of the identity content that needs safeguarding.

As a final example of concern with protecting the content of Ottoman Islamism, some believe celebration of the birth feels inauthentic when observed according to the Gregorian calendar, a Western-imported standard of practice that was implemented as part of Atatürk's reforms. An official who originally approved of the new holiday, thinking that observing the Birth Week around April 20 would ensure that schools could organize appropriate religious events for children, later regretted the shift, declaring that he "did not feel he was having an authentic emotional experience . . . out of the traditional time frame."

The official attributed this absence of authenticity to "cultural alienation: the severing of Islamic culture from its historical context," an enforced cleavage from their rightful past that Ottoman Islamists associate with Republican Nationalist reforms and have been vigorously working to repair.[131]

Conclusion

The AKP faced formidable domestic obstacles to any desired pursuit of hegemony for its Ottoman Islamist identity proposal upon coming to power in 2002. As my theory of identity contestation posits, however, individuals have strong sociopsychological and institutional motivations for spreading their particular proposals. As the inside-out element of the theory also stipulates, supporters of proposals whose identity contestation is blocked at the domestic level are motivated enough to take that contestation to the foreign policy arena if at all possible.

This study's analysis of Republican Nationalist and Ottoman Islamist identity proposals specifies the points of incompatibility among the content of these proposals, suggesting that Ottoman Islamist supporters would be blocked in their pursuit of hegemony by Republican Nationalist institutions with the power to do so. This chapter's discussion of the Turkish military, the Constitutional Court, and university rectors demonstrates that all three were strong repositories of Republican Nationalism, as well as direct obstacles—and even threats—to supporters of Ottoman Islamism. Having learned its lesson from the experiences of previous supporters, the AKP took its identity contestation to the realm of foreign policy, using EU-mandated reforms to reduce the power of the military, allow the makeup of the Constitutional Court to change in the AKP's favor, and indirectly, install a sympathetic president who will nominate future university rectors. With these obstacles thus mitigated, the AKP advanced a domestic and foreign policy agenda heavily laden with Ottoman Islamism, facilitating the proposal's spread across Turkey's population as well as the realization of the domestic and foreign interests it generates.

Taking the Theory "Outside"

State and Non-State Actors' Use of Inside-Out
Identity Contestation

One of the topics political science scholars can be sure they will have to address in response to questions from conference panel attendees, journal editors, and book reviewers is: How well does your theory travel? That is, how does your explanation/understanding of case X help us explain/understand an outcome in case Y?[1] Is your case sui generis, or is the theory you develop useful in analyzing cases outside of that which you have presented? Do we see the dynamics shaping outcomes in Turkey also at work in Turkmenistan? Tunisia? Tuvalu? The question of a theory's generalizability is an important one that ultimately gets to the heart of what we as political scientists aim to do in our work. Should we develop empirically rich, highly detailed, "thick" approaches that seek to provide deep insights into one case or a very small number of cases? Or is the nobler goal theoretically elegant, parsimonious, "thin" approaches that offer general insights into a large universe of cases? Thankfully for the greater good of our discipline, some political scientists reject the "either-or" premise of such questions, arguing that our analysis should be "puzzle-driven" rather than driven by a specific method or scope of research design.[2] Simply put, gaining a better insight through theory building, testing, and refinement requires the utilization of multiple methods across various settings of the analytical lens through which we zoom in on and zoom out from our cases of inquiry.

The approach I develop in this book is in large part designed to zoom in on the case of Turkey; indeed, the theory of inside-out identity contestation I present in these pages is built from an inductive, in-depth study of the identity politics and foreign policy orientations of this state. The puzzles I tease out tackle variations in the behavior prescribed and proscribed by differing identity proposals and in the presence of proposals in Turkey's institutions and societal discourse over time. However, while the empirical content detailed here is innately specific to Turkey, the concepts of identity red lines and institutions as identity-based obstacles, and the theoretical premises that supporters of an identity proposal pursue hegemony and will take their contestation to the foreign policy arena when blocked in their pursuit, are by no means unique to Turkey in their potential application. Taking inside-out theory "outside" of the case in which it is developed offers the potential for obtaining valuable insights into otherwise inexplicable foreign policy swings and dramatic shifts in identity discourses of states irrespective of their geographical region, level of economic development, particular religious or ethnic majority,[3] or other factors traditionally used to delimit an appropriate universe of cases.

Even regime type, which may at first glance seem to pose an important scope condition as closing or opening the domestic space in which actors can seek to struggle against a competing understanding of identity, does not hold. Consider the theory's premise that supporters of identity proposals use foreign policy as an arena—through engagement with international institutions, transnational civil society, diaspora groups, or a combination thereof—for advancing their proposal when blocked at home by institutions infused with a rival identity proposal. Even in democratic regimes considered to be highly institutionalized, universal consensus on the content of national identity is close to unthinkable, and those whose proposals for national identity are restricted on grounds of hate speech or are constrained by limited electoral appeal can reach out beyond their borders for solidarity and support. Far-right parties in Europe, for example, share mobilization tactics and financial resources with like-minded groups in other countries in their efforts to advance their own proposals back home.[4] Moving across the democracy-autocracy continuum, regimes that are less democratic by definition contain institutions such as educational systems, news media, and courts that are more restrictive in general. Important variation exists, however, in what hybrid and authoritarian regimes' leaders choose to restrict.[5] A regime whose identity understanding proscribes the recognition of minority rights, for example, will likely restrict media coverage pertaining to opposition on that issue but not necessarily on other issues. Thus we can expect to see more externalization of identity contestation in regimes with relatively restricted domestic public spheres in which debate cannot take place when compared to more democratic ones.[6] One exception to a claim of universal external validity might be regimes quite far along the authoritarian end of a regime continuum that are successful in preventing the externalization of identity struggles we might expect to exist in a constricted environment. Not stopping at suppressing public demonstrations domestically, highly authoritarian regimes may also restrict travel, cut off Internet access, and monitor other forms of correspondence with the outside world. This closure of access to the foreign policy arena effectively bars supporters of nonhegemonic proposals from contesting full stop.

In this penultimate chapter I provide glimpses into how future research could take the theory developed in this book "outside" the scope of the study of Turkey presented here to shed light on other countries in which foreign policy shapes, and is shaped by, identity contestation. Without extensive field-work I cannot parse out the content of competing identity proposals as I did in the research for this book, but I can highlight the foreign policy strategies used by actors who seek to achieve hegemony for their own understandings of na-tional identity. By drawing on secondary sources, including news accounts and the work of country specialists, this chapter offers a first-cut exploration of how inside-out identity contestation theory can elucidate potential linkages between identity politics and foreign policy in cases outside of the particularly intricate Gordian knot that is Turkish identity politics. Importantly, in doing so I explore both state and non-state actors' use of the foreign policy arena in advancing their understandings of identity back home. A major component of this book has been the study of how Turkey's ruling AKP was able to reduce the influ-ence of Republican Nationalist obstacles such as the military and the judiciary by adhering to EU accession criteria. While non-state actors generally do not have access to the leverage such institutional conditionality can generate, they can and do appeal to TANs[7] and diaspora populations[8] in seeking support for their own identity proposals. These two sources of support can often overlap, as members of a diaspora may engage directly with civil society activism to raise awareness of their grievances in their host country or may bring identity-related issues to the attention of extant information-sharing networks as an act of advo-cacy. As studies of diasporic media as "'extranational' space outside the control of national boundaries" show, for example, immigrants can use media in their vernacular language as a platform not only to vent against their host country but also to mobilize critical voices against their home country.[9] Here, both diasporic and transnational activist dynamics are at play.

In the following section I briefly investigate two cases of authoritarian regimes/illiberal democracies with highly polarized identity cleavages—Iran and South Africa—and two cases of democracies with similarly polarized cleavages, India and Israel. In the latter two cases, contestation over identity and the violence it produces contribute to less than fully democratic scores for both countries according to most assessments, but do not preclude either from being counted as a democracy.[10] The selection of these cases adds regional, ec-onomic, and cultural variation along with regime type to demonstrate that the inside-out theory of identity contestation developed in this book can usefully explain the use of foreign policy strategies by state and non-state actors outside of Turkey. In the final section of this chapter I return to the case of Turkey to explore the externalization of identity contestation, in which the Gülen and Kurdish movements engage.

Iran

The recent political struggles between moderates and conservatives in Iran evince a clear dynamic of identity contestation, with staunchly held views in competition over what norms of behavior in the domestic sphere should look like, and how and with whom Iran should engage in the international arena. An illiberal democracy in which elections are held but the candidates must be approved by a body known as the Guardian Council, whose members are directly or indirectly approved by the autocratic supreme leader, the Islamic Republic of Iran houses numerous debates over national identity that are intricately intertwined with beliefs about appropriate directions in foreign policy. As Suzanne Maloney notes, rivalry among elements of "great power" Persian nationalism, Islamism, and anti-imperialism has been a defining feature of struggles among diverse groups, each seeking, in this book's language, to attain identity hegemony through political power.[11] Whether these understandings best capture the current landscape of proposals for Iranian identity could be investigated through the methodology of intertextual analysis presented in chapter 2, before using process tracing to evaluate whether supporters of these proposals have attempted to circumnavigate domestic obstacles to their pursuit of hegemony by moving their contestation to the realm of foreign policy.

One major instance indicating that inside-out contestation along at least some line of identity may be taking place involves the dynamics of the Iranian nuclear deal, or P5 + 1 agreement (before the US withdrawal). Domestically, in the struggle over the deal moderate president Hassan Rouhani clashed with Iran's parliamentary conservatives, often known as Principlists.[12] Moderates in Iran hold a diverse set of beliefs about politics but are loosely united in opposition to such identity-related issues as the punishing actions of morality police against women seen not to adhere to Iran's Islamist dress code, the Islamic Revolutionary Guard's support of Shi'i militant groups such as Hezbollah in Syria and the Houthis in Yemen, and the perception of the West in general and the United States in particular as an evil enemy. An identity red line for Principlists, as Iran analyst Mehrdad Moarefian asserts, would be compliance with Western orders, such as inspection of Iran's military sites.[13] The signing of the deal on July 14, 2015, marked, or at least threatened, a violation of that red line, while simultaneously strengthening the role of Rouhani and the moderates who sided with him on pushing for an agreement with Western powers. Strongly reflected in the coverage of moderates' overwhelming victory in the February 2016 parliamentary and Assembly of Experts elections was a belief in the causal link between Rouhani's success in inking the P5 + 1 deal and his fellow moderates' success in the polls.[14] This domestic challenge to hardline conservatives, who had dominated Iranian politics since the late 1990s and were rattled by Rouhani's 2013 presidential win, might thus usefully be analyzed as a product of moderates' victories in the foreign policy arena.

Building on intellectual work focusing on identity contestation such as that of Maloney, recent treatments of the nuclear deal work and domestic political shifts hint at the potential analytical purchase and empirical insight to be gained by examining the link between identity and foreign policy in Iran. Ali Hossein Mahdavi, for example, argues that the 2016 elections should not be viewed from the perspective of democratization, a domestic issue, but rather in terms of how Iran will engage with the international community, a foreign policy one. In the same article, however, he also intimates that the election results would have been different had the P5 + 1 nuclear deal not take place. In the constructivist, "how possible" language of the questions this book seeks to answer, in understanding how reformists and conservatives came together in a structural shift in Iranian politics, "it was the nuclear deal that made the difference."[15] That is, reformists used foreign policy initiatives such as the nuclear deal and the purchase of Airbus airplanes, collaborations that Supreme Leader Ayatollah Khamenei and his hardliners saw as a threat to the Islamic revolution, to circumvent institutional obstacles and advance their own position in the domestic arena. It appears that reformists learned the lessons of 2009's unsuccessful Green movement, an uprising that challenged the re-election of hardline president Mahmoud Ahmedinejad, and chose to take their contestation to the foreign policy arena. As Mahdavi succinctly puts it: "Internationalization might be the most practical way for the Rouhani government and the nuclear deal supporters to achieve their goals."[16]

The Iran-Iraq War (1980–1988), in which Iraq's Sunni minority government struggled to defeat what it perceived as Iranian efforts to export its Shi'i Islamic revolution,[17] also provides a case ripe for inside-out analysis. Mohammad Ayatollahi Tabaar's work on this conflict points to domestic factional politics as a key factor in explaining Iran's actions in several stages, including the initial resistance to Iraqi occupation, aggressive behavior following the eviction of Iraqi forces in 1982, and the attrition phase prior to accepting a ceasefire in 1988.[18] Focusing on competing organizational interests in what might be termed a bureaucratic politics of identity approach, Tabaar parses out the rivalries between Iran's Islamists and nationalists, as well as between the Islamic Revolutionary Guard Corps (IRGC) and the army. A compelling account with useful glimpses into internal debates, Tabaar's explanation of how various groups sought to advance their relative position back home through their approach to the war could be enhanced with a clearer, more systematic capture of the intersection of identities and interests at play—and the identity red lines that shape the pursuit of those interests—offered in this book's conceptual framework of identity proposals.

Other examples of political struggles whose explanations could benefit from an inside-out identity contestation lens include the Green movement—would a greater ability to externalize the struggle to international audiences have made a difference in the outcome?—and the 1979 hostage crisis.[19] In the latter case, Iranian students took over the US embassy in Tehran and held fifty-two American diplomats hostage for more than a year. As Maloney suggests, this "most dramatic foreign policy step of the post-revolutionary era . . . was fueled by the contestation to assert institutional *and* ideational dominance over the state."[20] That is, in pursuit of identity hegemony for the proposal supported by the Islamist revolutionaries, foreign policy served as an arena for advancing their understanding of Iranian national identity.

South Africa

South Africa also constitutes a relevant case for an inside-out study of identity contestation, both because of its history as one of the most institutionalized cases of identity divides in recent years and because the role of anti-apartheid activists in seeking external normative support for their cause was critical in generating regime change. The racial apartheid system held firmly in place by successive National Party governments not only de facto but de jure disenfranchised nonwhite individuals of South Africa, revoking voting rights and then citizenship from the great majority of the people over whom it ruled based on identity. Although the Afrikaner minority-rule government held control over all institutions of power, the significance of this book's use of hegemony becomes clear in this case, in that by no means did the National Party enjoy identity hegemony as defined here. Employing the framework developed here to the South African case would first necessitate determining whether the identity proposal promulgated by the National Party either excluded nonwhite (black, Indian, and colored according to their categorizations) South Africans as an out-group or included them as a naturally inferior and therefore subordinate part of the in-group. Further, intertextual analysis may reveal that two or more proposals existed among the National Party, prescribing and proscribing what was possible, tolerable, and necessary behavior. The Afrikaner ethnic separatism of Prime Minister J. B. M. Hertzog, for example, contrasted greatly with the understanding of identity held by British and reformist (*verlighte*) Afrikaners.[21] It is clear that former president F. W. de Klerk, whether succumbing to domestic or international pressures or motivated by internal moral concerns in his efforts to transform South Africa's system into a multiracial democracy, found the prospect of majority rule by nonwhite South Africans tolerable, a belief of membership and representation that was shared by previous National Party leaders.

The lack of hegemony of any identity proposal relegating nonwhite South Africans to inferior status may be intuitive, but continual contestation of this proposal was clearly demonstrated by both whites and nonwhites.[22] The Progressive Party, for example, was formed by whites who declared themselves to be liberal supporters of "native rule." The great majority of those who opposed apartheid, however, had no institutional access to contest the National Party's racist identity proposal and the system of government prescribed by it—at least within the domestic sphere. In addition to lacking universal suffrage and citizenship, nonwhites also faced a repressive military apparatus made up of 85% ethnic Afrikaners,[23] a clear example of the domestic obstacles to contestation conceptualized in this book. Certainly debates about identity and appropriate behavior were manifest in many intra-opposition discussions among nonwhites that might necessitate parsing out two or more identity proposals. The Inkatha movement of Chief Buthelezi, for example, although at one point sympathetic to the Black Consciousness (BC) movement and the African National Congress (ANC), later isolated itself from them, advocating ethnic Zulu nationalism as opposed to BC's black unity and the ANC's nonracialism. Arguably for personal interests as a newly anointed homeland leader, Buthelezi distanced himself to the point that the National Party viewed him as an anti-ANC ally.[24] Despite internecine divisions, what those opposing apartheid shared was a domestic arena in which ongoing protest would mean continuous violent repression. Perhaps sociologist Gay Seidman most succinctly sums up the empirical potential the case holds for further study: "Faced with an intransigent regime at home, South Africans looked beyond their borders for help."[25]

Facing such obstacles at home, those promoting a more inclusive proposal for South African identity and thus an end to apartheid took their contestation outside to the foreign policy arena, attempting to gain support for their cause internationally when they could not do so domestically. They grafted onto TANs, particularly the pan-Africanist movement focusing African Americans' attention on African issues, which was gaining traction in the United States.[26] International dynamics, particularly the end of the Cold War and the collapse of the communist threat that had led Western leaders to support the Pretorian regime, opened up space for activists to call out to these leaders for their support. In getting the attention of the US government in particular, anti-apartheid activists engaged with what Locksley Edmondson calls black America's "mobilizing diaspora,"[27] thus exemplifying the intertwining of the TAN and diasporic strategies explored in this book. As a result of their efforts, supporters of a multiracial identity proposal not only succeeded in shaming those states that recognized South Africa's apartheid regime, but, as TAN scholar Audie Klotz argues, in reconstituting the interests of major players such that it became in their interest to adopt sanctions against the regime and support the transition to a multiracial democracy.[28] Key in this shift was convincing lawmakers that sustaining positive relations with an apartheid government violated what this book conceives of as an identity red line, a behavior fundamentally intolerable for a country that had just gone through its own civil rights movement for racial equality. Also moving this debate along were the actions of anti-apartheid activists calling attention to decolonization in neighboring Mozambique, Angola, and Namibia, outcomes that Nelson Mandela recalls as "influential" in building momentum for his own campaign.[29] There is an inside-out dimension here too, as Klotz notes that the victory of liberation movements in these countries was an important factor in the resurgent interest of African Americans in African affairs that would prove to be such a vital external constituency in pressing for South Africa's own liberation from apartheid.[30]

As the leading institution of South African activists contesting white rule/ Afrikaner nationalism, the ANC upon taking power through elections in 1994 had the opportunity to disseminate its own proposal for South African national identity, captured in spirit in the country's new, rainbow-colored flag. Interestingly for future studies applying identity hegemony theory, South Africa scholars Peter Vale and Sipho Maseko note that the ANC's leadership left the outgoing minority government "unable to deliver its own version of South Africa in Africa."[31] The South Africa case thus speaks clearly to the insights to be gained by further unpacking the dynamics of identity contestation at the domestic and international levels in a wider scope of cases. Indeed, given the many challenges South Africa's national unity project faced, from Afrikaner and Zulu nationalism to economic inequality and corruption in the ANC that can exacerbate identity divisions, those who opposed the ANC's attempts to establish hegemony for a "rainbow nation" proposal for South African could now seek outside support for and expression of their own proposals. As advocated throughout this book, popular culture is one especially important forum for locating identity contestation. In the Afrikaans case, for example, musical groups like Die Antwoord and websites such as www.watkykjy.com.za provide transnational outlets for contesting the destabilization and marginalization of white identity.[32]

India

Given its many overlapping identity dimensions—ethnicity, religion, language, caste, and so forth—and its role as a nuclear regional power, India has unsurprisingly provided fertile material for discussions of identity politics and foreign policy. In terms of scholarship examining how the two influence each other, the effects of postcolonial nation-building on foreign policy receive the majority of attention.[33] From the perspective of competing understandings of the nation and its international role, Jacques Hymans's psychological approach to nuclear policy includes a chapter on how shifts in understandings of national identity shape proliferation decisions;[34] and Sinderpal Singh examines how contestation among competing visions of India shaped the country's post–partition era foreign policy and how under the rule of Atal Bihari Vajpayee's Hindu nationalist Bharatiya Janata Party (BJP), Muslim-majority Pakistan and Bangladesh are framed as greater threats than they already were (particularly Pakistan) based on "Islamic orientations" and fears of terrorism.[35] While these studies focus on foreign policy variation based on shifts in party rule, that is, from the Indian National Congress Party to the BJP and back, extracting identity proposals irrespective of party lines may be helpful in elucidating important differences in beliefs about norms of membership and behavior, social purpose, relational meaning, and cognitive worldview across members of the same party. This is particularly the case in India, considering the many overlapping identity dimensions noted above. In the same vein, identifying identity red lines could help build on explanations of changes in coalition patterns among political parties.[36]

Another way of thinking about how actors in India use the foreign policy arena to advance their own identity proposals and contest rivals back home lies in the role of the Indian diaspora. Some reports indicate that anywhere from sixteen to twenty-five million individuals of Indian origin, now make up the world's largest diaspora, having recently surpassed China.[37] While outreach to diasporic populations is common, as they can provide valuable resources in the forms of remittances for development, votes for elections, and support in interstate diplomacy,[38] the inside-out approach advanced in this book could elucidate how Indian actors engage their diasporas as allies in their own particular domestic identity struggles back home. Scholars such as Latha Varadarajan engage the theme of "the domestic abroad,"[39] and critical studies pointing to Hindu nationalist movements' pursuit of hegemony for *Hindutva* as a politico-cultural ideology echo the identity hegemony motivation behind the contestation explored in this book.[40] Present throughout these works is the notion that Hindus are far from a monolithic group with a uniform view on Muslims, secularism, what it means to be Indian, and who India's allies should be; parsing out existing proposals for identity content would enrich studies of how and why a state's treatment of its diasporic populations may vary over time with shifts to a different proposal under a new government.

As an initial consideration, BJP prime minister Narendra Modi recently used his foreign policy travels to reach out to diasporic communities, calling on them to contribute to Indian development projects as well to "play a key role in shaping a positive image of India not just in American but around the world."[41] In addition to these desired contributions, however, Modi also seems to demonstrate identity-based motivations undergirding his visits to Indian audiences abroad, the great majority of whom were Hindu.[42] Claims that as chief minister of the state of Gujarat in 2002 Modi failed to prevent a systematic pogrom in which more than two thousand Muslims were killed by Hindu nationalists—an event Modi "flippantly dismissed" as a "Hindu backlash" against the murder of fifty-eight Hindus by an alleged Muslim mob, arguably demonstrating tacit approval of anti-Muslim violence[43]—led him to be denied a US visa in 2005; his ability to travel upon becoming prime minister opened up a new opportunity for him personally to advance his understanding of national identity abroad.

From a party standpoint, the BJP, more so than other parties, has long courted support from Indians in the diaspora. When in power in 2003, the party launched the first Pravasi Bharatiya Divas, a day of celebration for Indians living abroad meant to "help them stay in touch with their motherland."[44] This launch corresponded with a change in citizenship law to create an "overseas Indian" category that allowed those born of Indian descent overseas to be citizens, thus strengthening the principle of *jus sanguinis* introduced for those born in India in 1986.[45] Such moves not only expand the community of potential Hindus abroad who may support Hindu nationalists in India but also generate a social purpose of protecting Hindus abroad as members of the in-group. In November 2017, for example, the BJP government reached out to victims of an attack on a Hindu village in Bangladesh, promising compensation for the victims and visiting the village to view the damaged homes and extend support.[46] As the victims were Bangladeshi citizens, this outreach to Hindus abroad reflects a religion- and descent-based understanding of what it means to be Indian that differs from that of previous governments.

An inside-out contestation perspective could illuminate whether these efforts abroad opened space for advancing Modi's understanding of Indian identity, whether that eventually will be defined as "Hindu nationalist" or something else. Indeed, the dynamics of the December 2017 Gujarat election seem to reflect quite open forms of identity politics.[47] Following the nomination of Rahul Gandhi for party leader, a position currently held by his mother, Sonia Gandhi, Modi referred to the Congress Party's "Mughlai mentality" and "Aurangzeb rule," implying that it practices feudalism and dynastic politics.[48] Top officials, including BJP president Amit Shah, affirmed their staunchly Hindu nationalist stance by implying that the Congress Party was too "soft" on issues related to Muslim actors, including Kashmir and Rohingya refugees fleeing Myanmar.[49] More direct assertions of anti-Muslim sentiment also manifested themselves in campaign speeches; one candidate for an assembly seat in Dabhoi—a municipality that is approximately 38% Muslim—stated that if elected he would "not donate a single *paisa* to a masjid and madrasa" and that "there should be no population of Dubai in Dahoi."[50] Although given notice by election authorities for using strong communal language that included an epithet, the fact that the candidate used such language may indicate increasing support for and acceptance of Hindu nationalism. The opposite may be true, however, in that anti-Muslim rhetoric generates little to no increase in support for such an identity proposal; following Modi's claim that former Indian PM Manmohan Singh conspired with Pakistan to sink the BJP's chances, for example, the Congress candidate in the constituency in which the accusation was made defeated the BJP candidate.[51] Applying an inside-out perspective would prove useful in analyzing whether the appeal of Hindu nationalism is spreading and, if so, to what extent the BJP's efforts in reaching out to Indians abroad affect this shift.

Israel

Contestation over the content of Israeli national identity extends to the point of challenging whether the country should be categorized among other hybrid regimes or be considered a partial or "ethnic" democracy.[52] As Nadav Shelef's work on the evolution of conceptions of homeland and identity argues, for some Israel can be Jewish and democratic at the same time, while others contend that it is precisely the definition of Israel as a Jewish state that makes it an ethnic, partial, democracy.[53] From this perspective, Israeli Arabs who are Muslim, Christian, Druze, or any religion other than Jewish are culturally and legally disenfranchised, restricted from full participation in political and social life despite having citizenship. Further, many also see weak prospects for their kin living in the West Bank and Gaza or in refugee camps in Jordan, Lebanon, and elsewhere being able to return if the emphasis on the Jewish character of the state remains hegemonic.

Scholarship by Shelef and others such as Michael Barnett[54] debates many of the questions of identity this book engages in the case of Israel. These include who belongs to the in-group, what the group's goals are, and who can be trusted in the international arena. The answers to these questions prescribe and proscribe differing—and often incommensurable—courses of action on issues vital to national security as well as the protection of human rights, such as attitudes towards treatment of Palestinians.[55] Given the significance of this linkage for scholarship and policymaking alike, the profusion of categorizations among those researching identity in Israel reflects the same challenges encountered in previous analyses of understandings of Turkish national identity. By employing different methods of operationalization, we as scholars end up with more competing understandings of identity than those we study. Barnett, for example, specifies four constitutive strands of national identity—religion, nationalism, the Holocaust, and liberalism—and then examines how identity, narratives, frames, and institutions interact in the contestation over what it means to be

Israeli. Shelef identifies labor, revisionist, and religious forms of Zionism before specifying that an evolutionary dynamic—as opposed to one of elite imposition or rational adaptation—best explains change in how supporters of these different Zionisms defined their ideas about the shape of the homeland. Applying the framework of identity content and mechanism of contestation used in this book could help to synthesize the findings of these and other studies, establishing the basis for replicable and cross-case comparable studies.

In terms of identifying potential inside-out dynamics in Israeli domestic politics and foreign policy, the Oslo Accords are a useful case for consideration. A set of agreements signed between Israel and the Palestine Liberation Organization (PLO), named for the secret talks in Norway that paved the way for negotiations, Oslo I was signed in Washington, D.C., in 1993, and Oslo II in Taba, Egypt, in 1995. Thwarted by ultranationalists at home in his attempt to "instantiate an Israeli national identity that was Zionist and liberal,"[56] Labor prime minister Yitzhak Rabin led what would be know as the Oslo peace process as a form of international diplomacy. The famous handshake between him and PLO leader Yasser Arafat, apparently carefully orchestrated by US president Bill Clinton in 1993,[57] arguably would not have been possible on Israeli soil. Clinton was correct in calling this agreement a "brave gamble";[58] Rabin was assassinated in 1995 while leaving a peace rally by Jewish extremist Yigal Amir, who objected to the prime minister's proposal for Israeli national identity.

Although in many ways his political opposite, the man who would win the 1996 election following Rabin's death also engaged in using foreign policy as a means of attempting to sway identity politics in his favor back home. Right-wing Likud chairman Benjamin Netanyahu took over from acting prime minister Shimon Peres in a surprise victory with an extremely narrow margin and went on to hold several positions inside and outside government before returning to Israel's premiership in 2009. In a literal example of externalizing identity contestation, Netanyahu tried to circumvent internal obstacles to his efforts to have increased sanctions placed on Iran by taking his fight to the US Congress. Although the prime minister used his March 2015 speech and meetings with legislators as an attempt to gain international support for his position that Iran must be seen as a treacherous enemy, according to some reports he confronted a domestic institutional obstacle in doing so: Mossad.[59] Despite Netanyahu's objections, the Israeli intelligence agency briefed members of the US Senate Foreign Relations committee on the dangers of the Kirk-Menendez bill, which would have placed sanctions on Iran if it did agree to a long-term deal by June 30, 2015. Thus facing an audience that might be difficult to persuade, Netanyahu used his speech to portray Israel as the historical victim of aggression by Iran and its forebears:

We're an ancient people. In our nearly 4,000 years of history, many have tried repeatedly to destroy the Jewish people. Tomorrow night, on the Jewish holiday of Purim, we'll read the book of Esther. We'll read of a powerful Persian viceroy named Haman, who plotted to destroy the Jewish people 2,500 years ago. But a courageous Jewish woman, Queen Esther, exposed the plot and gave for [*sic*] the Jewish people the right to defend themselves.[60]

The speech's powerful references to Jews' history of both vulnerability and triumph sought to evoke an emotive connection in listeners that would motivate them to take action against Iran and thus protect the US and Israel's "common destiny."[61] Of course the intended listeners were by no means limited to those in the United States. By speaking from what he called "the most important legislative body in the world," the Israeli prime minister also intended to imbue his role as Israel's leader with international legitimacy in the eyes of his constituents back home. While he was unsuccessful in persuading the United States to increase sanctions on Iran, his contestation of moderation toward Iran in the foreign policy arena appears to have paid dividends in the elections that took place in Israel just two weeks later. Buoyed by last-minute campaign promises that no Palestinian state would be created under his Likud leadership, Netanyahu's party won a clear victory, "sweeping past" its chief rival, the center-leftist Zionist Union alliance.[62] Notable in the examples of Rabin and Netanyahu is that both are cases in which the externalization of identity contestation was led by individuals in power, as in the Turkish case of the AKP-led EU accession process, but that in the former the message delivered how Israel could be a full member in an international norm-abiding community, whereas in the latter Netanyahu emphasized how isolated Israel was and thus in need of protection.[63]

Non-state Actors within Turkey

The preceding sections of this chapter considered how the inside-out theory of identity contestation developed in this book can travel outside of Turkey to illuminate state and non-state actors' use of foreign policy strategies of institutional conditionality, transnational activism, and diaspora engagement to advance their identity contests back home. While by no means an exhaustive analysis of each of these strategies, I offer the brief discussions above in hopes that experts working across a wide variety of case studies will find the material presented ripe for analysis and cross-case comparison from an inside-out analytical perspective. In what remains of this chapter I turn the analysis back to Turkey to

examine two non-state actors that have effectively engaged actors through foreign policy in their struggle against Republican Nationalist institutions: the
Gülen movement and the Kurdish movement. As elements of both movements
at one time worked in collaboration with the AKP but now have extremely
hostile relations, Turkey's Gülenists and Kurds also demonstrate contestation
against Ottoman Islamism as part of their broader power struggles against the
party's increasingly authoritarian turn.

Turkish Calvinism

In the 2010s Gülenists, followers of US-based cleric Fethullah Gülen, have
become most famous for their explosive split with the AKP. Clashes between
the party and the movement began over issues such as the AKP's approach to
the Kurds and Israel, as well as the closure of university preparatory schools
(*dershaneler*) that were an immense source of income and recruitment for
the movement.[64] The December 2013 corruption scandal exposing top AKP
officials—a case of bribery and sanctions evasion surrounding Turkish-Iranian
gold trader Reza Zarrab that in late 2017 became a particular source of tension
in Turkish-US relations[65]—marked the official rupture, with Erdoğan claiming
that Gülenists who had secretly infiltrated the police and judiciary had created
a "parallel structure" (*paralel yapı*) seeking to undermine his rule.[66] Following
the botched coup in July 2016, Erdoğan accused anyone even remotely associated with the movement of being part of a terrorist organization (Fetullahçı
Terör Örgütü, FETÖ) that he blames for the attempt; picking up on *Star Wars*
lingo following the opening of the latest installment, a pro-government daily
compared Gülen to a "Sith lord."[67]

Prior to these animosities, however, in the first decade of AKP rule Gülenists
and AKP supporters worked in tandem in their contestation of Republican
Nationalist institutions, which both viewed as obstacles to the advancement of
their respective identity proposals: Ottoman Islamist for the AKP and Turkish
Calvinist for Gülenists, outlined below. In declaring his support for the AKP's
2010 referendum, which included a constitutional amendment revoking immu-
nity for military personnel involved in the 1980 coup from being tried for their
actions, Gülen stated: "First and foremost, it is a matter of shedding elements
of tutelage. Shedding this tutelage means that our people can think as themselves and that the path toward being themselves is opened."[68] This open display
of support marked a break from tradition for Gülen, who declares his mission
and that of his followers to be outside politics.[69] Similarly, during the *Ergenekon*
and *Balyoz* trials discussed in the previous chapter, Gülenists in the police and
judiciary, the same individuals who would later become the AKP's nemesis in
the corruption probe, were instrumental in prosecuting and jailing hundreds of

officers, journalists, and others on spurious charges but deemed to be threatening to the social purpose of opening the public sphere to Islam.[70] Gülen-sponsored media such as *Zaman* newspaper and the television networks Samanyolu TV and Mehtap TV, which generally broadcast television series that contain themes of piety and frequent references to Islam, were also used to provide supportive coverage of the AKP's initiatives. Between 2007 and 2013 *Today's Zaman*, the English-language newspaper of the Gülen-affiliated Feza Media Corporation, published an average of 1.6 stories a day supportive of the *Ergenekon* trials.[71]

Like Erdoğan, Gülen was also targeted during the February 28 Process, in which the RP was removed from power and Islamists were purged from public service, but he chose to leave Turkey, supposedly to seek medical treatment. It is precisely because of the two leaders' prior informal alliance, which Gülenists now largely deny,[72] that Erdoğan frequently claims that he and his followers were "betrayed" or "deceived."[73] As an indication of the relationship's devolution, publications from the pro-AKP Sabah media outlet shifted from referring to members as part of an innocuous *cemaat* (brotherhood/confessional community) led by "*Hocaefendi*" (term for a respected teacher/master) in 2011, to a shadowy *paralel yapı* in 2014, to a terrorist organization in 2018.[74]

Despite claims by both Erdoğan and Gülen that each is the better Muslim,[75] power struggles lie more at the center of the split than issues related specifically to identity. Indeed, a significant amount of overlapping identity content facilitated the leaders' collaboration in pushing back against Republican Nationalist institutions. Followers of both share the constitutive norm of being a pious Sunni Muslim and the common social purpose of expanding the place of Islam in the public sphere. The content of television shows on networks formerly owned by Gülenists represents a form of this expansion that mixes public and private spheres by, as Hikmet Kocamaner notes about Islamic-themed shows in general, "assisting the state in fighting social problems through their programming."[76] On the live cooking show *Yeşil Elma* (*Green Apple*), for example, host Oktay Usta uses dozens of Islamic phrases, such as *Allah razı olsun* and *Allah kabul etsin*, both meaning "may God approve/accept" and references to "our Prophet" ("*Peygamberimiz*") that stand out in their frequency when compared to other host-based shows.

The theme of piety running through the content of programming that appeared on Gülenist networks in many ways overlaps with that of Islamic media currently broadcast on AKP-affiliated networks to shape Erdoğan's "New Turkey," discussed in the concluding chapter. One of the ways in which Turkish Calvinism as a proposal for national identity differs, however, stems from how Gülenists pursue the social purpose of opening the public sphere to pious practices, partly because they come from a different tradition of Islam. Many of the highest ranking AKP leaders, for example, spent their early years as part of the Milli Görüş movement led by Erbakan and influenced by the Nakşibendi religious order. In contrast, Gülen is part of the Nurcu order, deriving his inspiration from the writings of Anatolian religious figure Bediüzzaman Said Nursi that were assembled by his followers into the volume *Risale-i Nur Külliyatı* (*The Epistles of Light*). Nursi strongly advocated promoting modernization, especially education and literacy, a theme that continue to influence followers of Nursi (Nurcular) today. A Gülen-friendly website, for example, emphasizes the role of Nursi in Turkey's modernization, quoting at length a historian who claims "today's modern Turkey isn't just the work of Atatürk, it is also Said Nursi's work."[77]

This emphasis on education, on spreading knowledge through reading and dialogue, manifests Gülenists' sense of *Hizmet,* or "service," the name members choose when referring collectively to themselves and their work. The component of service through education, which differentiates Gülenists from others, often takes the form of teaching abroad in the massive network of schools that finance Gülenists' work and serve as recruitment pools for the movement. Praise for the 2013 film *Selam* (*Greetings of Peace*) on Gülen's website, for example, lauds the "impressive stories of three Turkish teachers who are idealists working at schools opened by Turkish entrepreneurs on three different continents."[78] This Muslim missionary element represents the Calvinist part of the identity proposal. Although the term "Muslim Calvinists" has been used to describe the entrepreneurial spirit of pious Muslims in conservative Anatolian cities such as Konya and Kayseri,[79] I use the term Turkish Calvinism to characterize Gülenists' identity proposal because of their ardent focus on Turkish and Turkic culture. In this sense, while Gülenists share constitutive norms and social purpose with Ottoman Islamists, the relational meaning and cognitive worldview elements of their identity content overlap with Pan-Turkic Nationalists. Gülenists generally consider the faith of Muslim Turks' to be "true Islam," and that Arabs in former Ottoman territories negatively shaped Islam to reflect more of their own culture.[80] Evidence of efforts by the movement to convince Arabs themselves of this exists. An article describing an event at which Arab scholars discussed their experience with the Gülen movement, for example, quoted a Lebanese professor who declared that he felt he "had been reborn with *Hizmet*"; a Saudi professor speaks in a similar vein, stating: "Thanks to you, we learned how religion should be served, how service can be brought to people, to Muslims."[81] In sum, then, Turkish Calvinism is based on constitutive norms of piety, service, and Turkish culture; a social purpose of spreading Islam and knowledge of Turkish culture in the domestic and international spheres through education; a relational meaning oriented toward the Turkic world (but absent much of the anti-Westernism found in Pan-Turkic Nationalism); and a cognitive worldview of Turkey as home to the true version of Islam.

The engagement with Arabs mentioned above is one small part of the movement's massive international efforts through media, educational institutions, and events that Gülenists use to spread Turkish Calvinism abroad. Particularly in the wake of the 2016 coup attempt, Gülenists now have almost no space for their actions within Turkey, as their assets have been seized and movement members have been fired and jailed. This international outreach is by no means new, however, and is in fact integral to the movement's goals. While Gülen himself has quite literally taken his fight against Republican Nationalism outside by residing in exile in Pennsylvania, the global network of institutions he and his followers established also serves to advance Turkish Calvinism as a proposal for Turkey's national identity. Schools in more than 160 countries teach Turkish to students around the world and are highly competitive given the quality of education they are renowned for providing. They also serve as ambassadors for a particular understanding of Turkishness; a post on the official website of the Gülen schools states that "Turkish schools are excellent good will [*sic*] ambassadors for Turkey."[82] Gülen-affiliated organizations such as the Rumi Forum host events on Islam and trips for foreigners to visit Turkey. Events promoting Turkish culture, such as the Turkish Language Olympics (Türkçe Olimpiyatları), also provide an international platform for spreading interest in and knowledge of Turkish culture. The Turkish Language Olympics is an international forum in which fifteen thousand students up to age twenty-five from around the world compete to demonstrate their knowledge of Turkish language and culture by writing essays, singing songs, reciting poetry, and performing folk dances. The strong emphasis on education and Turkish culture is illustrative of the constitutive norms of the Turkish Calvinist proposal, while the competition's aim of spreading knowledge of Turkish culture illustrates one of its social purposes.[83]

Perhaps unsurprisingly given the purges of what the Turkish government calls FETÖcü individuals at home, the AKP has begun pushing back against Gülenist efforts abroad, suggesting an evolving contest between Ottoman Islamists and Turkish Calvinists for influence within the foreign policy arena. In Senegal, for example, the Turkish government established the Maarif Foundation (Maarif Vakfı) as an institution for overseeing Turkish education abroad—a move that would seem quite strange if one were unaware of the extensive network of schools established by Gülenists in more than thirty African countries. Starting with a school of only eight students in 1998, the Yavuz Selim network of educational institutions in Senegal grew to eleven schools with over three thousand students before the schools were taken over by the Maarif Foundation or closed in late 2017.[84] In Nigeria, the Turkish ambassador demanded that Gülen schools be closed amid massive protest from students and parents, whereas those in Somalia were shut within hours of the attempted coup.[85] The latter's rapid closure may have to do with the Somalian government's desire to continue benefiting from Turkish foreign aid; payments to Zanzibar, Tanzania's semiautonomous archipelago, were halted after the government's refusal to close the Gülen-affiliated Feza schools.[86] What began as efforts to pursue the social purpose of spreading Islamic education shared by Ottoman Islamists and Turkish Calvinists now suffers from the power struggle between the two groups' leaders. Students and teachers left without schools and/or funding now constitute unlikely but quite concrete victims of the externalization of that conflict to Africa.

Kurdish Nationalism/Western Liberalism

Whereas Gülenists were initially blocked in their efforts to spread Turkish Calvinism by the red line of secularism, and then by the AKP's post-putsch purges, Turkey's Kurdish population confronted the Republican and Pan-Turkic Nationalist red lines that prohibit the official recognition of Kurdish identity. Prior to the AKP era, in which no red line against recognition of the ethnicity of Kurds or any other group exists, the institutionally more powerful Republican Nationalists saw ethnicity as a conduit for separatist mobilization based on their experiences of Ottoman collapse, as discussed in chapter 4. Pan-Turkic Nationalists, whose supporters have carried out locally organized intimidation and violence against Kurdish targets, view the politicization of ethnicity by Kurds as a betrayal of their true Turkish ethnicity. Indeed, despite their many differences in identity content between their proposals, the shared view of Kurds as dangerous and/or traitorous united Republican and Pan-Turkic Nationalists in their support of the TSK's campaign against Kurdish YPG forces in Syria. This is an overlap the AKP used to thread the difficult needle of rallying nationalist support from otherwise disparate groups ahead of municipal, national, and presidential elections slated for 2019—the latter two of which were moved up to June 24, 2018.[87]

Blocked at the societal and institutional levels, Kurds varied as much in their strategies of resistance as they did in their desired goals. While perhaps bordering on the obvious, it is important to recognize that Kurds in Turkey do not share a monolithic identity proposal with consistent agreement on how to achieve a consistently agreed upon social purpose. Indeed, understanding Turkey's Kurdish question in its entirety required breaking down the differing forms of content supported by Kurds and identifying red lines among them. In Turkey alone, not to mention Kurdish groups in Syria, Iraq, and Iran, Kurds differ in constitutive norms of membership related to religion (Sunni, Alevi, other) and religiosity, as well as other factors related to language (whether knowledge of Kurdish is mandatory) and customs (traditional/rural versus modern/urban).

Social purpose varies from secession, to regional autonomy, to official minority status with protection of cultural rights, to being accepted as Turkish citizens without any special rights. Kurds also differ, if not as expressly as many citizens of Turkey would like, on the means of achieving that social purpose: the Kurdistan Workers' Party's armed assaults,[88] establishing political parties,[89] negotiations with the government,[90] or peaceful protest.[91]

Based loosely on these differences, among those who sought to externalize their struggle for Kurdish identity we could identify Kurdish Nationalists and Western Liberals, with the former supporting a specific proposal for Kurds' identity and the latter supporting a proposal for Turkey's national identity that accepts Kurds' rights to express their ethnicity if they so choose. Both groups have been highly effective in rallying support for their respective social purposes, particularly in their efforts to lobby within the EU. Indeed, one of Ankara's many complaints against the EU is that member states do not arrest Kurdish Nationalists that Turkey has identified as terrorists, a problem that evidence indicates Turkish intelligence officials tried to solve through assassinations of figures such as PKK cofounder Sakine Cansız in Paris in January 2013.[92] Irrespective of their belief in the use of violence, Kurds in Europe practice all the forms of inside-out identity contestation specified in this book: engagement with international institutions, diaspora groups, and activist networks in ways that intertwine the three.

Europe's large Kurdish diaspora, one that reflects many of the same identity divides present among Kurds in Turkey, provides a useful platform for trans-national efforts to advance Kurdish Nationalism and Western Liberalism by targeting institutions and civil society actors. With nearly half a million Kurds estimated to be living in Germany alone, they comprise a group that scholars consider one of the most politically active immigrant groups in Europe.[93] Catalyzed by Germany's outreach to Turkish citizens to come as guest workers (*Gastarbeiter*) for one year, nearly 200,000 individuals from Turkey entered Germany between 1961 and 1973, many of whom ended up staying and forming Turkish and Kurdish diasporas in the country.[94] Kurdish-language newspapers and television programming facilitated an Andersonian "imagined community" for Kurds and also provided a forum for collective mobilization.[95] Fiona Adamson and Madeleine Demetriou's discussion of the role of Kurds' activities in the European diaspora provides support for an inside-out identity contestation take on this mobilization: "[D]ispersed groups of Kurdish exiles and political exiles . . . interact[ed] and buil[t] dense networks across Europe in way that bypass, contest, and challenge official construction of national identity in Turkey."[96]

Although Kurdish Nationalists and Western Liberals cannot use the conditionality leverage of the EU in the same way a state actor such as the

AKP government can, their efforts to lobby EU institutions can help to put pressure on Ankara in its accession negotiations.[97] The European Commission's annual Regular Reports on Turkey, for example, reflect this pressure, urging Turkey to recognize minority rights and to solve the conflict waged between the Turkish military and the PKK since 1984.[98] Turkey's BDP established its own institutional presence to contribute to these discussions, including bringing then party leader Selahattin Demirtaş to speak to the European Parliament in December 2012.[99] Turkey's Kurds are not the only ones engaging in inside-out contestation in Europe. Other organizations claiming to represent all Kurds include the Kurdistan National Congress (Kongra Neteweyi ya Kurdistan, KNK), the successor to the Kurdish Parliament in Exile and an umbrella group that includes the Kurdish Institute of Brussels, founded in 1978 to be a "center for cultural and social development of our community here and in our homeland."[100] Within the European Parliament, a group called the European Friends of Kurdistan was created with twenty parliamentarians in 2014 to advance Kurdish causes mainly in Iraq, but also with the explicit support of the European branch of Turkey's HDP, a sister of and successor to the BDP.[101] In addition to putting pressure directly on the EU to apply its own pressure to Turkey, such organizations also offer Kurdish language courses, publish reports on the importance of the Kurdish question to democratization, and host international events such as the annual Brussels-based conference "The EU, Turkey, and the Kurds."[102] In sum, Kurds, although they may differ in terms of identity content across Kurdish Nationalists and Western Liberalists, constitute one of the most active diaspora groups in engaging in inside-out identity contestation to advance their understanding of national identity abroad and thus attempt to create space for that identity back home.

8

Conclusion

Just before midnight on July 15, 2016, I stood in a crowd of thousands in front of Turkey's parliament building in Ankara waiting for the arrival of President Erdoğan from Istanbul. The side of the building we faced was on İnönü Street, and it was flanked on another side by Atatürk Boulevard. The first two Turkish presidents after whom the streets were named, the leaders who crafted and institutionalized Republican Nationalism to the point of near hegemony, would have been displeased with the crowd around me, to put it mildly. The majority of women around me wore headscarves, and some were fully veiled; the crowd frequently shouted *allahu ekber* while waiting for the man many of them referred to as their *Reis* (captain). The tableau reflected some of the symbols of identity that Republican Nationalists had struggled ardently to eradicate.

The occasion for the gathering was the one-year anniversary of the defeat of a coup attempt undertaken by an improbable combination of ultra-secularist and Gülenist officers motivated by a mixture of personal and national interests. The occasion also marked nearly one year of AKP rule under a state of emergency that facilitated the purging of those suspected of supporting the putsch, those who signed the pro-Kurdish Academics for Peace (Barış için Akademisyenler) petition, and others in the opposition who were seen as threatening the vision of a "New Turkey" that Erdoğan seeks to institutionalize. In an ironic case of plus ça change,[1] the regime over which the Turkish leader presides recalls the authoritarianism of Republican Nationalist military tutelage, but the "stuff" or the content prescribing and proscribing policies could not be more different. Stark differences are manifested in foreign policy as well. Despite Erdoğan's sidelining of the creator of the strategic depth doctrine that prescribed a pivot to the East and South, under AKP rule Turkey continued to try to establish itself as a strong leader in the Middle East. Although mired in Syria by a shift in his approach to the Kurdish question, Erdoğan's Ottoman Islamist–laced advocacy of the Palestinian cause received a boost when, following his grandiose speech at the United Nations, 128 countries voted to reject the US recognition of Jerusalem as the capital of Israel;[2] a week earlier, Erdoğan had hosted an extraordinary meeting of the OIC to declare East Jerusalem as Palestine's capital. At this writing, Turkey-US and Turkey-EU relations are at an all-time low.

This book tackles the question of how this dramatic political and societal transformation was made possible in such a short amount of time, finding the answers in the actors' externalization of their identity contests. The theory of inside-out identity contestation I develop here posits that supporters of particular proposals for national identity struggle to spread their own versions across a population. By increasing the distribution of their own identity proposal, supporters not only increase individual self-esteem by achieving affirmation of their own understanding of national identity, but also increase their chances of realizing the interests generated by that identity—that is, of being in a position to carry out the domestic and foreign policies prescribed by that proposal. Crucial to this book's understanding of identity is that, just as the distribution of identity proposals across a population can shift through processes of contestation, the content of the proposals themselves is neither fixed nor exclusive. The elements of identity content constituting each composite proposal—from constitutive norms and social purpose to relational meanings and cognitive worldview—can change through contestation among supporters of competing proposals as well.

The preceding chapters examine two proposals' pursuits of identity hegemony in depth. Supporters of Republican Nationalism—a proposal that emerged among the majority (but not all) of military elites during the collapse of the Ottoman Empire and the struggle to liberate Turkey from Allied occupation, and whose content was fundamentally shaped by these constitutive experiences—strove to spread their proposal to the Turkish Republic's new citizens through drastic and far-reaching reforms affecting daily practices ranging from the clothes worn and the language used to the day of rest observed. With the institutions of Ottoman Islamism in decay and disrepute, Republican Nationalists faced few obstacles to their pursuit of hegemony that they could not overcome through brutal military suppression of ethnic- and religious-based rebellions. Although supporters progressed further in their attempt to achieve hegemony for Republican Nationalism than those of any other proposal in the republic's history, demonstrated in the relatively unchallenged presence of Atatürk in many (but not all) areas of public life and the embedding of his principles in Turkey's institutions of governance, their nationalizing project contained within it the seeds of its own demise. Contestation from within the proposal following the equally brutal 1980 military coup, when combined with the effects of Turkey's neoliberal economic opening, rising international criticism of the Kurdish problem, and the collapse of the Cold War order, weakened Republican Nationalism's position as an acceptable proposal for Turkey's national identity in many citizens' eyes.

Despite the contestation in the public sphere, the institutionalization of Republican Nationalism—in the military (via the MGK), the judicial system (via the Constitutional Court), and the higher education system (via university rectors), as analyzed in chapter 5—enabled its supporters to combat what were perceived as direct assaults on the principles of Atatürk by Ottoman Islamists prior to the AKP. The February 28 Process, initiated just five years before the AKP would take power, demonstrated the importance of identity-based obstacles in fending off the rise of political Islam: the MGK forced the increasingly successful Islamist RP out of power; the Constitutional Court shut down the party and banned its leader, Erbakan, from politics; and university rectors forbade female students wearing headscarves from entering university campuses. Thus, while Republican Nationalists were able to contest alternative proposals in the domestic sphere after abolishing the decrepit sultanate and caliphate, Ottoman Islamists under the newly formed AKP recognized the power of existing identity-based obstacles.

Choosing to take their identity contestation outside to the foreign policy arena, Ottoman Islamists not only circumvented domestic obstacles but also weakened them by engaging actively in the EU accession process. As chapter 6 demonstrates, electively carrying out the EU-mandated democratization reforms enabled the AKP to significantly reduce the military's influence in politics as well as to alter the makeup of the Constitutional Court. With a weakened military unable to block the selection of Gül as president in 2007, for the first time an Islamist filled the traditionally Republican Nationalist role, whose duties include selecting high court judges and university rectors. The AKP's ability to weaken identity-based obstacles by pursuing an EU-oriented foreign policy made it possible for the party to then begin realizing its Ottoman Islamist interests in domestic and foreign policy. Thus, in its second term, and much more aggressively in its third and fourth terms, the AKP began to act on its social purpose of opening space for Islam in the public sphere and reorienting Turkey's foreign policy toward Muslim populations and former Ottoman territories—a time lag and a degree of shift that serve as motivating puzzles for this research. While the AKP has enacted major changes in domestic and foreign policy in line with behaviors prescribed by Ottoman Islamist identity content, the Gezi Park protests and the withdrawal of support for the AKP by Gülenists represent serious and widespread challenges to its pursuit of hegemony. The radicalization of the rhetoric used and policies enacted by the AKP, exemplified by the open glorification of Hitler following Israel's 2014 attacks on Gaza, also serves to marginalize the proposal by making its support no longer tolerable for some. Although it is impossible to determine from this study whether this radicalization represents more of a change in constitutive norms of appropriate behavior among Ottoman Islamists, an increasing willingness to publicly express existing beliefs, or a combination of the two across the proposal's supporters, it has recently become clear that, like the case of Republican Nationalism, Ottoman Islamists' pursuit of hegemony may also become its own undoing.

In addition to these two cases of contestation among competing proposals that form the bulk of the book's case studies, chapter 4 also demonstrates that interaction through contestation from within a proposal can produce moderation among those recognizing inappropriate or anachronistic elements of their proposal's identity content. The content of Republican Nationalism in its current iteration is noticeably more moderate in terms of what are deemed to be threats to its principles than that of the Republican Nationalist identity proposal as it existed until the mid-1980s.[3] Further, chapter 4 also shows that new identity proposals may form through collectively recognized discontent with the content of existing proposals, as was the case for Western Liberalism. This may also be the case for some Gülenists who have removed their support from the AKP and its Ottoman Islamist identity project and distance themselves from the movement. As seen in chapter 7, although Gülenists share constitutive norms of Sunni Islam and piety with Ottoman Islamists, as well as the social purpose of opening space for Islam's role to guide domestic and foreign policy, identity content differences suggest that their proposal can be best understood as Turkish Calvinism. A conflict of interest between the most prominent figures leading the charge for each proposal eliminated all collaboration among their supporters against Republican Nationalism, at least for the moment. While power struggles can create temporary disruptions, the absence of identity red lines helps illuminate the potential for cooperation among supporters of different proposals in pursuit of a shared social purpose. Political alliances may form and fall apart, but one should not expect collaboration among Republican Nationalists and Ottoman Islamists (or Pan-Turkic Nationalists and Western Liberalists).

While most of the focus of this study has been on examining differences in identity that generate contestation among supporters of competing proposals, common elements of content can also be identified using the identity content framework outlined in chapter 2 and fleshed out chapter 3. Common elements, such as shared beliefs about the constitutive norms of membership in an in-group being based on civic rather than ethnic or religious criteria (e.g., Western Liberalism and Republican Nationalism); about the social purpose of increasing space for freedom of religious expression in the public sphere (e.g., Western Liberalism and Ottoman Islam); and about relational meanings that characterize the West as a hostile out-group (Ottoman Islamism and Pan-Turkic Nationalism) form points of convergence regarding issues of identity. These points of convergence can form the identity content basis—the "stuff" common to otherwise rival supporters—around which hybrid proposals can form through interaction while mutually contesting another group aspiring to hegemony.

As the conclusion to this book, I investigate the potential for such a proposal to shift the contours of Turkey's identity debates. As a result of the Gezi protests, it became clear that supporters of Western Liberalism and Republican Nationalism, as well as some Pan-Turkic Nationalists, were united in their rejection of Ottoman Islamism. While the identity contestation manifested during the protests primarily involved objections to the encroachment of Ottoman Islamism into daily lives, Gezi also served as a forum for contestation of foreign policy initiatives. In an interview during the protests, for example, Liberal Demokrat Partisi (Liberal Democrat Party, LDP) chairman Cem Toker stated that one of his main grievances with the AKP was that its prime minister and foreign minister were living in a "fantasyland . . . dreaming of the Ottoman Empire," refusing to see that "Western civilization" provides a much more appropriate model for Turkey's behavior in international relations.[4] Pan-Turkic Nationalists similarly ridiculed the AKP's attempts to extend Turkey's influence in former Ottoman territories, while criticizing its lack of support for Turkic Tatars in Crimea following Russia's annexation and for the peoples of Turkmen-populated Mosul in the light of ISIL's attack on and capture of Turkish embassy staff. Suggesting that former foreign minister Davutoğlu's foreign policy efforts were both misplaced and ridden with folly, a recent journal published by former MHP MP Ümit Özdağ's 21st Century Turkey Institute (21. Yüzyıl Türkiye Enstitüsü) contained articles with headings such as "Davutoğlu Syndrome or Alice in Wonderland" and "Ahmet Davutoğlu: A Don Quixote in the Balkans."[5] Republican Nationalists also expressed grave concerns over foreign policy initiatives they deemed to be overly aggressive to the point of bordering on irredentism, thus endangering Turkey's borders, a clear red line in terms of both constitutive norms of protecting Atatürk's legacy and the cognitive worldview of Turkey as a noninterventionist state focused on its own internal development. A former chairman of the Marmaris region's branch of the Atatürkist Thought Association (Atatürkçü Düsünce Derneği) articulated this sentiment well, arguing that the ubiquitous display of Atatürk's portrait during the protests was evidence of an AKP threat to the vision the republic's founding father had for Turkey.[6]

(Red) Lines at the Polls:
Identity Divides among the Opposition

Despite these supporters' common contestation of Ottoman Islamism's domestic and foreign policies, it would be a grave mistake to assume they comprise a united front that could pose a serious electoral challenge in the current climate. An examination of the points of intolerability among their identity proposals reveals significant challenges to the viability of a hybrid identity. For example, the constitutive norms of behavior for Pan-Turkic Nationalists do not differ dramatically from the Ottoman Islamist behavioral norms, whose translation into legislation was a point of intolerability for Republican Nationalists and Western Liberalists. In central Anatolia, an area in which many of the most ardent supporters of Pan-Turkic Nationalism reside, being a Sunni Muslim is widely considered to be "integral" to being a good Turkish nationalist.[7] Indeed, as Hakan Yavuz notes, in this region in particular "the re-lationship between Islam and Turkish nationalism is one not of contradiction and conflict but rather of mutual enhancement."[8] In contrast, the Republican Nationalist constitutive norm of respect for the legacy of Atatürk is unaccept-able to Pan-Turkic Nationalists, who, like Ottoman Islamists, view him as the figure responsible for the repression of their religious rights and their perse-cution as a collectivity under an absolutist secularist regime. The Republican Nationalist social purpose of protecting secularism domestically is thus in-compatible with pious Pan-Turkic Nationalists' belief in the importance of Islam in the public sphere as an integral part of traditional Turkish culture. As a member of the ultra-right-wing Hearths of Ideals (Ülkü Ocakları) posted on his highly religiously themed Facebook feed: "[T]here are two 'national' things we don't like: the National Lottery (Milli Piyango, considered to be a violation of Islamic morals) and the National Chief (Milli Şef, the name given to Republican Nationalist İsmet İnönü when he became president upon Atatürk's death in 1938)."[9] Members of Turkey's ultra-right-wing MHP echoed this sentiment in a lengthy discussion of the "natural fit" between being Muslim and being Turkish.[10]

Western Liberalists do not, in principle, object to Ottoman Islam's so-cial purpose of expanding the role of Sunni Islam in the public sphere or establishing closer ties with Muslim countries, or perhaps even with the cog-nitive worldview of Turkey as the leader of the Islamic world. Based on the constitutive norm of religious freedom, to take the most visible and highly contested example, Western Liberalists support the right of women to wear headscarves in public offices and in universities, as Ottoman Islamism's social purpose aimed to achieve. However, in line with their constitutive norms of equality, Western Liberalists share concerns that the gender-equality language used by supporters of Ottoman Islamism to justify the expansion of headscarf rights in terms of women's liberation is disingenuous. Western Liberalist and former CHP deputy chairman Şafak Pavey's speech in parliament on the day headscarved deputies took their oaths for the first time in the republic's his-tory, for example, noted critical areas in which women's rights that intersect with Islam have not been advanced, such as Turkish girls covering at the age of five and marrying at age fifteen. It is important to note, therefore, that the

Western Liberalist identity proposal's constitutive norms of freedoms and equality would indeed clash quite profoundly with the public expansion of Sunni Islam supported by Pan-Turkic Nationalists if (a) it was at the expense of individuals with other beliefs, such as Alevis, non-Muslims, and atheists; or (b) individuals, including women of all forms of belief, felt compelled to conform to the practices of pious Sunni Muslims due to familial, work, or societal/neighborhood pressures (*mahalle baskısı*).[11]

Moving from identity content related to religion to that connected with ethnicity, the exclusion of the constitutive norm of ethnocultural Turkishness from any proposal for Turkey's national identity constitutes a point of incommensurability for Pan-Turkic Nationalists. While they have much in common with Ottoman Islamists, Pan-Turkic Nationalists interviewed specifically criticized Erdoğan for failing to refer to the Turkish nation in his speeches, a point of significant consternation (addressed following an AKP-MHP electoral alliance). Tellingly from an identity contestation perspective, one interviewee in Trabzon quipped: "He doesn't know how to be Turkish."[12] Similarly, any recognition of Kurds as a separate ethnic group and the granting of Kurdish rights is, for Pan-Turkic Nationalists, a red line that cannot be crossed. Previously united on the common ground they found within the constitutive norm of Sunni Islam, many Pan-Turkic Nationalists—who generally vote for parties such as the MHP and the BBP but refused to vote for their common designated candidate in the August 2014 presidential election because they deemed him insufficiently nationalist[13]—also refused to vote for Erdoğan, in great part due to their objections to the AKP's 2013–15 efforts to make peace with the Kurds by negotiating with imprisoned leader of the PKK Abdullah Öcalan. A National Party (Ulusal Parti) deputy chairman used the familiar Pan-Turkic Nationalist phrase "Turkey belongs to Turks" in an interview to explain his contempt for the AKP's aborted peace process with the Kurds; he qualified this response using identity-based language, stating that the ones who are not Turks are the AKP.[14]

While moderated Republican Nationalists have become more tolerant toward recognizing Kurdish identity, in large part as a result of the contestation by the İkinci Cumhuriyetçiler of the reflexive interpretation and dogmatic application of Atatürk's principles, they remain staunchly opposed to any politicization of ethnic identity in the form of political parties or demands for regional autonomy. In demonstration of both politically anti-ethnic attitudes and their commitment to secularism, many Republican Nationalists, including former president Sezer—who became famous for his guardianship of Atatürk's principles by vetoing more legislation than any other president—boycotted the 2014 presidential election. Those boycotting, some of whom would later break off from the CHP and form the Anatolian Party (Anadolu Partisi), refused to vote for former OIC head Ekmeleddin İhsanoğlu because they deemed him an Islamist,

and found HDP candidate Selahattin Demirtaş's history with the Kurdish nationalist movement a red line they could not abide. One traditional CHP voter
commented, using the Turkish custom of repeating a word with an "m" in front
of it when speaking of something with disdain: "Ekmeleddin Mekmeleddin—
that's not Turkish, it's Arabic." This "Other-ization" of the candidate based on his
name in both religious and ethnolinguistic terms represents a dismissal of him as
an appropriate choice.[15] In contrast, these restrictive views on religion and ethnicity are viewed as limitations on freedoms of cultural expression by Western
Liberalists, among whom many were İkinci Cumhuriyetçiler.

Like the norm of Sunni Islam, Pan-Turkic Nationalists also share with
Ottoman Islamists a relational meaning depicting the West as a historically hostile Other, which is a red line for supporters of the other two proposals. Pan-
Turkic Nationalists oppose any but the most perfunctory relations with Europe
and generally view the United States as an imperialist enemy. Further, a core social
purpose for the latter group consists of promoting the well-being of Turkish and
Turkic peoples and ideally culminates in the formation of a cultural or even political union of the Turkic population scattered throughout Central Asia and the
Middle East. While a single political institution governing all Turkic peoples may
never materialize out of the "romantic desire for Turkish unity,"[16] subscribers to
this identity understanding share a belief in the desirability and even the naturalness of a union of Turkic peoples. Their relational meaning and cognitive worldview are thus incompatible with those of Republican Nationalists and Western
Liberalists. The former orient themselves westward—viewing the former Soviet
Turkic states as "backward"—and avoid international engagements when at all
possible in order to safeguard Turkey's territory and borders. In contrast with
Pan-Turkic and Republican Nationalisms, the latter strongly support active international engagement to promote democracy and human rights on a global
scale without any regional focus.

Although each of these three proposals contains points of intolerability
that motivate its followers to contest Ottoman Islamism, they all also contain
red lines when comparing each to the others. Furthermore, identities forming
around common points of interest can almost immediately become polarized
when one of the red lines of an identity proposal is crossed or a point of intolerability becomes manifest. To provide a concrete example, a very clear case of this
refortification of an identity proposal's constitutive norms of membership arose
among Republican Nationalists and Western Liberalists when several statues of
Atatürk were set on fire in the wake of Turkey's failure to protect the Kurdish-
majority Syrian town of Kobani from ISIL. The language used by Republican
Nationalists to condemn this insult evoked a hardening of boundaries among
groups that seemed to be finding common identity ground during the Gezi
protests in terms of social purpose, relational meaning, and cognitive worldview.

From a broader conceptual perspective, this erosion of the progress being made toward the formation of a new hybrid identity in Turkey provides insight into the challenges of fusing together groups who become united in their common opposition to a group with an even more different, less compatible identity proposal.[17] A brief discussion of the above-mentioned example of violence directed toward the Atatürk statues and their Republican Nationalist symbolism to protest the inaction of a distinctly non–Republican Nationalist government serves to illustrate this point. Kobani became a focal point of international attention when the radical group ISIL launched a major offensive against it on September 16, 2014, as part of its menacing spread across Syria. Despite numerous pleas from Kurdish political and civil society actors in Turkey as well as from the international community, as of the time of writing Turkey has refused to contribute militarily to the fight against ISIL in Syria, including in its neighboring Kobani. From many Kurds' perspectives, Turkey was "turning a blind eye" to ISIL and, at worst, has "stabbed [Kurds] in the back" by allowing ISIL fighters to flow across Turkey's borders and fights against an Erdoğan persona non grata, Bashar al-Assad.[18] Kurds and others in Turkey, appalled by Turkey's lack of action to shield residents of Kobani from what appeared to be an imminent massacre, staged widespread protests across Turkey's southeastern provinces as well as in large cities such as Ankara and Istanbul.

Demonstrations against the government's inaction in Kobani were generally less peaceful than the Gezi protests. During Gezi, participants made a deliberate point of self-policing to ensure that protesters didn't throw stones or damage property, thus delegitimizing the AKP government's claims that Gezi protesters were *çapulcular*, as discussed below.[19] Kobani protesters, however, not only damaged property but selected specific targets for destruction. While the torching and stoning of public buses may be interpreted as an act of rebellion against local branches of the AKP government, the burning of several Atatürk statues[20] targeted a very different source of grievance and, in turn, alienated supporters of a different identity proposal. Recalling the deeply seated, constitutive norm of respect for (sometimes bordering on adoration of) Atatürk among Republican Nationalists, and chapter 4's discussion of Atatürk's violent suppression of Kurdish uprisings in his efforts to disseminate his anti-ethnic,[21] civic-oriented proposal, defilement of Atatürk symbols by Kurds and their sympathizers becomes understandable as both an intolerable insult and a self-empowering act of violence against a formerly powerful pursuer of identity hegemony.

As an application of this book's framework of identity proposals makes clear, Turkey's protracted refusal to participate in military strikes targeted solely toward ISIL—a foreign policy action called for by Western Liberalists on the basis of human rights violations and concerns about ethnic cleansing of Kurds—were not based on any ethnic antipathy toward Kurds. An ethnic criterion of exclusion does not exist among the constitutive norms of the membership of the Ottoman Islamist proposal. Rather, Turkey's inaction until July 2015 stemmed from on Erdoğan's insistence that anti-ISIL strikes should also target Assad, whom Erdoğan viewed as stymying his vision of Turkey's regional leadership of Sunni Muslims—a clear Ottoman Islamist social purpose that may also help explain Turkey's arming of Jabhat al-Nusra and the accompaniment of Turkish military forces by Hay'at Tahrir al-Sham as they advanced into Syria in February 2018.[22] Importantly for an identity contestation perspective, as well as for any (however unlikely) future prospects for the resolution of the Kurdish question in Turkey under AKP rule, the 2015 reinitiation of war with the PKK and the TSK's related campaign against Kurdish YPG forces in Syria are not ethnically motivated. Rather, a combination of domestic political interests served to scuttle the 2013-2015 "solution process" (çözüm süreci) when Kurds, frustrated with the lack of support and even betrayal in Kobani, withdrew their support for Erdoğan's project to convert Turkey's parliamentary system of governance into a highly centralized presidency; former HDP co-chair (jailed as of this writing) declared "as long as there is an HDP we won't make you president."[23] His party's unprecedented gain of 13% of the vote in the June 7, 2015 general elections, while celebrated by Western Liberalists, was seen by AKP supporters as robbing them of the parliamentary majority they had sustained since coming to power in 2002.[24] As the AKP stalled in forming a coalition government and then called for fresh elections, the Turkish armed forces' renewed campaign against the PKK provided a rally around the flag effect that, when combined with newly nationalist rhetoric from Erdoğan and is supporters, contributed to the AKP's reclaiming a parliamentary majority in November.[25] As suggested in the previous chapter, Turkey's campaign against the YPG, while undoubtedly fueled by security concerns as Turkey rightly sees the Syrian militia as a branch of the PKK, threads a challenging needle by rallying support from both Republican and Pan-Turkic Nationalists in the run-up to local, parliamentary and presidential elections originally slated for 2019—the latter two of which were moved up to June 24, 2018.

Gezi Protests: The Makings of a Hybrid Proposal?

Electorally speaking, the AKP had faced little in terms of serious political competition throughout its first three terms in power, increasing its share of the vote and its seats in parliament in each general election since achieving its first parliamentary majority in 2002 as a newly formed party. Although founded by members of Erbakan's FP, the AKP seemed to represent a more progressive wing of the Islamist MGH. Its founders proclaimed that the AKP was a conservative democratic party, differentiating themselves from the Saadet Partisi (Felicity Party), an openly Islamist party founded by the traditionalists of the MGH. In its first years in power, the AKP appealed to domestic and international audiences alike as a party that was focused on tangible results for its constituents, as well as presenting a "Turkish model" for other countries in the region.[26] A common phrase used to explain why someone votes for the AKP is some version of "Look at what Tayyip [Erdoğan] did: the third bridge, the airport. . . . What did the other guys do? Nothing."[27]

As electorally successful as the AKP has been, even winning a referendum vote in 2010 that allowed the government to amend the constitution, the events comprising the Gezi Park protests of 2013 screamed the news that its attempts to spread Ottoman Islamism as a proposal for Turkey's identity had been ultimately unsuccessful. Previously politically apathetic individuals, including huge swathes of Turkey's youth, turned out in the millions to voice their criticism of the AKP, its increasingly illiberal actions, and its policies designed to raise a pious (*dindar*), conservative (*muhafazakar*) generation. The swell of opposition that was catalyzed and spread within hours of camera-phone images showing Turkish police forces beating peaceful demonstrators in Gezi Park and setting tents on fire while others slept in them unleashed a torrent of criticism against the AKP. The events collectively known as "Gezi," which began in May 2013 as an environmental sit-in to protect a park adjacent to Istanbul's Taksim Square from demolition, rapidly evolved into massive, countrywide protests. Demonstrations showing solidarity with the Gezi movement were recorded in all of Turkey's eighty-one provinces except Bayburt, located in Turkey's Black Sea region, and lasted over three months.[28]

Although the protests were initially mobilized by the images of police violence and the ensuing media silence resulting from a clampdown by outlets owned by large media conglomerates with financial ties to the AKP,[29] my analysis of the political culture of Gezi reveals that deep-seated issues of identity undergirded much of the outrage fueling protesters' return to the streets each evening after work. Based on the diagnostic evidence (to use the language of process tracing) that I refer to here, I argue that the Gezi protests represent the first major, sustained contestation of the Ottoman Islamist proposal for national identity in Turkey. Indeed, Gezi's genesis can be seen as a synecdoche of anti–Ottoman Islamist contestation: the social movement's roots lie in environmentalists' attempting to prevent a demolition project that would have made way for a reconstruction of Topçu Kışlası, the Ottoman-style military barracks destroyed in 1940. In terms of wider grievances, demonstrators referenced Erdoğan's sultanesque rule of his own political and media empires; the indiscriminate use of violence against peaceful demonstrators that Erdoğan hailed as acts of heroism by "*my* police" carried the Ottoman Islamist theme of a despot with his forces of oppression at his unchecked disposal.[30] Similar to the AKP's control of Ottoman imagery evidenced in its censure of the series *Muhteşem Yüzyıl* for its racy scenes and portrayal of alcohol consumption by palace notables, the AKP also appears to have tried to prevent one of the last descendants of the sultan's line from demonstrating at Gezi. Adile Osmanoğlu, the granddaughter of Abdülhamid II, stated in an interview with Bugün TV that a "figure close to Recep Tayyip Erdoğan threatened" her after she was seen visiting the site of the protest.[31] As an important if anecdotal indication that the events of Gezi pose a challenge to the AKP's Ottoman Islamist project, even the sultan's relative, who stated that before the events of Gezi "Erdoğan was a person whom [she] trust[ed] and respected," had lost respect for its identity proposal.

In addition to the Ottoman despot theme, discourse used by protestors throughout the ongoing demonstrations carried many other references to identity. Late Turkish and Ottoman history expert Halil İnalcık summed up all of the events surrounding the Gezi protests as an "identity issue" (*kimlik meselesi*) that represented the increasing polarization among secular and pious Turks. He noted that today there are "*Selamünaleyküm diyenler*" ("Those who say 'peace be with you,'" a greeting rooted in Islam) and "*Merhaba diyenler*" ("those who greet you with 'hello,'" a greeting with no religious connotation in Turkey), recounting a personal experience in which his insistence on using "*merhaba*" displeased colleagues (*pek hoşlanmadılar*) who invited him to a conference in the conservative city of Bursa, and who then treated him with disdain. He then elaborated on this theme by stating that Gezi was a gathering of those who wish to still be able to greet people by saying *merhaba* without being judged negatively or being excluded from a group.[32]

Along these lines, the rejection of Ottoman Islamism's social purpose of spreading Islam in the public sphere was prominent during Gezi. One of the most popular slogans of Republican Nationalists, "Turkey is secular and will remain secular!" ("*Türkiye laiktir, laik kalacak!*") was chanted hundreds of times.[33] A slogan spray-painted on a wall during Gezi mocks the questions posed to Islamic scholars during Ramadan, often broadcast live during programs shown before the *iftar* meal breaking the day's fast. While traditional questions asked during such broadcasts include whether brushing one's teeth or swearing breaks one's fast, the slogan at Gezi reads: "Teacher, does pepper spray break one's fast?"[34] Another spray-painted slogan reads, "You banned alcohol, people sobered up,"[35] an apt depiction of the many Islam-inspired incursions into daily life that provoked generally apathetic segments of Turkey's population into rising up against the spread of Ottoman Islamism. The restriction on the sale of alcohol, including a ban in all university campus facilities, is one of the many incursions to which Gezi protesters from many varied backgrounds objected. Alevis, non-Muslims, nonbelievers, and

Sunni Muslims gathered together to oppose the steps taken to restrict abortions and increase fertility in general, regulations against co-ed housing, conversion of some middle schools into *imam hatip* (preacher training schools), and other religiously oriented policies viewed as intolerable by supporters of alternative proposals for national identity in Turkey.

In addition to challenges of Ottoman Islamism's perceived threats to secular lifestyles, particularly raised by Republican Nationalists but also advocated by Western Liberalists who viewed the imposition of religion as a violation of personal liberties, Ottoman Islamism's constitutive norms of gender and sexual identity also constituted a widespread, unifying challenge by strikingly diverse groups of demonstrators. For Turkey's LGBTQ community, Gezi's concomitant diversity and solidarity represented a unique locus for the expression of sexual identities previously unthinkable in public spaces given the deep-seated prejudices against homosexuality discussed in chapter 3. Two LGBTQ activists expressed great hope about the newly created space for LGBTQs during the Gezi protests, stating that the supportive atmosphere among those demonstrating provided a safe space to protest Ottoman Islamists' open denunciation of homosexuality for people to whom "solidarity means a lot."[36] The communal spirit of Gezi and the breadth of its mobilizational capacity also facilitated numerous interactions among LGBTQs and those with admitted previous prejudices that, in true constructivist fashion, created "transformative contributions" to how actors viewed each other; by standing up against tear gas and water cannons, gay and trans community members showed they could be "as *delikanlı* (tough guy) as the rest."[37] The activist providing this insight noted that the LGBTQ Block's use of rainbow-colored banners, pamphlets, and slogans enabled the group to maintain "visibility in the daily life of the Park, and such attempts opened ways in which new acquaintances became possible." Responding to a question posed one month after the protests began about how Gezi affected the LGBTQ struggle in Turkey, one trans-activist sums up a change in behavior whose significance cannot be overstated:

> From now on, individuals who take to the streets in resistance will behave much differently toward LGBTQ individuals. In the first days many homophobic and sexist slogans were chanted and scrawled on our walls. Once feminist organizations and the LGBTQ Block began objecting to this together with other groups, representatives from the Çarşı group came to us to apologize with a bouquet of flowers in their hands. They said: "We're used to being this way. We were raised this way, but actually we really like you. We don't have anything against you [*Size bir lafımız yok*]." This was the beginning of a dialogue. People will stop and try to understand each other based on this.[38]

Çarşı is the group of fans supporting the Beşiktaş soccer club, one of Istanbul's three largest along with Fenerbahçe and Galatasaray, and it served as a massive mobilizer of demonstrators during the protests. The rivalry among the three clubs is notorious and long-standing, making the displays of solidarity among supporters of the three, with their arms around each others' shoulders, another image emblematic of the unique, if perhaps temporary, unifying power of Gezi. That Çarşı supporters also reached out to the LGBTQ community by apologizing for their previously bigoted language also represents a potential inflection point in which red lines delineating unacceptable behavior can be softened and even erased through the constitutive act of protesting together. One activist, commenting on the change in how gay and trans individuals are viewed and treated in Turkey, stated that "Gezi did in three weeks what otherwise would have taken us three years."[39]

Large numbers of women participating in the Gezi protests also posed numerous challenges to Ottoman Islamism's patriarchal view of women's role in society. When Istanbul's AKP mayor Hüseyin Avni Mutlu's demands that mothers come to collect their children from Gezi essentially reduced the role of women to that of submissive housewives, mothers turned up in droves to form a human chain around their supposedly "delinquent" children.[40] The spirit of defiance and independence of such women, incompatible with Ottoman Islamism's constitutive norms of appropriate behavior, also manifested itself in a razor-sharp and immensely creative use of wit to challenge Ottoman Islamism. One female protestor poked fun at Erdoğan's ardently socially conservative call for women to have three or more children and his aspiration of a new pious generation by spray-painting "Are you sure you want three kids like *us*?"[41] A similarly themed sign, held by a woman standing behind her smiling and headscarved mother, read "I'll have three kids, I promise!" and included stick-figure drawings of children named ÇapulCan, ÇapulNaz, and ÇapulNur[42]—adding common Turkish names to the insult "*çapulcu*" (hooligan). Protesters began defiantly calling themselves *çapulcu* after Erdoğan dismissed the Gezi protests as being the work of "*birkaç çapulcu*" ("a few hooligans").[43] Another woman, defying those who would characterize all headscarved women as Ottoman Islamists and providing ample caution to the researcher against making quick conclusions, held a sign reading "My head is covered but my eyes are not, *Tayyip be!*"[44]

By ridiculing particular aspects of Ottoman Islamism as promoted by the AKP government, supporters of other proposals engaged in a delegitimization campaign against the push for Ottoman Islamist identity hegemony with the limited tools at their disposal. Using their only really effective access to the foreign policy arena as a strategy for taking their contestation outside, opponents of Ottoman Islamism took to Twitter, Facebook, Instagram, YouTube, and other social media sharing sites to internationalize their discontent with the identity proposal being, as they viewed it, forced upon them. International solidarity movements in dozens of countries, inspired by and imitating the resilient wit displayed by Turkey's protesters in the face of disproportionate violence, put pressure on their respective governments to respond to the AKP's behavior. While harsh reprimands did come from individual countries and from the EU (in the form of the 2013 annual EU Progress Report on Turkey, whose criticism was deliberately toned down at the request of Turkey's Ministry for EU Affairs),[45] the potential effects of the boomerang model conceptualized by Keck and Sikkink were not realized,[46] due to many factors, including the AKP's extensive control over numerous media outlets;, the obstinacy of the prime minister himself; and crucially, a large proportion of Ottoman Islamist identity supporters who believe that the protesters' behavior was immoral and that their leader should have the authority to exercise complete control whenever he deems it necessary.

In the face of these obstacles to contestation of identity in both the domestic and foreign policy realms, the thousands of creative uses of humor in the easily accessible and relatively anonymous realm of social media that protesters employed to challenge the AKP's pursuit of hegemonic power recalls the strategies used by James Scott's subjects in *Weapons of the Weak*.[47] Scott enumerates the many strategies, including prank-pulling and name-calling, that those who are otherwise powerless in the face of repression use to incrementally erode the legitimacy of their repressors. Simultaneously, those engaged in seemingly minor acts of subversion of authority also strengthen their own sense of self-worth and create bonds of solidarity that unite them as a newly recognized "Us," or experientially constituted collectivity, in opposition to a common "Them."

The female protester's use of the word "us" in comically challenging Erdoğan by asking if he wanted three children like "us" noted above underscores well the of "Us versus Them" discourse that constitutes the recently catalyzed contestation by those challenging Ottoman Islamism and by those defending it. Erdoğan's many responses to the incredibly diverse group categorized all protesters as a monolithic and immoral "Them." Then-EU minister Egemen Bağış further "Other-ized"[48] dissenters by calling them terrorists,[49] and Erdoğan accused them of engaging in behaviors particularly offensive to supporters of an Ottoman Islamist identity proposal, such as drinking alcohol in a mosque and assaulting and urinating on a headscarved woman waiting for a ferry with her infant. Erdoğan's language describing the supposed attack on the woman, later proven to be false by camera footage along with the claims about alcohol,[50] is particularly notable from an "Us versus Them" perspective and even repetitive in its emphasis on the headscarf as a symbol of "us": "Is it now up to you [MHP

General Secretary Devlet Bahçeli] to defend the Gezi vandals against *our* head-scarved girl who was lynched with her headscarf and her 6-month child at her side?"[51] Conversely, using the language of Ottoman Islamism in an inclusive way, *Yeni Şafak* correspondent Süleyman Gündüz, who was present at the mosque when the supposedly alcohol-consuming protesters sought shelter from the tear gas being used by police, stressed that not only was alcohol not consumed but that those entering "took off their shoes" as a sign of respect.[52]

Through the use of Other-izing discourse, however, Ottoman Islamists si-multaneously delegitimized the peaceful civil protests in which citizens of Turkey were engaging while making it quite clear that they were excluded from being "our" citizens. Erdoğan even extended his hostile Other-izing line of thinking to the international realm, claiming that foreign forces, including a shady "interest lobby" (*faiz lobisi*),[53] were trying to prevent Turkey's rise as a strong state under his leadership by fueling the Gezi protests as a destabi-lization mechanism. In a speech to party supporters, Erdoğan called CNN International reporter Ivan Watson, who was taken into custody while filming the protests in Taksim despite showing his full press credentials, an intelli-gence agent (*ajan*) and a flunky (*dalkavuk*), receiving thunderous applause and cheering. Using language consistent with Ottoman Islamism's anti-Western re-lational meaning and cognitive worldview of Turkey as the legitimate inheritor of the imperial legacy with its leader in a sultan-esque role, Erdoğan answered his own question of why CNN International would show nonstop footage of the events at Gezi: "To mess with *my* country (*ülkemi karıştırmak için*), to show *my* country differently to the world."[54]

Ottoman Islamists were not alone in using "Us versus Them" rhetoric during Gezi, however; despite the overall diverse and inclusive atmosphere that characterized Gezi, some exclusionary elements of Pan-Turkic and Republican Nationalist identity content also manifested themselves during the protests. Some protesters displaying Kurdish colors and using Kurdish slogans were jeered at or threatened by those who insisted that all present were Turks. Pan-Turkic Nationalist interviewees stated they were at Gezi to defend the Turkish nation from corruption by an "Ottomanist" who misunderstands Turks' true Central Asian legacy, and that Kurdishness had no place there.[55] A warning posted for protesters from Istanbul's largely Republican Nationalist Fenerbahçe soccer club (Atatürk was a Fenerbahçe fan)[56] delineated what forms of iden-tity expression would be tolerated: "Attention please!!! During the march only the Turkish flag, the Fenerbahçe flag, and the flags of friends' teams we want to see beside us will be carried."[57] Although the welcoming of teams other than Fenerbahçe was a significant gesture, the message implicit in specifying the Turkish flag was that Kurdish flags must not be displayed. While some groups of

Western Liberalist protesters openly displayed their embrace of ethnic and racial diversity—a poignant photo shows several children holding up signs reading "Greek Orthodox (*Rum*) Çapulcu," "Kurdish Çapulcu," and "Turk Çapulcu"— such explicit recognition of ethnic difference is intolerable for supporters of Pan-Turkic and Republican Nationalism.[58] One publication documenting the Gezi experience stated its exclusionary vision quite clearly in a headline: "The Two Enemies of the Gezi Resistance: The AKP and the [Kurdish] BDP."[59] As discussed in the previous chapter, the BDP[60] is a Kurdish-based party that advocates increased cultural rights for Kurds, including education in their mother tongue, and that is often referred to as the political wing of the PKK. Another sign alluding negatively to ethnic and religious differences—that citizens of Turkey are stronger when they are united and weaker when such divides are artificially imposed upon them to separate them—read: "Now do you understand why they separated us as Turk-Kurd and Alevi-Sunni? Because by coming together we become like this—By uniting we will win!"[61]

As different from each other as they are in terms of identity content, supporters of each of the three alternative understandings of national identity discussed here posed significant and widespread challenges to the AKP's pursuit of hegemony for Ottoman Islamism for the first time during the Gezi protests. As the analysis presented above makes clear, this contestation was not just about the abuse of political power or the use of violence against protesters, but also about the identity content driving the objectionable policies implemented by the AKP and justifying the suppression of dissenters, precisely because "they" are "Them."

From the perspective of those seeking to derail the AKP in its institutionalization of a New Turkey at home and abroad, however, the infighting among those who were at Gezi and the lack of any sustained movement to emerge from it as a result paint a bleak picture. Even the 2017 Ankara-to-Istanbul Justice March (*Adalet Yürüyüşü*) led by CHP chairman Kemal Kılıçdaroğlu in protest against the jailing of party members failed to produce any noticeable increase in political solidarity. As united as groups with competing proposals were during the heady, often carnival-like atmosphere of Gezi, the above analysis also demonstrates that divisions related to identity persist. If these divisions prove to be red lines whose compromise cannot be tolerated, this may hinder the emergence of a hybrid identity that seemed poised to emerge from the recognition of common ground among groups that previously regarded each other with either apathy or antipathy. As vehement as is many individuals' rejection of Erdoğan's presidency, Ottoman Islamism in practice, and the populist authoritarianism he uses to sustain the two, the coalescence of opposition needed to challenge him seems highly unlikely to form any time soon.

Appendix 2.1

NOVELS AND MONOGRAPHS USED
AS SOURCES OF TEXTS

Novels

Sabahattin Ali, *Kürk Mantolu Madonna*

Nazan Bekiroğlu, *Nar Ağacı*

Eda Bildek, *1453 Fetih*

Hakan Günday, *Kinyas ve Kayra*

Yaşar Kemal, *İnce Mehmed 1*

Ayşe Kulin, *Veda*

Ömer Zülfü Livaneli, *Kardeşimin Hikayesi*

Ömer Zülfü Livaneli, *Mutluluk*

Ömer Zülfü Livaneli, *Serenad*

Orhan Pamuk, *Masumiyet Müzesi*

Berat Pekmezci and Levent Cantek, *Emanet Şehir*

Elif Şafak, *Baba ve Piç*

Şule Yüksel Şener, *Huzur Sokağı*

Canan Tan, *Hasret*

Hüseyin Tekinoğlu, *Fetih 1453*

Celal Temel, *Bir Dava İki Sevda*

Orkun Uçar and Burak Turna, *Metal Fırtına*

Ahmet Ümit, *İstanbul Hatırası*

Ahmet Ümit, *Sultanı Öldürmek*

Mete Yarar, *60 Yıllık İttifakta Son Günü*

Cenkut Yıldırım, *Devşirme*

Zekeriya Yıldız, *Sürgün Sultan*

Monographs

Mehmet Altan, *İkinci Cumhuriyetin Yol Hikayesi*

Anonymous, *Çapulcunun Gezi Rehberi: Gezi Parkı Direnişi'nden Aforizmalar*

Mustafa Armağan, *Satılık İmparatorluk: Lozan ve Osmanlı'nın Reddedilen Mirası*

Falih Rıfkı Atay, *Zeytindağı*

İsmail Şefik Aydın, *Uyan Türkiye*

Atılgan Bayar, *Müslüman Roma: Türkiye Cumhuriyeti Devleti'nin Yakın Geleceği*

İsmet Berkan, *Asker Bize İktidar Verir Mi?*

İpek Çalışlar, *Halide Edib*

A. Oğuz Çelikkol, *One Minute'ten Mavi Marmara'ya: Türkiye-İsrail Çatışması*

D. İsmet Çınkı, M. Cem Okyay, Erdinç Altıner, Ender Kahya, and F. Yavuz Uras, eds., *Er Mektubu Görülmüştür: Balyoz Mağduru Türk Subaylarına Gönderilen Destek Mektupları*

Ahmet Davutoğlu, *Stratejik Derinlik: Türkiye'nin Uluslararası Konumu*

Neşe Düzel, *Hesaplaşma*

Gökçe Fırat, *Mustafa Kemal'in Askerleriyiz*

Gökçe Fırat, *Türk Yurdu Anadolu*

Gökçe Fırat, Ali Özsoy, Kaya Ataberk, Serap Yeşiltuna, Özgür Erdem, Denizcan Dede, and Hazar Arısoy, *Taksim'de Kutsal Isyan*

Hurşit Güneş, *Adalet Çağrısı: CHP için Sosyal Demokrasi Seçeneği*

Uluç Gürkan, *Ermeni Sorunu'nu Anlamak: Önyargıları Aşmak ve Nefretten Arınmak*

Ezgi Gürses, *28 Şubat: Demokrasi Ters Şeritte*

İskender Öksüz, *Türk'üm Özür Dilerim*

Ümit Özdağ, *İkinci Tek Parti Dönemi*

Ali Rıza Özdemir, *PKK ve Korucular*

Saygı Öztürk, *Belgelerle 28 Şubat: Dünden Bügüne*

Saygı Öztürk and Kemal Yurteri, *MGK: Din ve Bügünüyle Milli Güvenlik Kurulu*

Cenk Sidar, *Türkiye Rüyası*

Oktay Sinanoğlu, *Bye Bye Türkçe: Bir Nev-York Rüyası*

H Bahadır Türk, *Muktedir: Türk Sağ Geleneği ve Recep Tayyip Erdoğan*

Fatih Yaşlı, *Kinimiz Dinimizdir: Türkçü Faşizm Üzerine bir İncelleme*

Ali Yıldırım, *Alevi Hukuku*

Appendix 2.2

TELEVISION SERIES AND FILMS USED AS SOURCES OF TEXTS

Television Series

Aşk-ı Memnu
Behẓat Ç
Bence Benim Annem
Benim İçin Üzülme
Fatma Gül'ün Suçu Ne?
Filinta
Huzur Sokağı
Karadayı
Kim Milyoner Olmak İster?
Kurtlar Vadisi
Kuzey Güney
Küçük Gelin
Leyla ile Mecnun
Medcezir
Muhteşem Yüzyıl
Osmanlı Tokadı
Öyle Bir Geçer Zaman Ki
Seksenler
Sofradayız
Survivor
Yalan Dünya
Yemekteyiz

Films

1299 Kuruluş
Babam ve Oğlum
Başka Dilde Aşk
Bir Bavul İki Dil
Dedemin İnsanları
Deli Deli Olma
Eşkıya
Fetih 1453
Gegen die Wand (German-Turkish)
Gönül Yarası
İncir Reçeli
Mutluluk
Nobetçi
Recep İvedik
Selam
Tatar Ramazan
Üç Maymun

NOTES

Chapter 1

1. Interview with AKP founding member and ministerial official, Ankara, July 20, 2013.
2. Philip Oltermann, "Erdoğan Accuses Germany of 'Nazi Practices' over Blocked Political Rallies," *Guardian*, March 5, 2017, https://www.theguardian.com/world/2017/mar/05/erdogan-accuses-germany-of-nazi-practices-over-blocked-election-rallies.
3. *Integrating Syrian Refugees in Turkey*, International Crisis Group, Europe and Central Asia Division, Report No. 241, November 30, 2016, https://www.crisisgroup.org/europe-central-asia/western-europemediterranean/turkey/integrating-syrian-refugees-turkey.
4. Explored in later chapters, the outcomes of these initiatives at the time of writing can be summarized as follows: Turkey became the most vocal opponent of the Syrian regime, staunchly refusing to participate in military campaigns against the Islamic State on Syrian territory unless the United States agreed to help oust Assad; Turkey failed to get international support for the nuclear deal and then enraged Iran by placing a NATO patriot missile on its southern border, intended to deter Syrian attacks but capable of reaching Iranian territory; and numerous instances of hostility, most prominently the Mavi Marmara flotilla crisis, led to downgraded diplomatic relations with Israel. Of these implosions, the third was arguably an outcome deliberately sought by the ruling party for domestic political reasons related to identity, discussed in chapter 6, but it cost Turkey tremendously in terms of regional influence and economic growth and thus has been rolled back.
5. See, for example, Bülent Aras, "Turkey's Rise in the Greater Middle East: Peace-Building in the Periphery," *Journal of Balkan and Near Eastern Studies* 11, no. 1 (2009): 29–41.
6. For the original argument, see John Mearsheimer, *The Tragedy of Great Power Politics* (New York: Norton, 2001). For an application to Turkey, see Ed Erickson, "Turkey as a Regional Hegemon—2014: Strategic Implications for the United States," *Turkish Studies* 5, no. 3 (2004): 25–45.
7. "Turkey to Go Ahead with Non-NATO-Integrated Missile Defense," *Hürriyet Daily News*, February 19, 2015, http://www.hurriyetdailynews.com/turkey-to-go-ahead-with-non-nato-integrated-missile-defense.aspx?PageID=238&NID=78566&NewsCatID=510.
8. "Turkey Wants to Get Russian S-400 Missiles Quickly, Defense Minister," *Reuters.com*, March 14, 2018, https://www.reuters.com/article/us-russia-turkey-missiles/turkey-wants-to-get-russian-s-400-missiles-quickly-foreign-minister-idUSKCN1GQ17A.
9. "*Suriye 'Tape'si Dünyayı Sarstı*," *Hürriyet Gazetesi*, March 29, 2014, http://www.hurriyet.com.tr/dunya/26102830.asp.
10. Sedat Ergin, "Erdoğan's 'Handshake and Ottoman Slap' Doctrine," *Hürriyet Daily News*, February 22, 2018, http://www.hurriyetdailynews.com/opinion/sedat-ergin/erdogans-handshake-and-ottoman-slap-doctrine-127697.

11. "Turkey-US Relations Hit All Time Low over Syria," *Reuters.com*, February 15, 2018, https://www.reuters.com/video/2018/02/15/turkey-us-relations-hit-all-time-low-ove?videoId=401368011.

12. See, for example, Meltem Müftüler Baç, "Turkey's Political Reforms and the Impact of the European Union," *Mediterranean Politics* 10, no. 1 (2005): 17–31. As the book explores, accession negotiations were opened in October 2005 and were put on hold in December 2006.

13. See, for example, Ziya Öniş, "The Triumph of Conservative Globalism: The Political Economy of the AKP," *Turkish Studies* 13, no. 2 (2012): 135–152.

14. A statement attempting to explain the AKP's support for Libyan dictator Muammer Qaddafi exemplifies such arguments: "[T[he government, influenced by Islamist sympathies, fell out of pace with NATO while resisting military action against Libya." See *France24 International News*, March 24, 2011, http://www.france24.com/en/20110324-turkey-allows-nato-command-libya-military-operations-vote.

15. H. Bahadır Türk, *Muktedir: Türk Sağ Geleneği ve Recep Tayyip Erdoğan* (Istanbul: İletişim Yayınları, 2014).

16. "Early Writings Reveal the Real Davutoglu,"*Al-Monitor*, August 13, 2014, http://www.al-monitor.com/pulse/originals/2014/08/zaman-davutoglu-ideologue-behlul-ozkan-academic-akp-islamic.html.

17. "Islamic Calvinists: Change and Conservatism in Anatolia," *European Stability Initiative Report*, September 19, 2005, http://www.esiweb.org/pdf/esi_document_id_69.pdf.

18. Tarık Oğuzlu, "Middle-Easternization of Turkey's Foreign Policy," *Turkish Studies* 9, no. 1 (2008): 3–20.

19. Of the dozens of op-ed-style interpretations of Turkey's regionally and Islamic-oriented foreign policy initiatives, see Tulin Daloğlu, "Davutoglu Invokes Ottomanism as New Mideast Order," *Al-Monitor*, March 10, 2013, http://www.al-monitor.com/pulse/originals/2013/03/turkey-davutologu-ottoman-new-order-mideast.html#; "Erdoğan and the Decline of the Turks," *Wall Street Journal*, June 2, 2010, http://online.wsj.com/article/SB1000142405274870487560457528139219525 0402.html; and Elmira Bayasli, "The Ottoman Revival Is Over," *New York Times*, March 30, 2014, http://www.nytimes.com/2014/03/31/opinion/the-ottoman-revival-is-over.html.

20. For noteworthy exceptions, see Nora Fisher Onar and Hakan Övünç Ongur, who focus on rival and evolving representations of Ottomanism, respectively, and Lerna Yanık, who highlights neo-Ottomanism's position as a hybrid representation of history. Nora Fischer Onar, "Echoes of a Universalism Lost: Rival Representations of the Ottomans in Today's Turkey," *Middle Eastern Studies* 5, no. 2 (2009): 229–241; and Hakan Övünç Ongur, "Identifying Ottomanisms: The Discursive Evolution of Ottoman Pasts in Turkish Presents," *Middle Eastern Studies* 51, no. 3 (2015), 416–432; and Lerna Yanık, "Constructing Turkish 'Exceptionalism': Discourses of Liminality and Hybridity in Post-Cold War Turkish Foreign Policy," *Political Geography* 30, no. 2 (2011): 1–10.

21. Ömer Taşpınar notes a difference between the two in a briefing, but does not account for the change. Ömer Taşpınar, *Turkey's Middle East Policies: Between Neo-Ottomanism and Kemalism* (Washington, DC: Carnegie Endowment for International Peace, 2008).

22. Sinan Ciddi, *Kemalism in Turkish Politics: The Republican People's Party, Secularism, and Nationalism* (London: Routledge, 2009), 13–30.

23. The list of demands included an official ban on the Islamic headscarf at universities, closing preacher-training (*imam hatip*) schools, and banning religious brotherhoods (*tarikatlar*). Erbakan was forced to approve the demands but subsequently resigned from the premiership under continuous pressure from the National Security Council (Milli Güvenlik Kurulu). The February 28 Process is discussed in detail in chapter 5.

24. *Selam*, September 26–October 2, 1999, cited in Sultan Tepe, *Beyond Sacred and Secular: Politics of Religion in Israel and Turkey* (Stanford, CA: Stanford University Press, 2008), 186.

25. Rawi Abdelal, *National Purpose in the World Economy: Post-Soviet States in Comparative Perspective* (Ithaca, NY: Cornell University Press, 2001).

26. Such Huntingtonian thinking reduces societal collectivities to exogenously determined units, as though they were tectonic plates, thus lacking agency among or variation across them, while also assuming that relations between these units are inherently conflictual. Huntington's subsequent conclusion that states (Turkey, Ukraine, Mexico) whose borders encompass more than one civilization are "torn countries" is, I assert, empirically incorrect

and normatively irresponsible. For the discussion of "torn countries," see Samuel Huntington, *The Clash of Civilizations and the Remaking of World Order* (New York: Simon and Schuster, 1996), 139–54.

27. Among the many arguments put forward, some of the most frequently cited are found in Şerif Mardin, *Religion and Social Change in Modern Turkey: The Case of Bediuzzaman Said Nursi* (Albany: State University of New York Press, 1989); Metin Heper, Ayşe Öncü, and Heinz Kramer, eds., *Turkey and the West: Changing Political and Cultural Identities* (London: I. B. Tauris, 1993); Soner Çağaptay, *Islam, Secularism, and Nationalism in Modern Turkey: Who Is a Turk?* (New York: Routledge, 2006); Jenny White, *Muslim Nationalism and the New Turks* (Princeton, NJ: Princeton University Press, 2013); Feroz Ahmad, *Turkey: The Quest for Identity* (London: Oneworld, 2014); and Sylvia Kedourie, ed., *Turkey: Identity, Democracy, Politics* (London: Routledge, 2014). Comparative studies engaging questions of Turkey's identity include Ayşe Zarakol, *After Defeat: How the East Learned to Live with the West* (Cambridge, UK: Cambridge University Press, 2011); and Şener Aktürk, *Regimes of Ethnicity and Nationhood in Germany, Russia, and Turkey* (Cambridge, UK: Cambridge University Press, 2012).

28. See "The Complete Transcript of Netanyahu's Address to Congress," *Washington Post*, March 3, 2015, http://www.washingtonpost.com/blogs/post-politics/wp/2015/03/03/full-text-netanyahus-address-to-congress/.

29. Ravish Tiwari, "BJP Calls for a Muscular Foreign Policy: Panchamrit to Replace Panchsheel," *India Today*, April 4, 2015, http://indiatoday.intoday.in/story/bjp-foreign-policy-national-executive/1/428383.html.

30. Manjari Chatterjee Miller, "Foreign Policy a la Modi," *Foreign Affairs*, April 3, 2014, http://www.foreignaffairs.com/articles/141095/manjari-chatterjee-miller/foreign-policy-a-la-modi. Miller, writing a year before the resolution noted above was introduced, predicted little change in foreign policy under Modi.

31. Based on my extensive search of political science and anthropological literature, this is a novel use of the term. The only reference I located was its use in an abstract on sexual and gender norms in Iran, but the term is not used in the body of the article. See Maryam Dezhamkhooy and Leila Papoli Yazdi, "Breaking the Borders/Violating the Norms: An Archaeological Survey of an Intersex in a Traditional Society, Bam (South Eastern Iran)," *Sexuality and Culture*, no. 17 (2013): 229–243.

32. Audie Klotz, "Norms Reconstituting Interests: Global Racial Equality and U.S. Sanctions against South Africa," *International Organization* 49, no. 3 (1995): 451–478.

33. Robert Cox, "Gramsci, Hegemony and International Relations," in *Gramsci, Historical Materialism, and International Relations*, ed. Stephen Gill (Cambridge, UK: Cambridge University Press, 1993), 42.

34. See, for example, Enze Han, *Contestation and Adaptation: The Politics of National Identity in China* (Oxford: Oxford University Press, 2013); and Gabriel Shaffer, ed., *Modern Diasporas in International Politics* (New York: St. Martin's, 1986).

35. Margaret Keck and Kathryn Sikkink, *Activists beyond Borders: Transnational Advocacy Networks in International Politics* (Ithaca, NY: Cornell University Press, 1998); and Klotz, "Norms Reconstituting Interests."

36. Neta Crawford's examination of the domestic and international normative dynamics at work in bringing about the end of colonialism demonstrates how persuasion through argumentation can lead to monumental shifts in both action and belief. Neta Crawford, *Argument and Change in World Politics: Ethics, Decolonization, and Humanitarian Intervention* (Cambridge, UK: Cambridge University Press, 2002). See also Thomas Risse-Kappen, ed., *Bringing Transnational Relations Back In: Non-State Actors, Domestic Structures, and International Institutions* (Cambridge, UK: Cambridge University Press, 1995).

37. Jeffrey Checkel, "Why Comply? Social Learning and European Identity Change," *International Organization* 55, no. 3 (2001): 553–588; and Sandra Lavenex and Frank Schimmelfennig, "EU Rules beyond Borders," *Journal of European Public Policy* 16, no. 6 (2009): 791–812.

38. These differences eventually produced two separate identity proposals, discussed later in this book as Western Liberalism and Republican Nationalism.

39. See, for example, Rogers Brubaker, *Nationalism Reframed: Nationhood and the National Question in the New Europe* (Cambridge, UK: Cambridge University Press, 1996); Sam

Kaplan, *The Pedagogical State: Education and the Politics of National Culture in Post-1980 Turkey* (Stanford, CA: Stanford University Press, 2006); Ronald Krebs, *Fighting for Rights: Military Service and the Politics of Citizenship* (Ithaca, NY: Cornell University Press, 2006); John Gillis, ed., *Commemorations: The Politics of National Identity* (Princeton, NJ: Princeton University Press, 1996); and Benedict Anderson, *Imagined Communities: Reflections on the Origin and Spread of Nationalism* (London: Verso, 2006), 167–91.

40. See Checkel, "Why Comply?"; Richard Herrmann, Thomas Risse-Kappen, and Marilynn Brewer, eds., *Transnational Identities: Becoming European in the EU* (Lanham, MD: Rowman and Littlefield, 2004); and Jelena Subotic, "Europe Is a State of Mind: Identity and Europeanization in the Balkans," *International Studies Quarterly* 55, no. 2 (2011): 309–330.

41. See Graham Macklin and Fabian Virchow, eds., *Transnational Extreme Right Networks* (Routledge, forthcoming); and Petra Vejvodova, "Transnational Cooperation of the Far Right," in *The Extreme Right in Europe: Current Trends and Perspectives*, ed. Uwe Backes and Patrick Moreau (Göttingen, Germany: Vandenhoeck & Ruprecht, 2011): 215–228.

Chapter 2

1. Jeffrey Checkel, "The Constructivist Turn in International Relations," *World Politics* 50, no. 2 (1998): 324–348. For arguments that this "turn" is in fact a "return" to the study of culture and identity in IR, see Friedrich Kratochwil and Yosef Lapid, eds., *The Return of Culture and Identity in IR Theory* (Boulder, CO: Lynne Rienner, 1996).

2. Rawi Abdelal, Yoshiko Herrera, Alastair Iain Johnston, and Rose McDermott, eds., *Measuring Identity: A Guide for Social Scientists* (Cambridge, UK: Cambridge University Press, 2009), 18.

3. Rogers Brubaker and Frederick Cooper, "Beyond 'Identity'," *Theory and Society* 29, no. 1 (2000): 1–47.

4. See Maja Zehfuss, *Constructivism in International Relations: The Politics of Reality* (Cambridge, UK: Cambridge University Press, 2001).

5. Samuel Huntington is perhaps the most common target of such objections. See Samuel Huntington, *The Clash of Civilizations and the Remaking of World Order* (New York: Simon and Schuster, 1996).

6. Henry Hale, *The Foundations of Ethnic Politics: Separatism of States and Nations in Eurasia and the World* (Cambridge, UK: Cambridge University Press, 2008), 25–30.

7. Examples of this approach include John Mueller, "The Banality of Ethnic War," *International Security* 25, no. 1 (2000): 42–70; Jack Snyder, *From Voting to Violence: Democratization and Nationalist Conflict* (New York: W. W. Norton, 2000); and Paul Brass, *Theft of an Idol: Text and Context in the Representation of Collective Violence* (Princeton, NJ: Princeton University Press, 1997).

8. David Laitin's work extensively employs an extraordinarily "thin" version of identity, conceptually speaking, as purely a coordination mechanism. See, inter alia, David Laitin, *Identity in Formation* (Ithaca, NY: Cornell University Press, 1998); and David Laitin, *Nations, States, and Violence* (Oxford: Oxford University Press, 2007). See also Russell Hardin, *One for All: The Logic of Group Conflict* (Princeton, NJ: Princeton University Press, 1995).

9. Shibley Telhami and Michael Barnett outline this concept as a common theme engaged in their edited volume. Shibley Telhami and Michael Barnett, eds., *Identity and Foreign Policy in the Middle East* (Ithaca, NY: Cornell University Press, 2002), 13–16.

10. Daniel Posner, *Institutions and Ethnic Politics in Africa* (Cambridge, UK: Cambridge University Press, 2005), 17.

11. Posner admits that he "strip[s] identity of its affect," thus leaving out any emotional or ontological commitments an individual may have with a particular identity and leaving him or her free essentially to pick up—or, crucially, discard—identities based on what a certain situation demands. Posner, *Institutions and Ethnic Politics*, 12.

12. Alexander Wendt's example of this is the difference to the United States in the meaning of British versus Soviet nuclear capabilities. Alexander Wendt, "Collective Identity Formation and the International State," *American Political Science Review* 88, no. 2 (1994): 389.

13. Defensive realists such as Stephen Walt suggest that threat perceptions of a potential adversary may be shaped by factors such as historical aggression, clearly an informational element.

Charles Glaser goes further by explicitly positing information about potential adversaries' motives as a variable influencing the severity of the security dilemma and therefore the relative prospects for cooperation and conflict among states. See Stephen Walt, *The Origins of Alliances* (Ithaca, NY: Cornell University Press, 1990); and Charles Glaser, *Rational Theory of International Politics: The Logic of Competition and Cooperation* (Princeton, NJ: Princeton University Press, 2010).

14. See Andrew Moravcsik, "Taking Preferences Seriously: A Liberal Theory of International Politics," *International Organization* 51, no. 4 (1992):515–553.

15. Michael Barnett, *Dialogues in Arab Politics: Negotiations in Regional Order* (New York: Columbia University Press, 1998).

16. Marc Lynch, *State Interests and Public Spheres: The International Politics of Jordan's Identity* (New York: Columbia University Press, 1999).

17. Rawi Abdelal, *National Purpose in the World Economy: Post-Soviet States in Comparative Perspective* (Ithaca, NY: Cornell University Press, 2001), 29.

18. David Campbell, *National Deconstruction: Violence, Identity, and Justice in Bosnia* (Minneapolis: University of Minnesota Press, 1992).

19. Both the comprehensive approach presented here and the particular ontological significance of identity in these debates, elaborated on below, differentiate this analysis from studies of competing foreign policy schools of thought. See, for example, Andrei Tsyganov, "From International Institutionalism to Revolutionary Expansionism: The Foreign Policy Discourse of Contemporary Russia," *Mershon International Studies Review* 41 (1997):247–268.

20. Peter Gourevitch, "The Second Image Reversed: The International Sources of Domestic Politics," *International Organization* 32, no. 4 (1978): 881–912.

21. For a classic analysis of Weber's dual concepts of lifestyle (personal) and life chances (structural), see Thomas Luckmann and Peter Berger, "Social Mobility and Personal Identity," *European Journal of Sociology* 5, no. 2 (1964): 331–344.

22. Arguing that they have experienced economic disenfranchisement as well as cultural suppression due to numerous factors, Kurds continue to push for education in Kurdish as one of their strategies to rectify both situations. See Frederike Geerdink, "Kurds Not Giving up on Education in Mother Tongue," *Al-Monitor*, September 23, 2014, http://www.al-monitor. com/pulse/originals/2014/09/turkey-kurds-education-in-mother-tongue-schools.html#.

23. The special privilege given to Buddhism in the Sri Lankan constitution has been cited as a main grievance of the country's Hindus, Muslims, and Christians. See Neha Sinha, "Sri Lanka: Hopes for Minorities?," *The Diplomat*, February 3, 2015, http://thediplomat.com/ 2015/02/sri-lanka-hope-for-minorities/. The country's flag symbolically represents this institutional inequality, with the Buddhist Sinhalese lion taking up two-thirds of the flag and small strips of green and saffron used to represent Muslims and (mostly Tamil) Hindus, respectively.

24. Waves of women's suffrage movements in the early twentieth century granting women equal voting rights and later institutionalizations of measures such as gender quotas notwithstanding, cases of women's unequal access to politics stemming from conservative beliefs about their role in the public sphere abound. See Georgina Waylen, "Women and Democratization: Conceptualizing Gender Relations in Transition Politics," *World Politics* 46, no. 3 (1994): 327–354.

25. See, for example, the comparative study of progress toward ensuring civil rights for LGBTQ individuals and marriage rights for couples in the United States and Canada: Miriam Smith, *Political Institutions and Lesbian and Gay Rights in the United States and Canada* (New York: Routledge, 2008).

26. Henry Tajfel, *Human Groups and Social Categories: Studies in Social Psychology* (Cambridge, UK: Cambridge University Press, 1981), 255.

27. See Anne Clunan, *The Social Construction of Russia's Resurgence: Aspirations, Identity, and Security Interests* (Baltimore, MD: Johns Hopkins University Press, 2009); and Deborah Welch Larson and Alexei Shevchenko, "Status Seekers: Chinese and Russian Responses to U.S. Primacy," *International Security* 34, no. 4 (2010): 63–95.

28. Leonie Huddy, "Contrasting Theoretical Approaches to Intergroup Relations," *Political Psychology* 25, no. 6 (2004): 956.

29. Clifford Geertz, *The Interpretation of Culture* (New York: Basic Books, 1973).

30. In Alexander Wendt's succinct terms, "identities are the basis of interests." See Alexander Wendt, "Anarchy Is What States Make of It," *International Organization* 46, no. 2 (1992): 398.

31. Robert Cox, "Gramsci, Hegemony, and International Relations: An Essay in Method," in *Gramsci, Hegemony, and International Relations*, ed. Stephen Gill (Cambridge, UK: Cambridge University Press, 1993), 42.

32. This political and societal institutionalization of an identity proposal's prescriptions for appropriate behavior—that is, how one with a certain identity should act—is in line with Robert Cox's discussion of a hegemonic actor's "mission." See Robert Cox, "Social Forces, States, and World Orders," in *Neorealism and Its Critics*, ed. Robert Keohane (New York: Columbia University Press, 1986), 219.

33. Antonio Gramsci, *Selections from the Prison Notebooks* (London: Lawrence and Wishart, 1971).

34. For a study applying passive revolution to explain Islamic deradicalization, see Cihan Tuğal, *Passive Revolution: Absorbing the Islamic Challenge to Capitalism* (Stanford, CA: Stanford University Press, 2009). Lustick also engages Gramsci in his study of ideological hegemony but does not engage the daily public contestation between competing ideologies or the obstacles that lead elites to choose one arena over the other as analyzed here. See Ian Lustick, "Hegemony and the Riddle of Nationalism: The Dialectics of Religion and Nationalism in the Middle East" *Logos* 1, no. 3 (2002): 18–44.

35. Cox, "Social Forces, States, and World Orders," 219.

36. See, for example, Michael Mann, *The Dark Side of Democracy: Explaining Ethnic Cleansing* (Cambridge, UK: Cambridge University Press, 2004); and H. Zeynep Bulutgil, *The Roots of Ethnic Cleansing in Europe* (Cambridge, UK: Cambridge University Press, 2016).

37. Brubaker's analysis stands as a seminal work on the dynamics of assimilation dynamics: Rogers Brubaker, *Nationalism Reframed: Nationhood and the National Question in the New Europe* (Cambridge, UK: Cambridge University Press, 1996). For a discussion of the conditions under which assimilation is used rather than annihilation, see Harris Mylonas, *The Politics of Nation-Building: Making Co-Nationals, Refugees, and Minorities* (Cambridge, UK: Cambridge University Press, 2013).

38. For an excellent summary, see Glaser, *Rational Theory of International Politics*, particularly 148–66.

39. See, for example, Enze Han, *Contestation and Adaptation: The Politics of National Identity in China* (Oxford: Oxford University Press, 2013); and Erin Jenne, *Ethnic Bargaining: The Paradox of Minority Empowerment* (Ithaca, NY: Cornell University Press, 2007).

40. For a discussion of the boomerang model of advocacy, see Margaret Keck and Kathryn Sikkink, *Activists beyond Borders: Advocacy Networks in International Politics* (Ithaca, NY: Cornell University Press, 1998). For a review of analyses of transnational civil society and its normative pressures, see Richard Price, "Transnational Civil Society and Advocacy in World Politics," *World Politics* 55, no. 4 (2003): 579–606.

41. See, for example, Frank Schimmelfennig, "Strategic Calculation and International Socialization: Membership Incentives, Party Constellations, and Sustained Compliance in Central and Eastern Europe," *International Organization* 59, no. 4 (2005): 827–860; and Jeffrey Checkel, "Why Comply?"

42. Abdelal et al., *Measuring Identity*, 17–32.

43. For a discussion of the need to tease out constructivist "logics of appropriateness" more specifically, see Martha Finnemore, *The Purpose of Intervention: Changing Beliefs about the Use of Force* (Ithaca, NY: Cornell University Press, 2004), 16.

44. See Ted Hopf, *Social Construction of International Politics: Identities and Foreign Policies, Moscow, 1955 and 1999* (Ithaca, NY: Cornell University Press, 2002), 24.

45. Ibid., 35.

46. Elif Şafak, *Baba ve Piç* (Istanbul: Metis Yayınları, 2007).

47. The article, whose newspaper has since been closed, notes that Şafak would be charged with the same crime as fellow writer Orhan Pamuk, who stated that he was the only one in Turkey talking about the killing of Kurds and Armenians. "*Elif Şafak da Yargılanacak,*" *Radikal Gazetesi*, July 29, 2006, http://www.radikal.com.tr/turkiye/elif-safak-da-yargilanacak-787336/. The writings of novelists Orhan Pamuk and Ahmet Altan have also been censored

due to their handling of traditionally "taboo" subjects such as the Kurdish and Armenian issues; both were likewise charged under article 301.

48. See "*İki Kadın Yazar, İki Kültür Ödülü*," Bianet, June 15, 2011, http://www.bianet.org/bianet/kultur/130759-iki-kadin-yazar-iki-kultur-odulu. I categorize this website as comprised of Western Liberalist content.

49. See Yazıcıoğlu's post "*Ülkücü Liderinden Elif Şafak'a Tepki*" on the ultranationalist website Milliyetciler (no date given), http://www.milliyetciler.com/haber/ulkuculerin-liderinden-elif-safak-a-tepki_206.html.

50. Celal Temel, *Bir Dava İki Sevda* (Istanbul: Hemen Kitap, 2012), 207–12.

51. The book also addresses taboo subjects such as incest and honor killings, about which little official information may be found and which may be impossible to broach openly in interviews. See Ömer Zülfü Livaneli, *Mutluluk* (Istanbul: Doğan Kitap, 2007).

52. A full list of the novels and monographs used as a source of texts for the intertextual analysis conducted is presented at the end of the book as appendix 2.1.

53. See, for example, Walter Armbrust, ed., *Mass Mediations: New Approaches to Popular Culture in the Middle East and Beyond* (Berkeley: University of California Press, 2000); and Lila Abu-Lughod, *Dramas of Nationhood: The Politics of Television in Egypt* (Chicago: University of Chicago Press, 2005). A full list of the movies and television series used a source of texts is presented as appendix 2.2 at the end of the book.

54. Hikmet Kocamaner, "Strengthening the Family through Television: Islamic Broadcasting, Secularism, and the Politics of Responsibility in Turkey," *Anthropological Quarterly* 90, no. 3 (2017): 683 (emphasis added).

55. The breakdown using Turkey's traditional geographical classification of regions is roughly as follows: Marmara 16%, Aegean 2%, Mediterranean 9%, Central Anatolia 42%, Black Sea 10%, Eastern Anatolia 10%, Southeast Anatolia 4%, and region unknown 7%.

56. The participant observation I conducted is in line with research methods used by scholars such as Lisa Wedeen and Jenny White to discern the underlying meanings structuring daily forms of individual practice and social interaction. See Lisa Wedeen, *Ambiguities of Domination: Politics, Rhetoric, and Symbols in Contemporary Syria* (Chicago: University of Chicago Press, 1999); and Jenny White, *Islamist Mobilization in Turkey: A Study in Vernacular Politics* (Seattle: University of Washington Press, 2002).

57. These differences eventually produced two separate identity proposals, discussed later as Western liberalism and Republican Nationalism.

58. David Collier, "Understanding Process Tracing," *PS: Political Science and Politics* 44, no. 4 (2011): 823–830.

59. Gavin D. Brockett, "When Ottomans Become Turks: Commemorating the Conquest of Constantinople and Its Contribution to World History," *American Historical Review* 119, no. 2 (2014): 411. See also Christine Philliou, "When the Clock Strikes Twelve: The Inception of an Ottoman Past in Early Republican Turkey," *Comparative Studies of South Asia, Africa, and the Middle East* 31, no. 1 (2011): 172–182.

60. See, for example, Kazım Yetiş, ed., *Türk Edebiyatında İstanbul'un Fethi ve Fatih* (Istanbul: Kitap Yurdu, 2005); and Gavin Brockett, *How Happy to Call Oneself a Turk: Provincial Newspapers in the Negotiation of a Muslim National Identity* (Austin: University of Texas Press, 2011), 67–80.

Chapter 3

1. Rawi Abdelal, Yoshiko Herrera, Alastair Iain Johnston, and Rose McDermott, *Measuring Identity: A Guide for Social Scientists* (New York: Cambridge University Press, 2009).

2. Soner Çağaptay, *Islam, Secularism, and Nationalism in Modern Turkey: Who Is a Turk?* (New York: Routledge, 2006).

3. Jenny White, *Muslim Nationalism and the New Turks* (Princeton, NJ: Princeton University Press, 2013).

4. Tanıl Bora, "Nationalist Discourses in Turkey," *South Atlantic Quarterly* 102, nos. 2/3 (2003): 433–451.

5. Şener Aktürk, "The Fourth Style of Politics: Eurasianism as a Pro-Russian Rethinking of Turkey's Geopolitical Identity," *Turkish Studies* 16, no. 1 (2015): 54–79.

6. For a critical analysis of this ideologically extremist, violence-oriented strand of Pan-Turkic Nationalism, appropriately titled *Our Enmity Is Our Religion*, see Fatih Yaşlı, *Kinimiz Dinimizdir: Türkçü Faşizm Üzerine Bir İnceleme* (Ankara: Tan Kitabevi Yayınları, 2009).

7. Interview with Haldun Solmaztürk, academic senior fellow for Turkey at the Chatham House and retired army general, Ankara, August 2013; and interview with Hakan Övünç Ongur, political theory professor, Ankara, August 2013. See also Niyazi Berkes, *Türk Düşününde Batı Sorunu* (Ankara: Bilgi Yayinevi, 1975), 64–65. Because *Turancılık*—though still embraced by a very small minority of Pan-Turkic Nationalists today (Yalçın Sarıkaya, Black Sea politics and nationalism expert and Giresun University professor, email correspondence with author, February 22, 2014)—has come to take on a derogatory meaning denoting naïve idealism, particularly since World War II (as discussed in the following chapter), the term is not used here.

8. See Guzel Maitdinova, "The Uyghur Diaspora in Tajikistan: History, Culture, and Current Situation" (paper presented at The Central Asia Program, International Conference on Uyghur Studies: History, Culture, and Society, September 2014).

9. See, among many, *Türkçülük-Turancılık*, https://www.facebook.com/pages/T%C3%BCrk%C3%A7%C3%BCl%C3%BCk-Turanc%C4%B1l%C4%B1k/513243655442161?fref=ts.

10. The gesture, made by pinching together the thumb, middle, and ring fingers and extending the index and little fingers to resemble a wolf, is ubiquitous at MHP rallies and other Pan-Turkic Nationalist gatherings. See the Facebook page of the *Bozkurtça Dergi* (*Grey Wolf-Language Journal*), whose headline next to a picture of Çakıroğlu and an image of the grey wolf states: "Heroes give their lives in order to make our home survive" ("*Kahramanlar can verir yurdu yaşatmak için*"), https://www.facebook.com/BozkurtcaDAVA?fref=ts; see also a commemorative page created for Çakıroğlu with different versions of the same symbols, https://www.facebook.com/bozkurtca.yasamak?fref=ts.

11. Turcology MA student Gamze, "*Bir millet iki devletiz biz. Doğu Türkistan'da Çinin yaptığı katliamlara diren kardeşim . . . Doğu Türkistan—Türk'ün kanayan yarası*," Facebook, date and link withheld. See Facebook pages using the flag as a profile photo, such as Uygur Doğu Türkistan Cumhuriyeti (Republic of Uyghur East Turkestan), https://www.facebook.com/uygurturkistan?fref=ts; and Doğu Türkistan, https://www.facebook.com/AnayurtTurkistan?fref=ts.

12. Interview with Ümit Özdağ, former MHP member and founder of the Twenty-First Century Turkey Institute (21. Yüzyıl Türkiye Enstitüsü), Ankara, August 2013.

13. "*Belli bir soydan gelen Türkler*"; "*ırkız Türkler*". Interview with MHP local government official and his supporters, Giresun, March 2014.

14. For a discussion of his and like-minded activists' thought traditions, see Ayşe Hür, "*Nihal Atsiz, Reha Oğuz Türkkan ve Turancılık Davası*," *Radikal Gazetesi*, February 10, 2013; and Mustafa Müftüoğlu, *Çankaya'da Kabus—1944 Turancılık Davası* (Ankara: Başak Yayınevi, 2005). In English, see Umut Uzer, "Racism in Turkey: The Case of Huseyin Nihal Atsiz," *Journal of Muslim Minority Affairs* 22, no. 1 (2002): 119–130.

15. Interview with *Ülkü Ocakları* member, Giresun, March 2014.

16. For broader academic discussions of the elements believed to constitute shared Turkic culture, see Anthony Hyman, "Turkestan and Pan-Turkism Revisited," *Central Asian Review* 16, no. 3 (1997): 339–351; and Jacob Landau, *Pan-Turkism: from Irredentism to Cooperation*, 2nd rev. ed. (London: C. Hurst, 1995).

17. "*Bahçeli: Kürt Sorunu Yoktur*," *Yurt Gazetesi*, November 4, 2012, http://www.yurtgazetesi.com.tr/politika/yenilendi-bahceli-kurt-sorunu-yoktur-h22080.html.

18. A subtitle from National Party (*Ulusal Parti*) chairman Gökçe Fırat's compilation of essays, entitled *Türk Yurdu Anadolu: Ermeni, Yunan, ve Kürt İddialarına Yanıtlar* (Istanbul: İleri Yayınları, 2012), 156. Tellingly, his book's title translates as *Anatolia, Home of the Turk: Responses to the Claims of Armenians, Greeks, and Kurds*.

19. Fırat, *Türk Yurdu Anadolu*, 168.

20. Ibid., 198.

21. Indicative of this sentiment, one survey respondent from Düzce stated that the characters in the film *Nefes: Vatan Sağolsun* (*Breath: Long Live the Homeland*) represented the best

examples for citizens of Turkey because they were nationalist (*milliyetçi*). The film depicts a group of Turkish soldiers valiantly defending a relay station in southeastern Turkey against attacks from the PKK.

22. Interview with *Ülkü Ocakları* member, Giresun, March 2014.

23. Interview with chairman of the Eskişehir branch of the Turkish Hearths (Türk Ocakları), Eskişehir, July 2013. Many, but not all, Pan-Turkic Nationalists are pious Muslims. As there is no significant contestation among Pan-Turkic Nationalists over the constitutive norm of piety—that is, fellow Pan-Turkic Nationalists sharing the other identity components outlined generally here do not question each other regarding their level of piety—I placed them both within the same identity proposal. Further, Türk Ocakları members are quick to distinguish themselves from the ultra-right-wing Ülkü Ocakları, but often manifest the same beliefs, if not the same zealous commitment to pursuing them. I therefore place them within the same proposal.

24. My translation from "*entelektüel namusu.*" İskender Öksüz, *Türküm Özür Dilerim* (Istanbul: Bilgi Kültür Sanat, 2013), 226.

25. The violence of the measures advocated to protect the Turkish nation against perceived threats such as secessionist Kurds and imperialist Americans manifests itself in pictures shared and comments made on Facebook pages devoted to Pan-Turkic Nationalist themes. See, among many others, Türkmeneli Cephesi (Turkmen Front), https://www.facebook.com/TurkmeneliCephesiResmiSayfa/.

26. Interview with three members of Ülkü Ocakları, Giresun, March 2014. Interview with two members of the MHP, Trabzon, March 2014. All members of the organizations spoken with during the interviews stressed the need for education and being informed about the prevalence of untruths in order to be an effective defender of the Turkish nation.

27. The Israeli government's view of the series' portrayal of Jews and Israelis as "offensive and "degrading" provoked (or became the excuse for, depending on the source consulted) the meeting now famous in the history of diplomatic protocol, in which Turkish ambassador to Israel Oğuz Çelikkol was seated in a chair lower than that of Israeli deputy foreign minister Danny Ayalon and at which only the Israeli flag was present. For his personal account, see Oğuz Çelikkol, *One Minute'ten Mavi Marmara'ya* (Istanbul: Doğan Egmont Yayıncılık, 2014), 90–94.

28. Twenty-one-year-old survey respondent from Sivas.

29. Twenty-one-year-old survey respondent from Adana.

30. Twenty-two-year-old survey respondent from Ankara.

31. David Kushner documents an "open and growing concern with the fate and well-being of all Turkic communities." See David Kushner, "Self-Perception and Identity in Contemporary Turkey," *Journal of Contemporary History* 32, no. 2 (1997): 228.

32. Bülent Aras, "Turkey's Policy in the Former Soviet South: Assets and Options," *Turkish Studies* 1, no. 1 (2000): 38.

33. Rory Finnin, "Captive Turks: Tatars in Pan-Turk Literature," *Middle Eastern Studies* 50, no. 4 (2014): 291–308.

34. Interview with Özgür Erdem, Ulusal Parti deputy chairman, Istanbul, August 2013.

35. Themes of a hostile "inferiority complex toward the West" because of Turkey's "traumatic past" pervade Pan-Turkic Nationalist discourse. Interview with Orkun, academic and self-described moderate Pan-Turkist, Ankara, August 2013.

36. See, for example, notices of rallies and signature campaigns shared on Facebook, such as "Recognize the 1992 Khojali Masscare—Demonstration by Young Turks," http://allevents.in/new%20york/recognize-the-1992-khojaly-massacre-demonstration-by-young-turks/257557920987937#; "*Hocalı Katliamı Soykırım Sayılsın—İmza Kampanyası*" ("Let the Khojali Massacre Be Counted as a Genocide—Campaign for Signatures"), https://www.facebook.com/hocalikatliami; "*Hocalı Katliamı Bir Soykırımdır*" ("The Khojali Massacre Is a Genocide"), https://www.facebook.com/pages/HOCALI-KATL%C4%B0AMI-B%C4%B0R-SOYKIRIMDIRB%C4%B0R-M%C4%B0LYON-%C3%9CYE-%C4%B0%C3%87%C4%B0N-DAVET-ED%C4%B0N-L%C4%B0STEN%C4%B0Z%C4%B0/111132045575482; and "*İki Devlet Bir Millet El Ele*" ("Two States, One Nation, Hand in Hand"), https://www.facebook.com/

NeverForgetKhojaly/photos/a.179676775471600.30415.179331222172822/191523644286913/.

37. Indeed, Republican Nationalist individuals who share the militancy and anti-Americanism of Pan-Turkists but have a social purpose of upholding Atatürk's principles rather than protecting the larger Turkic nation also read the book and enjoyed its precepts. I thank Berk Esen for this insight.

38. Orkun Uçar and Burak Turna, *Metal Fırtına* (Istanbul: Timaş Yayınları, 2012), 23–24.

39. Interview with Ülkü Ocakları member, Giresun, March 2014.

40. Turkish director Fatih Akın eventually abandoned the plan to make the movie due to a dearth of available actors. He has since received death threats from groups for his efforts to portray Dink's story, as well as for his recent film, *The Cut*, which addresses the Armenian genocide. Türkçü Turancılar Derneği, one of the groups mentioned above as established to protect Turkish identity, sent death threats via Twitter. See *"Agos'a ve Fatih Akın'a Tehdit,"* *Birgün Gazetesi*, August 4, 2014, https://www.birgun.net/haber-detay/agos-a-ve-fatih-akin-a-tehdit-66568.html.

41. *"Agos'a Beyaz Bereli Tehdidi,"* *Cumhuriyet Gazetesi*, August 4, 2014, http://www.cumhuriyet.com.tr/haber/turkiye/101561/Agos_a_beyaz_bereli_tehdidi.html#.

42. *"Hrant Dink'in 7. ölüm yılında Oguz Samastı saygı sevgi ve hayranlıkla tebrik ediyoruz,"* Facebook, January 19, 2014, https://www.facebook.com/TR.Milliyetci.TR/posts/637188273011459?stream_ref=10.

43. Kushner, "Self-Perception and Identity in Contemporary Turkey,", 228.

44. *Kesintisiz* was a term frequently used by interviewees to describe Turks' history. Two other interviewees emphasized, separately, that while some Turks seem to need to choose between glorifying Atatürk (as Republican Nationalists might do) or the Ottoman Empire (as Ottoman Islamists might do), there is no need for such a divisive dispute because they are both part of Turks' continuously glorious history. Interviews with Ülkü Ocakları member, Giresun, and Turcology MA student, Ankara, March 2014.

45. See Uzer's discussion of a "holistic Turkist *Weltanschauung"* in "Racism in Turkey," 124–25.

46. *"Türkiye'deki insanlar."* Survey respondent Özden from Mersin.

47. Ömer Zülfü Livaneli, *Serenad* (Istanbul: Doğan Kitap, 2011), 153.

48. The use of liberalism here should not be conflated with recent negative connotations of "liberal" when used to describe members of the Yetmez Ama Evet (It's Not Enough, But Yes) movement, who supported the AKP's initial promises to expand rights and liberties but later criticized the regime's increasing authoritarianism.

49. Interview with Yüksel Taşkın, Istanbul, August 2013. A Christian citizen of Turkey stated that she found the AKP's linkage of being Muslim with being Turkish exclusionary, relating a story in which Muslim Turks asked her how she could be Christian if her name was Zeynep (a highly traditional Turkish female name). Author's observation of a Turkish-language class, Washington, DC, March 2012.

50. For a discussion of the politics of introducing *"Türkiyeli"* into the constitution to refer to citizens of Turkey, see Ioannis Grigoriadis, *"Türk or Türkiyeli?* The Reform of Turkey's Minority Legislation and the Rediscovery of Ottomanism," *Middle Eastern Studies* 43, no. 3 (2007): 423–438.

51. A fascinating pro-Kurdish nationalist literature exists in Turkey as well, from monographs detailing the efforts of PKK leader Abdullah Öcalan to romantic novels narrating the journey of young female Kurds to rediscover their unknowingly suppressed Kurdish identity as they fall in love with Kurdish activists. See, for example, Celal Temel, *Bir Dava İki Sevda* (*One Cause, Two Loves*) (Istanbul: Hemen Kitap, 2012).

52. In the 2011 general elections, BDP members ran as independent candidates in order to circumvent the barrier, then formed a party wing once in parliament.

53. Interview with Güneş, political scientist, Ankara, August 2014.

54. Pinar Tremblay, *"Kürt Kadın Hareketi Türk Siyasetini Şekillendiriyor,"* *Al-Monitor*, March 25, 2015, http://www.al-monitor.com/pulse/tr/originals/2015/03/turkey-women-in-middle-east-figen-yuksekdag.html#.

55. Second Article of the Founding Bylaws established at the Halkların Demokratik Kongresi, http://www.halklarindemokratikkongresi.net/hdp/tuzuk/kurulus-tuzugu/492.

56. *"HDP Listelerinin Yarısı Kadın," Milliyet Gazetesi*, March 26, 2015, http://www.milliyet.com.tr/hdp-listelerinin-yarisi-kadin/siyaset/detay/2034500/default.htm.

57. Yıldız Tar, *"HDP'den Eşcinsel Milletvekili Adayı,"* KaosGL, April 7, 2015, http://www.kaosgl.com/sayfa.php?id=19133. This is an LGBTQ-friendly website.

58. It is important to note that party affiliation does not correspond directly to the identity proposals I have specified. I classify Nazlıaka, for example, as a Western Liberalist, as indicated by her extensive support of LBGT and women's rights and her service on the EU Harmonization and Turkey-EU Joint Parliamentary Committee, but is a member of the CHP, the party founded by Atatürk and the political representation of many Republican Nationalists. As this party and identity proposal overlap is common in the CHP, Turkey's main opposition party, analysis of party membership or preference would be unhelpful and, indeed, counterproductive to a study of identity contestation in Turkey.

59. Minutes of "Women and LGBTQ Rights in Turkey—Progressing or Regressing?," seminar, Istanbul, November 6, 2013.

60. "European Parliament Resolution of 22 May 2012 on a 2020 Perspective for Women in Turkey—par. 36," European Parliament, April 2013, http://www.europarl.europa.eu/sides/getDoc.do?pubRef=-//EP//TEX.

61. Author's observation of the speech of Gülay Barbarosoğlu (31st Conference of International University Women, Boğaziçi University, August 16, 2013).

62. *"Özgecan Eyleminde Alınan Kadınlara Polisten Küfür, Hakaret, ve Tehdit,"* Sendika, February 23, 2015, http://www.sendika.org/2015/02/ozgecan-eyleminde-gozaltina-alinan-kadinlara-polisten-kufur-hakaret-ve-tehdit/. I classify this as a labor-friendly, Western Liberalist website.

63. While prejudice toward LGBTQ individuals aligns neatly with the constitutive norms of membership and behavior of Pan-Turkic Nationalist and Ottoman Islamist proposals, it seems to fit awkwardly with the Western and modern norms of Republican Nationalism. This seeming incongruence served as a stark reminder to me in my research that pregiven assumptions and cognitive shortcuts must be avoided to the greatest extent possible in trying to extract actual, rather than neatly logical, identity proposals.

64. Menekşe Tokyay, "World Values Survey Reveals Important Trends in Turkey," *Southeast European Times*, May 8, 2011, http://www.setimes.com/cocoon/setimes/xhtml/en_GB/features/setimes/features/2011/08/05/feature-03.

65. See *"Erdoğan: Eşcinsel Çift Ahlaka Ters,"* Bianet, March 23, 2013, http://www.bianet.org/bianet/lgbti/145282-erdogan-escinsel-cift-ahlaka-ters.

66. See "Homophobic Prejudices Broken by Gezi Incidents in Turkey," *Hürriyet Daily News*, July 29, 2013, http://www.hurriyetdailynews.com/homophobic-prejudices-broken-by-gezi-incidents-in-turkey.aspx?pageID=238&nID=51567&NewsCatID=339.

67. Interviews with Erkut, legal activist, and Sezen, field coordinator for social policies, gender identity, and sexual orientation studies and activist, Istanbul, August 2013.

68. This commitment to sustaining and further developing active ties with the EU is present in texts collected from TÜSİAD, but does not seem as clear of a priority for its conservative counterpart, MÜSİAD. Interview with TÜSİAD foreign trade official, Istanbul, August 2013.

69. Interview with Şafak Pavey, former CHP deputy chairman and MP, Ankara, June 2013. As in the discussion of Aylin Nazlıaka, I also classify Pavey as a Western Liberalist member of the CHP, further supporting the assertion that party membership is not always a good sign of identity proposal support.

70. See *"Kim Milyoner Olmak İster'de Büyük Hata,"* Akşam Gazetesi, June 5, 2014, http://www.aksam.com.tr/televizyon/kim-milyoner-olmak-isterde-buyuk-hata/haber-313607.

71. Ulusalcılar, who in the extreme might still be reasonably classified as Kemalist in the way those using the term in a derogatory fashion intend—that is, dogmatic believers bordering on the cultish in their reverence of Atatürk and refusal to accept criticism of him or his actions—are discussed below.

72. The entire text of the speech is available as an e-book on the website of the Ministry of Culture and Tourism, at http://ekitap.kulturturizm.gov.tr/TR,81464/nutuk.html.

73. Hülya Adak, "Myths and Self Na(rr)ations: Mustafa Kemal's *Nutuk* and Halide Edib's *Memoirs and The Turkish Ordeal," South Atlantic Quarterly* 102, no. 2 (2003): 512.

74. The question was posed as: "*Sizce 'Türk' olmanın en önemli üç unsuru nedir?*" Survey respondent İpek from Istanbul.
75. Survey respondent Kortay from Izmir.
76. Atatürk's penning of the phrase decorates the institute's home page. See http://www.tdk. gov.tr/.
77. The "Speak Turkish!" campaign of the 1930s, for example, was used to assimilate Turkey's Jewish population. See Soner Çağaptay, *Islam, Secularism, and Nationalism in Turkey: Who Is a Turk?* (London: Routledge, 2006), 57–62.
78. Şener Aktürk argues that rather than being mono-ethnic, as many critics have claimed, Turkey has traditionally had an anti-ethnic regime, which refused to recognize identification along ethnic lines as part of state policy. See Şener Aktürk, *Regimes of Ethnicity in Germany, Russia, and Turkey* (Cambridge, UK: Cambridge University Press, 2012).
79. In this use of nationalizing projects, it is important to note, as Taras Kuzio does in his rebuttal to Rogers Brubaker, that these projects can be civic-oriented rather than solely assimilatory projects led by an ethnic core. See Taras Kuzio, "Nationalising' States or Nation-Building? A Critical Review of the Theoretical Literature and Empirical Evidence," *Nations and Nationalism* 7, no. 2 (2001): 136.
80. Survey respondent Cuneyt from Istanbul.
81. This desire for lack of dependence takes different forms; in its most extreme nationalist form, alliances with both the United States and the EU are seen as dangerous. A frequent chant at rallies organized by the Ataturkist Thought Association (Atatürkçü Düşünce Derneği) and the Association for Support of a Modern Lifestyle (Çağdaş Yaşamı Destekleme Derneği) is "*Ne ABD ne AB, tam bağımsız Türkiye!*" ("Neither the US nor the EU, a completely independent Turkey!). Interview with Türker Ertürk, retired admiral and frequent speaker on Atatürkist thought, Istanbul, August 2013.
82. This dismemberment narrative and its implications for the identity contestations that took place during the founding years of the Turkish War of Independence—fought in defiance of the terms of the Treaty of Sèvres—are analyzed in detail in the following chapter.
83. Author's observation, Ankara, October 2012. Notably for this book's theory of identity contestation, on this day the Ankara municipality government, run by the AKP, declared that the annual march to observe Republic Day and show respect to Atatürk's legacy would be prohibited. The first crowds attempting to march, which included CHP general secretary Kemal Kılıçdaroğlu, were blocked by barriers and sprayed with tear gas in an attempt to disperse them. The crowds persisted in their efforts, and the march eventually took place, in greater numbers than usual due to the perceived offense against Atatürk and the freedom of assembly.
84. *Çağdaşlaşma ütopyası*. Hurşit Güneş, *Adalet Çağrısı CHP İçin Sosyal Demokrasi Seçeneği* (Istanbul: Doğan Kitap, 2014), 75–78. The author explicitly states that he uses the term "utopia" in the sense of a never-ending goal (*sonsuz amaç*) rather than in the sense of an unrealistic dream (*gerekçi olmayan bir hayal*).
85. "*Laik*" means secular, while "*layık*" means "worthy." See https://www.facebook.com/ pages/Laiksiz-T%C3%BCrkiyeAtat%C3%BCrke-Lay%C4%B1k-De%C4%9Fildir/ 157826307577847?fref=ts.
86. Website of the Türk Dil Kurumu, http://www.tdk.gov.tr/index.php?option=com_ content&view=article&id=77.
87. "*Sahte Zafer*," *Cumhuriyet Gazetesi*, February 22, 2015, http://www.cumhuriyet.com.tr/ haber/dunya/219254/ Sahte_zafer.html.
88. Philip Robins, "Between Sentiment and Self-Interest: Turkey's Foreign Policy toward Azerbaijan and the Central Asian States," *Middle East Journal* 47, no. 4 (1993): 593–610.
89. "*Türkiye'nin İlk Güzeli*," *Hürriyet Gazetesi*, March 1, 1998, http://hurarsiv.hurriyet.com.tr/ goster/haber.aspx?id=-8265.
90. Interview with Hatice and Ersin, retired civil servants, Ankara, August 2013.
91. Survey respondent Ahmet from Istanbul.
92. Interview with foreign policy official, Ankara, July 2013; interview with Kazım Kurt, CHP MP, Eskişehir, August 2013; interview with Ümit Ülgen, self-described Atatürkist organization National Center (Milli Merkez) board member, Istanbul, August 2013; interview with Hakan Türker, CHP local MP, Giresun, March 2014.

93. Another word translated as "nationalist," but having a very different meaning than the ethnic, Pan-Turkic connotation of *"milliyetçi," ulusalcı* is used, sometimes in a derogatory fashion, to describe what are classified here as hardcore Republican Nationalist individuals who have not relaxed their beliefs to any degree regarding how secularism, nationalism, and Turkey's borders should be protected. As the identity content remains the same for both hardcore and moderate Republican Nationalists, and only the degree to which they view Atatürk's principles as threatened and the appropriate means for protecting these principles varies, I classify them as supporters of the same proposal.

94. Interview, ministry official, Ankara, November 2013.

95. Ibid.

96. A survey respondent specifically criticizes other television characters for encouraging alcohol consumption before stating that Behzat Ç, from the police detective series of the same name, is a character who promotes superior values (*üstün değerler*) for Turkish society. Survey respondent from Istanbul.

97. A recent debate in the Turkish Parliament erupted over the Turkish Language Institute's use of the word *"müsait,"* meaning "available," to imply a woman "ready to flirt, who can easily flirt" (*"flört etmeye hazır olan, kolayca flört edebilen"*). CHP deputy chairman Levent Gök stated that the expression's emergence in an institute under the supervision of the state actually reflects an understanding held by those in power (the AKP). *"TBMM'de 'Müsait' Tartışması: Şu Tokmala bir Şey mi Yapacağız Bilmiyorum,"* *Radikal Gazetesi*, March 11, 2015, http://www.radikal.com.tr/politika/tbmmde_musait_tartismasi_su_tokmakla_bir_sey_mi_yapacagiz_bilmiyorum-1310681. This understanding represents a remarkable shift for an institution founded by Atatürk, an adocate of women's equality, to protect the Turkish language and, by doing so, protect the Turkish people.

98. Survey respondent from Karaman.

99. Survey respondent from Nevşehir.

100. Fatma Aksu, *"Onları Tanıştıran Yazara Vefa Ziyareti,"* *Hürriyet Gazetesi*, November 13, 2012, http://www.hurriyet.com.tr/onlari-tanistiran-yazara-vefa-ziyareti-21913330.

101. Survey respondent from Karaman.

102. Survey respondent from Istanbul.

103. *"Dindar bir gençlik yetiştirme var . . . bu sözlerimin arkasındayım"* (speech delivered at a meeting of the AKP with province ministers, February 1, 2012). For a YouTube video of the live broadcast on *T24*, see http://www.youtube.com/watch?v=4vJbr0c0EUQ.

104. *"Dindar bir gençlik yetiştirme var."*

105. Ibid.

106. *"Dindar bir nesil çağdaş olamıyor mu?"* (speech to a group of businessmen to celebrate the opening of a new construction project, February 6, 2012). For a YouTube video of the live broadcast on *T24*, see http://www.youtube.com/watch?v=EuN55EL71_k.

107. See *"Erdogan: İçki İçen Alkoliktir,"* *Milliyet Gazetesi*, June 2, 2013, http://www.milliyet.com.tr/erdogan-icki-icen-alkoliktir/siyaset/detay/1717637/default.htm.

108. Cenkut Yildirim, *Devişrme* (Istanbul: *Neden Kitap*, 2010), 215.

109. See *"Erdoğan'dan Cem Özdemir'e: Haddini Bil,"* Haberler, May 27, 2014, http://www.haberler.com/erdogan-dan-cem-ozdemir-e-haddini-bil-6079186-haberi/; and *"Erdoğan: Kendini Bil, Haddini Bil,"* *Akşam Gazetesi*, March 23, 2015, http://www.aksam.com.tr/siyaset/erdogan-kendini-bil-haddini-bil/haber-392051.

110. A photograph of the test paper was included in Beyar Özalp, *"Din Sınavında Yanlış Şık Ali İsmail!,"* Evrensel, April 3, 2015, http://www.evrensel.net/haber/109480/din-sinavinda-yanlis-sik-ali-ismail#.VR51glVxF8w.facebook.

111. A TV presenter was fired after AKP spokesman Hüseyin Çelik declared that exposing décolleté was "unacceptable." "Bloomberg Cracks Down on Cleavage," BloombergView, October 9, 2013, http://www.bloombergview.com/articles/2013-10-09/turkey-cracks-down-on-cleavage.

112. A ban was put in place on the state-run air carrier, Turkish Airlines. *"THY'den Kırmızı Ruj Yasağı,"* *Akşam Gazetesi*, April 29, 2013, http://www.aksam.com.tr/yasam/thyden-kirmizi-ruj-yasagi/haber-200689.

113. "'The Simpsons Slapped' with Fine by Turkish TV Authority for Poking Fun at God," *Hürriyet Daily News*, December 3, 2012, http://www.hurriyetdailynews.com/turkish-tv-authority-fines-the-simpsons-for-poking-fun-at-god.aspx?pageID=238&nid=35981.

114. A top ministerial official and founding AKP member stated that he and other AKP members grew up with such principles, and that it is only natural that this upbringing, coupled with religious education, would shape the domestic and foreign policies they believed were appropriate for Turkey. Interview with ministerial official and AKP member, Ankara, August 2013.

115. See, for example, "Nihat Hatipoğlu—İftar," aired on ATV on July 27, 2014, https://www.youtube.com/watch?v=C_zhKM9rvWE.

116. See Meltem Özgenç, "*TRT Ekranlarında Şok Eden Sözler*," *Hürriyet Gündem*, July 25, 2013, http://www.hurriyet.com.tr/gundem/24389288.asp.

117. "*Arınc'ın 'Kadınlar Sokakta Kahkaha Atmayacak' Açıklması Dış Basında*," *Cumhuriyet Gazetesi*, July 30, 2014, http://www.cumhuriyet.com.tr/haber/dunya/100091/Arinc_in__Kadin_sokakta_kahkaha_atmayacak__aciklamasi_dis_basinda.html#.

118. The title of the column, which laments the moral decline of women in Turkey and their neglect of Islam's prescriptive codes, translates as "Immodesty, Lewdness, and Uncharitableness." M. Şevket Eygi, "*İffetsizlik, Hayasızlık, Mürüvvetsizlik*," *Gazete Vahdet*, March 2, 2015, http://www.gazetevahdet.com/iffetsizlik-hayasizlik-muruvvetsizlik-1146yy.htm.

119. The title of a recent article on the reasons conservative women stay out of the workforce—the belief that they are solely responsible for the rearing of children and the fear of harassment in the workplace by conservative men unused to interacting with women outside of their families—provides excellent insight into the spread of Ottoman Islamism's socially conservative constitutive norms and the potential outcomes of this spread: Ayşe Buğra, "*Muhafazakârlık Arttıkça Kadın İstihdamı Düşüyor*" ("As Conservatism Increases Women's Employment Falls"), *Akşam Gazetesi*, March 8, 2011, http://www.aksam.com.tr/roportaj/muhafazakarlik-arttikca-kadin-istihdami-dusuyor--24735h/haber-24735.

120. *Namus cinayetleri*, or "honor killings," are generally carried out by a family member of a girl or woman who is believed to have brought shame on the family—by being thought to have behaved promiscuously or to have been raped, for example. The best-selling novel *Mutluluk* attempts to bring to the public's attention the story of Meryem, raped by her uncle and ordered by her rapist to be killed by his son/her cousin. Zülfü Livaneli, *Mutluluk* (Istanbul: Remzi Kitabevi, 2008). Despite activists' efforts to change perceptions about honor killings to condemn them as unacceptable forms of behavior, recent research suggests that the reputations of 81% of those who have been imprisoned for carrying out an honor killing have increased among their families since they committed the killings (89 out of 110 inmates). See Damla Yur, "*Namus Cinayeti İtibar Artırıyor!*," *Milliyet Gazetesi*, December 2, 2013, http://www.milliyet.com.tr/namus-cinayeti-itibar-artiriyor-/gundem/detay/1800936/default.htm. The "great majority" of the inmates with whom the researcher spoke stated that they "did not feel any regret for the murders they had committed."

121. The television series *Küçük Gelin* (*Little Bride*) tells the tragic story of one of thousands of Turkey's child brides (defined in Turkey as a girl married under the age of seventeen), who are forced into marriages arranged by their parents—often through unofficial *nikah* ceremonies performed by imams—to expunge family honor or bring the family financial compensation.

122. In another telling title linking the rise of the AKP and its spread of socially conservative constitutive norms of behavior regarding women's place in society, many newspapers from a variety of ideological perspectives reported the finding that the murder of women had increased 1400% during AKP rule. For the details of the study conducted by the Turkish University Women's Association, see "*Kadin Cinayetleri Son 7 Yilda 1400% Artmistir*," Istanbul, http://www.tukd.org.tr/basinhaber07.asp.

123. Interview with Zeynep, AKP supporter and organizer, Trabzon, March 2014. The same language was used in an interview with an AKP supporter and local government official, Eskişehir, August 2013.

124. Interview with Hasan Cem Yılmaz, Pir Sultan Abdal Cultural Association general secretary, Ankara, July 2013.

125. See "*Sizin inancınızı binlerce kişi aynı anda hiç yuhaladı mi?*" ("Have Thousands Ever Jeered at Your Faith at the Same Time?"), *T24*, June 18, 2012, http://t24.com.tr/haber/sizin-inancinizi-binlerce-kisi-ayni-anda-hic-yuhaladi-mi/206585. To provide balance and demonstrate that supporters of competing proposals engage in the same strategies of contestation through delegitimization, Kılıçdaroğlu has also engaged in demeaning Erdoğan's religious identity, saying, "You're not pious, you're a trader/seller of religion" (*Sen dindar değilsin, din tüccarısın*). See "*Dindar Değilsin, Din Tüccarısın,*" *Milliyet Gazetesi*, February 1, 2012, http://www.milliyet.com.tr/dindar-degil-din-tuccarisin/siyaset/siyasetdetay/01.02.2012/1496376/default.htm.

126. While examples abound, Turkish journalist Amberin Zaman's case illustrates well this exclusion and delegitimization of women who speak against the AKP government. In the run-up to the presidential election on August 10, 2014, Erdoğan singled out Zaman for her criticisms, calling her a "shameless woman (*edepsiz kadın*)" and a "dressed-up militant (*kılıklı militant*)" and saying she "disrespectfully insults a 99% Muslim people (*saygısızca yüzde 99'u Müslüman olan bu halka hakaret ediyorsun*)," ordering her to "know her place! (*haddini bil!*)". "*Başbakan Hedef Gösterdi, Enis Berberoğlu İstifa Etti,*" *Zaman Gazetesi*, August 9, 2014, http://www.zaman.com.tr/gundem_basbakan-hedef-gosterdi-enis-berberoglu-istifa-etti_2236635.html.

127. "Ak Parti, Birinci Olağan Genel Kongresi, Genel Başkan R. Tayyip Erdoğan'ın Konuşması" ("Chairman R. Tayyip Erdoğan's Speech at the First Extraordinary General Assembly of the Ak Parti"), October 13, 2003, https://www.akparti.org.tr/upload/documents/tüzük-2013-1.pdf.

128. Şener Aktürk, "Persistence of the Islamic Millet as an Ottoman Legacy: Mono-Religious and Anti-Ethnic definition of Turkish Nationhood," *Middle Eastern Studies* 45, no. 6 (2009): 893–909.

129. Only after massive domestic protests by electorally powerful Kurds, involving multiple deaths, and accusations that the AKP had supported ISIL, the group that was carrying out the attacks on Kobani, did the government allow limited numbers of Iraqi Kurdish peshmerga forces to cross into Syria through Turkish territory. See "*Türkiye Peşmerge'ye Kapıları Açtı,*" *Hürriyet Gazetesi*, October 20, 2014, http://www.hurriyet.com.tr/gundem/27420112.asp.

130. "*Ak Parti'den 'Demokratik Açılım' Kitapçığı,*" *Hürriyet Gazetesi*, January 22, 2010, http://www.hurriyet.com.tr/gundem/13557237.asp.

131. Cüneyt Ülsever, "*Demokratik Açılımın Neresindeyiz?*" *Hürriyet Gazetesi*, February 17, 2010, http://www.hurriyet.com.tr/yazarlar/13813794.asp.

132. As Abdullah Öcalan remains in jail, Kurdish parliamentarians Pervin Buldan and Sırrı Süreyya Önder read the text of his message in Kurdish and Turkish, respectively.

133. The speech contains the remarkable phrase "Distinguished people of Turkey, the Turkish people who know ancient Anatolia as Turkey should know that the nearly one-thousand-year-old existence *they have shared with the Kurds under the flag of Islam* is based upon a legal order of brotherhood and solidarity" (emphasis added). For the full text of the speech, see "*İşte Öcalan'ın Nevruz Mesajı,*" *Sabah Gazetesi*, March 21, 2013, http://www.sabah.com.tr/gundem/2013/03/21/iste-ocalanin-nevruz-mesaji.

134. See Zeki Sarıgil and Ömer Fazlıoğlu, "Religion and Ethno-Nationalism: Turkey's Kurdish Issue," *Nations and Nationalism* 9, no. 3 (2013): 551–571.

135. For a discussion of how to move away from struggles for gender equality and focus on gender justice—a perspective that has enraged many Western Liberalist and Republican Nationalist women's rights activists—see E. Sare Aydın Yılmaz, "A New Momentum: Gender Justice in the Women's Movement," *Turkish Policy Quarterly* 13, no. 4 (2015): 107–115.

136. "*Başbakan: 'Bu Tayyip Erdoğan Değişmez'*" *Hürriyet Gazetesi*, June 12, 2013, http://www.hurriyet.com.tr/gundem/23479966.asp.

137. Questioning the identity-based nature of this aid, one ministry official rhetorically asked, "Why do we send aid to Somalia, but not the Philippines?" Interview with ministerial official, Ankara, November 2013.

138. Survey respondent from Ankara. The film depicts very strong moral themes of piety and charity and closely mirrors the path of Turkish teachers in schools affiliated with Islamic

cleric Fethullah Gülen, an ally of the AKP until the two movements' dramatic rupture in 2013.

139. "Istanbul Center for Cultural Education," IHH Humanitarian Relief Foundation, http://www.ihh.org.tr/en/main/activity/cultural-aid/5/istanbul-center-for-culture-and-education/142.

140. "Islam Rising in Brazil," IHH Humanitarian Relief Foundation, http://www.ihh.org.tr/EN/main/region/americas/76/islam-rising-in-brazil/619.

141. "Regards from Vietnamese Muslims," IHH Humanitarian Relief Foundation, http://www.ihh.org.tr/en/main/news/0/regards-from-vietnamese-muslims/2262.

142. Cited in Günther Seufert, "Self-Image and Foreign Policy in Turkey" (research paper for Stifting Wissenschaft und Politik, German Institute for International and Security Affairs, 2012), 13.

143. Ibid.

144. Interview with AKP member and local government official, Eskişehir, August 2013.

145. See "Charges against *Muhteşem Yüzyıl* Actors and Directors Dismissed," *Hurriyet Daily News*, March 13, 2013, http://www.hurriyetdailynews.com/charges-against-muhtesem-yuzyil-actors-and-directors-dismissed.aspx?pageID=238&nID=42904&NewsCatID=381.

146. Survey respondent from Artvin.

147. Survey respondent from Tunceli.

148. Survey respondent from Erzurum. Like-minded respondents critical of *Muhteşem Yüzyıl*'s perceived corruption of history praised Faruk Aksoy's film epic *Fetih 1453* (*The Conquest 1453*) for accurately portraying "one of the most important events in Turkish history." Survey respondent from Istanbul. Another respondent from Istanbul emphasized that Turkey didn't need to see Behlül, a character from *Aşk-ı Memnu* who has an affair with his uncle's second wife Bihter, but "needs to be shown an example of a personality such as Fatih Sultan Mehmet." The respondent underlined the vehemence of his beliefs, adding, "I wouldn't suppose there is any need to write down [the sultan's] qualities" and asking, "is there any need to explain" why Behlül was the worst role model for citizens of Turkey.

149. The website of state-run channel TRT 1, which broadcasts the show, states the following: "*Filinta*, the first Ottoman police drama in the history of television, is a series showcasing the concepts of fairness, justice, friendship, brotherhood, and love" (http://www.trt1.com.tr/filinta/39029).

150. Commentary and accompanying video displayed with the title "*Bir Osmanlı Poliyesi 'Filinta' Yakında Başlıyor!*" on the website of the AKP-supportive *Yeni Şafak Gazetesi*, at http://www.yenisafak.com.tr/video-galeri/bir-osmanli-polisiyesi-filinta-yakinda-basliyor/19273.

Chapter 4

1. As this study's analysis focuses on competing proposals for national identity within the Republic of Turkey, the state is used as the institutional collectivity about which various understandings are proposed by its citizens. This is by no means the only possible application of the theory of identity contestation that I develop here. As chapter 7's investigation of identity contestation among (substate) nationalist movements suggests, the unit of analysis for which various, competing identities are proposed need not be fixed.

2. Alexander Wendt, "Anarchy Is What States Make of It," *International Organization* 46, no. 2 (1992): 401.

3. Alexander Wendt, *Social Theory of International Politics* (Cambridge, UK: Cambridge University Press, 1999), 224–30. This categorization of four types of identities belonging to a state based on relevance should not be confused with this study's identity framework, which differs by breaking down competing proposals for an identity within a state. Doing so enables me to specify the differences causing friction among supporters of competing proposals, facilitating analysis of changes in support for particular proposals over time.

4. Wendt, *Social Theory of International Politics*, 195.

5. Sinan Ciddi, *Kemalism in Turkish Politics: The Republican People's Party, Secularism, and Nationalism* (London: Routledge, 2009), 13–30.

6. Robert Cox, "Gramsci, Hegemony, and International Relations: An Essay in Method," in *Gramsci, Hegemony, and International Relations*, ed. Stephen Gill (Cambridge, UK: Cambridge University Press, 1993), 42.

7. Ahmet Davutoğlu, *Stratejik Derinlik: Türkiye'nin Uluslararası Konumu* (Istanbul: Küre Yayınları, 2001), 69.

8. For a broad spectrum of discussions on various aspects of the reforms, see Jacob Landau, ed., *Atatürk and the Modernization of Turkey* (Boulder, CO: Westview Press, 1984). See also Erik Zürcher, *The Young Turk Legacy and Nation Building: From the Ottoman Empire to Ataturk's Turkey* (London: I. B. Tauris, 2010); Soner Çağaptay, *Islam, Secularism, and Nationalism in Modern Turkey: Who Is a Turk?* (London: Routledge, 2006); Suna Kili, *The Atatürk Revolution: A Paradigm of Modernization* (Istanbul: Türkiye İş Bankası, 2003); Nilüfer Göle, "Secularism and Islamism in Turkey: The Making of Elites and Counter-Elites," *Middle East Journal* 51, no. 1 (1997): 46–58; and Ali Kazancıgil and Ergun Özbudun, *Ataturk: Founder of a Modern State* (Hamden, CT: Archer Books, 1981). For collections of Turkish sources detailing the reforms and the philosophical precepts underlying them, see Leman Şenalp, *Atatürk Kaynakçası* (Ankara: Türk Tarih Kurumu Basımevi, 1984); and Kenan Akçay, *Kemalizm Üzerine* (Istanbul: ABeCe, 1981). For an example of how the subject of Atatürk and his reforms is taught in Turkish universities, see İhsan Güneş, ed., *Atatürk İlkeleri ve İnkılâp Tarihi I-II* (Eskişehir: Anadolu Üniversitesi Açıköğretim Fakültesi Yayınları, 1998); for an analysis how the subject is taught, see Betül Aslan, "*Türkiye'de Milli Tarih Anlayışı Bağlamında Dünden Bugüne İnkılâp Tarihi Dersleri*," *Kazım Karabekir Eğitim Fakultesi Dergisi*, no. 9 (2004), http://e-dergi.atauni.edu.tr/ataunikkefd/article/view/1021003872.

9. The acronym ATAMER (essentially "Atatürk Center") is used for various research centers in Turkish universities, such as Süleyman Demirel University (Isparta), Sakarya University (Sakarya), Galatasaray University (Istanbul), and Çanakkale On Sekiz Mart University (Çanakkale); what the acronym stands for can vary slightly from university to university. The acronym is also used by the Anadolu Tarih Araştırmaları Merkezi (Center for Anatolian History Studies); see http://www.atukad.org.tr/index.html.

10. Rogers Brubaker, *Nationalism Reframed: Nationhood and the National Question in the New Europe* (Cambridge, UK: Cambridge University Press, 1996), 79–83.

11. Donald Everett Webster, *The Turkey of Atatürk: Social Process in the Turkish Reformation* (Philadelphia, PA: American Academy of Political and Social Science, 1939), 244–45. For an analysis by a government-appointed language expert of Armenian descent, to whom Atatürk gave a surname fittingly implying "he explains (*açar*) language (*dil*)," see Agop Dilaçar, *Atatürk ve Türkçe, Atatürk ve Türk Dili* (Ankara: Türk Dil Kurumu, 1963), 47–49.

12. See "*II. Mahmut Dönemi Islahatlar*," January 19, 2014, http://www.ataturkilkeveinkilaplari. com/osmanlida-islahat-hareketleri/ii-mahmut-donemi-islahatlari.html.

13. "*İslam dünyasının önderi tavrı takınmaya başladı*," "*yeni kurulmuş cumhuriyet yönetimi için tehlikeli olabileceği*." See http://www.atamer.sakarya.edu.tr/ink-03.htm.

14. For a discussion of Balkan politics during the Ottoman and Atatürk eras, see Ahmet Eyicil, "*Atatürk Devrinde Türkiye'nin Balkan Politikası*," Atatürk Araştırma Merkezi (Atatürk Research Center), Atatürk Kültür, Dil, ve Tarih Yüksek Kurumu (Atatürk Higher Institute of Culture, Language, and History), http://www.atam.gov.tr/dergi/sayi-59/ataturk-devrinde-turkyenin-balkan-politikasi.

15. Vural Savaş, *Atatürkçü İdeoloji ve Çağdaş İdeolojiler*, Atatürk Araştırma Merkezi (Atatürk Research Center), Atatürk Kültür, Dil, ve Tarih Yüksek Kurumu (Atatürk Higher Institute of Culture, Language, and History), http://www.atam.gov.tr/dergi/sayi-11/ataturkcu-ideoloji-ve-cagdas-ideolojiler.

16. See, for example, Suna Kili, *Ataturk Revolution: A Paradigm of Modernization* (London: Milet Publishing, 2004); Andrew Davison, "Secularism and Modernization in Turkey: The Ideas of Ziya Gökalp," *Economy and Society* 24 (May 1995): 189–224; G. L. Lewis, "Ataturk's Language Reform and Modernization," in *Atatürk and the Modernization of Turkey*, ed. Jacob Landau (Boulder, CO: Westview Press, 1984), 195–214; S. N. Eisenstadt, "The Kemalist Regime and Modernization: Some Comparative and Analytical Remarks," in Landau, *Atatürk and the Modernization of Turkey*, 3–16; and Kemal Karpat, *Turkey's Politics* (Princeton, NJ: Princeton University Press, 1959).

17. See http://www.resulullah.org/kutsal-emanetler-nerelerde-sergileniyor.
18. Eda Bildek, *1453 Fetih* (Konya: Mola Kitap, 2012), 139–40.
19. Like the works of Zülfü Livaneli, the Istanbul-based plots of Ümit's crime novels, starring his hero Chief Inspector Nevzat, serve as a forum in which numerous debates over identity take place in the course of solving the murder(s). His Republican Nationalist deputy inspector Ali's stories about his "*Atatürkçü*" father (p. 190) and his negative childhood experiences with a stern Islamist schoolteacher recount the reasons he views pious Muslims as "backward" (*örümcek kafalı*, literally "spider-headed") and feels he is "coming to another country" when entering Istanbul's conservative Çarşamba neighborhood (pp. 140–43).
20. See Erol Koroğlu, *Ottoman Propaganda and Turkish Identity: Literature in Turkey during World War I* (London: IB Tauris, 2007), 183.
21. Construction of the first Turkish parliamentary building in the Ulus neighborhood of Ankara began in 1915 under the direction of the Committee of Union and Progress. The small structure is now a museum featuring displays of Atatürk's personal effects and correspondence as well as those of the second and third presidents of the republic, İsmet İnönü and Celal Bayar.
22. Speech of İsmet İnönü, October 9, 1923, cited in Hamze Eroğlu, "*Cumhuriyetin İlanının Hazırlıkları,*" Atatürk Araştırma Merkezi (Atatürk Research Center), Atatürk Kültür, Dil, ve Tarih Yüksek Kurumu (Atatürk Higher Institute of Culture, Language, and History), http://www.atam.gov.tr/dergi/sayi-16/turkiye-cumhuriyetinin-ilani. All translations are the author's.
23. İsmet İnönü, *Hatıralar: İkinci Kitap* (*Memories: Second Book*) (Ankara: Bilgi Yayınevi, 1987), 167.
24. Osman Okyar, "Atatürk's Quest for Modernism," in Landau, *Ataturk and the Modernization of Turkey*, 50.
25. For an Ottoman Islamist interpretation of the life and exile of Mehmet VI Vahideddin, which suggests that the rainy day on which the sultan leaves his home signifies that Istanbul is crying in despair at the loss of the empire (*"İstanbul ağlıyor"*), see the novel by Zekeriya Yıldız, *Sürgün Sultan* (Istanbul: Nesil, 2012).
26. Mustafa Kemal Atatürk, *Nutuk* (speech presented on October 15–20, 1927, in Ankara), chronological sections at Türkiye Cumhuriyeti Kültür ve Turizm Bakanlığı (Republic of Turkey's Ministry of Culture and Tourism), http://ekitap.kulturturizm.gov.tr/TR,81466/turk-yurdunun-genel-durumu.html.
27. "*Halifeliğin Kaldırılması*" ("The Abolition of the Caliphate"), Sakarya University's ATAMER research center, http://www.atamer.sakarya.edu.tr/ink-03.htm.
28. *Nutuk*, full version, Atatürk Araştırma Merkezi (Atatürk Research Center), Atatürk Kültür, Dil, ve Tarih Yüksek Kurumu (Atatürk Higher Institute of Culture, Language, and History), http://www.atam.gov.tr/nutuk/hilafet-konusunda-halkin-suphe-ve-endisesini-gidermek-icin-yaptigim-aciklamalar.
29. Atatürk, *Nutuk*, chronological sections at Türkiye Cumhuriyeti Kültür ve Turizm Bakanlığı, http://ekitap.kulturturizm.gov.tr/TR,82434/muslumanlari-bir-halife-hayaliyle-hala-yaniltmaya-calis-.html.
30. Ibid. Cited section at http://ekitap.kulturturizm.gov.tr/TR,82431/halifeligin-kaldirilmasinin-zamani-gelmisti.html.
31. Osman Okyar, "Atatürk's Quest for Modernism," in Landau, *Atatürk and the Modernization of Turkey*, 45.
32. *Türkiye Büyük Millet Meclisi, 671 No'lu Şapka İktisası Hakkında Kanun*, November 25, 1925, published in *Resmi Gazete*, November 28, 1925.
33. *Tutanak Dergisi*, Dönem 4, c. 24'e ek, cited in Özdemir İnce, "*Bazı Kisvelerin Giyilemeyeceğine Dair Kanun,*" *Hürriyet Gazetesi*, December 3, 2010, http://hurarsiv.hurriyet.com.tr/goster/haber.aspx?id=16436998&yazarid=72.
34. The first decision made by the first party to take power from the CHP, the Democratic Party (Demokrat Parti) led by Republican Nationalist Adnan Menderes but comprising a loose coalition that included center-right conservatives, was to reinstitutionalize the *ezan* in Arabic. See Hakan Yavuz, *Islamic Political Identity in Turkey* (Oxford: Oxford University Press, 2003), 33.
35. İsmet İnönü, *Hatıralar: Cilt 2* (Ankara: Bilgi Yayınevi, 1985), 223.

36. Falih Rıfkı Atay, a writer and friend of Atatürk, fondly recollected the rigorous implementation of the Latin alphabet. See *Çankaya* (Istanbul: Doğan Kardeş Matbaası, 1969), 2:439, cited in Binnaz Toprak, *Islam and Political Development in Turkey* (Leiden: E. J. Brill, 1981), notes to ch. 3, 145n20.

37. Mustafa Kemal Atatürk, "*Ülkesini, yüksek istiklalini korumasını bilen Türk millet, dilini de yabancı diller boyunduruğundan kurtarmaılıdır*," cited at Türk Dil Kurumu, http://www.tdk. gov.tr/.

38. The commentary under the cartoon in a monograph lamenting the "sale" of the empire and the deliberate disposal of its legacy states that Atatürk is "trampling on/chewing up" Arabic letters under his feet ("*Atatürk'ü Arap harflerini ayakları altında çiğnerken gösteren bu karikatür*"), a decidedly critical interpretation of a cartoon intended to glorify the language reform. See Mustafa Armağan, *Satılık İmparatorluk: Lozan ve Osmanlının Reddedilen Mirası* (Istanbul: Timaş Yayınları, 2013), 190.

39. See Andrew Mango, *Atatürk: The Biography of the Founder of Modern Turkey* (New York: Overlook Press, 2002), 41–42.

40. See the "Who Are We?" ("*Biz Kimiz?*") page, http://turkcesivarken.com/biz-kimiz/.

41. Interview with the owner of a small shop, Ankara, December 2012. The shop owner was careful to emphasize that he did not resent foreigners themselves and appreciated being able to speak with them in Turkish.

42. See Oktay Sinanoğlu, *Bye Bye Türkçe Bir Nev-Türk Rüyası* (Istanbul: Bilim+Gönül, 2012), 8. The spelling of New York as *Nev-York* is rare in Turkish usage and likely indicates a strict following of the language laws that until recently had prohibited use of the Kurdish letter "w" in Turkish writing, as described below.

43. Mustafa Yürekli, "*Nutuk'u Orijinalinden Okuyamayan Nasıl Atatürkçü Olur?*," Haber7, October 15, 2009, http://www.google.com/url?sa=t&rct=j&q=&esrc=s&source=web&cd=2&ved=0CCc QFjAB&url=http%3A%2F%2Fwww.haber7.com%2Fyazarlar%2Fmustafa-yurekli%2F444759-nutuk8217u-orjinalinden-okuyamayan-nasil-ataturkcu-olur&ei=9ZgmVYuqM6OxsASb5oGwC g&usg=AFQjCNEajGGDVOG-KRTgCT-tkKsg0UCfvg&bvm=bv.90237346,d.cWc.

44. During a speech in which he defended the benefits of the mandatory Ottoman Turkish classes, given at an event titled "An Evening of Respect for Calligraphist Hasan Çelebi," Erdoğan declared to the guest of honor: "Not just for what you have written or read or the letters you teach, God willing may my Lord (*Rabbim*) reward you for each letter you have poured out through calligraphy." See "*Erdoğan'dan Sert Osmanlıca Çıkışı*," InternetHaber, December 13, 2014, http://www.internethaber.com/erdogandan-sert-osmanlica-cikisi-747129h.htm.

45. "*Erdoğan 'Ecdadın Mezar Taşları Okunmuyor' Dediği Mezarlar Risk Altında*," T24, January 13, 2015, http://t24.com.tr/haber/ecdadin-okunamayan-mezar-taslari-risk-altinda,283586. The article contains a quote from Erdoğan indicative of attempts to spread Ottoman Islamism across more of Turkey's society: "Whether they want to or not, [the students] will learn" ("*İsteseler de istemeseler de, öğrenecekler*").

46. Namık Açıkgöz, "Liselere Osmanlıca Dersleri," HaberVaktım, April 14, 2012, http:// m.habervaktim.com/author_article_detail.php?id=49640.

47. "'Osmanlıca Zor ve Karışık Değil,'" *Sabah Gazetesi*, December 9, 2014, http://www.sabah. com.tr/gundem/2014/12/09/osmanlica-zor-ve-karisik-degil.

48. Cited in "*Zorunlu Osmalıca Dersi Tartışma Yarattı*," *Posta Gazetesi*, December 5, 2014, https:// twitter.com/yusufhalacoglu/status/580191242266546176.

49. Cited from a copy of the law posted at Ministry of National Education (Milli Eğitim Bakanlığı), http://mevzuat.meb.gov.tr/html/112.html.

50. See "*Q, W, X Kimliklere Girecek*," Memurlar, October 31, 2013, http://www.memurlar.net/ haber/422057/.

51. Türkiye Büyük Millet Meclisi Bakanlığına, "*Bingöl İlini Adının Çewlig Olarak Değiştirilmesi Hakkında Kanun Teklifi*" (submitted by BDP Bingöl Milletvekili İdris Baluken, November 13, 2013), 4.

52. The results of the study, conducted by Fırat University professor Harun Tunçel, are cited in Tarık Işık, "*12 Bin 211 Köyün Adı Değiştirilmiş*," *Radikal Gazetesi*, May 13, 2009, http://www. radikal.com.tr/turkiye/12_bin_211_koyun_adi_degistirilmis-935681.

53. Türkiye Büyük Millet Meclisi Bakanlığına. *"Bingöl İlini Adının Çewlig Olarak Değiştirilmesi Hakkında Kanun Teklifi"* (submitted by BDP Bingöl Milletvekili İdris Baluken, November 13, 2013), 4. The line cited from the memorandum was originally *"yabancı dil ve köklerden gelen ve kullanılmasında büyük karışıklığa yol açan yerleşme yerleri ile tabii yer adlarının Türkçe adlarla degiştirilmesi."*

54. *"Burası Türkiye Kürtçe Yasak,"* Evrensel, February 5, 2014, http://www.evrensel.net/haber/ 77785/burasi-turkiye-kurtce-isim-yasak. This is a Kurdish-friendly website.

55. See Ömer Şahin, *"'Q, W, X'in 85 Yıllık Yasağı Bitiyor,"* *Radikal Gazetesi*, September 27, 2013, http://www.radikal.com.tr/turkiye/q_w_xin__85_yillik_yasagi_bitiyor-1152737.

56. Celal Temel, *Bir Dava İki Sevda* (Istanbul: Hemen Kitap, 2012).

57. Tunceli province was named Dersim until the government believed a name change was needed as part of the Republican Nationalization of the country in 1936. Among other actions, the name change served to spark the Dersim Rebellion (Dersim İsyanı) against the government, in which thousands of Kurdish civilians were killed, in 1937–1938.

58. Temel, *Bir Dava İki Sevda*, 73.

59. For an in-depth discussion of the concept of active neutrality and Turkey's struggle to stay out of the conflict, see Selim Deringil, *Turkish Foreign Policy during the Second World War: An 'Active' Neutrality* (Cambridge, UK: Cambridge University Press, 1989).

60. Democrat Party (Demokrat Parti) cofounder and leader Adnan Menderes, for example, was arguably a Republican Nationalist who was opposed to the CHP-proposed land reform, which threatened his own land interests and thus, with the support of CHP leader İnönü, split off to form a separate party in 1946. See Mustafa Altınoğlu, *Geçmişin Yüküyle Yenilik Arayışı: CHP'de Lider, Tavan Taban Analizi* (Ankara: SETA Yayınları, 2014), 24.

61. The main outlier in the Republican Nationalist narrative of avoiding international conflicts at all costs so as to protect Turkey's borders and the nation they surround is the 1974 invasion of Cyprus, undertaken following years of hesitation in response to the intercommunal violence being waged among the Greek Cypriots. The invasion, authorized by Republican Nationalist prime minister Bülent Ecevit and carried out by the military displays a clear tension between the overlapping Republican Nationalist social purposes of protecting the Turkish nation, as many of those on the Turkish side of the de facto border were Turkish citizens (as opposed to Turkic populations in Crimea or Xinjiang, which would constitute an in-group for Pan-Turkic Nationalists), and protecting its borders. For an in-depth analysis of the dynamics of the conflict and its motivations, see William Hale, *Turkish Foreign Policy since 1774*, 3rd ed. (London: Routledge, 2012); and Clement Dodd, *The History and Politics of the Cyprus Conflict* (New York: Palgrave Macmillan, 2010).

62. For an analysis of the economic and societal effects of this opening, including the emergence of the pious "Anatolian Tigers" who would form part of the financial backbone of Ottoman Islamism's support base, see Evren Hoşgör, "Islamic Capital/Anatolian Tigers: Past and Present," *Middle Eastern Studies* 47, no. 2 (2011): 343–360; Ziya Öniş, "Turgut Özal and His Economic Legacy: Turkish Neoliberalism in Critical Perspective," *Middle Eastern Studies* 40, no. 4 (2004): 113–134; and Ziya Öniş, "Neoliberal Globalization and the Democracy Paradox: The Turkish General Elections of 1999," *Journal of International Affairs* 54, no. 1 (2000): 283–306.

63. See, for example, Ali Balcı, "The Kurdish Movement's EU Policy in Turkey: An Analysis of a Dissident Ethnic Bloc's Foreign Policy," *Ethnicities*, October 9, 2013, http://etn.sagepub. com/content/early/2013/10/08/1468796813504551. I suggest further research on this dynamic as a strategy of "take it outside" identity contestation in the concluding chapter.

64. İhsan Dağı, "Democratic Transition in Turkey, 1980–83: The Impact of European Diplomacy," *Middle Eastern Studies* 32, no. 2 (1996): 124–141.

65. The constitution was accepted by 92% of the voters in a public referendum on November 7, 1982, which likely speaks more to the repressiveness of the era than it does to any level of near unanimous support for the military's actions and its regulation of Turkey's society.

66. Mustafa Kemal Atatürk, *Atatürk'ün Söylev ve Demeçleri* (Ankara: Türk İnkılâp Tarihi Enstitüsü, 1952), 226, cited in Frank Tachau and Metin Heper, "The State, Politics, and the Military in Turkey," *Comparative Politics* 16, no. 1 (1983): 20.

67. The older father and son finally reconcile shortly before Sadık's death, an act whose significance is demonstrated by nine survey respondents' selecting Hüseyin as an "ideal example" for Turkish people (survey respondent from Ankara), citing his "family values" (survey respondent from Istanbul) and his willingness to "do anything for his son" (survey respondent from Amasya).

68. Ertuğrul Günay, "*CHP Neden Başarısız?,*" *Radikal Gazetesi*, February 1, 2004, http://www. radikal.com.tr/ek_haber.php?ek=r2&haberno=3021.

69. Ahmet Altan, for example, is the founder of the liberal and openly pro-Kurdish newspaper *Taraf Gazetesi*. For a full discussion of the movement and its origins, see Mehmet Altan, *İkinci Cumhuriyetin Yol Hikayesi* (Istanbul: Hayykitap, 2008). See also Metin Sever and Cem Dizder, eds., *Yeni Arayışlar, Yeni Yönelimler, İkinci Cumhuriyet Tartışmaları* (Ankara: Başak, 1993).

70. Sinan Ciddi, *Kemalism in Turkish Politics: The Republican People's Party, Secularism, and Nationalism* (London: Routledge, 2009), 97. The use of the term "red lines" here underscores the utility of applying a framework that can identify such red lines across competing identity proposals, as well as those that are questions from within. Ciddi provides an analysis of the İkinci Cumhuriyetçiler from the perspective of answering why social democracy has failed to take shape in Turkey. Ibid., 97–107.

71. Mehmet Altan, "Türkiye'nin Bütün Sorun Politik Devletten Liberal Devlete Geçememesidir," in *Yeni Arayışlar, Yeni Yönelimler, İkinci Cumhuriyet Tartışmaları*, ed. Metin Sever and Cem Dizder (Ankara: Başak, 1993), 56, cited in Ciddi, *Kemalism in Turkish Politics*, 105.

72. The full text of his piece was posted on the liberal website Bianet in a symposium of works related to "Rights struggles of the 90s" ("*90'larin Hak Mücaderleri*") on December 17, 2014, http:// www.bianet.org/bianet/siyaset/160861-ahmet-altan-yazisina-atakurt-basligini-attiginda.

73. Ahmet Altan, "Ah, Ahparik," *Taraf Gazetesi*, September 6, 2008, *Taraf Gazetesi*, http://arsiv. taraf.com.tr/yazilar/ahmet-altan/ah-ahparik/1820/.

74. "Ahmet Altan: Taboo-Breaking Journalist," *Today's Zaman*, December 31, 2010, http://www. todayszaman.com/national_person-of-the-year-ahmet-altan-taboo-breaking-journalist_ 231129.html.

75. "Jailed Turkish Journalists Nazlı Ilıcak and Altan Brothers Sentenced to Life in Jail," *Hürriyet Daily News*, February 16, 2018, http://www.hurriyetdailynews.com/istanbul-court-hands-down-aggravated-life-sentences-to-journalists-nazli-ilicak-altan-brothers-three-others-127438.

76. Interview with columnist at *Cumhuriyet Gazetesi*, Ankara, August 2013.

77. Deniz Baykal, interview with Güneri Civaoğlu in *Milliyet Gazetesi*, September 26, 2000, cited in Ciddi, *Kemalism in Turkish Politics*, 96.

78. Even if the motivation behind Baykal's shift in stance was purely electoral, the thinking guiding the more conciliatory tone arguably reflects a recognition of the evolving, moderated preferences among CHP voters.

79. Interview with Haldun Solmaztürk, retired infantry officer, Ankara, August 2013. The officer clearly separated being pro-European and being pro-EU, stating that he sees a shift from the former to the latter. Other, hardcore Republican Nationalist military retirees reject the prospect of EU membership as a European project of "imperialism." Interview with Türker Ertürk, retired admiral, Istanbul, August 2013.

80. Electoral failure and identity red lines are intertwined at the heart of this split, with Anadolu Partisi members frustrated with the selection of former OIC leader Ekmeleddin İhsanoğlu, whom they suspected of being an Islamist, as the "tent candidate" (*çatı aday*) supported by the CHP in what turned out to be an unsuccessful bid for the presidency in August 2014. See Vedat Özdan, "*Anadolu Partisi'yle Sol Şerit Doldu Mu?,*" *T24*, November 17, 2014, http://t24. com.tr/yazarlar/vedat-ozdan/anadolu-partisiyle-sol-serit-doldu-mu,10619.

81. Ciddi, *Kemalism in Turkish Politics*, 104.

82. Leftists (*solcular*), some of whom are also known as revolutionaries (*devrimciler*), comprised one side of an immensely violent ideological struggle that left thousands dead. In addition to street killings carried out by groups of right-wing thugs, prominent leftists who viewed themselves as part of Turkey's 1968 generation—some of whom also engaged in killing, robbery, and hostage-taking—were executed by the government, including Deniz Gezmiş, Yusuf Aslan, and Hüseyin İnan. While the leftist movement was decimated in large part following the

1980 coup, residual leftist sentiment manifests itself in political parties such as the Worker's Party of Turkey (Türkiye İşçi Partisi, TIP) and the Communist Party of Turkey (Türkiye Komunist Partisi, TKP); the Revolutionary People's Liberation Party Front (Devirmci Halk Kurtuluş Partisi-Cephesi, DHKP/C, which was responsible for the attack on the US embassy in Ankara in 2013); and the PKK (classified as a terrorist group by the United States and Turkey), as well as many Alevi and Kurdish politico-cultural organizations. Interviews with Erkan, TKP member, Ankara, November 2013; Besim Can Zırh, expert in Alevis, Ankara, August 2013; and Ekrem Güzeldere, expert on Kurds, August, Istanbul 2013. On the other side of the struggle, ultra-right-wing Pan-Turkic Nationalists viewed communists as anathema in their ideology and tyrannical in their political oppression of fellow Turkic brothers in Soviet Socialist Republics such as Azerbaijan and Turkmenistan. Interview with three members of the Ülkü Ocakları, Giresun, March 2014, and two members of the MHP, Trabzon, March 2014. The near-civil war conditions into which Turkey had devolved by the end of the 1970s in large part motivated the Turkish military to intervene and restore order.

83. See Sam Kaplan, *The Pedagogical State: Education and Politics of National Culture in Post-1980 Turkey* (Stanford, CA: Stanford University Press, 2006), 76.

84. Despite Kaplan's claims that the group seeks to "convert Ottoman Turkish heritage in political reality" (*Pedagogical State*, 76), the explanation of the group's emblem on its website evidences content much more in line with what I term Pan-Turkic Nationalism: the white background represents the spotlessness/purity and original authenticity of Turkish civilization (*Türk Medeneiyetinin Temizliğini, Orijinalliğini*); the red shaft symbolizes the eternal span of Turkishness (*Ebed Müddeti*), consistent with the Pan-Turkic narrative of pre-Ottoman and pre-Islamic roots; the blue of the three tiles stands for Turkishness (*Türklüğü*); and the arrangement of the three tiles represents the aesthetics of Islam (*İslam Estetistiğini*). See http://aydinlarocagi.org/amblemimiz/#.VShbz0bfYU0.

85. Interview with Nedim Ünal, hairman of the Eskişehir branch of the Turkish Hearths (Türk Ocakları, a similar but decidedly non-Ottoman-oriented sociopolitical group), Eskişehir, July 2013. A document issued by the State Planning Office (Devlet Planlama Teşkilatı, DPT) states: "Turkish culture and later Islamic culture" are "the sources of our national culture." Cited in Kaplan, *Pedagogical State*, 77.

86. See, for example, Deniz Kandiyoti, "The Travails of the Secular: Puzzle and Paradox in Turkey," *Economy and Society* 4, no. 1 (2012): 513–531.

87. Kaplan, *Pedagogical State*, 83.

88. See, for example, Ümit Cizre Sakallıoğlu, "Parameters and Strategies of Islam-State Interaction in Republican Turkey," *International Journal of Middle East Studies* 28, no. 2 (1996): 231–251; and Binnaz Toprak, "Religion as State Ideology in a Secular Setting: The Turkish-Islamic Synthesis," in *Aspects of Religion in Modern Turkey*, ed. Malcolm Wagstaff (Durham: University of Durham's Center for Middle Eastern and Islamic Studies, 1990). Volume 4 in Occasional Working Paper Series.

89. For a highly critical appraisal of Evren's usage of Islam, see a column posted in the leftist newspaper *Birgün* on the coup's anniversary: Nazım Alpman, "*12 Eylül İşçi Katliamlarıyla Sürüyor,*" *Birgün Gazetesi*, September 11, 2014, http://birgun.net/news/view/12-eylul-isci-katliamlariyla-suruyor/5302.

90. Ottoman Islamists targeted by the military regime refer to themselves as the "*12 Eylül mağdurları,*" or "those unjustly treated by the 12 September events"; the same expression is use in reference to the secularization process of February 28, 1997, as discussed in the next chapter. A common theme among Republican Nationalists is that at least part of the motivation behind the Ottoman Islamists' rise to power and how they have used that power is a desire for revenge (*intikam*) or a settling of accounts (*hesaplaşma*). Author's observations, Ankara, 2012–2014. At a gathering of some of these individuals to celebrate the guilty verdict issued against Kenan Evren as part of the *Ergenekon* trials of those deemed to be plotting to overthrow the AKP, an operator of a printing business stated: "I saw Kenan Evren while he was being sentenced, that's enough for me." Cited in Celil Kırnapcı, "*12 Eylül Mağdurları 32 Yıl Sonra Aynı Karede,*" *Zaman Gazetesi*, November 28, 2012, http://www.zaman.com.tr/gundem_12-eylul-magdurlari-32-yil-sonra-ayni-karede_2021764.html.

91. For an in-depth discussion of the inadvertent support the 1980 military coup and its after-math provided to Turkey's Islamists, see Banu Eligür, *The Mobilization of Political Islam in Turkey* (Cambridge, UK: Cambridge University Press, 2014).

92. William Armstrong, "The Mobilization of Turkish Islamism," *Hürriyet Daily News*, March 27, 2014, http://www.hurriyetdailynews.com/the-mobilization-of-turkish-isla-mism.aspx?pageID=238&nID=64129&NewsCatID=474.

93. See Sultan Tepe, *Beyond Sacred and Secular: Politics of Religion in Israel and Turkey* (Stanford, CA: Stanford University Press, 2008), 184.

94. See the breakdown of votes, posted on Secim-Sonuclari, http://www.secim-sonuclari.com/1987.

95. Tepe, *Beyond Sacred and* Secular, 185.

96. For a deeply informative ethnographic analysis of these processes, see Jenny White, *Islamist Mobilization in Turkey: A Study in Vernacular Politics* (Seattle: University of Washington Press, 2002). See also Ruşen Çakır, *Ne Şeriat Ne Demokrasi: Refah Partisini Anlamak* (Istanbul: Metis Kitap, 1994); and Sencer Ayata, "Patronage, Party, and the State: The Politicization of Islam in Turkey," *Middle East Journal* 50 (Winter 1996): 40–56.

97. White, *Islamist Mobilization in Turkey*, 55–56. A more recent "counter-reaction" to the rise of Ottoman Islamism during the later years of AKP rule is also quite evident; displaying a rep-lica of Atatürk's signature, from decals on car windows to tattoos on left arms (to connote a commitment to social democracy as opposed to the social conservatism of the political "Right") became an increasingly popular form of expressing Republican Nationalist solidarity since my first period of language study in Istanbul in 2010. While distinctions between identity proposals can at times be murky, the Atatürk signature provides a good litmus test that an individual is a Republican Nationalist (although of course not all supporters of the proposal have the tattoo).

98. Interview with Erhan, Ülkü Ocakları member, Giresun, March 2014.

99. Interviews with Erhan, Ülkü Ocakları member, Giresun; and Gamze, Gazi University Turcology MA student, Ankara, March 2014.

100. See the discussion of a "holistic Turkist *Weltanschauung*" in Umut Uzer, "Racism in Turkey."

101. Interviews with Özgür Erdem, Ulusalcı Parti deputy chairman, Istanbul, August 2013; and an MHP politician, Trabzon, March 2014.

102. Interview with Yonca, Hacettepe University faculty member, Ankara, March 2014.

103. Oral Sander, "Turkey and the Turkic World," *Central Asian Survey* 13, no. 1 (1994): 42 (emphasis added).

104. Ciddi, *Kemalism in Turkish Politics*, 106.

105. Interviews with MHP provincial party official, Trabzon; Mehmet Öz, chairman of the Türk Ocakları, Ankara; and Gamze, Gazi University MA student of Turcology, March 2014.

106. Philip Robins, "Between Sentiment and Self-Interest: Turkey's Foreign Policy toward Azerbaijan and the Central Asian States," *Middle East Journal* 47, no. 4 (1993): 599.

107. Graham Fuller, Ian Lesser, Paul Henze, and James Brown, *Turkey's New Geopolitics: From the Balkans to Western China* (Oxford, UK: Westview Press/RAND, 1993), 67.

108. Gülay Mutlu, "Turkey and the Turkic Republics: Is There a New Vision?," *Eurasia Review*, October 31, 2011, https://www.eurasiareview.com/31102011-turkey-and-the-turkic-republics-is-there-a-new-vision-analysis/.

Chapter 5

1. Sam Kaplan, *The Pedagogical State: Education and the Politics of National Culture in Post-1980 Turkey* (Stanford, CA: Stanford University Press, 2006).

2. Ronald Krebs, *Fighting for Rights: Military Service and the Politics of Citizenship* (Ithaca, NY: Cornell University Press, 2006).

3. John Gillis, ed., *Commemorations: The Politics of National Identity* (Princeton, NJ: Princeton University Press, 1996).

4. Benedict Anderson, *Imagined Communities: Reflections on the Origin and Spread of Nationalism* (London: Verso, 2006), 167–91. Anderson is perhaps best known for his 1983 analysis of the role of print capitalism and the emergence of vernacular languages in forming shared ideas of national identities among individuals who would never meet, but his exegesis on the effects of identity codification in the postcolonial era in the revised edition is well worthy of note.

5. See Venelin I. Ganev, *Preying on the State: The Transformation of Bulgaria after 1989* (Ithaca, NY: Cornell University Press, 2013).

6. Given the increasingly diverse makeup of the CHP in terms of identity proposals, a circumstance resulting from multiple factors such as party disintegration and reformation as well as the emergence of Western liberalism, as discussed in the previous chapter, I do not analyze the party as a Republican Nationalist identity obstacle here. It is worth re-emphasizing I deliberately avoid the reduction of identity to party membership.

7. "*Kapatılan Televizyonlar ve Gazeteler Belli Oldu!*," *Hürriyet Gazetesi*, July 28, 2016, http://www.hurriyet.com.tr/3-ajans-16-tv-45-gazete-23-radyo-kapatildi-40172869.

8. Interview with Kazım Kurt, CHP MP and Republican Nationalist, Eskişehir, August 2013. To illustrate the shift using numbers, during the 2014 local (March) and presidential (August) campaigns, 90% of the coverage by the state public broadcaster Turkish Radio and Television Corporation (Türkiye Radyo ve Televizyon Kurumu) was of then prime minister and presidential candidate Erdoğan. See *Diminishing Press Freedom in Turkey*, Rethink Institute, Washington, DC, November 2004, http://www.rethinkinstitute.org/diminishing-press-freedom-turkey-2/.

9. Kemal Kılıçdaroğlu, "Çıkarılan yeni düzenlemeyle referanduma kadar sadece kandi boruları ötecek, televizyonlar sadece bir taraf lehine özgürce yayın yapılacak," Çıkarılan yeni düzenlemeyle referanduma kadar sadece kendi boruları ötecek, televizyonlar sadece bir taraf lehine özgürce yayın yapabilecek. Twitter, February 9, 2017, https://twitter.com/kilicdarogluk/status/829617363188334592.

10. Hikmet Kocamaner, "Transformation of Islamic Television in Turkey from the Era of the Secularist State Monopoly to Family-Focused Programming under the Conservative-Muslim AKP Government," *Project on Middle East Political Science Studies* 23 (February 2017), https://pomeps.org/2017/01/19/transformation-of-islamic-television-in-turkey-from-the-era-of-secularist-state-monopoly-to-family-focused-programming-under-the-conservative-muslim-akp-government/.

11. Nurhan Yentürk, "Measuring Turkish Military Expenditure," *SIPRI Insights on Peace and Security* 1 (2014): 14.

12. For a discussion of Turkey's traditionally strong state and weak society and the military's primary role within the state apparatus, see Metin Heper, *The State Tradition in Turkey* (North Humberside: Eothen Press, 1985).

13. The founding narrative or myth is a common theme in many studies of nationalism but lacks the clear delineation of elements such as membership and behavioral norms, goals, and relations with various out-groups that can provide cross-proposal and cross-time analysis of identity understandings, and that is provided in this study's use of an identity content framework. Foundational works on foundational myths include George Schöpflin, "The Functions of Myth and the Taxonomy of Myths," in *Myths and Nationhood*, ed. Geoffrey Hosking and George Schöpflin (London: Hurst and Co., 1997); E. J. Hobsbawm, *Nations and Nationalism since 1780: Programme, Myth, Reality* (Cambridge, UK: Cambridge University Press, 1990); and Benedict Anderson, *Imagined Communities: Reflections on the Origins and Spread of Nationalism* (London: Verso, 1983.

14. Atatürk was also deemed by those supportive of Republican Nationalism to be the country's Hero of Turkishness and Civilization (Türklük ve Medeniyet Kahramanı). See Hasan Ünder, "*Atatürk İmgesinin Siyasal Yaşamdaki Rölü*," in *Modern Türkiye'de Siyasi Düşünce: Kemalizm*, ed. Ahmet İnsel (Istanbul: İletişim Yayınları, 2001), 143.

15. Atatürk's most famous biographer provides evidence calling this narrative into question, including the teacher's being a "hard man" in Atatürk's own words and thus unlikely to bestow such a title of honor upon a student. As with all national narratives and myths, however, the most interesting part is the persistence and impact of beliefs, rather than their truth or falsehood. See Andrew Mango, *Atatürk: The Biography of the Founder of Modern Turkey* (New York: Overlook Press, 2002), 36–37.

16. According to biographer Andrew Mango, Mustafa Kemal chose the surname Atatürk (Father of the Turk) in line with his parental sentiment toward the republic' new citizens, passing a law that it could not be used by anyone else, including his family members. See Mango, Atatürk, 498.

17. See "*Bir Ülkenin Kaderini Değistiren Saat,*" *Sabah Gazetesi,* March 9, 2012, http://www.sabah.com.tr/gundem/2012/03/09/bir-ulkenin-kaderini-degistiren-saat.

18. "*Dante'nin cehenneminde yananların gözleri gibi.*" İpek Çalışlar, *Halide Edib: Biyografisine Sığmayan Kadın* (Istanbul: Everest Yayınları, 2010), 252.

19. Thomas Smith, "Between Allah and Atatürk: Liberal Islam in Turkey," *International Journal of Human Rights* 9, no. 3 (2005): 307–325.

20. See Reşat Kasaba, "Kemalist Certainties and Modernist Ambiguities," in *Rethinking Modernity and National Identity in Turkey,* ed. Sibel Bozdoğan and Reşat Kasaba (Seattle: University of Washington Press, 1997), 22.

21. While the focus here is on domestic institutions and the legitimacy with which citizens imbue their agents of governance, Ian Hurd's study of legitimacy and international institutions provides an excellent discussion of the concept. See Ian Hurd, *After Anarchy: Legitimacy and Power in the United Nations Security Council* (Princeton, NJ: Princeton University Press, 2007), 7–12.

22. Mark Tessler and Ebru Altnoğlu, "Political Culture in Turkey: Connections among Attitudes toward Democracy, the Military, and Islam," *Democratization* 11, no. 1 (2004): 25. As polls conducted in 2013–2014 (discussed in the following chapter) demonstrate, this level of confidence would drop, due in part to the efforts of the AKP to weaken and discredit the institution of the armed forces as an identity-based obstacle.

23. Michael Wuttrich, "Factors Influencing Military-Media Relations in Turkey," *Middle East Journal* 66, no. 2 (2012): 258.

24. Author's observation, Bursa, June–August 2011.

25. Kaplan, *Pedagogical State,* 183.

26. Ibid., 180.

27. Nilüfer Narlı, "Civil-Military Relations in Turkey," *Turkish Studies* 1, no. 1 (2000): 107.

28. For two of the most frequently cited discussions, see William Hale, *Turkish Politics and the Military* (London: Routledge, 1994); and Frank Tachau and Metin Heper, "The State, Politics, and the Military in Turkey," *Comparative Politics* 16, no. 1 (1983): 17–33.

29. The AKP's outreach to the Kurds, in efforts to solve the ongoing civil war that contributed to Turkey's "lost decade" and to meet EU accession criteria, constituted a threat to the third of these principles for Turkey's lingering hardcore Republican Nationalists. Nothing about the identity content of Ottoman Islamism prescribes recognition of minority groups such as the Kurds—as does Western liberalism—but nothing proscribes it either, as discussed in chapter 3.

30. The term was apparently coined by journalist Cengiz Çandar, due to the TSK's continuous pressuring of the RP through warnings and demands rather than calling the military out of its barracks to run it out of office. Cengiz Çandar, "Postmodern Darbe," *Sabah Gazetesi,* June 28, 2007, http://arsiv.sabah.com.tr/1997/06/28/y12.html. See also Tanel Demirel, "Lessons of Military Regimes and Democracy: The Turkish Case in Comparative Perspective," *Armed Forces and Society* 31, no. 2 (2005): 245–271.

31. *211 Sayılı Türk Silahlı Kuvvetleri İç Hizmet Kanunu, Madde 35,* enacted January 4, 1961. Government of Turkey, statutes section, http://www.mevzuat.gov.tr/MevzuatMetin/1.4.211.pdf.

32. Narlı, "Civil-Military Relations in Turkey," 115.

33. Sultan Tepe, *Beyond Sacred and Secular: Politics of Religion in Israel and Turkey* (Stanford, CA: Stanford University Press, 2007), 185. For an in-depth discussion of the RP and its roots (along with the other parties listed above) in the Milli Görüş Hareketi, see ibid., 181–94.

34. For a comprehensive and highly critical take on the process, see Ezgi Gürses, *28 Şubat: Demokrasi Ters Şeritte* (Istanbul: Şule Yayınları, 2012).

35. Hakan Yavuz, *Islamic Political Identity in Turkey* (Oxford: Oxford University Press, 2003), 243.

36. For an outstanding ethnographic study of these networks and their efficacy, see Jenny White, *Islamist Mobilization in Turkey: A Study in Vernacular Politics* (Seattle: University of Washington Press, 2002).

37. For a collecton of these headlines, see "*28 Şubat Karanlığına Götüren Manşetler,*" *Son Haberler,* http://www.sonhaberler.com/28-subat-karanligina-goturen-mansetler-p1-aid,9761.html?page=1.

38. Soner Yalçın, *Hangi Erbakan?* (Ankara: Başak Yayınları, 1994), 223.

39. For a discussion of the TSK's attempts to roll back Islam's perceived incursions into society following the coup, see Şevket Kazan, *Öncesi ve Sonrasıyla 28 Şubat* (Ankara: Keşif Yayınları, 2001).

40. The General Staff Office's chief of operations, Çetin Dogan, stated: "Today the number one threat is internal security; it's Islamic reactionism" (*"Bugün bir numaralı tehdit artık iç güvenliktir, irticadir."* Quoted in Fatih Çekirge, *"Genelkurmay'da Düşman Değişti,"* Sabah Gazetesi, April 30, 1997, http://arsiv.sabah.com.tr/1997/04/30/.

41. Narlı, "Civil-Military Relations in Turkey."

42. Yavuz, *Islamic Political Identity in Turkey,* 202.

43. Fikret Bila, *"Binlerce Irticacı Var,"* Milliyet Gazetesi, August 31, 2000, http://gazetearsivi.milliyet.com.tr/Ara.aspx?araKelime=kivrikoglu%20gulen&isAdv=false.

44. *"Değiştirilemez ve değiştirilmesi teklif edilemez."* Article 4 of the Constitution of the Republic of Turkey, Turkish Grand National Assembly, http://www.tbmm.gov.tr/anayasa/anayasa82.htm.

45. Firat Cengiz, "The Future of Democratic Reform in Turkey: Constitutional Moment or Constitutional Process?," *Government and Opposition* 49, no. 4 (2014): 682–703.

46. Ceren Belge, "Friends of the Court: The Republican Alliance and Selective Activism of the Constitutional Court of Turkey," *Law Society and Review* 40, no. 3 (2006): 653–692.

47. Hale, *Turkish Politics and the Military,* 258.

48. "Bugün hepimize düşen görev, Atatürkçülüğü . . . geleceğe taşımak." *"Atatürkçülüğü Gelecege Taşımak Hepimizin Görevi,"* Archives of ATVMSNBC, November 10, 2001, http://arsiv.ntvmsnbc.com/news/118183.asp#BODY.

49. *"Türkiye Cumhuriyetinin kurucusu, ölümsüz önder ve eşsiz kahraman Atatürk'ün belirlediği milliyetçilik anlayışı."* Preamble to the Constitution of the Republic of Turkey, Turkish Grand National Assembly, http://www.tbmm.gov.tr/anayasa/anayasa82.htm.

50. Belge, "Friends of the Court," 654. In addition to Islamist parties, the court also shut down multiple iterations of Kurdish parties, seen as equally unacceptable, at least to hardcore Republican Nationalists and Kemalists.

51. Constitution of the Republic of Turkey, Turkish Grand National Assembly, http://www.tbmm.gov.tr/anayasa/anayasa82.htm.

52. *"Türkiye Cumhuriyetinin Anayasa ile belirtilen laiklik ilkesine aykırı davranışlarda."* Anayasa Mahkemesi Kararlar Dergisi, Sayı 9 (Ankara: Ankara Yarıaçık Cezaevi Maatbası, 1971).

53. White, *Islamist Mobilization in Turkey,* 115.

54. "Siyasi Partiler," Ministry of Library and Archive Services, Turkish Grand National Assembly, http://www.tbmm.gov.tr/kutuphane/siyasi_partiler.html.

55. Gürses, *28 Şubat,* 23.

56. "1997'deki Refah Partisi Kapatma Davası İddianamesi," full indictment, Hurriyet Gazetesi, March 14, 2008, http://www.hurriyet.com.tr/dunya/8460645.asp

57. For an in-depth discussion of this decision and its repercussions, see Richard Peres, *Headscarf: The Day Turkey Stood Still* (Reading, UK: Garnet Publishing, 2012).

58. "Siyasi Partiler," Ministry of Library and Archive Services, Turkish Grand National Assembly, http://www.tbmm.gov.tr/kutuphane/siyasi_partiler.html.

59. Unlike many of its predecessors, the Saadet Partisi still exists—perhaps because it receives a very small percentage of the vote and as such has remained a relatively marginal actor—and very deliberately distances itself from the AKP. Interview with SP member at party headquarters, Giresun, March 2014.

60. Sultan Tepe, "Turkey's AKP: A Model 'Muslim Democratic' Party?," *Journal of Democracy* 16, no. 3 (2005): 69–82. The timing of this decision is fascinating and underlines the book's argument well. The court's decision to uphold the columnist's conviction came just after a decision overturning another columnist's sentence for similar charges—a highly contested decision made by a vote of 14 to 13. One observer characterized the court's latter decision upholding the sentence as "revenge of laicism/secularism." See Oya Armut, *"Yargıtay'da Laiklik Rövanşı,"* Hürriyet, March 16, 2005, http://www.hurriyet.com.tr/gundem/yargitay-da-laiklik-rovansi-304165.

61. Yüksel Aytuğ, ". . . Ve Rektör Kırcaali Öldürüldü," Sabah Gazetesi, April 1, 2008, http://www.sabah.com.tr/yazarlar/gunaydin/aytug/2008/04/01/ve_rektor_kircaali_olduruldu.

62. Kaplan, *Pedagogical State.*

63. See, for example, Salih Can Açıksöz, "Kaplan Sam, *The Pedagogical State: Education and the Politics of National Culture in Post-1980 Turkey*," *International Journal of Middle East Studies* 42, no. 3 (2010): 526–528.

64. Himmet Umunç, "In Search of Improvement: The Reorganisation of Higher Education in Turkey," *Minerva* 24, no. 2 (1986): 453. Rectors of private universities, of which there were relatively few until the last ten years, are selected by an administrative board and must be approved by YÖK.

65. "*Yeni KHK ile Rektörlük Seçimleri Kaldırıldı . . . Erdoğan'a Atama Yetkisi Geldi*," *Cumhuriyet Gazetesi*, October 29, 2016, http://www.cumhuriyet.com.tr/haber/egitim/623503/Yeni_ KHK_ile_rektorluk_secimleri_kaldirildi..._Erdogan_a_atama_yetkisi_geldi.html#.

66. Ümit Cizre and Menderes Çınar note that "appointments of university [rectors] since 1997 were pointedly made from among staunch Kemalists." Ümit Cizre and Menderes Çınar, "Turkey 2002: Kemalism, Islamism, and Politics in the Light of the February 28 Process," *South Atlantic Quarterly* 102, nos. 2/3 (2003): 312.

67. Gareth Jenkins, "Muslim Democrats in Turkey?," *Survival* 45, no. 1 (2003): 56.

68. Kamuran Zeren and Erhan Göğem, "*Tarikatçı Rektör Açığa Alındı*," *Hürriyet Gazetesi*, September 20, 1997, http://www.hurriyet.com.tr/tarikatci-rektor-aciga-alindi-39265157.

69. "*Harran'a Rektör Dayanamadı*," *Hürriyet Gazetesi*, December 14, 1998, http://www.hurriyet. com.tr/harrana-rektor-dayanmiyor-39052729.

70. AKP MPs whose headscarved wives were not invited refused to attend in protest, declaring they hoped to be able to go with their wives next year—a not so subtle hint about their wish for an Ottoman Islamist president to replace President Sezer at the end of his term. "*Türban Seneye Çankaya'da Diyorlar*," HaberTürk, October 29, 2006, http://www.haberturk.com/ polemik/haber/4198-turban-seneye-cankayada-diyorlar.

71. In the same remarks, Safran also stated that he "believed President Abdullah Gül will make such decisions based on much sounder and healthier measures." See "*Sezer'de Neredeydiniz?*," HaberVaktim, July 9, 2010, http://www.habervaktim.com/haber/130403/sezerde- neredeydiniz.html.

72. Yakup Bulut, "Bir Oyla Rektör," *Yeni Şafak Gazetesi*, May 19, 2007, http://www.yenisafak. com/gundem/bir-oyla-rektor-46187.

73. Ahmet Altan, cited at memurlar.net, October 29, 2003, http://www.memurlar.net/ haber/3028/.

74. User "Olmakyadaolmamak" ("To be or not to be"), Mezun Forum, September 29, 2006, http://forum.mezun.com/showthread.php?30528-M%C3%9CSiAD-T%C3%BCrkiye- nin-istikrar%C3%BDn%C3%BD-bozmak-i%C3%A7in-d%C3%BD%C3%BEarda-Papa- i%C3%A7eride-rekt%C3%B6rler-rol-al%C3%BDyor-dedi/page2.

75. Law 8/5105, *Kamu Kurum ve Kuruluşlarında Personelin Kılık ve Kıyafetine Dair Yönetmelik*, July 16, 1982, http://www.memurlar.net/haber/1094/.

76. Emelie Olsun, "Muslim Identity and Secularism in Contemporary Turkey: The Headscarf Dispute," *Anthropological Quarterly* 58, no. 4 (1985): 161–62.

77. Before the Islamic headscarf took on a political meaning as a result of the increased polarization between Republican Nationalists and Ottoman Islamists, beginning in the 1980s and intensifying throughout the 1990s, *türban* was used to refer to the garment that pious Muslim women pinned around their faces and secured at the back of the head to hide all of their hair and neck in accordance with their religious beliefs. The *başörtüsü* was a head covering that secular women would fasten at the neck to protect their hair when going outside. The word *türban* has generally fallen out of usage, and *başörtüsü* has taken on an Islamist connotation.

78. Beards and mustaches have immense political significance in Turkey. In addition to the identifiable Muslim beard signifying an Islamist, a small, *badem* (almond) mustache may often indicate a pious individual; a handlebar mustache with the tips pointed downward is often associated with ultranationalist MHP members (most of whom I identify here as Pan-Turkic Nationalists); and a bushy mustache with no tips or a goatee generally signifies a leftist. See "Facial Hair Politics in Turkey: A Tale of Moustaches and Men," *Hürriyet Daily News*, August 6, 2010, http://www.hurriyetdailynews.com/default.aspx?pageid=438&n=facial-hair-in- turkish-politics-a-tale-of-moustaches-and-men-2010-08-06.

79. *Turkey: Situation of Women Who Wear Headscarves*, Immigration and Refugee Board of Canada, Report TUR102820.E, May 20, 2008, http://www.refworld.org/cgi-bin/texis/vtx/rwmain?page=country&category=&publisher=IRBC&type=&coi=TUR&rid=&docid=4885a91a8&skip=0.
80. Recep Tayyip Erdoğan, cited in *"Başbakan: Bu Tayyip Erdoğan Değismez,"* *Hürriyet*, June 12, 2013, http://www.hurriyet.com.tr/gundem/23479966.asp.

Chapter 6

1. Vocativ, "The Turkish 'Game of Thrones' Has Fans Bringing Out Their Swords!" Twitter, https://twitter.com/vocativ/status/975386595317592064.
2. Elif Batuman, "Ottomania," *New Yorker*, February 17, 2014, http://www.newyorker.com/magazine/2014/02/17/ottomania.
3. This refers to the group of individuals, mostly intellectuals, who called themselves part of the Yetmez Ama Evet (It's Not Enough, But Yes) movement, discussed in detail later in the chapter.
4. See *"Bu Edepsizliği Sandık Temizleyemez,"* *Milli Gazetesi*, March 20, 2014, http://www.milligazete.com.tr/yazdir/1035990.
5. See *"Bin 400 Liralık Ne İçtin Egemen Bağış?,"* *Aydınlık Gazetesi*, October 24, 2013, http://www.aydinlikgazete.com/mansetler/26659-bin-400-liralik-ne-ictin-egemen-bagis.html.
6. See *"Başbakan Erdoğan, Egemen Bağış'a Sahip Çıktı,"* AktifHaber, April 4, 2012, http://www.aktifhaber.com/basbakan-erdogan-egemen-bagisa-sahip-cikti-960870h.htm.
7. See Enze Han, *Contestation and Adaptation: The Politics of National Identity in China* (Oxford: Oxford University Press, 2013).
8. See Margaret Keck and Kathryn Sikkink, *Activists beyond Borders: Transnational Advocacy Networks in International Politics* (Ithaca, NY: Cornell University Press, 1998).
9. Tellingly, former foreign minister, current prime minister, and foreign policy architect Ahmet Davutoğlu criticized neo-Ottomanism for being "too Western-oriented" in his own works. Interview conducted by an *Al-Monitor* correspondent with Davutoğlu's former student and current analyst of his works, Behlül Özkan, "Early Writings Reveal the Real Davutoglu," *Al-Monitor*, August 13, 2014, http://www.al-monitor.com/pulse/fr/originals/2014/08/zaman-davutoglu-ideologue-behlul-ozkan-academic-akp-islamic.html#.
10. The controversial line in the poem was: "Our minarets are our bayonets, Our domes are our helmets, Our mosques are our barracks." See "Erdogan Goes to Prison," *Hurriyet Daily News*, March 27, 1999, www.hurriyetdailynews.com/erdogan-goes-to-prison.aspx?pageID=438&n=erdogan-goes-to-prison-1999-03-27.
11. See http://alkislarlayasiyorum.com/icerik/130020/cumhuriyet-gazetesi-tehlikenin-farkinda-misiniz.
12. For the YouTube video of the speech given in 1997, see https://www.youtube.com/watch?v=GdBAUNQ5b2w.
13. A list compiled by a blogger counts well-known journalists, writers, musicians, politicians, academics, and lawyers among the "Yetmez Ama Evetçi"ler." For the full list and quotes used to defend the classification of these individuals, see *"Yetmez Ama Evetçi'lerin Listesi,"* November 23, 2013, http://yetmezamaevetciler.blogspot.com.
14. Interview with EU ministerial official, Ankara, November 2013.
15. See Linda Michaud-Emin, "The Restructuring of the Military High Command in the Seventh Harmonization Package and its Ramifications for Civil Military Relations in Turkey," *Turkish Studies* 8, no. 1 (2007): 25–42. Writing in 2007, Michaud-Emin argued that the balance of political power is still in favor of the TSK. For arguments asserting that the military's influence over politics has indeed significantly decreased, in line with this book's argument, see, for example, Tuba Eldem, Guardians Entrapped: The Demise of the Turkish Armed Forces as a Veto Player (PhD diss., University of Toronto, 2013); Ersel Aydınlı, "Turkey under the AKP: Civil-Military Relations Transformed," *Journal of Democracy* 23, no. 1 (2012): 100–108; and Zeki Sarıgil, "Europeanization as Institutional Change: The Case of the Turkish Military," *Mediterranean Politics* 12, no. 1 (2007): 39–57.

16. *2004 Regular Report on Turkey's Progress Toward Accession* (Brussels: Commission of the European Communities, October 2004), 22.
17. Sarıgil, "Europeanization as Institutional Change," 45.
18. Ibid., 11–12.
19. *118. Madde, 1982 Türkiye Cumhuriyeti Anayasa,* full text, http://www.hukuki.net/kanun/2709.15.text.asp.
20. Lale Sarıibrahimoğlu, "Turkish Armed Forces," in *Democratic Oversight and Reform of the Security Sector in Turkey,* ed. Ümit Cizre (Geneva: Democratic Centre for Control of the Armed Forces, 2008), 71.
21. The blogger headlined a section *"AB demokrasisi yoluyla ordu tasfiye ediliyor."* Filiz Doğan, *"Böl-parçala, AB'ye uy,"* Turksolu, May 26, 2003, http://www.turksolu.com.tr/31/dogan31.htm.
22. *Turkey 2007 Progress Report,* Commission of the European Communities, November 6, 2007, 9, http://ec.europa.eu/enlargement/pdf/key_documents/2007/nov/turkey_progress_reports_en.pdf.
23. The "e-memorandum" posted on the Turkish Armed Forces website on April 27, 2007, expressed its displeasure at the nomination of Gül and intimated that the military would intervene if Turkey's secular system was threatened.
24. "Analysis: Turkey's Divisive Ergenekon Trial," *Al Jazeera,* August 12, 2013, http://www.aljazeera.com/indepth/features/2013/08/201381175743430360.html.
25. "*Balyoz'a Microsoft Darbesi,*" *Milliyet Gazetesi,* April 16, 2013, http://www.milliyet.com.tr/balyoz-a-microsoft-darbesi-gundem-1694244/.
26. Bülent Serim, "*Ergenekon Sanıkları Neden Şimdi Tahliye Edildi,*" OdaTV, March 14, 2014, http://odatv.com/ergenekon-saniklari-neden-simdi-tahliye-edildi-1403141200.html.
27. "*Kurumlara Güven Derecesi,*" in *Türkiye Sosyal-Siyasal Eğilimler Araştırması* (Istanbul: Kadir Has Üniversitesi, 2015), 17, http://www.khas.edu.tr/uploads/pdf-doc-vb/news/TSSEA20OCAK2015.pdf.
28. D. İsmet Çınkı, M. Cem Okyay, Erdinç Altıner, Ender Kahya, and F. Yavuz Uras, eds., *Er Mektubu Görülmüştür: Balyoz Mağduru Türk Subaylarına Gönderilen Destek Mektupları* (Istanbul: Kırmızı Kedi Yayınevi, 2014).
29. "*Türk Ordusunun Siyasetteki Gücünde Olan Değişimin Değerlendirmesi,*" in *Türkiye Sosyal-Siyasal Eğilimler Araştırması* (Istanbul: Kadir Has Üniversitesi, 2015), 18, http://www.khas.edu.tr/uploads/pdf-doc-vb/news/TSSEA20OCAK2015.pdf
30. Yavuz, *Islamic Political Identity in Turkey,* 248.
31. While the amendment guaranteeing that students couldn't be denied access to education for wearing a headscarf was in place, some university rectors refused to obey it and continued to force female students to remove their headscarves before entering campus. See "Rectors Disobey Lifting of Headscarf Ban," *University World News,* March 8, 2008, http://www.universityworldnews.com/article.php?story=2008022910002217.
32. See "*AK Parti'yi Kapatma Kararı Askeri Darbeden Farksız Olur,*" *Yeni Şafak Gazetesi,* May 10, 2008, http://yenisafak.com.tr/yorum-haber/ak-partiyi-kapatma-karari-askeri-darbeden-farksiz-olur-10.05.2008-116288.
33. Istanbul Bilgi University professor of constitutional law Serap Yazıcı, cited in "Yazıcı: Any Crack in This System Would Bear Positive Results for Society," *Today's Zaman,* April 13, 2010, http://www.todayszaman.com/interviews_yazici-any-crack-in-this-system-would-bear-positive-results-for-society-2_207254.html.
34. Mustafa Akyol, "Turkish Universities Latest Domino in Erdogan's Path," *Al-Monitor,* November 7, 2016, http://www.al-monitor.com/pulse/originals/2016/11/turkey-erdogan-took-full-control-of-universities.html.
35. "*İstanbul Üniversitesi Rektörlüğüne Prof. Dr. Mahmut Ak Atandı,*" *Radikal Gazetesi,* April 2, 2015, http://www.radikal.com.tr/turkiye/istanbul_universitesi_rektorlugune_prof_dr_mahmut_ak_atandi-1327362.
36. "*Rektörlük Seçiminde İkinci Olan Mahmut Ak Masada mı Kazanacak?,*" *Radikal Gazetesi,* March 13, 2015, http://www.radikal.com.tr/turkiye/rektorluk_seciminde_ikinci_olan_mahmut_ak_masada_mi_kazanacak-1312715.

37. Yusuf Ulcay, updated profile, Facebook, February 26, 2015, https://www.facebook.com/profile.php?id=580536594.

38. *"Tayyip Erdoğan Süfyan, Fethullah Gülen Mehdi, Öyle Mi?,"* Yeni Akit Gazetesi, March 12, 2015, http://www.yeniakit.com.tr/yazarlar/hasan-karakaya/tayyip-erdogan-sufyan-fetullah-gulen-mehdi-oyle-mi-9835.html.

39. See the foundation's website, http://www.hayratvakfi.org/2014/.

40. *"Cumhurbaşkanı kendi rektörünü seçiyor,"* Cumhuriyet Gazetesi, April 2, 2015, http://www.cumhuriyet.com.tr/haber/turkiye/232935/Cumhurbaskani_kendi_rektorunu_seciyor.html#. The title of the article, published in a strongly Republican Nationalist newspaper, is telling: "The President Chooses His Own Rector."

41. A. Kadir Yıldırım,"The Slow Death of Turkish Higher Education," Al Jazeera, July 10, 2014, http://www.aljazeera.com/indepth/opinion/2014/07/turkish-higher-education-reform-20147106282924991.html.

42. *Karar Sayısı,* KHK/676, Resmi Gazete, October 29, 2016, http://www.resmigazete.gov.tr/eskiler/2016/10/20161029-5.htm.

43. *"Boğaziçi Akademisyenleri 'Atame Rektör'e Karşı: Ülkeye Zarar Verir,"* Diken, November 1, 2016, http://www.diken.com.tr/bogazici-akademisyenleri-atama-rektore-karsi-ulkeye-zarar-verir/.

44. "Turkish University Rector Claims Shaking Hands with Women 'More Horrific than Holding Fire,' " Hürriyet Daily News, October 16, 2017, http://www.hurriyetdailynews.com/turkish-university-rector-claims-shaking-hands-with-women-more-horrific-than-holding-fire-120913.

45. For a discussion of the similarities between forms of authoritarianism guided by two very different identity proposals, see Hakan Övünç Ongur, "Plus Ça Change . . . Re-Articulating Authoritarianism in the New Turkey," Critical Sociology, February 29, 2016, doi:10.1177/0896920516630799.

46. Esra Ülkar, *"'1982'den Daha da Geriye Gittik,"* Hürriyet Gazetesi, November 2, 2016, http://www.hurriyet.com.tr/1982den-daha-da-geriye-gittik-40265716.

47. Fülya Özerkan, "Controversy on Campus as Erdogan Handpicks Turkey Rectors," France24, November 21, 2016, http://www.france24.com/en/20161121-controversy-campus-erdogan-handpicks-turkey-rectors.

48. "Turkey: 2013 Progress Report," European Commission, Brussels, October 16, 2014, p. 4, https://www.google.com/url?sa=t&rct=j&q=&esrc=s&source=web&cd=2&ved=0ahUKEwj725q38fvZAhVLpFkKHUztAbkQFggtMAE&url=https%3A%2F%2Fec.europa.eu%2Fneighbourhood-enlargement%2Fsites%2Fnear%2Ffiles%2Fpdf%2Fkey_documents%2F2013%2Fpackage%2Ftr_rapport_2013_en.pdf&usg=AOvVaw1bl4TWZNtvI8CEWkrHQdjE.

49. Ahmet Davutoğlu, *Stratejik Derinlik: Türkiye'nin Uluslararası Konumu* (Istanbul: Küre Yayınları, 2001).

50. Cited in Ayşe Zarakol, "Problem Areas for the New Turkish Foreign Policy," Nationalities Papers 40, no. 5 (2012): 739.

51. See Orhan Selçuk, "Turkish Airlines: A Foreign Policy Tool," Today's Zaman, December 17, 2012, http://www.todayszaman.com/news-301432-.html.

52. Calls by Turkey for aid provision from both international actors and its own citizens tend to increase during the holy month of Ramadan, during which there is an emphasis on piety and the plight of the poor. Author's observation, Ankara, July 2012. See also "Turkey Urges 57-Country of Organization of Islamic Cooperation to Aid Somalia," Ahlul Bayt News Agency, August 7, 2011, http://www.abna.ir/data.asp?lang=3&Id=258087.

53. Bilge Sarıtaş Ercan, *"Türkiye-İsrael İlişkileri"* (working paper for the Stratejik Düsünce Enstitüsü, October 2011), https://www.academia.edu/6196134/Stratejik_D%C3%BC%C5%9F%C3%BCnce_Enstit%C3%BCs%C3%BC_Uluslararas%C4%B1_%C4%B0li%C5%9Fkiler_Koordinat%C3%B6rl%C3%BC%C4%9F%C3%BC_T%C3%BCrkiye-%C4%B0srail_%C4%B0li%C5%9Fkileri.

54. Erdal Şafak. *"Davos Seçim Değil Tarih Malzemesi* (Davos Isn't a Choice, It's a Requisite of History)," Sabah, February 15, 2009, http://www.sabah.com.tr/Yazarlar/safak/2009/02/15/Davos_secim_degil_tarih_malzemesi.

55. Interview with ministerial official, Ankara, July 2013.

56. See "Erdogan Hailed as New Champion for Arabs Who Hope to Emulate the Turkish Model," *Al Arabiya*, September 14, 2011, http://www.alarabiya.net/articles/2011/09/14/166780.html.

57. Interview with journalist from major newspaper, Ankara, July 2013.

58. See *"Erdoğan'dan Vatandaş'a İnanilmaz Hakaret,"* *Sözcü Gazetesi*, May 15, 2014, http://sozcu.com.tr/2014/gundem/erdogan-iste-boyle-dovdu-510209/. For the YouTube video of the confrontation, see http://www.youtube.com/watch?v=b48rj-EUOXM.

59. See Rifat Bali, "Present-Day Anti-Semitism in Turkey," Jerusalem Center for Public Affairs, July 23, 2009, http://jcpa.org/article/present-day-anti-semitism-in-turkey/.

60. See the second open letter, posted on the website of the Turkish Jewish Community (Türk Musevi Cemaatı) (n.d., but references first letter, dated March 23, 2012), http://www.turkyahudileri.com/content/view/1856/279/lang,en/.

61. "İnadına Osmanlı Torunlarıyız," https://www.facebook.com/InadinaOsmanliTorunlariyiz?fr ef=photo. The phrase "İnadına" could be translated in numerous ways, including "out of spite" and "by the irony of fate," but the intent to deliberately promote Ottoman Islamism with no holds barred is clear.

62. The comment was posted June 5, 2014, by a user with a Turkish name, but identities cannot be verified. See https://www.facebook.com/InadinaOsmanliTorunlariyiz/photos/a.468520 779901317.1073741826.468516019901793/651055291647864/?type=1&theater.

63. "Yeni Akit Hitler'i Arıyor!," *Radikal Gazetesi*, July 19, 2014, http://www.radikal.com.tr/turkiye/yeni_akit_hitleri_ariyor-1202754.

64. "Yıldız Tilbenin Hitler Tweetleri Ortalığı Karıştırdı," *Cumhuriyet Gazetesi*, July 10, 2014, http://www.cumhuriyet.com.tr/haber/turkiye/92831/Yildiz_Tilbe_nin_Hitler_tweetleri_ortaligi_karistirdi.html#.

65. See "Gökçek'ten Yıldız Tilbe'ye Destek," EnSonHaber, July 11, 2014, http://www.ensonhaber.com/melih-gokcekten-yildiz-tilbeye-destek-2014-07-11.html.

66. "Gökçek: Helal Olsun Yıldız Tilbe'ye," *Yeni Şafak Gazetesi*, July 11, 2014, http://www.yenisafak.com.tr/politika/gokcek-helal-olsun-yildiz-tilbeye-666057. A similar response from the pro-AKP news website HaberVaktim was titled "Melih Gökçek Came out behind Yıldız Tilbe!" See "Melih Gökçek Yıldız Tilbe'ye Arka Çıktı!," HaberVaktim, July 11, 2014, http://www.habervaktim.com/haber/378201/gokcek-yildiz-tilbeye-arka-cikti.html.

67. See "Young Turkish Jews Emigrating to Israel Cue to Anti-Semitism, Tensions with Israel," *Haaretz News*, October 23, 2013, http://www.haaretz.com/jewish-world/jewish-world-features/1.553964.

68. "İsrail, Melih Gökçek'in Afişlerini Konuşuyor," *Akşam Gazetesi*, March 26, 2013, http://www.aksam.com.tr/dunya/israil-melih-gokcekin-afislerini-konusuyor/haber-180747.

69. "İsrail Basını: Teslim Olduk, Hamas ve Türkiye Kazandı," *Yeni Şafak Gazetesi*, June 27, 2016, http://www.yenisafak.com/dunya/israil-basini-teslim-olduk-hamas-ve-turkiye-kazandi-2487428.

70. Yasın Altıntaş and Berrin Naz Önsiper, "Türkiye-İsrail Anlaşması: Zafer mi Hezimet mi?," *Tesnim Haber Ajansı*, August 22, 2016, https://www.tasnimnews.com/tr/news/2016/08/22/1164807/t%C3%BCrkiye-israil-anla%C5%9Fmas%C4%B1-zafer-mi-hezimet-mi.

71. Sibel Ekin, "More Turkish Jews Seek New Life in Israel," *Ahval News*, March 3, 2018, https://ahvalnews.com/turkey/more-turkish-jews-seek-new-life-israel.

72. The AKP also attempted to open the highly contentious border with Armenia, but abandoned its plans when its closest cultural brother, Azerbaijan, pushed back against its attempts, demanding that the opening be linked to Armenian concessions on the Nagorno-Karabakh "frozen" conflict.

73. Mehmet Tan, Aziz Belli, and Abdullah Aydın, "2002 Sonrası ve Arap Baharı Kapsamında Türkiye Suriye İlişkileri ve Bölgesel Yansımaları" (report from II. Bölgesel Sorunlar ve Türkiye Sempozyumu, October 1–2, 2002, Kahramanmaraş, Turkey), 73, http://iibfdergisi.ksu.edu.tr/Imagesimages/files/10.pdf.

74. Yaşar Anter, "Hem Tatil Hem Siyaset için Bodrum'da," *Hürriyet Gazetesi*, August 5, 2008, http://www.hurriyet.com.tr/index/ArsivNews.aspx?id=9588900.

75. See Meliha Benli Altunışık and Özlen Tür, "From Distant Neighbors to Partners? Changing Syrian-Turkish Relations," *Security Dialogue* 37, no. 2 (2006): 229–248.

76. Interview with Foreign Ministry official, Ankara, August 2013; interview with Energy Ministry official and AKP founding member, Ankara, July 2013; and interview with EU ministry official, Ankara, July 2013.
77. "*Davutoglu: Esad'a 7 Saat Dil Döktüm*," *Hürriyet Gazetesi*, September 28, 2014, http://www.hurriyet.com.tr/gundem/27291393.asp.
78. "*MİT Tırları Soruşturması: Neler Olumştu?*," BBC Türkçe, November 27, 2015, http://www.bbc.com/turkce/haberler/2015/11/151127_mit_tirlari_neler_olmustu.
79. Mona Alami, "Jabhat al-Nusra's Rebranding Is More than Simple Name Change," *Al-Monitor*, August 5, 2016, http://www.al-monitor.com/pulse/originals/2016/08/jabhat-al-nusra-sever-al-qaeda-focus-local-syria.html; and "Syria Islamist Factions, Including Former al Qaeda Branch, Join Forces: Statement," *Reuters*, January 28, 2017, https://www.reuters.com/article/us-mideast-crisis-syria-rebels/syria-islamist-factions-including-former-al-qaeda-branch-join-forces-statement-idUSKBN15C0MV.
80. Yaroslav Trofimov, "Porous Turkey-Syria Border Poses Challenge in Fight against Islamic State," *Wall Street Journal*, February 19, 2015, http://www.wsj.com/articles/porous-syria-turkey-border-poses-challenge-in-fight-against-islamic-state-1424334057.
81. "Syrian War Monitor Says 465,000 Killed in Six Years of Fighting," *Reuters*, March 13, 2017, https://www.reuters.com/article/us-mideast-crisis-syria-casualties/syrian-war-monitor-says-465000-killed-in-six-years-of-fighting-idUSKBN16K1Q1.
82. Phillip Connor, "Most Displaced Syrians Are in the Middle East, and about a Million Are in Europe," Pew Research Center, January 29, 2018, http://www.pewresearch.org/fact-tank/2018/01/29/where-displaced-syrians-have-resettled/.
83. "*Erdoğan'dan Flaş Musul Açıklaması*," *Hürriyet Gazetesi*, October 18, 2016, http://www.hurriyet.com.tr/erdogan-akademik-yil-acilisinda-konusuyor-40251805.
84. "*Erdoğan'dan İnönü'ye Sert Lozan Eleştirisi*," *Cumhuriyet Gazetesi*, September 29, 2016, http://www.cumhuriyet.com.tr/haber/siyaset/607804/Erdogan_dan_Ataturk_ve_inonu_ye__iki_ayyas_tan_sonra__birileri_..._Lozan__Zafer_mi_bu_.html#.
85. Nick Danforth, "Turkey's New Maps are Reclaiming the Ottoman Empire," *Foreign Policy*, October 23, 2016, http://foreignpolicy.com/2016/10/23/turkeys-religious-nationalists-want-ottoman-borders-iraq-erdogan/.
86. "*Cumhurbaşkanı Erdoğan: 1923 Psikolojisiyle Hareket Edemeyiz*," Yeni Şafak, October 19, 2016, http://www.yenisafak.com/gundem/cumhurbaskani-erdogan-1923-psikolojisiyle-hareket-edemeyiz-2550170.
87. Interview with journalist at major newspaper, Ankara, July 2013.
88. "*Okulları İmam Hatip Yapma Şansını Yakaladık* (We Seized the Chance to Make Schools Imam Hatip Schools)," NTVMSNBC, August 24, 2012, http://www.ntvmsnbc.com/id/25376553.
89. "*Zorunlu Osmanlıca Dersi Kararı Tartışma Yarattı*," *Hürriyet Gazetesi*, December 5, 2014, http://www.hurriyet.com.tr/gundem/27714841.asp.
90. "*Osmanlıca Zorunlu Ders Oluyor*," Yeni Çağ *Gazetesi*, December 9, 2014, http://www.yenicaggazetesi.com.tr/osmanlica-zorunlu-ders-oluyor-106478h.htm.
91. "*Abdülhamid'in Torununa 'Atatürk'ü Seviyor Musunuz' Sorusu*," aHaber, December 10, 2015, http://www.ahaber.com.tr/gundem/2014/12/10/abdulhamidin-torununa-aturkun-seviyor-musunuz-sorusu.
92. Hakan Övünç Ongur, "Identifying Ottomanisms: The Discursive Evolution of Ottoman Pasts in Turkish Presents," *Middle East Studies* 51, no. 3, 2015.
93. See "*Padişah Buyurdu, Rektör Duyurdu: İTÜ'ye Cami Geliyor*," Sendika, March 27, 2015, http://www.sendika.org/2015/03/padisah-buyurdu-rektor-duyurdu-ituye-cami-geliyor/. This is a labor-friendly website.
94. "*Üniversite Sosyal Tesislerinde İçki Yasak!*," *GazeteVatan*, October 4, 2012, http://www.gazetevatan.com/universite-sosyal-tesislerinde-icki-yasak--485184-gundem/.
95. Fulbright English teaching assistant James, email correspondence with author; and Fulbright English teaching assistant Adnan, telephone interview with author, February 2015.
96. "*İçki Yasağı Başladı!*," *Sözcü Gazetesi*, October 5, 2012, http://www.sozcu.com.tr/2012/gundem/basbakan-talimatiyla-icki-yasagi-basladi-68783/.

97. For the distinction between *ilim*, which comes from the Koran, and scientific *bilim*, see a discussion by Islamic cleric Fethullah Gülen, "*Ilim ve Bilim*," September 27, 2001, http://tr.fgulen.com/content/view/11577/3/. Gülen is a previous ally of the AKP, whose own identity proposal's subtle content differences suggest the possibility of defining a Turkish Islamism separate from Ottoman Islamism if a more fine-grained comparison of the two would be useful, but who publicly supported the realization of Ottoman Islamist interests up until a split between the two factions.

98. E. Sare Aydın Yılmaz, "A New Momentum: Gender Justice in the Women's Movement," *Turkish Policy Quarterly* 13, no. 4 (2015): 107–115.

99. "*Kadın ile Erkek Eşit Konuma Getiremezsiniz, Çünkü o Fıtrata Terstir*," *Milliyet Gazetesi*, November 24, 2014, http://www.milliyet.com.tr/erdogan-batsin-bu-dunya/siyaset/detay/1974189/default.htm.

100. The repeated use of *fıtrat* to explain away disastrous outcomes came under intense criticism following the mining disaster in Soma, in which more than three hundred miners lost their lives due to shoddy construction of the mine and failure to heed multiple safety warnings. In a speech referring to the disaster, Erdoğan, to the shock and horror of his opponents, pointed to the example of miners' deaths in the 1800s, saying, "These things happen all the time, it's in the nature of this job" ("*Bunlar sürekli olan şeyler, bu işin fıtratında bu var*"). See "*Erdoğan: Bu İşin Fıtratında Var*," HaberSol, May 14, 2014, http://haber.sol.org.tr/devlet-ve-siyaset/erdogan-bu-isin-fitratinda-var-haberi-92417. Thsi is a Western liberal, leftist website.

101. For commentary on and a video of the television appearance, see "*AKP'nin Adayı Uğur Işılak: Kadının Fıtratında Köle Olmak Var*," *Cumhuriyet Gazetesi*, April 9, 2015, http://www.cumhuriyet.com.tr/video/video/248019/AKP_nin_adayi_Ugur_Isilak__Kadinin_fitratinda_kole_olmak_var.html#.

102. "*AKP'nin Geleneği: Mecvut Yapılara Hasar Ver, Yerlerine Taklitlerini İnşa Et* ("The AKP's Tradition: Do Damage to Existing Buildings and in Their Places Construct Imitations)," HaberSol, August 3, 2012, http://haber.sol.org.tr/kultur-sanat/akpnin-gelenegi-mevcut-yapilara-hasar-ver-yerlerine-taklitlerini-insa-et-haberi-57908.

103. Kadir Tambar, *The Reckoning of Pluralism: Political Belonging and the Demands of History in Turkey* (Stanford, CA: Stanford University Press, 2014), 26.

104. Can Erimtan, "Turkey's Culture Wars: The Yavuz Sultan Selim Bridge, the Topçu Barracks, and the AKM," *Istanbul Gazette*, June 3, 2013, http://istanbulgazette.com/turkeys-culture-wars-the-yavuz-sultan-selim-bridge-the-topcu-barracks-the-akm/2013/06/03/.

105. Pir Sultan Abdal Cultural Association deputy chairman, quoted in "*Demokratleşme Paketine ilk Tepki!*," *Milliyet Gazetesi*, September 30, 2013, http://gundem.milliyet.com.tr/-demokratiklesme-paketi-ne-ilk/gundem/detay/1770585/default.htm. Scholars of the Alevi experience assert that the "Alevi stigma is quite powerful in Turkey," leading many to migrate to Europe rather than face exclusion in their home country. Interview with Besim Zırh, sociologist and Alevi expert, Ankara, August 2013.

106. Laki Vingas, "Non-Muslim Minorities in Modern Turkey," *Turkish Policy Quarterly* 13, no. 1 (2014): 111–119.

107. Sibel Hürtaş, "Çanakkale Savaşı ve Öteki Şehitler," *Al-Monitor*, March 27, 2015, http://www.al-monitor.com/pulse/tr/originals/2015/03/turkey-gallipoli-war-other-m.html.

108. "*Erdoğan: Ruhban Okulu'nun Açılması İçin Batı Trakya'da Müftü Seçimini Bekliyorum*," *Azınlıkça*, October 6, 2013, http://www.azinlikca.net/yunanistan-bati-trakya-ozel-haber/erdogan-ruhban-okulunun-acilmasi-icin-bati-trakya-da-muftu-secimini-bekliyorum-1062013.html.

109. "Turkey: 2013 Progress Report," 6.

110. Interview with EU ministry official, Ankara, November 2013.

111. "*Görev mahallinde başının daima açık . . .*" was removed from Law 8/5105 on the administration of public institutions, initially put in place by the military government in 1982. Exceptions were made for individuals wearing uniforms, such as military, police, and judicial personnel. Decision 2013/5443, full transcript, *Resmi Gazete*, October 8, 2013, http://www.resmigazete.gov.tr/eskiler/2013/10/20131008-10.htm.

112. High-school teacher Gülderen Gültekin, cited in "*Kamuda Başörtüsüne Özgür Geldi*," Anadolu Ajansı, October 8, 2013, http://www.aa.com.tr/tr/turkiye/237534--kamuda-basortusune-ozgurluk-geldi.

113. Birgül Ünlü (profession not provided), cited in *"Kamuda Başörtüsüne Özgür Geldi,"* Anadolu Ajansı, October 8, 2013, http://www.aa.com.tr/tr/turkiye/237534--kamuda-basortusune-ozgurluk-geldi.

114. For an in-depth account of Kavakçı's experience, see Richard Peres, *Headscarf: The Day Turkey Stood Still* (Reading, UK: Garnett Publishing Limited, 2012). The Fazilet Partisi was the reincarnation of Necmettin Erbakan's Refah Partisi, which had been closed down by the Constitutional Court, as discussed in the previous chapter. While banned from engaging in politics, Erbakan exercised significant influence over party strategy and the selection of candidates. Kavakçı's selection may be read as an earlier attempt to contest Turkish national identity with an Ottoman Islamist proposal. Kavakçı's inability to take her oath in parliament and the subsequent closure of FP by the Constitutional Court demonstrate the domestic obstacles to this contestation in 1999 and underscore this chapter's argument that the AKP needed to take its contestation to the foreign policy arena.

115. *"Şafak Pavey ve Kirli Provokasyonu"* ("Şafak Pavey and Her Dirty Provocation,"), Sevilay Yükselir, *Sabah Gazetesi*, November 3, 2013, http://www.sabah.com.tr/Yazarlar/yukselir/2013/11/03/safak-pavey-ve-kirli-provokasyonu. Yükselir's editorial admits in hindsight that questioning the reason for Pavey's disability—initially published via a tweet that Yükselir subsequently erased on a friend's advice—was inappropriate, but insists controversy about this questioning has overtaken the more important issue of Pavey's "deceit, instigation, and provocation."

116. *"İnancımız, kimliğimiz pazarlığa tabi değildir."* Rıdvan Kaya, cited in *"Okullarda Kıyafet Zorunluluğu Yok, Başörtüsü Serbest,"* T24, November 27, 2012, http://t24.com.tr/haber/okullarda-kiyafet-zorunlulugu-yok-turban-serbest,218326.

117. Social media critical of the AKP quickly spread word of the "Ottoman circus" with which Abbas was welcomed, as tweeted sardonically by *Milliyet Gazetesi* columnist Kadri Gürsel, emphasizing both what they viewed as the absurdity of the display as well as its anachronistic nature if understood to represent the Ottoman Empire. The sixteen costumed warriors represented the sixteen Turkish empires, including the Mughal and the Seljuk Empires, dating back to 200 B.C.—that is, long before Osman I (Osman Gazi) founded in 1299 what would be known in English through faulty transliteration as the Ottoman Empire. Mainstream Turkish media outlets did not carry discussion of the tweet, but a website shared by the government-friendly Star TV network blamed a foreign media outlet, the British newspaper *The Guardian*, for quoting the tweet in a headline, calling the newspaper's action "a great show of impoliteness to the historical ceremony." See *"The Guardian'dan Tarihi Törene Büyük Terbiyesizlik,"* Akademik Perspektif Enstitüsü, January 13, 2015, http://haber.akademikperspektif.com/2015/01/13/guardiandan-tarihi-torene-buyuk-terbiyesizlik/. For the original *Guardian* article, see "Abbas Welcomed at Turkish Presidential Palace by Erdogan—and 16 Warriors," *Guardian*, January 12, 2015, http://www.theguardian.com/world/2015/jan/12/abbas-erdogan-16-warriors-turkish-presidential-palace.

118. *"Osmanlı'nın Ayak Sesleri: Filistin Başbakanı Mahmud Abbas Karşılandı,"* YouTube, January 15, 2015, https://www.youtube.com/watch?v=uKDY1ORbNIE.

119. Yalçın Akdoğan, "Tarihimiz gururumuzdur," Twitter, April 11, 2015, https://twitter.com/Y_Akdogan/status/586783044331315201.

120. Yalçın Akdoğan, "Şanlı bir gelenekten gelen Emniyet Teşkilatımıza nice yıllar diliyorum, Rabbim muhafaza eylesin," Twitter, April 10, 2015, https://twitter.com/Y_Akdogan/status/586501860376322048.

121. Author's observations, 2012–2014.

122. *"Helal Facebook Salamworld Geliyor,"* Gazete5, July 30, 2012, http://www.gazete5.com/haber/helal-facebook-salamworld-geliyor-231779.

123. It is possible the "reader" is a fictional device used by the columnist to draw attention to a practice she deems inappropriate herself. In any case, the policing of Ottoman Islamism against Western and impious behavior remains clear.

124. Fatma Barbarosoğlu, *"Her Güne Yeni bir Adet: Baş Örtme Törenleri,"* Yeni Şafak Gazetesi, October 24, 2014, http://www.yenisafak.com.tr/yazarlar/fatmakbarbarosoglu/her-gune-yeni-bir-adet-bas-ortme-torenleri-56576.

125. Ibid. The reader's letter that Barbarosoğlu refers to in her cautionary piece criticizes not only the ostentatious rented hall (*salon*) in which the event took place but also the residences in her religiously conservative neighborhood: "There's no end to the luxury" (*"lüksün sonu yok"*). The reader then makes explicit the link to condemnation of the West and the sense of anomie its secular, materialist lifestyle creates, stating that when "strangers on the street fail to smile at her in America, Canada, or Europe," she is "mortified by the fact that people do not deign to greet each other."

126. "*Kuran-ı Kerim Şeklindeki Pastaya Soruşturma*," *Milliyet Gazetesi*, April 19, 2015, http://www.milliyet.com.tr/kur-an-i-kerim-seklindeki-pastaya-gundem-2046540/.

127. *Diyanet Basın* (Press), "'Müftülükte Kuran-ı Kerim Tasarımlı Pasta Skandalı' başlıklı haberle ilgili açıklama," Twitter, April 19, 2015, https://twitter.com/diyanetbasin/status/589804191830450176.

128. "*Tuzla'da Hicret Yolu Yapıldı*," *Milliyet Gazetesi*, April 22, 2015, http://www.milliyet.com.tr/tuzla-da-hicret-yolu-yapildi-gundem-2047793/. Perhaps looking to best Üsküdar's example, the subsequently opened display in Tuzla includes a pilgrimage path (*"Hicret parkuru"*) on which visitors can view replicas of other holy icons in addition to the Kabe.

129. Although the name of the communication service, by which individuals can call toll-free with questions regarding religion and suspected violations of Islamic law, was officially changed in 2012 to Alo 190 Din Danışması (Hello 190 Religion Adviser, with the 190 referring to the telephone number), the news media continue to use the name Alo Fetva. See "*Diyanet'ten Ücretsiz Fetva Hattı*," Dunya Bülteni, March 8, 2012, http://www.dunyabulteni.net/haberler/200834/diyanetten-ucretsiz-fetva-hatti.

130. "*Diyanet'in Kabe Maketi ve Kuran Pastası Açıklaması*," *Sabah Gazetesi*, April 22, 2015, http://www.aksam.com.tr/guncel/diyanetin-kabe-maketi-ve-kuran-pastasi-aciklamasi/haber-400161.

131. The official's comments are discussed in Hakki Gurkas, "Claiming the Public Space for the Prophet Muhammad," in *Turkey: A Regional Power in the Making*, ed. Kenan Aksu (Newcastle upon Tyne, UK: Cambridge Scholars Publishing, 2013), 240.

Chapter 7

1. The epistemological question of explaining versus understanding as distinct forms of knowledge production is addressed well in Martin Hollis and Steve Smith, *Explaining and Understanding International Relations* (Oxford, UK: Oxford University Press, 1990).

2. Although writing as a comparativist, Michael Coppedge convincingly makes an argument along these lines that travels to the study of IR as well. Michael Coppedge, "Thickening Thin Concepts: Combining Large N and Small in Comparative Politics," *Comparative Politics* 31, no. 4 (1999): 465–476.

3. The distribution of these identities, rather than the specific nature of their content (beliefs, language, etc.), can be an influential factor in the level and nature of contestation.

4. See Graham Macklin and Fabian Virchow, eds., *Transnational Extreme Right Networks* (forthcoming from Routledge); and Petra Vejvodova, "Transnational Cooperation of the Far Right," in *The Extreme Right in Europe: Current Trends and Perspectives*, ed. Uwe Backes and Patrick Moreau (Göttingen, Germany: Vandenhoeck & Ruprecht, 2011), 215–228.

5. See, for example, Georgy Egorov, Sergei Guriev, and Konstantin Sonin, "Why Resource-Poor Dictators Allow Freer Media: A Theory and Evidence from Panel Data," *American Political Science Review*, 103, no. 4 (2009): 645–668.

6. For a study of how debates over identity vary with respect to the level of restriction of the public sphere, see Marc Lynch, *State Interests and Public Spheres: The International Politics of Jordan's Identity* (New York: Columbia University Press, 1999).

7. For non-state actors' roles in particular, see Thomas Risse-Kappen, ed., *Bringing Transnational Relations Back in: Non-State Actors, Domestic Structures, and International Institutions* (Cambridge, UK: Cambridge University Press, 1995).

8. See, for example, Gabriel Shaffer, ed., *Modern Diasporas in International Politics* (New York: St. Martin's, 1986).

9. Amy Foerster and Jennifer Miller, "Extranational Spaces and the Disruption of National Boundaries: Turkish Immigrant Media and Claims against the State in 1980s West Germany," *Nations and Nationalism* 23, no. 4 (2017): 2.

10. For a discussion see Larry Diamond, "Thinking about Hybrid Regimes," *Journal of Democracy* 13, no. 2 (2002): 21–35.

11. Suzanne Maloney, "Identity and Change in Iran's Foreign Policy," in *Identity and Foreign Policy in the Middle East*, ed. Shibley Telhami and Michael Barnett (Ithaca, NY: Cornell University Press, 2002), 94.

12. Mehrdad Moarefian, "Rouhani's Impromptu Alliance May Transform the Political Field in Iran," *CriticalThreats*, November 23, 2015, https://www.criticalthreats.org/team/mehrdad-moarefian.

13. Ibid.

14. See, for example, Max Fisher, "How the Nuclear Deal Boosted Iran's Moderates—and Showed Iranian Elections Can Matter," *Vox*, 2 March 2, 2016, https://www.vox.com/2016/3/2/11147102/iran-election-moderates-nuclear-deal; and Thomas Erdbrink, "Iranian President and Moderates Make strong Gains in Elections," *New York Times*, February 29, 2016, https://www.nytimes.com/2016/03/01/world/middleeast/iran-elections.html.

15. Amir Hossein Mahdavi," Iran's Election Wasn't about Moderation or Democracy. It Was about How Iran Will Re-Engage with the World," *Monkey Cage* (blog),*Washington Post*, March 3, 2016, https://ovipot.hypotheses.org/1630.

16. Ibid.

17. R. K. Ramazani, "Iran's Islamic Revolution and the Persian Gulf," *Current History* (January 1985): 5–8.

18. Mohammad Ayatollahi Tabaar, "Factional Politics in the Iran-Iraq War," *Journal of Strategic Studies*, August 9, 2017, http://www.tandfonline.com/eprint/r89yv6kfu9MFqF8BqMtB/full.

19. Similar to his take on the Iran-Iraq War, Tabaar's work on the factional politics behind Iran's behavior during the crisis, and particularly the co-optation by Iran's Islamists of anti-US rhetoric from the country's leftists, indicates domestic contestation that could be further illuminated with an inside-out identity perspective. See "Causes of the US Hostage Crisis in Iran: The Untold Account of the Communist Threat," *Strategic Studies* 26, no. 4 (2017): 665–697.

20. Maloney, "Identity and Change in Iran's Foreign Policy," 104 (emphasis original).

21. Anthony W. Marx, *Making Race and Nation: A Comparison of the United States, South Africa, and Brazil* (Cambridge, UK: Cambridge University Press, 1998), 205.

22. See, for example, John Comaroff, *Body of Power, Spirit of Resistance* (Chicago: University Chicago Press, 1985).

23. Cynthia Enloe, *Ethnic Conflict and Political Development* (Boston: Little, Brown, 1973), 216–58.

24. Anthony Marx, interview with National Party member Gerrit Viljoen, 1994, cited in Marx, *Making Race and Nation*, 205.

25. Gay Seidman, "Guerrillas in Their Midst: Armed Struggle in the South African Anti-Apartheid Movement," *Mobilization: An International Journal* 6, no. 2 (2001): 117.

26. See, for example, Bernard Makhosezwe Magubane, *The Ties That Bind: African-American Consciousness of Africa* (Trenton, NJ: Africa World Press, 1987).

27. Locksley Edmondson, "Black America as Mobilizing Diaspora: Some International Implications," in *Modern Diasporas in International Politics*, ed. Gabriel Shaffer (New York: St. Martin's, 1986).

28. Audie Klotz, "Norms Reconstituting Interests: Global Racial Equality and U.S. Sanctions against South Africa," *International Organization* 49, no. 3 (1995): 451–478. For her book-length discussion, see Audie Klotz, *Norms in International Relations: The Politics of Apartheid* (Ithaca, NY: Cornell University Press, 1999).

29. Nelson Mandela, *Long Walk to Freedom* (Boston: Little, Brown, 1994), 435.

30. Klotz, "Norms Reconstituting Interests," 463. She notes the resurgence follows the inhibition of activism during the McCarthy era.

31. Peter Vale and Sipho Maseko, "South Africa and the African Renaissance," *International Affairs* 74, no. 2 (1998): 271.

32. See Hannelie Marx and Viola Candice Milton, "Bastardised Whiteness: 'Zef' Culture, *Die Antwoord*, and the Reconfiguration of Contemporary Afrikaans Identities," *Social Identities* 17, no. 6 (2011): 723–745.

33. See, for example, Priya Chacko, *Indian Foreign Policy: The Politics of Postcolonial Identity from 1947 to 2004* (Abingdon, UK: Routledge, 2012); and Manu Bhagavan, *The Peacemakers: India and the Quest for One World* (New York: Palgrave Macmillan, 2013).

34. Jacques Hymans, *The Psychology of Nuclear Proliferation: Identity, Emotions, and Foreign Policy* (Cambridge, UK: Cambridge University Press, 2006).

35. Sinderpahl Singh, *India in South Asia: Domestic Politics and Foreign Policy from Nehru to the BJP* (Abingdon, UK: Routledge, 2013), 110.

36. See, for example, Adam Ziegfeld, "Coalition Government and Party System Change: Explaining the Rise of Regional Political Parties in India," *Comparative Politics* 45, no. 1 (2012): 69–87.

37. United Nations Department of Economic and Social Affairs, "Trends in International igrant Stock," cited in *The Times of India*, January 14, 2016, https://timesofindia.indiatimes.com/nri/other-news/India-has-largest-diaspora-population-in-world-UN-report-says/articleshow/50572695.cms. Measurements of the size of a diaspora, coming from the Greek for "to scatter," will depend on the definition given, such as whether the individual was forced to leave the home country and whether he or she feels return is possible. The UN numbers, based on individuals living outside the country of their birth, thus represent a broad definition used by the newspaper.

38. In the Indian case, see, respectively, Liesl Riddle, "Diasporas: Exploring their Development Potential," *ESR Review* 10, no. 2 (2008): 28–35; Kathleen Newland, "Voice after Exit: Diaspora Advocacy," Migration Policy Institute, November 2010, https://www.migrationpolicy.org/pubs/diasporas-advocacy.pdf; and Arthur J. Rubinoff, "The Diaspora as a Factor in U.S.-India Relations," *Asian Affairs: An American Review* 32, no. 3 (2005): 169–187.

39. Latha Daravarajan, *The Domestic Abroad: Diasporas in International Relations* (Oxford: Oxford University Press, 2010).

40. See, for example, Catarina Kinnvall and Ted Svensson, "Hindu Nationalism, Diasporic Politics, and Nation-Building in India," *Australian Journal of International Affairs* 64, no. 3 (2010): 274–292; and Christophe Jaffrelot and Ingrid Therwath, "The Sangh Pariver and the Hindu Diaspora in the West: What kind of 'Long-Distance Nationalism,'" *International Political Sociology* 1, no. 3 (2007): 278–295.

41. Rama Lakshmi, "Narendra Modi Urges the Indian Diaspora to Become and Extension of Foreign Policy," *Guardian*, March 2, 2015, https://www.theguardian.com/world/2015/mar/02/narendra-modi-india-overseas-diaspora-united-states.

42. Shoaib Danyal, "From Indian to Hindu Nationalism: Why the Modi Government Commented on a Communal Riot in Bangladesh," *Dhaka Tribune*, November 23, 2017, http://www.dhakatribune.com/bangladesh/foreign-affairs/2017/11/23/indian-hindu-nationalism-modi-government-commented-communal-riot-bangladesh/.

43. Sangeeta Kamat and Biju Mathew, "Mapping Political Violence in a Globalized World: The Case of Hindu Nationalism," *Social Justice* 3, no. 3 (2003): 4–16.

44. Pravasi Bharatiya Divas, http://www.pbd-india.com/.

45. Anupama Roy, "Between Encompassment and Enclosure: The 'Migrant' and the Citizen in India," *Contributions to Indian Sociology* 42, no. 2 (2008): 219–248.

46. Danyal, "From Indian to Hindu Nationalism."

47. Milan Vaishnav, "Modi's Going to Have a Much Tougher 2018 than Anyone's Expecting," *Print*, December 19, 2017, https://theprint.in/2017/12/19/get-ready-mr-modi-2018-battles-tough-bruising/.

48. "PM Modi Congratulates Congress on 'Aurangzeb Raj,'" *Abplive*, December 4, 2017, http://www.abplive.in/india-news/pm-modi-congratulates-congress-on-aurangzeb-raj-612345?ani.

49. "Clear Stand on Kashmir, Rohingya: Amit Shah to Rahul Gandhi," NDTV, November 22, 2017, https://www.ndtv.com/india-news/amit-shah-to-rahul-gandhi-clear-stand-on-kashir-rohingya-1778375.

50. Aditi Raja, "Gujarat Elections 2017: *Dadhi-topi* Numbers Have to Be Brought Down, Says a BJP Candidate," *Indian Express*, December 8, 2017, http://indianexpress.com/elections/

gujarat-assembly-elections-2017/gujarat-elections-dadhi-topi-numbers-have-to-be-brought-down-says-a-bjp-candidate-4973258/.

51. "Gujarat Results: Seat Where Modi Made 'Pakistan' Hand Claim Remains with Congress," *Indian Express*, December 18, 2017, http://indianexpress.com/elections/gujarat-assembly-elections-2017/palanpur-narendra-modi-gujarat-assembly-elections-2017-results-congress-4988427/.

52. See, for example, Sammy Smooha, "Minority Status in an Ethnic Democracy: The Status of the Arab Minority in Israel," *Journal of Ethnic and Racial Studies* 13, no. 3 (1990): 389–413.

53. Nadav G. Shelef, *Evolving Nationalism: Homeland, Identity, and Religion in Israel, 1925–2005* (Ithaca, NY: Cornell University Press, 2010). For a counterargument, see Yoav Peled "Ethnic Democracy and the Legal Construction of Citizenship: Arab Citizens of the Jewish State," *American Political Science Review* 86, no. 2 (1992): 432–443.

54. Michael Barnett, "The Israeli Identity and the Peace Process: Re/Creating the Un/Thinkable," in *Identity and Foreign Policy in the Middle East,* ed. Shibley Telhami and Michael Barnett (Ithaca, NY: Cornell University Press, 2002), 58–87.

55. See, for example, Amir Lupovici, "Ontological Dissonance, Clashing Identities, and Israel's Unilateral Steps towards the Palestinians," *Review of International Studies* 38, no. 4 (2012): 809–833.

56. Barnett, "Israeli Identity and the Peace Process," 61.

57. Gary Hershorn, "The Arafat-Rabin Handshake 20 Years On," Reuters, September 13, 2013, http://blogs.reuters.com/photographers-blog/2013/09/13/the-arafat-rabin-handshake-20-years-on/.

58. Simon Tisdall, "Shalom, Salam, Peace," *Guardian,* September 14, 1993, https://www.theguardian.com/world/1993/sep/14/israel.

59. Massimo Calabresi, "Exclusive: Netanyahu Canceled Intel Briefing for Senators on Iran," *TIME Magazine*, March 14, 2015, http://time.com/3744265/benjamin-netanyahu-israel-iran-nuclear-talks-obama/.

60. Benjamin Netanyahu, "The Complete Transcript of Netanyahu's Address to Congress," *Washington Post*, 3 March 3, 2015, https://www.washingtonpost.com/news/post-politics/wp/2015/03/03/full-text-netanyahus-address-to-congress/?utm_term=.6d4065d05fbc.

61. Ibid.

62. Jodi Rudoren, "Netanyahu Soundly Defeats Chief Rival in Israeli Elections," *New York Times*, March 17, 2015, https://www.nytimes.com/2015/03/18/world/middleeast/israel-election-netanyahu-herzog.html.

63. I am indebted to Yehonatan Abramson for this point.

64. For a summary, see İsmet Berkan, "9 *Soruda Cemaat-Hükümet Kavgasının Arkeoloji ve Geleceği,*" Hürriyet, November 30, 2013, http://www.hurriyet.com.tr/9-soruda-cemaat-hukumet-kavgasinin-arkeolojisi-ve-gelecegi-25243707.

65. Sezin Öney, "The Question: 'How Important Is the Zarrab Case in Corroding U.S.-Turkey Relations?'," *Ahvalnews*, November 20, 2017, https://ahvalnews.com/question/question-how-important-zarrab-case-corrosion-us-turkey-relations.

66. "*Erdoğan'dan 'Paralel Yapı' Açıklaması: Bize İhanet Ettiler, Bazı Özel Adımlar Var,*" Habertürk, November 18, 2015, http://www.haberturk.com/gundem/haber/1155174-cumhurbaskani-erdogan-aciklama-yapiyor.

67. Betül Özel Çiçek, "'Designated Survivor' Destined to Fail," *Daily Sabah*, December 13, 2017, https://www.dailysabah.com/arts-culture/2017/12/14/designated-survivor-destined-to-fail.

68. See Gülen's comments, March 6, 2012, http://tr.fgulen.com/content/view/20398/172/.

69. The official separation from the political realm follows the tradition of Nursi, who refused to comment on politics or encourage his followers to mobilize around issues of political debate. A post on Gülen's official website in answer to the self-posed question of "Does Fethullah Gülen have a political goal?" quotes Gülen as saying "political movements are things that come and go (*gelip geçicidir*)" but that the legacy of the Koran is "forever" (*daima*), and that "we never dove into politics" (*biz hiçbir zaman siyasete dalmadık*." See the piece posted on March 6, 2012, http://tr.fgulen.com/content/view/20398/172/.

70. In the wake of the corruption scandal, Erdoğan reversed his position on this collaboration with Gülen, expressing a willingness to have all those jailed in the case retried. See Tülin Daloğlu, "The Trials of Turkey's Legal System," *Al-Monitor*, January 6, 2014, https://www. al-monitor.com/pulse/originals/2014/01/ergenekon-turkey-gulen-akp-trial.html.

71. Joshua Hendrick, *The Ambiguous Politics of Market Islam in Turkey and the World* (New York: NYU Press, 2013), 176.

72. In-person and online conversations with the author, names withheld, November 2017.

73. Recep Tayyip Erdoğan, interview with AHaber news outlet, YouTube, October 4, 2016, https://www.youtube.com/watch?v=Sl2RtkW6A0Y.

74. See, respectively, Mahmut Övür, "*Başbakan Erdoğan: Bahçeli'nin Hocaefendi'ye Saldırısı İhanet*," Sabah, May 14, 2011, https://www.sabah.com.tr/yazarlar/ovur/2011/05/14/ basbakan-erdogan-bahcelinin-hocaefendiye-saldirisi-ihanet; Fatih Ulaş, "'*Paralel Yapı, Çok Karanlık bir Örgüt*,'" Sabah, March 14, 2014, https://www.sabah.com.tr/yazarlar/barlas/ 2011/04/19/sanki-tek-cemaat-fethullah-guleninki-mi; and "*İşte Fetullahçı Terör Örgütü'nün (FETÖ) Amacı, Taktik, ve Strategisi*," Sabah, June 6, 2017, https://www.sabah.com.tr/ fotohaber/gundem/iste-fetullahci-teror-orgutunun-feto-amaci-taktik-ve-stratejisi.

75. See, for example, Esra Kaya, "*Erdoğan'dan Fethullah Gülen'e Beddua Yanıtı*," *Hürriyet Gazetesi*, December 22, 2013, http://www.hurriyet.com.tr/erdogandan-fethullah-gulene-beddua-yaniti-25422263.

76. Hikmet Kocamaner, "Strengthening the Family through Television: Islamic Broadcasting, Secularism, and the Politics of Responsibility in Turkey," *Anthropological Quarterly* 90, no. 3 (2017): 676.

77. Murat Tokay, "*Modern Türkiye, Said Nursi'nin de Eseri*," Aksiyon, December 12, 2011, http:// www.aksiyon.com.tr/kitap/modern-turkiye-said-nursi-nin-de-eseri_531228.

78. See https://fgulen.com/en/home/1323-fgulen-com-english/press/news/34842-todays-zaman-turkish-movie-selam-received-with-great-interest-at-istanbul-gala.

79. See, for example, Nicholas Birch, "Turkey: 'Muslim Calvinists' in Anatolia Show How Piety Can Blend with Modernity," *Eurasianet*, July 23, 2008, http://www.eurasianet.org/ departments/insight/articles/eav072408a.shtml.

80. Interview with Ekrem Güzeldere, academic, Istanbul, August 2013.

81. Özdemir Özkan and Veysel Engi, "*Arap âlimler: Hizmet, İslam'ın İtibarını Kurtarıyor*," *Zaman Gazetesi*, March 15, 2015, http://www.zaman.com.tr/fethullah-gulen-hocaefendi_arap-alimler-hizmet-islamin-itibarini-kurtariyor_2283320.html.

82. http://gulenschools.org/.

83. See the event's website at http://www.turkceolimpiyatlari.com.tr/.

84. Stephanie Fillon, "A Battle for Power in Turkey Faces Resistance in Senegal," *QuartzAfrica*, December 6, 2017, https://qz.com/1147965/a-battle-for-power-in-turkey-faces-resistance-in-senegal/.

85. Philipp Sander, "Turkey Targets Gulen Schools in Africa," *DW*, August 4, 2016, www. dw.com/en/turkey-targets-gulen-schools-in-africa/a-19448457.

86. Ibid.

87. Laura Pitel, "Erdogan Rides Nationalist Wave in Support of Afrin Offensive," *Financial Times*, January 24, 2018, https://www.ft.com/content/d5d91dd6-011c-11e8-9650-9c0ad2d7c5b5.

88. Interview with PKK supporter from Bingöl in Antalya, July 2016. For an academic overview, see Güneş Murat Tezcür, "Violence and Nationalist Mobilization: The Onset of the Kurdish Insurgency in Turkey," *Nationalities Papers* 43, no. 2 (2015): 248–266.

89. See, for example, *Nicole Watts, Activists in Office: Kurdish Politics and Protest in Turkey* (Seattle: University of Washington Press, 2010).

90. "Selahattin Demirtaş'tan Çözüm Süreci Çağrısı," NTV, April 20, 2016, https://www.ntv.com. tr/turkiye/selahattin-demirtastan-cozum-sureci-cagrisi,swqKW7sqRkecMnx5WEh vRw.

91. Interview with Kurdish employee from Diyarbakır in Antalya, July 2016. For an academic perspective, see Fırat Bozcalı and Çağrı Yoltar, "A Look at Gezi Park from Turkey's Kurdistan," *Cultural Anthropology*, October 31, 2013, https://culanth.org/fieldsights/ 396-a-look-atgezi-park-from-turkey-s-kurdistan.

92. Accusations made based on leaked documents that the killings are linked to Turkey's National Intelligence Organization (Milli İstihbarat Teşkilatı) caused a major rift in the AKP government's negotiations with the PKK. See Orhan Kemal Cengiz, "New Developments in Paris Killings Threaten to Derail PKK Peace Talks," *Al-Monitor*, January 20, 2014, http://www.al-monitor.com/pulse/originals/2014/01/turkey-military-mit-kurds-murder-paris-activists.html#.

93. See, for example, Bahar Baser, *Kurdish Diaspora Political Activism in Europe, with a Particular Focus on Great Britain* (Berlin: Berghof Peace Support, 2011).

94. Foerster and Miller, "Extranational Spaces and the Disruption of National Boundaries," 5.

95. Benedict Anderson, *Imagined Communities: Reflections on the Origins and Spread of Nationalism* (New York: Verso, 1983). On Kurdish media in Europe, see Amir Hassanpour, "Satellite Footprints as National Boundaries: MED-TV and the Externality of State Sovereignty," *Journal of Muslim Minority Affairs* 18, no. 1 (1998): 53–72.

96. Fiona Adamson and Madeleine Demetriou, "Remapping the Boundaries of State and National Identity: Incorporating Diasporas into IR Theorizing," *European Journal of International Relations* 13, no. 4 (2007): 509.

97. Lenka Berkowitz and Liza M. Mügge, "Transnational Diaspora Lobbying: Europeanization and the Kurdish Question," *Journal of Intercultural Studies* 35, no. 1 (2014): 74–90.

98. Dilek Kurban, *Europe as an Agent of Change: The Role of the European Court of Human Rights and the EU in Turkey's Kurdish Policies* (Berlin: Stiftung Wissenschaft und Politik, 2014).

99. See "Demirtaş'tan Brüksel Açıklaması," *Özgür Gündem*, December 10, 2012, https://ozgurgundem.wordpress.com/2012/12/10/demirtastan-bruksel-aciklamasi-baris-ve-demokrasi-partisi-bdp-genel-baskani-selahattin-demirtas-avrupa-parlamentosunda-ap-yaptigi-konusmanin-carpitildigini-ileri-surdu. Demirtaş became cochair of the BDP's sister/successor HDP. He and his previous cochair Figen Yüksekdağ are in jail as of this writing.

100. See "About Us," Kurdish Institute of Brussels, http://www.kurdishinstitute.be/kurdish-institute-of-brussels-1/.

101. See a statement on the Kurdish Friendship Group-EP, Peoples' Democratic Party—Representation in Europe, October 16, 2014, http://en.hdpeurope.com/?p=826.

102. See Kurdish Institute of Brussels, http://www.kurdishinstitute.be/eu-turkey-and-the-kurds/.

Chapter 8

1. Hakan Övünç Ongur, "*Plus Ça Change . . .* Rearticulating Authoritarianism in the New Turkey," *Critical Sociology*, February 29, 2016, doi:10.1177/0896920516630799.

2. "UN Resolution: How Each Country Voted," *Al Jazeera*, December 21, 2017, https://www.nytimes.com/2017/12/21/world/middleeast/trump-jerusalem-united-nations.html?mtrref=www.google.com&gwh=2F2D643BBB405457F4A0FB5CA2FC0687&gwt=pay.

3. The exact point at which shifts in identity content constitute a measurably different identity proposal necessitating a new designation seems an analytical decision rather than an empirical question. As the degrees of importance of the content elements in the Republican Nationalist proposal have altered (the emphasis on where and how secularism must be protected, the evolving willingness to engage the Armenian and Kurdish questions) rather than the fundamental content elements themselves, I use the term Republican Nationalism throughout the historical period analyzed in the book.

4. Interview with Cem Toker, LDP chairman, Istanbul, August 2013.

5. Bülent Şener, "*Davutoğlu Sendromu ya da Alice Hariklar Diyarında,*" *21. Yüzyıl*, no. 46 (October 2012): 23–27; and Gözde Kılıç Yaşın, "*Balkanlarda Bir Don Kişot: Ahmet Davutoğlu,*" *21. Yüzyıl*, no. 46 (October 2012): 28–34.

6. Interview with former chairman of Marmaris regional branch of Atatürkist Thought Association, Istanbul, August 2013.

7. Interview with chairman of the Eskişehir branch of the Türk Ocakları (Turkish Hearths), cultural organization dedicated (in the interviewee's words) to producing educated, "quality Muslim Turks," Eskişehir, July 2013.

8. Hakan Yavuz, *Islamic Political Identity in Turkey* (Oxford: Oxford University Press, 2003), 262.

9. Name and link withheld, Facebook, April 18, 2015.

10. Interview with members of MHP, Trabzon, April 2014.

11. For an excellent study of individuals (particularly Alevis) who felt compelled to conceal their own religious identity and even participate in Sunni practices due to fear of being ostracized or even harmed, see Binnaz Toprak, *Türkiye'de Farklı Olmak: Din ve Muhafazakârlık Ekseninde Ötekileştirilenler* (Istanbul: Metis Yayınları, 2008).

12. Interview with MHP party member, Trabzon, March 2014.

13. İhsanoğlu was the designated mutual candidate ("*çatı adayı*") of the CHP, MHP, BBP, and other opposition parties but insufficiently appealed to all of them. Many MHP members, accustomed to the fiery nationalist rhetoric of MHP leader Devlet Bahçeli, found İhsanoğlu's quiet demeanor and lack of nationalist sentiment unacceptable and, finding no appropriate candidate, boycotted the election.

14. Interview with Özgür Erdem, Istanbul, August 2013.

15. Interview with Turkish academic, Ankara, July 2014.

16. Bülent Aras, "Turkey's Policy in the Former Soviet South: Assets and Options," *Turkish Studies* 1, no. 1 (2000): 38.

17. For a discussion of the temporality of coalitions forged solely based on opposition to a common other, see Lisel Hintz, "Explaining Democratic Failure in the Post-Soviet Space," *Washington Review of Turkish and Eurasian Affairs* (December 2011), http://www.thewashingtonreview.org/articles/explaining-democratic-failure-in-the-post-soviet-space.html.

18. Kurdish and Syrian affairs analyst Mutlu Çiviroğlu, speaking at "Turkey: ISIS and the Middle East" Conference, Georgetown University, September 24, 2014.

19. Kobani protesters in provinces with large Kurdish populations across southeastern Turkey, including Batman, Diyarbakır, Muş, Siirt, Şırnak, and Van, lit fireworks, threw Molotov cocktails and stones at police, and set fire to city buses. See "*Kobani için Otobüs Yaktılar,*" *Hürriyet Gazetesi,* October 7, 2014, http://www.hurriyet.com.tr/gundem/27340297.asp.

20. See "*İstanbul'da Atatürk Heykelini Yaktılar,*" *Haber3,* October 7, 2014, http://www.haber3.com/istanbulda-ataturk-heykelini-yaktilar-2941096h.htm.

21. Building on the case of Turkey, Şener Aktürk uses "anti-ethnic" to describe a regime that explicitly excludes ethnicity as a defining component of a state's citizens, as discussed in chapter 4. Şener Aktürk, *Regimes of Ethnicity and Nationhood in Germany, Russia, and Turkey* (Cambridge, UK: Cambridge University Press, 20120).

22. Sedat Ergin, "When Tahrir al-Sham Forces Accompany a Turkish Military Convoy in Idlib," *Hürriyet Daily News,* February 16, 2018, http://www.hurriyetdailynews.com/opinion/sedat-ergin/when-tahrir-al-sham-forces-accompany-a-turkish-military-convoy-in-idlib-127381.

23. "Demirtaş: HDP Var Oldukça Seni Bakan Yaptırmayacağız," *Hürriyet,* March 18, 2015, http://www.hurriyet.com.tr/gundem/demirtas-hdp-var-oldukca-seni-baskan-yaptirmayacagiz-28481582.

24. "As It Happened: Turkey's Ruling AKP Loses Majority in Blow for Erdoğan," *Hürriyet Daily News,* June 7, 2015, http://www.hurriyetdailynews.com/as-it-happened-turkeys-ruling-akp-loses-majority-in-blow-for-erdogan-83585.

25. "Cumhurbaşkanı Erdoğan: '1 Kasım'da 550 Tane Yerli ve Milli Milletvekili İstiyorum,'" *Hürriyet,* September 21, 2015, http://www.hurriyet.com.tr/gundem/cumhurbaskani-erdogan-1-kasimda-550-tane-yerli-ve-milli-milletvekili-istiyorum-30124611.

26. The Western world's fascination with Turkey as a model of democracy and economic development has dramatically waned as Ottoman Islamism has become increasingly present in the public sphere and institutions of governance. In its heyday, however, numerous academic articles and conferences as well as policy pieces were devoted to Turkish democracy. In August 2011, for example, *The Economist* favorably cited "Muslim democracy *alla Turca*" in a discussion of the Arab Spring, stating that "Turkey's Islamists seem to have got things right." See "The Turkish Model: A Hard Act to Follow," *Economist,* August 6, 2011, http://www.economist.com/node/21525408.

27. Conversation with a taxi driver in Ankara, March 2014:

28. See Tolga Şardan, "*Gezi'ye Katılmayan Tek İl,*" *Milliyet Gazetesi,* November 25, 2013, http://www.milliyet.com.tr/geziye-katilmayan-tek-il/gundem/detay/1797621/default.htm.

29. In a post published just a month before Gezi, *Al-Jazeera* rightly and presciently referred to this situation, characterized as indirect censorship—in which the ties of media barons to profitable industries such as construction and the benefits they receive from favorable government contracts lead them to censor their own news outlets—as the Turkish "media muzzle." See "The Turkish Media Muzzle," *Al Jazeera*, April 2, 2013, http://www.aljazeera.com/programmes/listeningpost/2013/04/201342104340948788.html.

30. "*Erdoğan: Polis Kahramanlık Destanı Yazdı,*" *NTVMSNBC*, June 24, 2013, http://www.ntvmsnbc.com/id/25450862/. The title of the article deserves translation: "Erdoğan: The Police Wrote an Epic of Heroism."

31. "*Adile Osmanoğlu: Erdoğan'a Yakın bir İsim Beni Tehdit Etti,*" Bugün, December 11, 2014, http://www.bugun.com.tr/gundem/tehdit-edildim-haberi/1386513.

32. Interview with Halil İnalcık, Turkish and Ottoman history expert, Ankara, August 2013.

33. Author's observations of protests in Ankara (Kuğulu Park) and Istanbul (Nişantaşı), both June 2013.

34. Photo of the slogan used in *Çapulcu'nun Gezi Rehberi* (Istanbul: Hemen Kitap, 2013), 151.

35. Ibid., 13.

36. Interview with lawyer/university professor and LGBTQ activist, Istanbul, August 2013.

37. Bade Okçuoğlu, "The LGBTQ Block" (presented at Talk Turkey Conference: Re-Thinking Life since Gezi, The New School University, October 4–5, 2013), transcript, *Jadaliyya*, http://www.jadaliyya.com/pages/index/15037/rethinking-gezi-through-feminist-and-lgbt-perspect.

38. Esmeray, speaking with interviewer Burcu, posted as "*Esmeray Ameliyat Oldu,*" Türk Eşcinsel Kulübü LGBTQ Haber Sitesi, July 9, 2013, http://news.turkgayclub.com/yasam/4848-esmeray-ameliyat-oldu.html.

39. See "Homophobic Prejudices Broken by Gezi Incidents in Turkey," *Hurriyet Daily News*, July 29, 2013, http://www.hurriyetdailynews.com/homophobic-prejudices-broken-by-gezi-incidents-in-turkey.aspx?pageID=238&nID=51567&NewsCatID=339.

40. "Rethinking Gezi through Feminist and LGBTQ Perspectives," *Jadaliyya*, November 3, 2013, http://www.jadaliyya.com/pages/index/15037/rethinking-gezi-through-feminist-and-lgbt-perspect.

41. Photo taken by author in Kuğulu Park, Ankara, June 2013. Similar photo in "*Direnince Çok Eğlenceli Oluyorsun Türkiye!,*" *Milliyet Gazetesi*, June 9, 2013, http://www.milliyet.com.tr/direnince-cok-eglenceli-oluyorsun/pazar/haberdetay/09.06.2013/1720366/default.htm. Emphasis added.

42. Photo in *Çapulcu'nun Gezi Rehberi* (Istanbul: Hemen Kitap, 2013), 169.

43. "*Başbakan Erdoğan: Biz Birkaç Çapulcunun Yaptıklarını Yapmayız,*" *Radikal Gazetesi*, June 9, 2013, http://www.radikal.com.tr/politika/basbakan_erdogan_biz_birkac_capulcunun_yaptiklarini_yapmayiz-1136875.

44. The (in this case intentionally disrespectful) use of Erdoğan's familiar name Tayyip and the slang word "*be*" by the young headscarved girl here also serve as a direct rebuke to his authority and thus a further challenge to his promotion of an Ottoman Islamist identity. Photo in *Çapulcu'nun Gezi Rehberi* (Istanbul: Hemen Kitap, 2013), 163.

45. Interview with EU ministry official, Ankara, November 2013.

46. Margaret Keck and Kathryn Sikkink, *Activists beyond Borders: Transnational Advocacy Networks in International Politics* (Ithaca, NY: Cornell University Press, 1998).

47. James Scott, *Weapons of the Weak: Everyday Forms of Peasant Resistance* (New Haven, CT: Yale University Press, 1985).

48. See Iver B. Neuman, *Uses of the Other: "The East" in European Identity Formation* (Minneapolis: University of Minnesota Press, 1999).

49. Bağış declared all those going to protest in Taksim Square would be considered terrorists. See "*Egemen Bağış: Taksim'e Çıkan Terorist Muamelesi Görür,*" *Radikal Gazetesi*, June 16, 2013, http://www.radikal.com.tr/politika/egemen_bagis_taksime_cikan_terorist_muamelesi_gorur-1137822. http://www.radikal.com.tr/politika/egemen_bagis_nekrofiller_mesajinin_muhatabini_acikladi-1181010.

50. See "Recording Shows Erdoğan Refused to Ease Tensions During Gezi Park Protests," *Today's Zaman*, March 14, 2014, http://www.todayszaman.com/news-342132-recording-shows-erdogan-refused-to-ease-tensions-during-gezi-park-protests.html.

51. *"Erdoğan: Kabataş'taki Gezi'cileri Savunmak Sana mı Kaldı ey Bahçeli?,"* *T24*, February 19, 2014, https://t24.com.tr/haber/erdogan-kabatastaki-gezicileri-savunmak-sana-mi-kaldi-bahceli,251453 (emphasis added).

52. *"Erdoğan 'Camiye İçkiyle Girdiler' İddiasını Tekrarladı,"* *Hürriyet Gazetesi*, June 10, 2013, http://www.hurriyet.com.tr/gundem/23468860.asp.

53. Erdoğan is generally unspecific in his use of the term, but paints frightening pictures of foreign currency speculators looking to profit from a collapse of the Turkish economy. This resonates very strongly with citizens of Turkey, who experienced a devastating economic crisis in 2000–2001. The government-friendly newspaper *Sabah Gazetesi* offers a description for readers supporting Erdoğan's claims. See Süleyman Yaşar, *"Nedir Faiz Lobisi? Erdoğan Niye Lobbiyi İşaret Etti?,"* *Sabah Gazetesi*, June 10, 2013, http://www.sabah.com.tr/yazarlar/yasar/2013/06/10/nedir-faiz-lobisi-erdogan-niye-lobiyi-isaret-etti.

54. Cumhuriyet embedded a video of the speech, which was broadcast on CNN Turk, along with its report, posted on June 3, 2014 at http://www.cumhuriyet.com.tr/video/video/78603/Erdogan_dan_CNN_muhabirine__Dalkavuk_ajan.html# (emphasis added).

55. Interview with three Ülkü Ocakları members, Giresun, March 2014.

56. See the *"Atatürk ve Fenerbahçe"* post on the soccer club's website at http://www.fenerbahce.org/hedef1milyonuye.asp?q=/kurumsal/detay.asp?ContentID=10.

57. Posted in a summary of the march as *"Fenerbahçeliler Taksim'e Yürüdü,"* *EverywhereTaksim*, June 8, 2013, http://everywheretaksim.net/tr/t24-taraftarlar-gezi-parki-icin-taksimde/.

58. Photo in *Çapulcu'nun Gezi Rehberi*, 121.

59. *Taksim'de Kutsal İsyan* (Istanbul: İleri Yayınları, 2013), 70.

60. Since the local elections of March 2014, the BDP was largely supplanted by the HDP, discussed in chapters 3 and 7.

61. Photo in *Çapulcu'nun Gezi Rehberi*, 26.

INDEX

Tables are indicated by an italic *t* following the page number.